PSYCHOPATHOLOGY IN ANIMALS

Research and Clinical Implications

PSYCHOPATHOLOGY IN ANIMALS
Research and Clinical Implications

Edited by

J. D. KEEHN

Department of Psychology
York University
Atkinson College
Downsview, Ontario, Canada

ACADEMIC PRESS

A Subsidiary of Harcourt Brace Jovanovich, Publishers

New York   London   Toronto   Sydney   San Francisco

ACADEMIC PRESS, INC.
111 Fifth Avenue, New York, New York 10003

United Kingdom Edition published by
ACADEMIC PRESS, INC. (LONDON) LTD.
24/28 Oval Road, London NW1 7DX

Library of Congress Cataloging in Publication Data
Main entry under title:

Psychopathology in animals.

    Includes bibliographies.
    1. Comparative psychiatry. 2. Animal
psychopathology. 3. Psychology, Pathological.
4. Psychology, Pathological––Animal models.
I. Keehn, J. D. [DNLM: 1. Psychopathology.
2. Disease models, Animal. 3. Models,
Psychological. WM100.3 P9765]
RC455.4.C6P74   616.8'9'070724   79–51679
ISBN 0–12–403050–5

PRINTED IN THE UNITED STATES OF AMERICA

79 80 81 82   9 8 7 6 5 4 3 2 1

Contents

7 The Kindling Effect: An Experimental Model of Epilepsy?   169

JOHN GAITO

8 Behavioral Anomalies in Aversive Situations   197

HANK DAVIS

9 Experimental Depression in Animals   223

V.A. COLOTLA

10 Fears in Companion Dogs:

Characteristics and Treatment   239

DAVID HOTHERSALL

DAVID S. TUBER

List of Contributors

Numbers in parentheses indicate the pages on which the authors' contributions begin.

V. A. COLOTLA (223), National School of Professional Studies, Iztacala and Faculty of Psychology, National Autonomous University of Mexico, Mexico City 13, D. F., Mexico

HANK DAVIS (197), Department of Psychology, University of Guelph, Guelph, Ontario, Canada

GAYLORD D. ELLISON (81), Department of Psychology, University of California, Los Angeles, Los Angeles, California 90024

C. B. FERSTER (279), The American University, Department of Psychology, Washington, D. C. 20016

JOHN L. FULLER (61), Department of Psychology, State University of New York at Binghamton, Binghamton, New York 13901

JOHN GAITO (169), Department of Psychology, York University, Downsview, Ontario M3J 1P3, Canada

DAVID HOTHERSALL (239), Department of Psychology, The Ohio State University, Columbus, Ohio 43212

J. D. KEEHN (1), Department of Psychology, York University, Atkinson College, Downsview, Ontario M3J 2R7, Canada

DONALD J. LEVIS (257), Department of Psychology, State University of New York at Binghamton, Binghamton, New York 13901

MELVIN LYON (103), Psychopharmacological Research Laboratory, Sct.Hans Hospital, Roskilde, Denmark, and Psychological Laboratory, University of Copenhagen, Copenhagen, Denmark

F. L. MARCUSE (305), Department of Psychology, University of Manitoba, Winnipeg, Manitoba R3T 2N2, Canada

ERIK BARDRUM NIELSEN (103), Psychopharmacological Research Laboratory, Sct. Hans Hospital, Roskilde, Denmark

J. J. PEAR (305), Department of Psychology, University of Manitoba, Winnipeg, Manitoba R3T 2N2, Canada

RONALD K. SIEGEL (29), Department of Psychiatry, University of California, Los Angeles, Los Angeles, California   90024

SHEPARD SIEGEL (143), Department of Psychology, McMaster University, Hamilton, Ontario L8S 4K1, Canada

DAVID S. TUBER (239), Department of Psychology, The Ohio State University, Columbus, Ohio   43212

Preface

After a lull following early optimistic attempts to create "experimental neurosis" in animals, interest in animal models of human psychopathology is once again rising. This book illustrates several advances in the analysis and genesis of abnormal behavior that make the study of animal psychopathology intellectually exciting and reports some clinical applications that make it practically rewarding as well. It should appeal to students of animal, clinical, and abnormal psychology, to psychiatrists, and to veterinarians whose practices include more than ordinary physical ailments.

First, behavioral, ethological, and genetic methods and concepts are applied to animal and human disorders of behavior; then biochemical, pharmacological, physiological, and psychological procedures that generate such disorders are reviewed. All chapters relate human to animal disorders by way of structural or functional concordances. These relationships clarify mechanisms that may be involved in a variety of human psychological disablements. Accounts of treatment of these disablements appear near the end of the volume.

Chapter 1 is a survey of psychopathologies in animals. It relates them to human symptomatology and compares a behavioral analysis with diagnosis. A wide range of drug-related aspects of natural animal behavior are discussed by Ronald K. Siegel in Chapter 2. In Chapter 3, John L. Fuller analyzes alcohol-related behaviors and audiogenic seizures in rodents and separation syndromes in monkeys and dogs from a genetic point of view.

The next six chapters are concerned with particular behavioral anomalies. In Chapter 4, Gaylord D. Ellison elucidates sociopathological characteristics of norepinephrine and serotonin levels in rats in connection with schizophrenic reactions in humans. The evidence linking amphetamine psychosis with schizo-phrenia is reviewed in Chapter 5 by Melvin Lyon and Erik Bardrum Nielsen, who also propose a new theory of amphetamine-action, and in Chapter 6 Shepard Siegel clarifies the status of drug-tolerance and dependence as a condi-tioned response. In Chapter 7, John Gaito relates the ''kindling effect'' of repeated brain stimulation to human epilepsy; anomalous behaviors that testify to the power of negative reinforcement are analyzed by Hank Davis in Chapter 8 in a number of experimental situations. V. A. Colotla in Chapter 9 reviews the two literatures of experimental depression—learned helplessness and isolation-rearing—showing how one seeks a human analogue of an experimental phenomenon and the other is sought as an animal analogue of the childhood separation syndrome.

Not all abnormal animal behaviors originate in the laboratory. Howard Liddell once wrote: ''Perhaps the most intriguing problem for the investigator of animal behavior is the biological basis of psychic trauma. No one believes that susceptibility to mental injury is an unique human frailty. The gun-shy dog, the spoiled race-horse are familiar examples.'' Several other cases of mental injuries to animals are to be found in the present volume, although the emphasis is directed more to the biological bases of the injuries than to their nature as psychic trauma.

In Chapter 10, David Hothersall and David S. Tuber exhibit a clinical psychology of animals in which human discoveries in the animal laboratory are used to help animals in distress; in Chapter 11 Donald J. Levis recounts the laboratory basis of implosive therapy in man; and in the penultimate chapter C. B. Ferster explains the nature of generic reinforcement and its importance for psychotherapy from the standpoint of a behaviorist. Clinical benefits, applied to animals as well as to humans, must be weighed against discomforts caused by experimental methods used to gain them. A unique feature of this book is that it addresses the problem of ethical treatment of experimental animals. This is the topic of the final chapter in which F. L. Marcuse and J. J. Pear delineate the ethics of animal experimentation.

J. D. KEEHN

Psychopathology in Animal and Man

1

I. The Psychopathology of Animal Life

Although psychology was originally the study of human mentality, modern psychological theory is heavily indebted to experiments with animals. Mostly these experiments concern themselves with explanations of normal behavioral processes, but psychological aberrations are evident in animals just as they are in humans. Tinklepaugh (1928) describes a case of agitated depression and self-mutilation in a captive male rhesus monkey when his mate was replaced by other females; Hebb (1947) attributes spontaneous neurosis to two caged female chimpanzees; and ulcerative colitis among Siamang gibbons distressed by social disruption during care and maintenance routines is reported by Stout and Snyder (1969). It is inaccurate to call these psychopathologies, because psychopathology implies a particular one of several models of madness (Siegler & Osmond, 1966). But as the same inaccuracy pervades psychology, psychosomatics, and psychiatry, psychopathology is as acceptable as these other descriptors so long as it does not hinder functional analyses of the phenomena it describes.

Behavioral abnormalities in animals have been observed by veterinarians, psychologists, ethologists, zoologists, farmers, husbandrymen, and animal attendants. Among abnormalities encountered in veterinary practice, Croft (1951), Chertok and Fontaine (1963), and Schmidt (1968) include hysteria in

PSYCHOPATHOLOGY IN ANIMALS
Research and Clinical Implications

goats and cows; collective epilepsy among dogs; nymphomania in cats; emotional trauma in dogs, horses, and cats; dyspepsia, anorexia, and paroxysmal hypotenia in dogs and cats; and impotence in the bull. In addition, Christian and Ratcliffe (1952) report fatal convulsive seizures in otters, minks, a cheetah, a serval, and a lynx. Tonic immobility in farm animals (Fraser, 1960); intromission phobia in the bull (Fraser, 1957); hysteria in hens (Sanger & Hamdy, 1962); neurotic fears in pets (Hothersall & Tuber, Chapter 10 of this volume); sudden deaths in guinea pigs (Lane-Petter, 1953) and rats (Richter, 1959); and psychosis among cats (J. M. Mitchell, 1953) and dogs (Newton & Gantt, 1968) have also been described.

Meyer-Holzapfel (1968) lists many abnormalities of animals in zoos. The list includes nonadaptive escape reactions, food refusal, excessive aggression, stereotyped motor reactions, displacement scratching, self-mutilations, homosexuality, sexual perversions, perversions of appetite, apathy, and defective mother–infant interactions. In the wild, van Lawick-Goodall (1971) instances behavioral aberrations in an orphaned chimpanzee:

> When he was four years old Merlin was far more submissive than other youngsters of that age: constantly he approached adults to ingratiate himself, turning repeatedly to present his rump, or crouching pant-grunting before them. At the other end of the scale, Merlin was extra-aggressive to other infants of his own age. . . . As Merlin entered his sixth year his behavior was becoming rapidly more abnormal. Sometimes he hung upside down . . . suspended almost motionless for several minutes at a time. Hunched up with his arms around his knees, he sat often rocking from side to side with wide open eyes . . . [p. 227].

Examples of bizarre motor reactions have appeared in animals isolated for experimental purposes. Katz (1937) describes frenzied activity by chicks used by Brückner in a Kasper Hauser experiment; Thompson, Melzack, and Scott (1956) report whirling behavior in isolation-reared dogs; Startsev (1976) describes convulsions in young baboons moved from a small cage in a quiet indoors location to an outdoor larger one in public view of older males; Berkson (1967) gives an account of huddling in infant crab-eating macaques separated from their mothers; and Mitchell (1970) reports an apparent dissociation and hallucination in an adult rhesus monkey raised in partial social isolation:

> One . . . male slowly moved his right arm toward his head while in a rigid seated pose and, upon seeing his own approaching hand, suddenly appeared startled by it. His eyes slowly widened and he would at times fear grimace toward, threaten or even bite the hand. . . . If he did not look directly at the hand or did not bite it, "it" would continue to move toward him. . . . As "it" approached him his eyes became wider and wider until the hand was clasping his face. There he would sit for a second or two, with saucer-sized eyes staring in terror between clutching fingers [p. 228].

There are several kinds of animal behaviors that are bizarre from the human standpoint but which are not statistically abnormal. These include audiogenic seizures (Finger, 1944), tonic immobility (Crawford & Prestrude, 1977), displacement activities (Tinbergen, 1952) and schedule-induced phenomena (Staddon, 1977). Some have likened these to human psychopathologies: audiogenic seizures resemble hysterical convulsions (Finger, 1944); tonic immobility resembles catatonia (Gallup & Maser, 1977); displacements are like psychosomatic disorders (Barnett, 1955); and schedule-induced drinking models alcoholism (Gilbert, 1976).

I prefer to call these peculiarities lawful misdemeanors instead of pathologies because they are specific responses to specific situations common to most members of a species, not defects. As such, they invite analysis rather than cure. An analysis of one lawful misdemeanor, schedule-induced polydipsia, is offered below, and alternative human disablements that it could model are indicated.

II. Treatment of Abnormal Animals

Alleviation of distress may be accomplished by therapy or by prosthetic devices. In physical medicine, treatment by therapy implies an injured or temporarily unhealthy organism, whereas treatment by prosthesis implies an organism that is permanently impaired. The former treatment aims to readjust an organism to an existing environment; the latter aims to arrange an environment that enables an organism to cope. Crutches, wheelchairs, and spectacles are common prosthetic devices.

Psychological treatment can also be therapeutic or prosthetic. With therapeutics, behavior is changed either by direct assault on the offending responses (Seligman, Maier, & Geer, 1968), by modification of mood (Staddon, 1977), or by the elimination of a pathological defensive dominant (Bowden, 1976). Psychological treatment by prosthesis requires adjustment of a maintaining or initiating environment, as when repetitive stereotypes disappear in oversized cages (Draper & Bernstein, 1963) or when deprivation syndromes are attenuated with swinging instead of stationary surrogate monkey mothers (Mason, 1968).

A mere change of companions may be a prosthetic device for the alleviation of distress. Scott, Steward, and De Ghett (1973) report such a case:

> Terriers reared [with littermates] frequently gang up on one member of the group and attack it persistently (Fuller, 1953). This particular animal had long been the object of such persecution. In the run, it stood listlessly, head and tail down, seldom ate, and appeared to be sick. We therefore transferred it into a litter of nonaggressive cocker spaniels in a nearby run. Within half an hour, it had recovered, holding its head and tail up, interacting constantly with the cockers, and eating. Left in the group of cockers, it continued to behave normally [p. 15].

In this case the terrier is not cured ("recovered") by a change of companions, because the original "symptoms" would surely return if the dog were put back into the original situation. But the terrier behaves normally with the new group, and it is in this respect that I call the new situation prosthetic rather than curative. Prosthesis is a general characteristic of psychological environments, for example, schedules of reinforcement, and a pivotal issue in abnormal psychology is the extent to which abnormalities are features of abnormal (impaired) organisms or features of environments that maintain unprofitable behaviors (cf. Adams, 1964; Davis, Chapter 8 of this volume; Sidman, 1960). Lawful misdemeanors fall at the latter extreme.

Known environmental conditions elicit lawful misdemeanors so these behaviors are easily controlled by environmental prosthesis. In such cases, however, it is not a matter of preventing the behavior from appearing but of analyzing the mechanisms through which it occurs.

Concerning therapy, although experimental analogues of psychoanalytic mechanisms have been explored (J. McV. Hunt, 1941; Miller, 1939; Mowrer, 1940) there cannot be, as Liddell (1965) points out, a psychodynamics of animal behavior. Masserman (1942) describes treatment of experimental animal neurosis in psychodynamic language—transference, reassurance, and working through—but the behavioral methods he employs to modify behavior are not unlike those described by Wolpe (1958) in learning-theory terms. It is unnecessary to give animals psychiatric labels (Brion & Ey, 1964; H. F. Hunt, 1964), and there is no alternative for changing behavior than direct manipulation of organism–environment interactions.

Several procedures have been used. Merrill (1945) employed extinction to cure two Great Danes of killing sheep. He repeatedly exposed them to penned lambs that the dogs could not reach, and found that when, after a few weeks the lambs were released, the dogs ignored them. A Dalmatian was cured of killing chickens with a similar technique. Tuber, Hothersall, and Voith (1974) employed classical and operant-conditioning methods with three misbehaving dogs. With one, they desensitized emotional responses to thunderstorms with reciprocal inhibition therapy based on the counterconditioning method used by Wolpe (1958) to alleviate experimental neurosis in cats. With the second case they eliminated child-nipping during play by means of operant shaping (Skinner, 1953); and with the third case they transferred the stimulus control of acceptable behavior of an unattended Afghan from its owner to a rock-radio program by means of a classical conditioning stimulus-transfer procedure devised by Wickens (1973) with cats.

Harlow and Suomi (1971; Suomi, Harlow, & McKinney, 1972) used younger monkeys as therapists to overcome social deficits in older monkeys reared in social isolation. The 6-month-old patients exhibited typical motor stereotypies of the isolation syndrome—self-clasping, huddling, and rocking—and retreated to huddle in a corner when first exposed to the 3-month-old therapists. The therapists were not social isolates. They were normally developed for their age and persisted in approaching and clinging to the isolates. "Within a week," Harlow and Suomi (1971) report, "the isolates were reciprocating the clinging."

Other examples of animals as "therapists" are reported by Mason and Kenney (1974) who used dogs as companions to reestablish filial attachments in socially deprived infant rhesus monkeys, by Ellison (1977), who describes complex interactions between social and neurophysiological factors in determining depression and hyperactivity in rats, and by Rosenblum and Kaufman (1968), who report how the behavior of other females in a group affects the separation syndrome of protest and despair (Bowlby, 1976). With pigtail monkeys, separated infants are ignored by other females and they adopt a typical huddled posture of despair; with bonnet monkeys, comparable infants are accepted by other females, to whom they cling without appearing to be disturbed. In these cases, the therapists are more prosthetic devices than they are curative agents.

Drug treatment has been used to control abnormal animal behaviors, beginning with bromine, caffeine, and veronal-induced prolonged narcosis therapy for experimental neurosis by Pavlov and his associates and continuing with alcohol treatment of experimental neurosis in cats by Masserman and Yum (1946). More recent instances of drug treatment of animals thought to be modeling human psychopathologies are the attenuation of tonic immobility in chickens by amphetamine (Boren & Gallup, 1976) and by imipramine (Maser & Gallup, 1974); the alleviation of learned helplessness in rats by pargyline (Weiss, Glazer, & Pohorecky, 1976); the control of hyperkinesis in dogs (Corson, Corson, Arnold, & Knopp, 1976) and rats (Campbell & Randell, 1975) with amphetamine, and the treatment with chlorpromazine of the postisolation syndrome found in dogs (Fuller & Clark, 1966).

By means of reserpine injections, Duncan and Wood-Gush (1974) reduced stereotyped pacing by frustrated chickens, and Keehn and Matsunaga (1972) attenuated palatability-induced alcohol ingestion by rats with trihexyphenidyl injections. Oral administration of the same drug reduced schedule-induced alcohol-polydipsia in this species (Keehn, 1974). With rhesus monkeys traumatized by partial isolation rearing, McKinney *et al.* (1973) found that 3-month's treatment with chlorpromazine significantly reduced a number of behavioral disturbances. Suomi and Harlow (1977) report improvement in isolation-induced depression in the same monkey species after 10–14 days treatment with imipramine. For the same condition, Morrison and McKinney (1976) say that electroconvulsive shock therapy serves to elevate motor and exploratory activity but does not increase social responsiveness in afflicted animals.

Suomi and Harlow (1977) acknowledge an affinity between depression engendered by isolation-rearing and depression as modeled by learned-helplessness experiments (Seligman, 1975). In the latter paradigm, forced reality testing was employed by Seligman *et al.* (1968) to establish escape responses in three dogs previously submitted to inescapable shocks. The helpless animals were repeatedly dragged on leashes from shock to safe sides of a double-compartment box until they eventually learned to escape shock by themselves.

Masserman (1943) applied a similar forced-solution method to the cure of experimental neurosis in cats. The hungry cats refused to approach food at a location where they had previously been shocked, exhibiting conditioned emotional responses instead. Masserman forced the cats toward the food container with a moveable barrier until more or less normal eating behavior reemerged. The technique of extinguishing fear by flooding with unreinforced fear-arousing stimuli is a comparable therapy employed by Stampfl and Levis (1967). (The basis of this technique is described by Levis in Chapter 11 of this volume.) At the other extreme is Wolpe's (1958) more persuasive approach to the same result by reciprocal inhibition of fear by feeding.

Behavioral treatment is uncommon in veterinary practice, but drug and hormone treatments are standard. These latter are becoming standard in laboratory investigations. On the one hand, benzodiazapenes that are effective with humans are under test for their anxiety-reducing properties with animals (Wise, Berger, & Stein, 1972); on the other hand, testosterone propionate administration is used to offset femininization of male rats by prenatal stress (Ward, 1974). Effects of hormone treatment, like those of drug treatment (Ellison, 1977), depend on the social situation. Androgen potentiates ejaculation by a femininized male rat in the presence of a female partner; but when the partner is male, androgen elicits lordosis instead.

III. Similarities, Diagnoses, and Animal Models

"No one believes," Liddell (1956) remarks, "that susceptibility to stress is an unique human frailty [p. 19]," and the examples of spontaneous and experimental animal psychopathologies surveyed earlier in this chapter should bear him out (cf. Keehn, 1979a). No one should believe, either, that psychopathology explains these abnormalities, either in animals (Zubin & Hunt, 1967) or in their human counterparts (Ferster, 1966). But belief in discoverable parallels between animal and human psychologies is essential. In this respect, the studies of animal and human psychopathologies are complementary because the one can expose originating situations while the other presents resulting symptoms. As Liddell (1956) said in connection with experimental neurosis,

> Because of man's incredibly complicated cognitive machinery, his neurotic symptoms may exhibit a bewildering diversity. Nevertheless, our emotionally disturbed animals under careful observation show many of the same or closely similar symptoms. The physician is in a much better position, however, to explore and analyse his psychoneurotic patient's symptomatology than is the behaviorist in the case of his experimentally neurotic animal. When it comes to analyzing the *originating situations* . . . the shoe is on the other foot. The behaviorist can *create and rigorously control* the situations in which experimental neuroses originate [p. 59; emphasis added].

The similarities between human neurosis and canine experimental neurosis first reported from Russian laboratories emphasized excessive emotionality under stress (Pavlov, 1927). Now, with primates, psychosomatic disturbances are prominent parts of experimental neurotic syndromes (Startsev, 1976). In the later cases, gastric achylia and hyperglycemia, for example, correspondences between animal and human injuries are easily recognized; but in the earlier cases, identification of animal emotionality under stress with human neurotic ill-ness is now thought to have been premature (Broadhurst, 1973). The principle difference between the late and early cases lies in the relative difficulties in diagnosing organic and psychological disorders.

Psychiatric diagnoses depend on symptomatology: They are category labels assigned to groups of disabling behaviors as though they share a common origin. That this is an unprofitable tactic is evidenced by the variety of diagnoses possi-ble for childhood schizophrenia (Tinbergen, 1974), by the absence of a common international diagnostic standard (Kendell, 1975), and by the presence of similar symptoms in more than a single category (Zigler & Phillips, 1961). Particularly disturbing are the different conceptions of schizophrenia employed within and between Britain and the United States, and their consequent effect on diagnostic habits (Kendell, 1975), that makes it difficult to collate information on schizophrenia generated by these sources.

Similar difficulties exist in the categorization of disturbances in the behavior of animals. Pavlov (1927), for instance, cites hyperemotionality as being in-dicative of experimental neurosis. His account of the neurosis of a dog exposed to the difficult discrimination procedure of Shenger-Krestovnikova includes reference to squealing, wriggling, and violent barking after prolonged exposure to the difficult discrimination. Contrariwise, the long-term experimental neurosis produced in cats by Thomas and de Wald (1977) with an analogue of the Shenger-Krestovnikova procedure was manifested not by hyperactivity but by rigid immobility. Moreover, Thomas and de Wald equate experimental neurosis with learned helplessness which is also supposed to model exogenous depression in humans (Seligman, 1975), the separation syndrome in human and monkey infants (Suomi & Harlow, 1977), and catatonia (Gallup & Maser, 1977). The state of affairs concerning diagnosis is no less confusing with animals than it is with humans, although with respect to origination, the relationships between specific behaviors and environmental contingencies at least are open to investigation in the case of animals.

Such an investigation could be applied to the Thomas and de Wald (1977) method for creating experimental neurosis in cats. Ostensibly the method follows that of Shenger-Krestovnikova, but it actually conforms to an operant- rather than to a respondent-conditioning paradigm. The animals must press a lever to expose two other levers, one bright, one dark. Then, a press on the bright lever secures a food reward while a press on the dark lever is unreinforced. When the discrimination is reliably established, the dark lever is brightened bit by bit toward the level of the bright lever. Eventually, after an initial display of agitated aggression, the animals stopped pressing the bar that initiated trials and ''sat or lay immobile with their shoulders rigidly hunched in a distinctly depressive posture that is characteristic of experimental neurosis [Thomas & de Wald, 1977, p. 222].''

These behaviors resemble some characteristics of human neuroses and could be construed as psychopathological, but they also resemble behaviors found in studies of normal animal learning, particularly schedule-induced aggression during time-out from positive reinforcement (Azrin, Hutchinson, & Hake, 1966; Hutchinson, Azrin, & Hunt, 1968), and preratio pauses with multiple and chained fixed-ratio reinforcement schedules (Keehn, 1966). In these instances, exploration of controlling variables has taken precedence over exploration of pathological implications.

Because of the low reliability of psychiatric diagnoses with humans, the variety of animal behaviors believed to model human neuroses (Shagass, 1975), and the range of human disabilities thought to be modeled by the paradigm of learned helplessness in animals, it could be unprofitable to seek animal models of general psychiatric syndromes directly. An alternative strategy is the analysis of specific maladaptations in animal behavior. Such an analysis in the case of humans has already been proposed by Shapiro (1975).

IV. Models of a Maladaptive Behavior: Alcoholism in the Rat

There are three basic questions to be answered by animal addiction models:

1. Why are drugs taken in the first place?
2. Why is drug-taking maintained despite social and physical harm?
3. Why, after withdrawal, does readdiction occur?

Six models have been proposed for answering these questions: the nutritional model, the genetic model, the physiological model, the pharmacological model, the reinforcement model, and the adjunctive-behavior model. Some of them try, but none of them answers all three questions. Question 1 obviously cannot be answered according to actual effects of drugs, or, with animals, drug experience expectations. The question can only be answered by appeal to accident, either chance discovery through direct first-hand experience or the accident of a forceful or persuasive social introduction. The answers to Question 2 are the distinguishing features of the animal models; each proposes a different mechanism for the question's answer. Some models retain the same mechanism to answer Question 3, but, as Isbell (1955) quickly saw, this is not always sensible. A pharmacological model suitable for Question 2 cannot apply to Question 3 any more than it can to Question 1. Question 3 could have the same answer as Question 1 but this is unlikely, and the answer to this question may be the one that solves the riddle of addiction. I believe the solution will involve jointly the pharmacological, reinforcement, and adjunctive-behavior models.

A. EXPERIMENTAL PROCEDURES

The imperative of all models is to devise a situation in which the experimental animal either drinks or otherwise secures a drug. The classical method of studying alcohol consumption is the two-bottle self-selection technique of Richter

(1956), where subjects are given bottles of water and alcohol concentrations in their living quarters. A later refinement (Myers & Holman, 1966) uses three bottles, any one of which is randomly left empty, to minimize the bottle or position preferences that some experimental animals adopt. Richter found that rats do not generally drink alcohol in concentrations much over 5–7%, and that they select it according to nutritional needs. On the basis of this, it was thought that with man alcohol selection is a perversion of appetite. The malnutrition of certain alcoholics is taken as evidence of this. Alcohol provides the alcoholic with calories so, the argument goes, he or she eats less of more suitable foodstuffs and then becomes undernourished.

Mello (1972) claims now from laboratory evidence that this is not the reason that alcoholics are undernourished. She thinks that alcoholics eat less than they need because alcohol intoxicates more quickly on an empty stomach. A simple nutritional model of alcoholism does not account for the repeated cycles of inebriation in humans and does not even produce inebriation in rats. It might, though, interact with a genetic component of alcohol selection. Strains of mice have been shown by Rodgers and his colleagues (Rodgers, 1967) to differ in their preferences for alcohol over water in the two-bottle free-choice situation, and to regulate alcohol consumption in accordance with speed of alcohol metabolism. Presumably, the animals drink enough alcohol to make up caloric deficiencies but not enough or so quickly as to exceed the rate of metabolism and cause intoxication. This is not like the human state of affairs.

The fact of a genetic contribution of alcohol self-selection is confirmed by Eriksson's (1972) success in breeding alcohol-preferring rats at the Alko laboratories in Finland. But genetics alone do not lead rats or mice to drink to intoxication. Self-selection only shows that some animals take more of their fluid as alcohol than as plain water. The method has not generated excessively high alcohol intakes, nor has it shown that alcohol is preferred to other fluids.

Generally, water sweetened with saccharin or sucrose is preferred by rats over unsweetened alcohol solutions (Lester & Greenberg, 1952), and self-selection among alcohol concentrations and competitors depends on the nature of the alternatives and the strengths of the alcohol solutions. Strain membership is a factor in this choice. But this does not bear on whether there are strain differences in voluntary or involuntary intoxication; only on strain differences in taste, nutritional requirements, physiological status, or whatever. According to Rodgers, mice apparently *limit* their alcohol intakes according to their rate of metabolism; they do not drink themselves beyond it as is required by an alcoholism model.

A physiological model of alcoholism could overcome this problem if alcohol causes physiological changes, or if physical disturbances exist already that stimulate further alcohol selection (Myers, 1972). Various possibilities have been suggested, from serotonin depletion (Myers & Cicero, 1969) to injury to the hypothalamus (Amit & Stern, 1971) but none has produced demonstrations of animal intoxication.

Sinclair (1974) added a motivational condition to the two-bottle free-choice situation and thinks he has a closer approximation to the requirements of a model of alcoholism. He showed that Sprague–Dawley rats and rats of the alcohol-prone strains developed by Eriksson (1972) barpress for alcohol in operant-conditioning boxes. Sinclair obtained a parallel result to the human studies of Mendelson and Mello (Mello, 1972) in that less alcohol was consumed by the rats the harder they had to work to get it but the amounts that his animals drank were not enough to intoxicate them. Despite its technical advance over the original self-selection method it is doubtful if Sinclair's refinement provides a superior alcoholism model, for free choice means freedom from constraint not freedom from the exercise of effort. By adding a barpressing requirement to the effort of approaching a bottle and drinking, Sinclair could manipulate the effort needed for the rats to get alcohol. He showed that for rats that prefer alcohol, alcohol is a reinforcer. But he did not expose the nature of the reinforcement or induce his rats to drink to inebriation.

Sinclair adopted a reinforcement model. A different reinforcement model was proposed by Keehn (1969). He did not appeal to alcohol as a reinforcer but to another reinforcer that alcohol drinking might secure. In an experimental arrangement that required rats to drink alcohol for food-pellet reinforcers, the animals increased their alcohol intakes to intoxicating blood alcohol levels around 200 mg% in half-hour sessions, and maintained this level of alcohol drinking for over 2 months. When other options were open, however, the animals did not get drunk. Intoxication did not fixate as a motive for drinking; the animals became drunk only when the environment reinforced alcohol drinking.

This state of affairs also applies to humans (Giffen, 1966). Given the persistence of a reinforcing environment, drunkenness persists; change the environment appropriately and drunkenness disappears. This conception of alcoholism underlies a social-reinforcement model that differentiates the pharmachological reinforcing properties of alcohol from the social reinforcement of drinking. The social-reinforcement model accounts for the initiation of drinking and readdiction (Questions 1 and 3), but not for the harmful social and physical effects of alcoholism (Question 2).

A social-reinforcement model of alcoholism is not acceptable to Lester and Freed (1973). They claim that

> It is no difficult feat to achieve high blood alcohol concentrations in rats constrained to drink alcohol by fluid or food deprivation, but where the alcoholic drinks from strong inner motivation, the rat is constrained to do so by equally compelling external manipulations alien to man [p. 105].

And what is this strong inner motivation? To Lester and Freed it is the need for tension reduction. They summarize with an earlier statement of Lester:

> If stress and anxiety are involved in the mechanism of addiction, then the ingestion of alcohol to reduce these states seems eminently reasonable. In the absence of any showing

that enough alcohol has been ingested to produce such a reduction, however, the nexus of alcohol ingestion and degree of stress is nebulous. Experiments directed to the production of various levels of stress or anxiety and its concomitant measurement of alcohol selection might well illuminate this relationship [p. 105].

Another reinforcement model is implied by this statement, this time a negative-reinforcement model of anxiety or stress reduction. The model was first proposed by Conger (1951) on the basis of data that has since been disputed. Most studies of animals find that they do not drink alcohol in stressful situations (Cappell & Herman, 1972) and human alcoholics, as Mello (1972) showed, get more anxious while drunk, not less.

As Lester and Freed state, it is easy to produce high levels of alcohol intake in rats. Direct reinforcement of drinking has already been mentioned, but a better method is by schedule-induction. The method was first used with alcohol by Lester (1961) and is based on an accidental discovery by Falk (1961). He found that rats food-reinforced on a short variable-interval schedule drank after nearly every food pellet eaten and rapidly became polydipsic. After Lester, several groups have reported alcohol induction with the method (e.g., Hawkins, Schrot, Githen, & Everett, 1972), and its role as a model for alcoholism has been speculated upon by Gilbert (1976). This is the adjunctive-behavior model of alcoholism, named after Falk's (1972) description of his discovery. It focuses addiction not on the properties of the substance of addiction, but first on the causal conditions for excessive consumption. With the method, monkeys (Barrett & Weinberg, 1975) have been induced to consume alcohol to intoxication, and mice (Ogata, Ogata, Mendelson, & Mello, 1972) and rats (Falk, Samson, & Winger, 1972) have drunk themselves to the point of alcohol dependence, with blood alcohol levels up to 200 mg%.

It is possible that schedule-induced drinking turns initially unpalatable alcohol into a positive reinforcer (Meisch & Thompson, 1971), supporting the reinforcement model of alcoholism that Sinclair (1974) adopted, but with adjunctive drinking instead of genetic determination as a second component. However, rats that drink more 9% alcohol than water in home cages choose water instead of alcohol for adjunctive drinking (Keehn & Coulson, 1975), and even physically dependent rats starved almost to the point of death choose 25% saccharin over 5% alcohol (Samson & Falk, 1974a). To alter an alcohol–water preference an extraneous contingency is needed. Keehn and Coulson (1972) induced adjunctive drinking in rats by periodic feeding with water and alcohol available together. The rate of feeding depended on the fluid chosen, and the animals drank most of whichever fluid produced the higher feeding rate.

Falk and his colleagues produced alcohol dependence, evidenced by audiogenic seizures and convulsions in withdrawal, by means of multiple daily experimental sessions 1 hr long and 3 hr apart in which food pellets are delivered to hungry rats at 2-min intervals. The only fluid available is 5% alcohol, and the animals drink it excessively in the usual polydipsic postpellet pattern. By contrast, in home cages with single daily food rations and only 5% alcohol for drinking, dependence does not develop (Samson & Falk, 1974a, b). Apparently, it is not the amount of alcohol drunk that produces dependence but the temporal pattern in which it is taken. Mello (1972) reports the same observation with humans.

A possible combination of adjunctive-drinking, pharmacological, and social-reinforcement models might answer the questions with which I began. Accident apart, social reinforcement is necessary for the introduction to drinking (Question 1) and readdiction (Question 3), or at least for the recommencement of drinking that makes readdiction possible. Adjunctive behavior accounts for drinking to excess; extraneous (social) reinforcement directs the excessive behavior to alcohol drinking rather than to some other pastime, like tennis, golf, or chess. The pharmacological model differentiates true addiction from devotion, and answers Question 2: What maintains the excessive behavior when it is harmful and no longer socially reinforced?

B. TOLERANCE AND DEPENDENCE

How could the pharmacological model function? It appeals to the principles of tolerance and dependence, which describe the respective observations that with some drugs repeated usage requires higher doses for constant effectiveness and that withdrawal of the drug causes physical disturbance and psychological stress. Beyond the pharmacological level the model can be dissected into two behavioral components. The first pertains to dependence and withdrawal and relates to the reinforcement model of stress reduction. Once dependence is acquired the only way to remove withdrawal distress is by further use of the drug of dependence, or a closely related compound. Stress reduction, in this case, refers not to the general control of tension by the drug, as happens with relaxants like meprobamate or chlordiazepoxide, but to the specific avoidance of anticipated withdrawal symptoms. This is why alcoholics become anxious when they start drinking and why they are reluctant to stop.

The second behavioral component of tolerance relates it to dependence. Tolerance has both cellular, which are pharmacological, and behavioral, which are psychological, implications. The relationship here of interest is at the psychological level. The argument is in three steps:

1. An addicting drug is an unconditional stimulus for an unconditioned physiological reaction. This physiological reaction is in two parts. The first is a direct disturbance caused by the drug; the second is a neutralizing response to this disturbance, a kind of rebound effect.

2. The first drug response is purely physiological; its magnitude is a direct monotonic fixed function of dosage. The rebound response is conditionable to the drug administration procedures. It grows with repeated drug administration. Therefore, larger drug doses are needed for initial responses to overcome the conditioned rebound. This is tolerance.

3. In the absence of the drug after the rebound response is conditioned,

only this response occurs to the spatio-temporal conditioned stimuli associated with drug administration. This is the syndrome of withdrawal. It may occur in unexpected situations by the mechanism of stimulus generalization. By this account, dependence on a drug is not dependence on effects the drug directly produces, but dependence on the drug to counteract conditioned rebound responses to these effects. The argument resembles one that Wikler (1965) applied to morphine addiction, that Solomon (1977) applied to acquired motivation in general, and that Siegel elegantly supports by evidence and argument in Chapter 6 of this volume.

V. Analysis of a Maladaptive Behavior: Polydipsia in the Rat

When food and water are freely available to laboratory rats they normally eat and drink at night (Siegel & Stuckey, 1947) and consume in the vicinity of 40 ml of water, mostly at the times they choose to eat (Kissileff, 1969). Figure 1.1 displays the eating and drinking rhythms of two mature male albino rats throughout a typical 24-hr day. The animals were maintained undeprived in experimental chambers in which barpresses were reinforced with 45-mg Noyes pellets on a fixed-interval 60-sec schedule. Water was available all the time. The graph shows, hour by hour, the number of pellets that each rat ate and the number of drinks that it took in the hour. No hour passed without some food being eaten (the food and water were replenished and the animals were weighed between 1700 and 1800 hr, which may explain the high intake values at that time), but there were several hours in which no drinks occurred.

Figure 1.2 shows selected 30-min segments of cumulative barpress records of one of the animals. They indicate eating and drinking occasions at times that the animal was active. (Pellet deliveries appear as spurs on the lower records.) Records A, B, D, E were collected when the animal was totally undeprived. Record C was obtained after the animal had, for the first time, been deprived of food, but not water, for 40 hr. More drinking appears in Record C, when the rat was temporarily underweight, than in the other records.

Underweight rats with some experience of food-pellet deliveries at intervals between about 15 sec and up to 4 min usually drink almost every time they eat. An example of this behavior is depicted in Figure 1.3 which contains cumulative licking records of a rat food-reinforced at fixed-intervals of 15, 30, 60, and 120 sec.

The repetitive sequence of eating and drinking depicted in Fig. 1.3 can lead to supernormal fluid intakes. In 3.17-hr-long sessions with food reinforcement scheduled once per minute on the average, Falk (1961) reported water intakes in excess of 90 ml, or over three times the normal daily consumptions of his rat subjects. This excessively high water consumption (schedule-induced polydipsia) led Falk (1972) to describe his finding as absurd. In his own words:

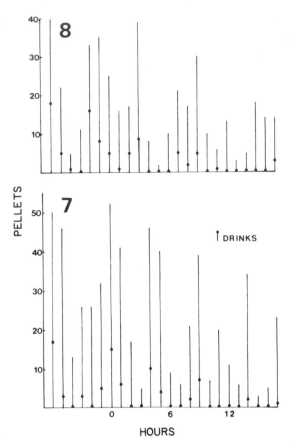

Figure 1.1 *Numbers of pellets eaten and drinks taken by each of two rats (Nos. 7 and 8) in a typical 24-hour period. The heights of bars represent numbers of pellets and the solid circles, numbers of drinks. Note that in every hour some pellets were eaten but that in many hours there were no drinks.*

It was absurd because food deprivation in rats yields a decrease in water intake, not an increase. It was absurd because heating a large quantity of room-temperature water to body heat and expelling it as copious urine is wasteful for an animal already pressed for energy stores. It is absurd for an animal to drink itself into a dilutional hyponatremia bordering on water intoxication. But perhaps most absurd was . . . the lack of an acceptable behavioural account [p. 149].

The earliest behavioral accounts of schedule-induced polydipsia appeal either to adventitious reinforcement (Clark, 1962) or to postprandial drinking that slaked a dry mouth (Stein, 1964). Neither of these accounts has survived experimental challenges: Drinking occurs after reinforcement (see Figure 1.3) not before it as the adventitious reinforcement theory requires, and drinking is not initiated by the consumption of a food pellet, as the dry-mouth theory demands,

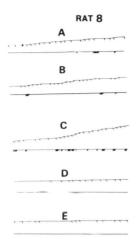

Figure 1.2 *Thirty-minute segments of cumulative barpress records produced in 24-hour-long sessions without food deprivation (A, B, D, E) and after 40 hours of food deprivation (C). Reinforcers (food pellets) were scheduled at fixed 1-min intervals and are marked by spurs on the cumulative records. Event marks on the lower graphs indicate drinks.*

but by the onset of a period when food becomes unavailable (Keehn & Colotla, 1971a).

More recent theories assign schedule-induced polydipsia to a broad class of adjuncts to responses maintained directly by reinforcement schedules (Falk, 1972; Staddon, 1977). These theories do not concentrate on the prominent maladaptive aspects of schedule-induced responses (e.g., Gilbert, 1976), but focus instead on adaptive functions that adjunctive behaviors may serve. Falk (1977) classifies adjunctive behaviors along with displacement activities in general and argues that these behaviors function as stabilizing influences on agonistic, mating, parental, and feeding activities in threatening environments. In contrast, I propose to consider schedule-induced polydipsia as specifically food-related and to show how it serves to facilitate food consumption by a food-depleted animal.

We see in Figure 1.3 that when single food pellets are scheduled intermittently, a bout of drinking follows nearly every pellet. If several pellets are available in succession, however, drinks are postponed until all the pellets are secured. This is visible in Figure 1.4, which contains cumulative licking records of two rats that were reinforced with a schedule that provided continuous reinforcement for 1, 6, 9, or 21 barpresses at the end of every 30 sec. Within these meal sizes it is apparent that eating takes precedence over drinking whenever that is possible even though the reinforcement schedule generates overdrinking, not overeating.

More evidence that schedule-induced drinking is subordinate to eating is

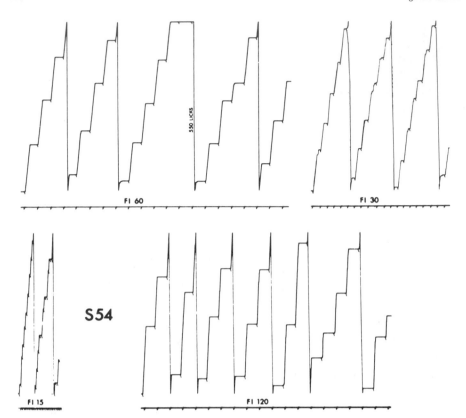

Figure 1.3 *Cumulative licking records of a hungry rat food reinforced on the designated schedules for bar-pressing. Spurs on the records indicate pellet deliveries. [From Colotla, V. A., Keehn, J. D., & Gardner, L. L. Control of schedule-induced drink durations by interpellet intervals. Psychonomic Science, 1970, 21, 137–139. Reprinted by permission.]*

provided by Millenson, Allen, and Pinker (1977). They demonstrated that levels of schedule-induced drinking generated by a variable-interval reinforcement schedule, in which momentary probabilities of food reinforcement are predictable to a certain extent, are not obtained with a comparable random-interval schedule in which occasions of food reinforcement are entirely unpredictable. With fixed-ratio schedules, Colotla (1973) likewise found that schedule-induced drinking is confined to occasions when food reinforcement is unlikely. Additional data supporting this conclusion are reviewed by Staddon (1977).

Falk (1961) remarked on two kinds of maladaptation in his discovery of schedule-induced drinking: supernormal drinking and the tendency for prolonged drinks to retard reinforcement. The evidence reviewed earlier shows that the second of these maladaptations is insubstantial, but it does not pertain to the question of excessive drinking. This question can be addressed by determining how eating entrains drinking over long periods of time.

The magnitude of schedule-induced polydipsia is determined by the

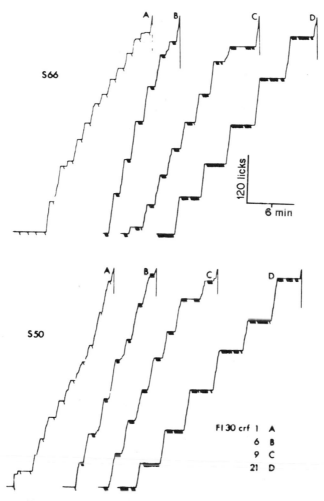

Figure 1.4. *Typical cumulative records of schedule-induced licks by hungry rats when 1, 6, 9, or 21 successive barpresses were food reinforced on a fixed interval 30-sec schedule. Spurs on the records indicate pellet deliveries. [From Keehn, J. D., & Colotla, V. A. Stimulus and subject control of schedule-induced drinking. Journal of the Experimental Analysis of Behavior, 1971, 16, 257–262. Copyright 1971 by The Society for the Experimental Analysis of Behavior, Inc. Reprinted by permission.]*

number of drinking bouts between food pellets, and by bout length. Up to a point, bout length depends on interpellet interval (see Fig. 1.3; Falk, 1967; Hawkins, Schrot, Githens, & Everett, 1972) and on the volume of fluid consumed per drink (Freed, Mendelson, & Bramble, 1976). Bout frequency depends on interpellet interval (Keehn & Colotla, 1971b), fluid composition (Keehn, Colotla, & Beaton, 1970), pellet composition (Christian, 1976), body weight (Keehn, 1979b), and session length (Keehn & Riusech, 1978).

Figure 1.5 shows the percentage of food pellets followed by drinks in suc-

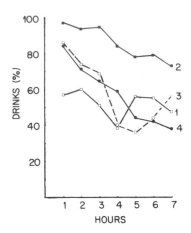

Figure 1.5 *Mean percentages of pellets followed by drinks in successive hours of 7-hour-long sessions in which hungry rats barpressed for food-pellets scheduled at fixed 60-sec intervals. [From Keehn, J. D., & Riusech, R. Schedule-induced drinking facilitates schedule-controlled feeding. Animal Learning and Behavior, 1979, 1, 41-44. Reprinted by permission.]*

cessive hours of 7-hour-long sessions in which each of four rats was maintained on a fixed-interval 60-sec food-reinforcement schedule for barpresses. For the first hour, three of the animals drank after more than 80% of the pellets that they ate; the other drank after about 60% of its pellets. In all cases drink frequencies declined steadily over the first 4 hours. After that, drink frequencies rose with two animals and continued to fall with the others, but every animal drank less frequently in the seventh than in the first hour of the sessions. Thus schedule-induced drinking is not impervious to satiation even though it continues well beyond normal limits.

Schedule-induced drinking is not infinitely maladaptive, but can it serve an adaptive function? Falk (1977) classifies schedule-induced drinking with displacement activities and other behavioral adjuncts to schedule-controlled responses and argues that these activities serve to stabilize approach–avoidance tendencies. Another possibility is that schedule-induced drinking cannot be categorized with other adjunctive activities (Heyman, 1977; Penney & Shull, 1977) and that it functions specifically to help food-depleted animals eat (Keehn & Riusech, 1979). Figure 1.6 supports this possibility. It shows the hourly average food-pellet intakes of the four rats who produced the data in Figure 1.5. The upper and lower curves display the rate of eating in the presence and absence of water in the experimental chamber, respectively. For about 3 hours the animals secured food at close to the maximum rate of 60, 45-mg pellets every hour. Thereafter, unless water was available, the rate of eating by the animals, who averaged 78 gm underweight, declined precipitously, such that significantly fewer pellets were consumed in the seventh hour when water was absent than when it was present.

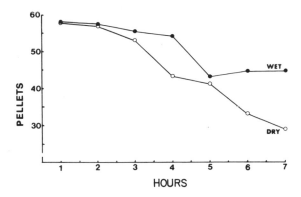

Figure 1.6   *Average number of food pellets secured per hour by four hungry rats reinforced for barpresses on a fixed 60-sec interval schedule with (WET) and without (DRY) water available in the experimental chamber.*

The maintenance of eating by underweight animals is an adaptive basis for schedule-induced drinking but not for schedule-induced polydipsia: The 7-hour water intakes of Rats 1, 2, 3, 4, respectively, averaged 56.3, 144.4, 85.8, and 66.1 ml, or from two to four times normal water intakes for this time span. Cohen (1975) believes that such excessive drinking occurs because eating raises the reinforcement value of drinking water. Keehn and Riusech (1977, 1979) argue the converse: that water increases the reinforcement value of dry food pellets, as sweeteners improve certain foods and beverages as reinforcers. Some support for this proposal appears in Figure 1.7.

Figure 1.7 displays numbers of barpresses, accumulated hourly, of the four rats individually in two experimental sessions with water (WET) and two sessions without water (DRY). With water present, barpressing typically continues fairly steadily for the whole 7-hour session; without water, sharp declines in barpressing for food appear after 3 or 4 hours with three of the animals. The exception, Rat 1, was the least prolific drinker.

An abrupt decline in barpressing by Rat 3 appears after 2 hours in the lower of its wet–dry records. This decline coincides with a break in the animal's drinking, which registered as 2965, 2449, *192, 163, 189,* 1117, and 884 licks in successive hours corresponding to the barpress record in Figure 1.7. The "break" between Hours 4 and 5 in the upper wet-dry barpress record of Rat 4 was also accompanied by a reduction in drinking: 588 licks in that hour as against an average of 1350 licks per hour in the rest of the session (range: 975–1768). Thus, eating and drinking together maintain barpressing at a higher rate than that maintained by eating alone.

A likely reason for this result is that food-plus-water is a more potent reinforcer for a hungry organism than is food alone. In this case, not only would schedule-induced drinking be expected but it would be expected to correspond with eating. It is precisely the entrainment of drinking by eating that is the basis of schedule-induced polydipsia. When an alternative method of enhancing rein-

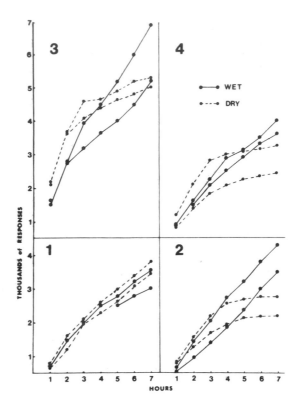

Figure 1.7 *Numbers of barpresses, accumulated hour by hour, by each of four rats food reinforced with a fixed-interval 60-sec schedule, on two sessions with (WET) and two sessions without (DRY) water available.*

forcement potency is employed, such as sweetening the food pellets (Christian, 1976), schedule-induced polydipsia does not occur. I propose, then, that the maladaptive aspect of schedule-induced polydipsia with respect to fluid consumption is a side effect of an adaptive function of schedule-induced drinking with respect to the intake of food, and that schedule-induced polydipsia can be construed as a demonstration of the power of positive reinforcement in opposition to homeostatic mechanisms in control of eating and drinking. Concerning similar conditions in humans, alcoholism, obesity, and other excessive indulgences are called to mind (Gilbert, 1976).

VI. Abnormal Behavior and Normal Theory

Schedule-induced polydipsia appears to be a maladaptive accompaniment of an otherwise adaptive activity. It illustrates a subtle operation of the law of effect in opposition to homeostatic controls of drinking (Epstein, Kissileff, & Stellar, 1973). As such, schedule-induced polydipsia exposes limits to the explanatory power of homeostasis in connection with the physiological bases of motivation. Conversely, other forms of maladaptive behaviors (Breland & Breland, 1966; Davis, 1977; Hearst & Jenkins, 1974), in which effects of reinforcement are overridden by phylogenetic determinants of behavior, expose limitations of the law of effect. In both cases, unnatural circumstances generate unnatural responses in lawful ways that force laws of normal behavior to be reassessed (Davis & Hurwitz, 1977).

Some behaviors are abnormal not because they are "pathological," but because they violate social or theoretical expectations or because their origins are poorly understood. As Ferguson (1968) says about abnormalities in domestic birds,

> The term "abnormal" in relation to the behavior of domestic birds is susceptible to different usages by husbandrymen, veterinary clinicians and behaviorists. Thus the commercial egg producer . . . may insist on classifying as alarmingly abnormal . . . broodiness, which seriously compromises egg production targets. The behaviorist records greater respect to . . . this normal maternal trait. . . . Similarly, increased exploratory pecking . . . in calcium-deprived birds, is normal by a behaviorist's definition. . . . The same activity . . . would appear to the clinician as an abnormal behavior resulting from the abnormal nutritional status [p. 190].

If, in Ferguson's example, the behaviorist's analysis is mistaken and the clinician's treatment is ineffective the bird may be labeled "compulsive" and treated as mentally ill. Thus a change in emphasis occurs from analysis of the origins of the bird's behavior to characterization of the status of the bird. This change fails to explain the bird's behavior and, in addition, misses an opportunity to examine how else the bird's behavior could be controlled. Such missed opportunities impede the scientific analysis of behavior and the clinical application of general behavioral laws, as also could the demand for "hi-fidelity" models of human psychopathologies (Russell & Burch, 1959) instead of the attempt at direct analysis of anomalous behaviors that animals display (cf. Davis, Chapter 8 of this volume).

REFERENCES

Adams, H. "Mental illness" or interpersonal behavior? *American Psychologist*, 1964, *19*, 191–197.

Amit, Z., & Stern, M. H. A further investigation of alcohol preference in the laboratory rat induced by hypothalamic stimulation. *Psychopharmacologia*, 1971, *21*, 317–327.

Azrin, N. H., Hutchinson, R. R., & Hake, D. P. Extinction-based aggression. *Journal of the Experimental Analysis of Behavior*, 1966, *9*, 191–204.

Barnett, S. A. "Displacement behavior" and "psychosomatic" disorder. *Lancet*, 1955, *2*, 1203–1208.

Barrett, J. E., & Weinberg, E. S. Effects of chlordiazepoxide on schedule-induced water and alcohol consumption in the squirrel monkey. *Psychopharmacologia*, 1975, *40*, 319–328.

Berkson, G. Abnormal stereotyped motor acts. In J. Zubin & H. F. Hunt (Eds.), *Comparative psychopathology: Animal and human*. New York: Grune & Stratton, 1967. Pp. 76–94.

Boren, J. L., & Gallup, G. G. Amphetamine attenuation of tonic immobility in chickens. *Physiological Psychology*, 1976, *4*, 429–432.

Bowden, D. M. Editor's introduction. In V. G. Startsev, *Primate models of human neurogenic disorders*. Hillsdale, New Jersey: Erlbaum, 1976. Pp. 1–10.

Bowlby, J. Human personality development in an ethological light. In G. Serban & A. Kling (Eds.), *Animal models in human psychobiology*. New York: Plenum, 1976.

Breland, K., & Breland, M. *Animal behavior*. New York: Macmillan, 1966.

Brion, A., & Ey, H. (Eds.). *Psychiatrie animale*. Paris: Desclée de Brouwer, 1964.

Broadhurst, P. L. Animal studies bearing on abnormal behavior. In H. J. Eysenck (Ed.), *Handbook of abnormal psychology* (2nd ed.). London: Pitman, 1973. Pp. 721–754.

Campbell, B. A., & Randall, P. K. Paradoxical effects of amphetamine on behavioral arousal in neonatal and adult rats: A possible animal model of the calming effect of amphetamine on hyperkinetic children. In N. R. Ellis (Ed.), *Aberrant development in infancy: Human and animal studies*. Hillsdale, New Jersey: Erlbaum, 1975. Pp. 105–112.

Cappell, H., & Herman, C. P. Alcohol and tension reduction. *Quarterly Journal of Studies on Alcohol*, 1972, *33*, 33–64.

Chertok, L. & Fontaine, M. Psychosomatics in veterinary medicine. *Journal of Psychosomatic Research*, 1963, *7*, 229–235.

Christian, J. J., & Ratcliffe, H. L. Shock disease in captive wild mammals. *American Journal of Pathology*, 1952, *28*, 725–737.

Christian, W. P. Control of schedule-induced polydipsia: Sugar content of the dry food reinforcer. *Psychological Record*, 1976, *26*, 41–47.

Clark, F. C. Some observations on the adventitious reinforcement of drinking under food reinforcement. *Journal of the Experimental Analysis of Behavior*, 1962, *5*, 61–63.

Conger, J. J. The effects of alcohol on conflict behavior in the albino rat. *Quarterly Journal of Studies on Alcohol*, 1951, *12*, 1–29.

Cohen, I. L. The reinforcement value of schedule-induced drinking. *Journal of the Experimental Analysis of Behavior*, 1975, *23*, 37–44.

Colotla, V. A. *Analysis of schedule-induced drinking with ratio schedules of reinforcement*. Unpublished doctoral dissertation, York Univ., 1973.

Colotla, V. A., Keehn, J. D., & Gardner, L. L. Control of schedule-induced drink durations by interpellet intervals. *Psychonomic Science*, 1970, *21*, 137–139.

Corson, S. A., Corson, E. O., Arnold, L. E., & Knopp, W. Animal models of violence and hyperkinesis. Interaction of psychopharmacologic and psychosocial therapy in behavior modification. In G. Serban & A. Kling (Eds.), *Animal models in human psychobiology*. New York: Plenum, 1976. Pp. 111–139.

Crawford, F. T., & Prestrude, A. M. (Eds.). Animal hypnosis. *Psychological Record*, 1977, *27*, (special issue).

Croft, P. G. Some observations on neurosis in farm animals. *Journal of Mental Science*, 1951, *97*, 584–588.

Davis, H. Response characteristics and control during lever-press escape. In H. Davis & H. M. B. Hurwitz (Eds.), *Operant–Pavlovian interactions*. Hillsdale, New Jersey: Erlbaum, 1977. Pp. 233–266.

Davis, H., & Hurwitz, H. M. B. (Eds.). *Operant–Pavlovian interactions*. Hillsdale, New Jersey: Erlbaum, 1977.

Draper, W. A., & Bernstein, I. S. Stereotyped behavior and cage size. *Perceptual and Motor Skills*, 1963, *10*, 231–234.

Duncan, I. J. H., & Wood-Gush, D. G. M. The effect of a Rauwolfia tranquilizer on stereotyped movements in frustrated domestic fowl. *Applied Animal Ethology*, 1974, *1*, 67–76.

Ellison, G. D. Animal models of psychopathology. The low-norepinephrine and low-serotonin rat. *American Psychologist*, 1977, *32*, 1036–1045.

Epstein, A. N., Kissileff, H. R., & Stellar, E. (Eds.). *The neuropsychology of thirst: New findings and advances in concepts*. Washington: Winston, 1973.

Eriksson, K. Behavioral and physiological differences among rat strains specifically selected for their alcohol consumption. *Annals of the New York Academy of Sciences,* 1972, *197,* 32–41.

Falk, J. L. Production of polydipsia in rats by an intermittent food schedule. *Science,* 1961, *133,* 195–196.

Falk, J. L. Control of schedule-induced polydipsia: Type, size, and spacing of meals. *Journal of the Experimental Analysis of Behavior,* 1967, *10,* 199–206.

Falk, J. L. The nature and determinants of adjunctive behavior. In R. M. Gilbert & J. D. Keehn (Eds.). *Schedule effects: Drugs, drinking and aggression.* Toronto: Univ. of Toronto Press, 1972. Pp. 148–173.

Falk, J. L. The origin and functions of adjunctive behavior. *Animal Learning and Behavior,* 1977, *5,* 325–335.

Falk, J. L., Samson, H. H., & Winger, G. Behavioral maintenance of high concentrations of blood ethanol and physical dependence in the rat. *Science,* 1972, *177,* 811–813.

Ferguson, W. Abnormal behavior in domestic birds. In M. W. Fox (Ed.), *Abnormal behavior in animals.* Philadelphia: Saunders, 1968. Pp. 188–207.

Ferster, C. B. Animal behavior and mental illness. *Psychological Record,* 1966, *16,* 345–356.

Finger, F. W. Experimental behavior disorders in the rat. In J. McV. Hunt (Ed.), *Personality and the behavior disorders* (Vol. II). New York: Ronald, 1944. Pp. 413–430.

Fraser, A. F. Intromission phobia in the bull. *Veterinary Record,* 1957, *69,* 621–623.

Fraser, A. F. Spontaneously occurring forms of tonic immobility in farm animals. *Canadian Journal of Comparative Medicine,* 1960, *24,* 330–333.

Freed, W. J., Mendelson, J., & Bramble, J. M. Intake-volume regulation during schedule-induced polydipsia in rats. *Behavioral Biology,* 1976, *16,* 245–250.

Fuller, J. L., & Clark, C. D. Genetic and treatment factors modifying the postisolation syndrome in dogs. *Journal of Comparative and Physiological Psychology,* 1966, *61,* 251–257.

Gallup, G. G., & Maser, J. D. Tonic immobility: Evolutionary underpinnings of human catalepsy and catatonia. In J. D. Maser & M. E. P. Seligman (Eds.), *Psychopathology: Experimental models.* San Francisco: Freeman, 1977. Pp. 334–357.

Giffen, P. J. The revolving door: A functional interpretation. *Canadian Review of Sociology and Anthropology,* 1966, *3,* 154–166.

Gilbert, R. M. Drug abuse as excessive behavior. *Canadian Psychological Review,* 1976, *17,* 231–240.

Harlow, H. F., & Suomi, S. J. Social recovery by isolation-reared monkeys. *Proceedings of the National Academy of Science,* 1971, *68,* 1534–1538.

Hawkins, T. D., Schrot, J. F., Githens, S. H., & Everett, P. B. Schedule-induced polydipsia: An analysis of water and alcohol ingestion. In R. M. Gilbert & J. D. Keehn (Eds.), *Schedule effects: Drugs, drinking and aggression.* Toronto: Univ. of Toronto Press, 1972. Pp. 95–128.

Hearst, E., & Jenkins, H. M. *Sign-tracking: The stimulus–reinforcer relation and directed behavior.* Austin, Texas: Psychonomic Society, 1974.

Hebb, D. O. Spontaneous neuroses in chimpanzees: Theoretical relations with clinical and experimental phenomena. *Psychosomatic Medicine,* 1947, *9,* 3–16.

Heyman, G. M. *The hedonic value of polydipsia for rats.* Paper presented at the annual meeting of the American Psychological Association, San Fransisco, September 1977.

Hunt, H. F. Problems in the interpretation of 'experimental neurosis.' *Psychological Reports,* 1964, *15,* 27–35.

Hunt, J. McV. The effects of infant feeding–frustration upon adult hoarding in the albino rat. *Journal of Abnormal and Social Psychology,* 1941, *36,* 338.

Hutchinson, R. R., Azrin, N. H., & Hunt, G. M. Attack produced by intermittent reinforcement of a concurrent operant response. *Journal of the Experimental Analysis of Behavior,* 1968, *11,* 484–495.

Isbell, H. Craving for alcohol. In World Health Organization Report, *Quarterly Journal of Studies on Alcohol,* 1955, *16,* 38.

Katz, D. *Animals and man; studies in comparative psychology.* London: Longmans Green, 1937.

Keehn, J. D. Maintenance of behaviour by secondary reinforcement. *Acta Psychologica*, 1966, *25*, 314–333.

Keehn, J. D. "Voluntary" consumption of alcohol by rats. *Quarterly Journal of Studies on Alcohol*, 1969, *30*, 320–329.

Keehn, J. D. Psychological sciences and the treatment of alcoholism. *Alcoholism*, 1973, *9*, 29–38.

Keehn, J. D. *Control of drinking by oral administration of trihexyphenidyl*. Paper presented at the fifteenth annual meeting of the Psychonomic Society, Boston 1974.

Keehn, J. D. *Origins of madness: Psychopathology in animal life*. Oxford: Pergamon, 1979. (a)

Keehn, J. D. Schedule-induced polydipsia, schedule-induced drinking, and body weight. *Bulletin of the Psychonomic Society*, 1979, *13*, 78–80. (b)

Keehn, J. D., & Colotla, V. A. Stimulus and subject control of schedule-induced drinking. *Journal of the Experimental Analysis of Behavior*, 1971, *16*, 257–262. (a)

Keehn, J. D., & Colotla, V. A. Schedule-induced drinking as a function of inter-pellet interval. *Psychonomic Science*, 1971, *23*, 69–71. (b)

Keehn, J. D., Colotla, V. A., & Beaton, J. M. Palatability as a factor in the pattern and duration of schedule-induced drinking. *Psychological Record*, 1970, *20*, 433–442.

Keehn, J. D., & Coulson, G. E. Schedule control of alcohol versus water selection by rats. *Quarterly Journal of Studies on Alcohol*, 1972, *33*, 395–399.

Keehn, J. D., & Coulson, G. E. Schedule induced choice of water versus alcohol. *Psychological Record*, 1975, *25*, 325–328.

Keehn, J. D., & Matsunaga, M. Attenuation of rats' alcohol consumption by trihexphenidyl. In O. Forsander & K. Eriksson (Eds.), *Biological aspects of alcohol consumption*. Helsinki: Finnish Foundation for Alcohol Studies, 1972. Pp. 251–257.

Keehn, J. D., & Riusech, R. Schedule-induced water and saccharin polydipsia under haloperidol. *Bulletin of the Psychonomic Society*, 1977, *9*, 413–415.

Keehn, J. D., & Riusech, R. Schedule-induced drinking facilitates schedule-controlled feeding. *Animal Learning and Behavior*, 1979, *7*, 41–44.

Kendell, R. E. *The role of diagnosis in psychiatry*. Oxford: Blackwell, 1975.

Kissileff, H. R. Food associated drinking in the rat. *Journal of Comparative and Physiological Psychology*, 1969, *67*, 284–300.

Lane-Petter, W. Some behaviour problems in common laboratory animals. *British Journal of Animal Behaviour*, 1953, *1*, 124–127.

Lester, D. Self-maintenance of intoxication in the rat. *Quarterly Journal of Studies on Alcohol*, 1961, *22*, 223–231.

Lester, D., & Freed, E. X. Criteria for an animal model of alcoholism. *Pharmacology, Biochemistry and Behavior*, 1973, *1*, 103–107.

Lester, D., & Greenberg, L. A. Nutrition and the etiology of alcoholism; the effect of sucrose, saccharin and fat on the self-selection of ethyl alcohol by rats. *Quarterly Journal of Studies on Alcohol*, 1952, *13*, 553–560.

Liddell, H. S. *Emotional hazards in animals and man*. Springfield, Illinois: Thomas, 1956.

Maser, J. D., & Gallup, G. G. Tonic immobility in the chicken: Catalepsy potentiation by uncontrollable shocks and alleviation by imipramine. *Psychosomatic Medicine*, 1974, *36*, 199–205.

Mason, W. A. Early social deprivation in the non-human primates: Implications for human behavior. In D. C. Glass (Ed.), *Environmental influences*. New York: Russell Sage Foundation, 1968. Pp. 70–100.

Mason, W. A., & Kenney, M. D. Redirection of filial attachments in rhesus monkeys: Dogs as mother surrogates. *Science*, 1974, *183*, 1209–1211.

Masserman, J. H. Psychobiologic dynamisms in behavior: An experimental study of neuroses and therapy. *Psychiatry*, 1942, *5*, 341–347.

Masserman, J. H. *Behavior and neurosis: An experimental psychoanalytic approach to psychobiologic principles*. Chicago: Univ. of Chicago Press, 1943.

Masserman, J. H., & Yum, K. S. An analysis of the influence of alcohol on experimental neurosis in cats. *Psychosomatic Medicine*, 1946, *8*, 36–52.

McKinney, W. T., Young, L. D., Suomi, S. J., & Davis, J. M. Chlorpromazine treatment of disturbed monkeys. *Archives of General Psychiatry,* 1973, *29,* 490–494.

Meisch, R. A., & Thompson, T. Ethanol intake in the absence of concurrent food reinforcement. *Psychopharmacologia,* 1971, *22,* 72–79.

Mello, N. K. Behavioral studies of alcoholism. In H. Begleiter & B. Kissin (Eds.), *Biology of alcoholism. Physiology and behavior.* New York: Plenum, 1972.

Merrill, G. G. Breaking the killing habit in dogs by inhibiting the conditioned reflex. *Journal of the American Veterinary Medicine Association,* 1945, *107,* 69–70.

Meyer-Holzapfel, M. Abnormal behavior in zoo animals. In M. W. Fox (Ed.), *Abnormal behavior in animals.* Philadelphia: Saunders, 1968. Pp. 476–503.

Millenson, J. R., Allen, R., & Pinker, S. Adjunctive drinking during variable and random interval food reinforcement schedules. *Animal Learning and Behavior,* 1977, *5,* 285–290.

Miller, N. E. Experiments relating Freudian displacement to generalization of conditioning. *Psychological Bulletin,* 1939, *36,* 516–517.

Mitchell, G. Abnormal behavior in primates. In L. Rosenblum (Ed.), *Primate behavior: Developments in field and laboratory research.* New York: Academic Press, 1970.

Mitchell, J. M. A psychosis among cats. *Veterinary Record,* 1953, *65,* 254.

Morrison, H., & McKinney, W. T. Environments of dysfunction: The relevance of primate models. In R. N. Walsh & W. T. Greenough (Eds.), *Environments in therapy for brain dysfunction.* New York: Plenum, 1976. Pp. 132–170.

Mowrer, O. H. An experimental analogue of "regression" with incidental observations on "reaction formation." *Journal of Abnormal and Social Psychology,* 1940, *35,* 56–87.

Myers, R. D. Brain mechanisms involved in volitional intake of ethanol in animals. In E. Forsander & K. Eriksson (Eds.), *Biological aspects of alcohol consumption.* Helsinki: Finnish Foundation for Alcohol Studies, 1972.

Myers, R. D., & Cicero, T. J. Effects of serotonin depletion on the volitional alcohol intake of rats during a condition of psychological stress. *Psychopharmacologia,* 1969, *15,* 373–381.

Myers, R. D., & Holman, R. B. A procedure for eliminating position habit in preference–aversion tests for ethanol and other fluids. *Psychonomic Science,* 1966, *6,* 235–236.

Newton, J. E. O., & Gantt, W. H. History of a catatonic dog. *Conditional Reflex,* 1968, *3,* 45–61.

Ogata, H., Ogata, F., Mendelson, J. H., & Mello, N. K. A comparison of techniques to induce alcohol dependence and tolerance in the mouse. *Journal of Pharmacology and Experimental Therapeutics,* 1972, *180,* 216–230.

Pavlov, I. P. *Conditioned reflexes.* London: Oxford Univ. Press, 1927.

Penney, J., & Schull, J. Functional differentiation of adjunctive drinking and wheel running in rats. *Animal Learning and Behavior,* 1977, *5,* 272–280.

Richter, C. P. Production and control of alcoholic craving in rats. In H. A. Abramson (Ed.), *Neuropharmacology.* Transactions of the Third Conference, Princeton. New York: Josiah Macy Foundation, 1956.

Richter, C. P. The phenomenon of unexplained sudden death in animals and man. In H. Feifel (Ed.), *The meaning of death.* New York: McGraw-Hill, 1959.

Rodgers, D. A. Alcohol preference in mice. In J. Zubin & H. F. Hunt (Eds.), *Comparative psychopathology: Animal and human.* New York: Grune & Stratton, 1967. Pp. 184–201.

Rosenblum, L. A., & Kaufman, I. C. Variations in infant development and responses to maternal loss in monkeys. *American Journal of Orthopsychiatry,* 1968, *38,* 418–426.

Russell, W. M. S., & Burch, R. L. *The principles of humane experimental technique.* London: Methuen, 1959.

Samson, H. H., & Falk, J. L. Alteration of fluid preferences in ethanol-dependent animals. *Journal of Pharmacology and Experimental Therapeutics,* 1974, *190,* 365–376. (a)

Samson, H. H., & Falk, J. L. Schedule-induced ethanol polydipsia: Enhancement by saccharin. *Pharmacology, Biochemistry and Behavior,* 1974, *2,* 835–838. (b)

Sanders, M. J. An experimental demonstration of regression in the rat. *Journal of Experimental Psychology,* 1937, *21,* 493–510.

Sanger, V. L., & Hamdy, A. H. A strange fright/flight behavior pattern (hysteria) in hens. *Journal of the American Veterinary Medicine Association,* 1962, *140,* 455–459.

Schmidt, J. P. Psychosomatics in veterinary medicine. In M. W. Fox (Ed.), *Abnormal behavior in animals.* Philadelphia: Saunders, 1968.

Scott, J. P., Steward, J. M., & DeGhett, V. J. Separation in infant dogs: Emotional response and motivation consequences. In J. P. Scott & E. C. Senay (Eds.), *Separation and depression: Clinical and research aspects.* Washington: American Association for the Advancement of Science, 1973. Pp. 3–32.

Seligman, M. E. P. *Helplessness.* San Francisco: Freeman, 1975.

Seligman, M. E. P., Maier, S. F., & Geer, J. The alleviation of learned helplessness in the dog. *Journal of Abnormal and Social Psychology,* 1968, *73,* 256–262.

Shagass, C. Experimental neurosis. In A. M. Freedman, H. I. Kaplan, & B. J. Shadok (Eds.), *Comprehensive textbook of psychiatry* (2nd ed.). Baltimore: Williams & Wilkins, 1975. Pp. 428–445.

Shapiro, M. B. The requirements and implications of a systematic science of psychopathology. *Bulletin of the British Psychological Society,* 1975, *28,* 149–155.

Sidman, M. Normal sources of pathological behavior. *Science,* 1960, *132,* 61–68.

Siegel, P. S., & Stuckey, H. L. The diurnal course of water and food intake in the normal mature rat. *Journal of Comparative and Physyiological Psychology,* 1947, *40,* 365–370.

Siegler, M., & Osmond, H. Models of madness. *British Journal of Psychiatry,* 1966, *112,* 1193–1203.

Sinclair, J. D. Rats learning to work for alcohol. *Nature,* 1974, *249,* 590–592.

Skinner, B. F. *Science and human behavior.* New York: Macmillan, 1953.

Solomon, R. L. An opponent-process theory of acquired motivation: The affective dynamics of addiction. In J. D. Maser & M. E. P. Seligman (Eds.), *Psychopathology: Experimental models.* San Francisco: Freeman, 1977. Pp. 66–103.

Staddon, J. E. R. Schedule-induced behavior. In W. K. Honig & J. E. R. Staddon (Eds.), *Operant behavior.* New York: Prentice-Hall, 1977. Pp. 125–152.

Stampfl, T. G., & Levis, D. J. Essentials of implosive therapy: A learning theory-based psychodynamic behavioral therapy. *Journal of Abnormal Psychology,* 1967, *72,* 496–503.

Startsev, V. G. *Primate models of human neurogenic disorders.* Hillsdale, New Jersey: Erlbaum, 1976.

Stein, L. S. Excessive drinking in the rat: Superstition or thirst? *Journal of Comparative and Physiological Psychology,* 1964, *58,* 237–242.

Stout, C., & Snyder, R. L. Ulcerative colitis-like lesion in Siamang gibbons. *Gastroenterology,* 1969, *57,* 256–261.

Suomi, S. J., & Harlow, H. F. Production and alleviation of depressive behaviors in monkeys. In J. D. Maser & M. E. P. Seligman (Eds.), *Psychopathology: Experimental models.* San Francisco: Freeman, 1977. Pp. 131–173.

Suomi, S. J., Harlow, H. F., & McKinney, W. T. Monkey psychiatrists. *American Journal of Psychiatry,* 1972, *128,* 928–932.

Thomas, E., & de Wald, L. Experimental neurosis: Neurophysiological analysis. In J. D. Maser & M. E. P. Seligman (Eds.), *Psychopathology: Experimental models.* San Francisco: Freeman, 1977. Pp. 214–231.

Thompson, W. R., Melzack, R., & Scott, T. H. "Whirling behavior" in dogs as related to early experience. *Science,* 1956, *123,* 939.

Tinbergen, N. Derived activities: Their causation, biological significance, origin and emancipation during evolution. *Quarterly Review of Biology,* 1952, *27,* 1–32.

Tinbergen, N. Ethology and stress diseases. *Science,* 1974, *185,* 20–27.

Tinklepaugh, O. L. The self-mutilation of a male macacus rhesus monkey. *Journal of Mammalogy,* 1928, *9,* 293–300.

Tuber, D. S., Hothersall, D., & Voith, V. L. Animal clinical psychology: A modest proposal. *American Psychologist,* 1974, *29,* 762–766.

Van Lawick-Goodall, J. *In the shadow of man.* Boston: Houghton Mifflin, 1971.

Ward, I. L. Sexual behavior differentiation: Prenatal hormonal and environmental control. In R. C. Friedman, R. M. Richart & R. J. Van de Wiele (Eds.), *Sex differences in behavior.* New York: Wiley, 1974.

Weiss, J. M., Glazer, H. I., & Pohorecky, L. A. Coping behavior and neurochemical changes: An alternative explanation for the original "learned helplessness" experiments. In G. Serban & A. Kling (Eds.), *Animal models in human psychobiology.* New York: Plenum, 1976. Pp. 141-173.

Wickens, D. D. Classical conditioning, as it contributes to the analyses of some basic psychological processes. In F. J. McGuigan & D. B. Lumsden (Eds.), *Contemporary approaches to conditioning and learning.* Washington: Winston, 1973. Pp. 213-243.

Wikler, A. Conditioning factors in opiate addiction and relapse. In D. M. Wilner & G. G. Kassebaum (Eds.), *Narcotics.* New York: McGraw-Hill, 1965. Pp. 85-100.

Wise, C. D., Berger, B. D., & Stein, L. Benzodiazepines: Anxiety reducing activity by reduction of serotonin turnover in the brain. *Science,* 1972, *177,* 180-183.

Wolpe, J. *Psychotherapy by reciprocal inhibition.* Stanford: Stanford Univ. Press, 1958.

Zigler, E., & Phillips, L. Psychiatric diagnosis and symptomatology. *Journal of Abnormal and Social Psychology,* 1961, *63,* 69-75.

Zubin, J., & Hunt, H. F. (Eds.). *Comparative psychopathology: Animal and human.* New York: Grune & Stratton, 1967.

RONALD K. SIEGEL

Natural Animal Addictions: An Ethological Perspective

2

I. Introduction

The cause of the worldwide consumption of hashish, opium, wine, and to-bacco," wrote Leo Tolstoy (1890/1975), "lies not in the taste, nor in any pleasure, recreation, or mirth they afford, but simply in man's need to hide from himself the demands of conscience . . . for man is a spiritual as well as animal being [p. 45]." Such behavior is termed *intoxication* and a widely held belief is that man is the only species that intoxicates itself through the administration of psychoactive drugs. Indeed, it is a traditional, albeit tacit, assumption of psychological thinking that man is the only animal that becomes addicted to drugs outside of laboratory settings. Hence, man's drug addictions are un-natural, deviant, and pathological, if not immoral as well. In the *Art of Intoxication,* author Reverend Crane (1871) expressed this thinking in the following passage: "Intoxicants are also within reach of the brute, but his better instinct warns him, and he obeys. . . . By what law, then, is any intoxicant needful for us? The narcotic indulgences of men are the contrivance of evil ingenuity, a perversion, an abuse, a crime [pp. 77–78]." Despite the evidence of laboratory studies wherein animals self-administer and become addicted to numerous psychoactive drugs, modern psychopharmacologists still believe that "man shares with lower forms the ability to react with pleasure to such drugs, but only man has had the ingenuity to identify these pleasure-producing substances by his own initiative [Brill, 1972, p. 6]."

PSYCHOPATHOLOGY IN ANIMALS
Research and Clinical Implications

Recent ethological studies, discussed later, suggest that numerous species besides man self-administer psychoactive plants in natural habitats. Many of these self-administrations are marked by both intoxication and addiction. Furthermore, analyses of the stimulus control in such behaviors suggest that some animal addictions may reflect natural biologic responses to cues from the internal and external environments. Moreover, these studies reveal that man has learned much of his knowledge of plant drugs and medicines from observations on and modeling of these animal behaviors. In this sense, man is much closer to his "animal being" than even Tolstoy may have guessed.

A. Definitions and Examples

The term *intoxication* (which comes from the Latin *intoxicatio,* 'poisoning' or 'inebriation') is far from precise, but one definition that is generally accepted in psychopharmacology is "the abnormal state induced by a chemical agent . . . excitement or exhilaration beyond self-control [*Webster's Third New International Dictionary*]." By this definition, it is likely that many animals have been intoxicated through the ingestion of plant toxins and allied substances. Grazing cattle, horses, and sheep on the Great Plains of North America sometimes browse locoweed (*Astragulus* spp.) and become unusually excited and "drunk" as the result of the mineral selenium found in the plant. Some animals appear to seek out drug intoxications, as is the case with elephants in Africa and Asia that show a "passion" and "addiction" for alcohol, either in the form of fermented fruit or beverages. Under the right circumstances, the intoxications may be regarded as pleasurable and even hallucinatory. Several members of the cat family repeatedly eat catnip *(Nepeta cataria)* containing hallucinogenic nepetalactone oils and appear to play with imaginary butterflies and mice. Horses and cattle in many parts of the world browse opium poppies and become excited and disoriented. Conversely, many animals will actively avoid ingestion of plant drugs like henbane (*Hyoscyamus niger,* containing atropine and scopolamine) that have nauseating odors, tastes, or other aversive properties.

In the present context, the word *addiction* (from the Latin *addicere,* 'to be fond of') can refer to an animal's natural fondness and craving for a preferred plant substance (positive addiction). Many animals display specific hungers for plant drugs, and ethologists have described many such preferences as "passions," "cravings," and "addictions." For example, in Australia the koala bear is known as a drug addict since it feeds almost exclusively on *Eucaplyptus* which has a "narcotic effect" and reportedly produces long periods of sleep. Pigeons and other birds have a distinct preference for marihuana seeds (*Cannabis* spp.), and the subsequent ingestion often results in altered behavior. Many other animals appear to be "addicted" to psychoactive substances produced by other animals. For example, a number of ants lick intoxicating attractants secreted by beetles and become stuporous, only to repeat the administration once the "narcotic" effects have worn off (cf. Siegel, 1973). Yet other species clearly have "negative addictions" and actively avoid ingestion of psychoactive substances. For example, grazing animals on ranges in the Hawaiian Islands will actively avoid ingestion of *Datura stramonium* (jimsonweed) unless other forage is unavailable. And some wild baboons in Africa are alleged to have an almost innate avoidance of psychoactive mushrooms and other fungi.

Do the drug-seeking and drug-avoiding behaviors of animals have anything in common with those of man? The present chapter attempts to answer this question in light of recent ethological findings. The first section examines the origins of plant drugs and their coevolution with animal life. The inevitable ecological encounters between animals and plant drugs is traced by examples from folklore, mythology, and ethology. The human modeling of this animal behavior is discussed in terms of the discovery and use of psychoactive drugs as foods, medicines, and religious-magical agents. The second section attempts to integrate these findings in terms of the stimulus control variables in animal addictions. These variables include botanical, biochemical, and behavioral factors. Fostered by some speculation and guided by recent empirical findings in the field and laboratory, a general explanation of natural addiction is developed in terms of an animal model. Such a model may prove valuable in the study of drug dependency in man and it would have the advantage over others of greater experimental control over biological, environmental, and pharmacological variables without the addition of untestable mentalistic constructs.

The search for a natural model of animal addiction is based on a historic tradition of applying principles of animal behavior to parallel human events. Indeed, man learned much of the rudiments of medicine, including the therapeutic application of psychopharmacologic agents, by observing which plants and treatments were used by animals suffering from wounds, fever, or infection. The symbol of the serpent as an emblem of medicine played an important part in the healing of Egyptians and Babylonians and dates to 4000 B.C. Many medicines and charms were derived from the behavior and feeding habits of snakes. Even Aesculapius, the mythological patron saint of medicine, was taught the pharmaceutical art by an animal. The actual practice of studying medicine through observations of animal behavior dates back to Hindu writings of 1000 B.C. There, observations of the powerful jaws of large ants remaining firmly attached to objects even after the ant was beheaded led to the custom of using ants to close and "clampstitch" wounds (Clausen, 1954). Observations of dogs healing themselves led to the Eskimo custom of lapping cuts and wounds with the tongue (Murphy, 1954). The wise Avicenna of Cordoba, one of the most famous physicians of the twelfth century, and the famous Spanish pharmacist Avenzoar, discovered many medicines and treatments by observations of animals (Lewinsohn, 1954). Others, such as Signior Jaquinto, physician to Queen Anne, would often follow animals for long periods of time in order to be led to healing herbs (Northcote, 1912/1971). Even the modern French herbalist Mességué describes how he learned about the healing properties of plant drugs by observing wild animals in natural habitats (Mességué, 1970). It is in this spirit that we embark here on an ethologic search for an understanding of natural animal addictions.

II. Self-Administration of Psychoactive Plants

A. EVOLUTION OF PLANT DRUGS

In the beginning of the Mesozoic Era, some 225 million years ago, the coal-swamp flora and fauna were disappearing, while the angiosperms and the reptiles began their evolutionary advance. The angiosperms, which cover the major groups of flowering plants, rapidly became dominant in the plant kingdom because of their superior reproductive mechanisms and broad range of adaptable forms. Two major changes occurred in their plant chemistry during this period that would eventually give rise to the phenomena of drug addiction.

First, angiosperms started to produce hydrolysable tannins. There is little knowledge concerning the role of tannins in plants, but these substances do act as antifungal agents for the plants and, for animals, are bitter tasting, inhibit protein digestion and enzyme activity, and cause liver lesions if taken in excess. Second, angiosperms started to produce aromatic amino-acid-based alkaloids, substances which constitute the major groups of psychoactive agents. As a general rule, alkaloids have no known function in plants, and no one really knows why plants produce these drugs. However, alkaloids taste bitter like the tannins but have a wider range of physiologic activity including psychologic, tetragenic, and toxic effects. They act as extremely effective feeding deterents, and it has been argued that many of the naturally occurring plant drugs are evolutionarily justified in terms of the maladaptive effects that they could have on herbivores (Bever, 1970; Eisner & Halpern, 1971). Indeed, Swain (1974) has noted that these major changes in plant chemistry coincided with the sudden extinction of the dominant life in the animal kingdom, the dinosaurs. These giant reptiles, unlike the birds and mammals which followed them, failed to evolve effective mechanisms with which to detect and/or detoxify these alkaloids. Subsequently, changes occurred in the thickness of dinosaurs' egg shells, there was an increase in the size of their hypothalamus, and their fossils have been found in contorted positions suggestive of alkaloid poisoning.

Today, some 65 million years later, veterinarians are well acquainted with the contorted bodies of grazing horses, cattle, and other animals that have accidentally ingested lethal amounts of highly toxic alkaloidal plants, such as species of *Senecio, Datura,* and *Nicotiana.* Similar accidents have occurred in man. For example, a group of soldiers, sent to Jamestown in 1676 to put down Bacon's Rebellion, ate the young shoots of *Datura* as a pot green and became severely intoxicated for several days. *Datura* (containing scopolamine, atropine, and hyoscyamine) has since been known as "Jamestown" or jimson weed. Anthony's legion had a similar *Datura* experience during a retreat in 38–37 B.C.

Periodic outbreaks of ergotism, resulting from accidental ingestion of a rye fungus *Claviceps purpurea,* were common in the Middle Ages and even in this century. Epidemics occurred in France as far back as A.D. 857 and as recently as 1951. In A.D. 944, 40,000 people died of the disorder. In many such cases, the death of dogs and other animals fed on the rye fungus was equally unavoidable and dramatic.

Ingestion of plant alkaloids and allied substances did not always result in death. For example, locoweed intoxication is characterized by paresis, ataxia, dullness, and a tendency of the animals to isolate themselves from social groupings, but death is rare. The animals appear to act crazy, hence the name *loco* which means 'cracked brain'. There are no documented deaths in man due to locoweed, but intoxication is marked by stupor, ataxia, fixed gaze, hyperactivity, and a tendency to isolate oneself (Marsh, 1909).

Even when ingestion of plant drugs did not result in death or even intoxication of the animals, it did contribute to the dispersal of these plants throughout the world (cf. Ridley, 1930). The *Strychnos* (containing the highly poisonous alkaloid, strychnine) is particularly interesting in these phenomena. Although animals rapidly learn which fruits are edible and which are not, monkeys, civetcats, and elephants will readily devour the intensely bitter pulp of *Strychnos,* swallowing the seeds and then evacuating them. Interestingly, they refuse to eat the pleasant-tasting seeds of the cocoa *(Theobroma cacao),* but ingest the bitter seeds and fruits of other psychoactive plants such as *Coffea.* Horses as well as cattle constantly swallow spores of hallucinogenic fungi (e.g., *Psilocybe* spp.) in the grass they eat and pass them in a germinating condition. Other psychoactive plants ingested and dispersed by animals throughout the world include: *Opuntias* (cattle, pigs, emus, crows); *Daturas* (goats, cattle, horses, ants); *Atropa belladonna* (birds, pigs); *Solanum nigrum* (birds), *Senecio vulgaris* (sparrows); *Digitalis purpurea* (earthworms); *Claviceps purpurea* (flies); *Physostigma venenosum* (caterpillars); *Cicuta* spp. (deer); *Amanita muscaria* (deer, rodents, insects); *Duboisia hopwoodii* (birds); *Papaver somniferum* (grazing animals); *Sophora secundiflora* (grazing animals); among others.

B. DISCOVERY OF PLANT DRUGS BY OBSERVATIONS ON ANIMALS

Not all of man's encounters with naturally occurring drugs were accidental. Ritual, magical, religious, or medicinal uses of drugs date back into the early history of both Old World and New World peoples. Anthropologists have traced the use of hallucinogens, for example, as far back as Paleolithic Europe and Neolithic Asia Minor (La Barre, 1975). Archaeologically, hallucinogen use has been dated to 8500 B.C. in the New World. Man's use of other drugs may be older than that. Throughout recorded history, there are abundant instances of such plant use being surprisingly discriminative and efficacious. Early man learned much of this basic psychopharmacology from observations on animal-plant interactions.

Folklore and mythology are replete with examples of man's discovery of plant drugs through observations on animal behavior (cf. Siegel, 1973). For example, in Australia, the aborigines knew of leaves that fell into water holes and killed both the fish and emu in the area. For centuries, the natives ate these animals without ill effects. Later, expeditions to the area revealed that the leaves of the plant *(Duboisia)* contain the alkaloids atropine and scopolamine, which have useful anesthetic effects. Similarly, the ancient Hawaiians discovered the stupefying effects of "auhuhu" on fish and the plant was later identified as *Tephrosia purpurea* (Arnold, 1944). In the East Indies, natives discovered and used *Anamirta cocculus* berries (containing picrotoxin) to stun fish and cause them to rise to the surface for easy capture (Esplin & Zablocka-Esplin. 1970). And in tropical Asia, observations of birds falling down after flying over the "upas" trees gave rise to the discovery of *Rauwolfia serpentina* (reserpine).

In India, folklore maintains that the mongoose, when bitten by a cobra, retires to the jungle to look for a plant known as Mungo root *(Ophiorrhiza mungos)*, which it eats as an antidote to the venom. Mongooses have also been reported to pretreat themselves by rubbing the root over the head and body parts which the snake might bite. This treatment usually results in a "drugged sleep" from which the animal quickly recovers (Hinton & Dunn, 1967). Natives of northern Rhodesia observed cobras peeling and eating the bark of *Strophanthus welsitschii-Mimbapanda*. This naturally enough evolved as a charm against snake bites as did the Mungo root (Gilges, 1955). However, while infusion teas of the roots of both plants have been used as treatment for gonorrhea and scabies, there is no evidence to indicate that they are effective against snake bites. After watching koalas become sleepy from eating *Eucalyptus,* Australian aborigines adopted the custom of using the leaves to sooth and heal wounds (Mathison, 1958). Although the sleepy behavior may be more easily explained by the normal biological rhythms of the nocturnal koala, they do feed exclusively on *Eucalyptus* giving support to the native belief that koalas are true drug addicts. Nonetheless, analysis of the leaves revealed high concentrations of various oils with local anesthetic properties as well as marked germicidal effects (Penfold & Willis, 1961).

Many stories are told about the discovery of stimulant drugs by animals. The legendary discovery of coffee was purportedly around A.D. 900 by an Abyssinian tending his herd of goats. The herder noticed that his animals became abnormally "frisky" after eating the bright red fruit of a tree that was later isolated and identified as coffee (Taylor, 1965). In Yemen, a shepherd discovered that one of his goats would leave the herd at a certain point to eat some leaves, after which it ran very fast and exhibited signs of extraordinary stimulation. The shepherd tried the leaves himself and found them quite stimulating and reviving after a day's work. Since that time, the use of these "qat" leaves *(Catha edulis,* containing the alkaloids cathine, cathedine, and cathenine) spread throughout the entire country (Abdo Abbasy, 1957).

Almost identical stories are told of the discovery coca *(Erythroxylum coca,* containing cocaine) based on modeling of animal behaviors. One story claims that coca was first used by pack animals traveling in the mountains of Peru that were deprived of their normal forage. The coca leaves sustained the animals, prompting humans to copy the coca-eating behavior. Indeed, Mortimer (1901) notes that coca was used by man, and perhaps by beast, when traveling in the mountains where ingestion was probably induced by irregular eating, improper diet, and lack of oxygen at higher altitudes. Such use is similar to that of peyote cactus (*Lophophora williamsii*, containing mescaline) used in small doses by Huichol Indians traveling in the Sierra Madre mountains of Mexico (Lumholtz, 1902). Recent nutritional analysis has revealed that 100 gm of coca leaves contains 305 calories, 18.9 gm of protein and 46.2 gm of carbohydrates, and satisfies the Recommended Dietary Allowance for calcium, iron, phosphorus, vitamins A, B_2, and E (Duke, Aulik, & Plowman, 1975). Thus, the coca leaves could have sustained the travelers. However, the full complement of nutrients present in coca leaf may not be fully absorbed in the normal chewing–sucking ingestion employed by man.

Another Peruvian story claims that a number of birds and insects are fond of coca seeds and leaves, and the speed with which they devour the plant suggested stimulant properties to early human observers. Mortimer (1901/1974) indicated that ants and other insects avidly devoured the leaves, but there was no indication of psychoactive effects from this ingestion. However, he did note that "the birds are great lovers of coca seeds, and when these are lightly sown on the surface of the nursery it is necessary to cover the beds at night with cloths to guard against 'picking and stealing' [p. 238]." One may speculate that early man modeled his coca use after such observations.

A folktale told by Huichol Indians in Mexico claims that tobacco was first used by birds which favored the yellow flowers of the wild varieties (e.g., *Nicotiana rustica*). The story states that the tobacco enabled the birds to fly high and strong and to see great visions. Accordingly, early man copied the behaviors in their quest to communicate with their gods and see visions. Indeed, Furst (1972, p. 176) notes that according to Huichol mythology, tobacco was once a hawk and "is said to give one visions [Myerhoff, 1974, p. 126]." And among the myths of the Warao Indians, tobacco is intimately associated with the initial discovery "through the conscious act of a bird spirit [Wilbert, 1972, p. 65]." Recent anthropological work has revealed that tobacco functions as an hallucinogen among many primitive peoples, especially the Huichol Indians, and the psychotomimetic effects may be due to high concentrations of nicotine or hallucinogenic harmine alkaloids (Janiger & Dobkin de Rios, 1973; Siegel, Collings, & Diaz, 1977).

Another story told by natives from Mexico claims that a number of insects are fond of tobacco leaves, and the speed with which they devour the leaves suggested the presence of stimulants. In addition, when eaten by a particular type of worm, tobacco has the magical ability to transform the worm into a small hawk. Wolf (1962) has listed the insect pests of tobaccos and these include: the tobacco flea beetle (which prefers tobacco but also feeds on *Datura* and related plants), cutworms, tobacco thrips, wireworms, budworms, aphids, cigarette beetles, and tobacco moths. Interestingly, one insect pest, the hornworm, is the larval stage of the "hawk moth" (*Protoparce* spp.). Thus, it remains possible that early man's myths may have been based on observations of real natural phenomena.

Numerous stories also detail the discovery of hallucinogens from observations of animal behavior. Pope (1969) suggests that *Tabernanthe iboga,* a hallucinogenic plant containing ibogaine, may have been discovered by boars, porcupines, and gorillas in Africa: "Several accounts mention that the natives saw boars dig up and eat the roots of the plant, only to go into a wild frenzy, jumping around and perhaps fleeing from frightening visions [p. 174]." In Czechoslovakia, peasant stories tell that man learned of the stimulant properties of *Cannabis* by observing the abnormally high jumps of grasshoppers that fed on local varieties of this plant. And the ancient Greeks adopted the habit of eating hempseeds after watching finches ingest them and become extremely tame and sedate (cf. Schultes, 1970).

The mythology of many peoples suggest that fruit may have been one of the earliest intoxicants for both animals and man. The word *fruit,* from *frui* meaning 'to enjoy', figures prominently in many legends of intoxication (cf. Stevens, 1949). Chinese folklore tells of a sacred apple tree surrounded by dragons. Ancient Sumerian pottery depicts a serpent protecting the sacred orange tree of life. Similar myths are found in the Babylonian and Hebraic Gardens of Eden. Indeed, it may be speculated that the original Hebraic apple tree was "thorn-apple," a vernacular name for *Datura,* also known as Devil's Trumpet. The myth would thus function to help man avoid an unpleasant, if not lethal, intoxication.

The relative ease of discovering fermentation in the normal course of storing foods (fruits and grain) probably accounted for alcohol being the first drug used and developed by man. According to an old Chinese legend, a flock of sparrows once picked some grains of rice to store for the winter in a tube of bamboo. The autumn rains came and flooded the tube causing the rice to ferment into wine. This was accidentally eaten by both birds and man (Lehner & Lehner, 1962). Even today the Chinese ideograph for *samshu* (rice wine) consists of the ideographs of birds and water. Another legend tells that "Noah became the first viniculturist after he had observed a male goat eating the grapes of the *labrusca* and becoming drunk and gay as a result [Janson, 1952, pp. 245–246]." Interestingly, goats in ancient Greece were sacrificed to Dionysus as punishment for injuring the vine. Another version of this story tells of Adam modeling the alcohol-seeking behavior of monkeys in the Garden of Eden. And the Greek historian Timotheus mentions that monkeys were loved by Dionysus because they did not destroy the vines in satisfying their fondness for fermented grapes.

The names given by early man to many plants also reveal much about their observed effects on animals (cf. Folkard, 1884). The etymology of such terms provides us with an instructive lesson in the natural history of animal drug use. Many plants were named for their apparent aversive properties. Henbane (*Hyoscyamus niger,* containing atropine and scopolamine) seems to have derived its name from the baneful effects its seeds have upon poultry. When eaten by man, henbane produced sleepy and drowsy behavior and thus acquired the alternative name "Insana." Similarly, Leopold's Bane *(Doronicum pardalianches)* caused the death of leopards that ate it; Sheep's Bane *(Hydrocotyle vulgaris)* poisoned sheep; Swine Bane *(Chenopodium rubrum)* killed swine; fly-agaric *(Amanita muscaria)* killed the flies that landed on it; wormwood *(Absinthium* spp., containing thujone which is similar to tetrahydrocannabinol found in *Cannabis)* drove away insects and insect larvae; Flea Bane (marigolds) repulsed fleas and other insects; and Cow Bane *(Cicuta virosa* or water hemlock) killed cattle and other grazing animals. Indeed, the Iroquois Indians observed these latter effects and subsequently employed hemlock roots in their numerous suicides.

Other plants were identified by the attraction that animals displayed toward them. Catnip *(Nepeta cataria)* attracted cats that eagerly ingested it; Hare's Lettuce *(Lactuca* spp.) was allegedly used by rabbits for stimulant and medicinal effects, later by man as an opium substitute for its narcotic and stimulant properties; Dog Grass *(Triticum caninum),* Swine Grass *(Polygonum aviculare),* Pigeon Grass *(Vervain),* and Goose Grass *(Galium aparine)* all attracted their respective namesakes. Pigeon Candy was an early vernacular name for hempseeds derived from stimulating effects on pigeons and for its "great assistance in taming birds and in training them for shows as all fears seem to be set aside when they know that hempseed is being offered [Levi, 1957, p. 499]."

C. DISTRIBUTION OF ANIMAL ADDICTIONS IN NATURE

I have collected over 1546 cases of animals self-administering plant drugs in natural habitats. Many cases represent unconfirmed folklore and mythology; others are clearly accidental in nature. Nonetheless, there are reports of animals self-administering plant drugs and confirming observations that this behavior is often repeated by the same individual animals. Many accounts and descriptions of these observed behaviors have used terms such as "craving," "passion," and "addiction" to describe the self-administrations. In 310 cases there are sufficient observations and data to suggest that ingestions are both intentional and "addicting." These cases involve mammals (122), birds (58), insects (56), reptiles (12), fish (5), as well as other groups of animals (12). The vast majority of these animals are herbivores, which are divided between domesticated (41%) and feral (59%) species.

The nature of this animal self-administration appears uncannily similar to that of man. In an analysis of 144 hunting and gathering groups of man, Blum and associates (1969) have noted that 47% of the plant drug self-administrations are for psychoactive effects, whereas the remainder are used for social, religious, magical, or medicinal purposes. In the 310 instances of intentional animal self-

Table 2.1

Comparative Distribution of Major Groups of Psychoactive Plant Drugs Used by Cultural Groups of Man (N = 144) and Species of Animals (N = 109) in Natural Habitats[a]

Man		Animal	
Plant drugs	Number of cultures	Plant drugs	Number of species
Tobacco	57	Alcohol	28
Alcohol	52	Tobacco	20
Hallucinogens	40	Hallucinogens	19
Stimulants	15	Cannabis	18
Cannabis	7	Stimulants	9
Opium	3	Opium	9
Coca	1	Coca	6

[a] The human data are adapted from Blum (1969.) Correlation with animal data is r = .90, p < .01.

administrations, 45% are marked by observable psychoactive effects and the rest are used in the natural foraging of social groups or for medicinal effects by sick or wounded animals.

The 310 cases involve 109 different animal species. The distribution of drugs used by these animals is compared to those drugs used by the hunting and gathering groups of man in Table 2.1. Here it can be seen that both animals and man choose similar plant drugs for self-administration in their natural habitats. Only those examples with confirmed ethological observations from several sources are discussed as prototypical examples of natural animal addictions.

D. OBSERVATIONS OF ANIMAL ADDICTIONS

1. Catnip

Several members of the cat family *(Felidae)* repeatedly self-administer catnip *(Nepeta cataria)*. Catnip, a member of the mint family, has been used by man as a treatment for amenorrhea, chlorosis, and flatulent colic in infants. Recently, it has been used by man as a hallucinogen with effects similar to those of *Cannabis* (Jackson & Reed, 1969). Catnip contains nepetalactone oils (Waller, Price, & Mitchell, 1969), and sensitivity to these oils is a genetically inherited response among *Felidae* (Todd, 1963). The catnip response in cats is characterized by sniffing, licking, chewing with head shaking, chin and cheek rubbing, and headover and body rolls accompanied by some salivation. Hatch (1972) describes frequent signs of apparent hallucinations such as "phantom butterflies" above the cat and "phantom mice" in the cat's cage as indicated by the cat's behavior. In the domestic cat, *Nepeta* induces EEG changes similar to those found following tetrahydrocannabinol (THC) administration. Since the behavioral changes are virtually identical to the oestrous behavior cycle and catnip-like activity has been found in urine extracts from tomcats, it has been argued that catnip mimics a pheromone produced to reinforce or release courtship behavior (Palen & Goddard, 1966; Todd, 1963). Sensitive *Felidae* self-administer *Nepeta* in natural environments when available, but there is no correlation between the distribution of plants having catniplike activity and that of cats that are sensitive to them. Nonetheless, domesticated male and female cats which possess the autosomal dominant gene for the catnip response will readily self-administer catnip (when provided by man) without additional reinforcement. Since tolerance develops rapidly without concomitant increases in dose, it is difficult to assess the frequency of such self-administration (Todd, 1963).

Leyhausen (1973) describes cats' reactions to both *Nepeta* and *Actinidia polygama* as one of addiction. Indeed the reaction to *Actinidia* appears even more dramatic than the reaction to catnip. The large cats tested in his experiments would interrupt all ongoing activities (including eating and sexual intercourse) and seek out the *Actinidia* when they detected its smell. At the completion of the reaction they rolled onto their backs "and stayed there for some time in complete ecstasy. I believe the animals became truly addicted to this smell, because they continued to react although it affected their sense of smell and in the end damaged the brain [Leyhausen, 1973, p. 62]." Leyhausen agrees that such consequent variables should normally aversively condition the cat to avoid the substance in the future. However, he argues that the pleasure induced by both *Nepeta* and *Actinidia* overshadow these effects and prevent negative feedback mechanisms from operating, thus permitting positive addiction to occur.

2. Tobacco

A number of animals besides man seem capable of tobacco addictions. In Africa, both human children and young baboons seem to be particularly fond of sucking the flowers of wild tobacco plants (Watt & Breyer-Brandwijk, 1962). Cowan (1870) adds the tobacco worms and the African rock goat to the list of animals that are fond of the plant. Charles Darwin, in his famous 1871 monograph on the descent of man, reported that many monkeys "smoke tobacco for pleasure" and others develop a strong taste for eating tobacco. The great ethologist Eugene Marais, who lived among baboons in Africa for many years, reported on the similarity between baboon and bushman in their attraction for tobacco:

> The South African baboon in captivity is singularly like the Bushman in its predilection for tobacco and alcohol. It needs little observation to convince one that the taste for tobacco is not instinctive and hereditary. Wild baboons certainly never make use of it even where there is every opportunity for doing so. . . . In captivity, on the other hand, the chacma's taste for tobacco is so common that it was almost impossible for us to determine when any particular individual had first acquired it. All captive baboons beg for tobacco and eat or chew it with all the zest of a long-established habit. One old male showed a greak liking for pipe oil similar to the craving of the Hottentots. He had taught himself to scratch the oil out of a pipe stem with a blade of grass which he then cleaned on to a piece of paper, rolled up and chewed [Marais, 1936/1969, p. 129].

There are numerous other folktales and stories about captive primates developing such habits related to tobacco and even smoking. Cassell (1861) related a story of a circus mandrill which was accustomed to sit in a chair and smoke a pipe and drink wine:

> All his maneuvers were performed with great slowness and composure. When his keeper lighted his pipe and presented it to him, he inspected it minutely, sometimes feeling it with his fingers, as if to know it was lighted before putting it into his mouth. It was then introduced almost up to the bowl, with that part generally downwards, and it was retained without any smoke appearing for some minutes. Meanwhile Jerry (the mandrill) was not dormant; he was actually filling to repletion, not only his capacious mouth, but his cheek-pouches, and this was soon evident, by his exhaling a volume of smoke from his mouth, nose, and sometimes his ears, which was sufficient to fill his cage. Still he does not appear to have greatly relished smoking—an acquired and not a natural taste to humanity itself—a bribe of gin and water being always promised before the commencement of the process, as if to remind spectators of the actual fact that, at that time, smoking and drinking spirits and water, generally went together [p. 63].

Many more contemporary stories are told of domesticated and/or captive animals using tobacco. For example, a terrier living on a farm in Indiana was reported to be "addicted to smoking: begging and whining whenever the usage struck, the dog consumed several cigarettes, and an occasional cigar, daily [Anonymous, 1976, p. 2]."

In natural habitats, a large number of animals appear to accidentally ingest tobacco; these include elephants, cattle, horses, sheep, goats, deer, poultry, rabbits, ostrichs, dogs, and insects. But why do animals only accidentally self-administer tobacco in natural habitats and yet readily and intentionally ingest it in captive or domesticated situations? Marais (1936) tried to solve this puzzle by suggesting that, in the case of the captive baboon, it does so in order to alleviate depression or despair: "In captivity, the chacma has a powerful psychological predisposition to the use of intoxicants, and it may be argued that this predisposition is due to the same cause as in man—namely, some kind of suffering inseparable from the new mind which, like man, it has acquired in the course of its evolution [p. 128]." Nonetheless, while Marais' explanation has some theoretical merit and will be discussed in a later section of this chapter, it is more parsimonious to assume that captive and domesticated animals self-administer tobacco and its products only because they are provided by man and such animals are used to having all foods provided by human keepers.

3. Alcohol

It is well known that elephants ingest a wide variety of psychoactive plants. Some plants, like tobacco, are accidentally browsed, while others, such as *Sansevieria* leaves, are probably used for their moisture rather than for their legendary cathartic effects (Sikes, 1971). However, a number of accounts note that elephants are passionately fond of and addicted to alcohol in the form of fermented fruit and "become quite tipsy, staggering about, playing huge antics, screaming so as to be heard miles off, and not seldom having tremendous fights [Carrington, 1959, p. 68].'' In Tanzania, elephants tend to favor the wild fruit of the mgongo tree and sometimes become intoxicated when it purportedly ferments on the ground or in their stomachs. In other areas of Southeast Africa, similar behavior has been noted following ingestion of the doum palm and marula fruit. Sometimes elephants will raid African villages and even city distilleries in search of fermented grain or alcoholic preparations. And elephant handlers and trainers are well acquainted with the use of beer and beverage alcohol as ''treats'' for the animals. In a series of controlled observations, Sikes (1971) notes that the migratory patterns of African elephants span a life of some 70 years and are marked by special areas with favored foods that are revisited at ''appropriate times'' when the Borassus palm fruits ferment. When this happens, hunters in the African bush can scent the fermented fruits which they seek out for refreshment. Sikes maintains that elephants also detect the scent and repeatedly migrate to these areas and self-administer the fermented fruit. However, his observations suggest that the highly attractive olfactory cues rather than the psychoactive effects of the alcohol reinforce and maintain this behavior.

In a further study of this phenomena, I studied this behavior among a herd of African elephants on a wild game preserve in Southern California (Siegel, in preparation). In a series of controlled studies, it was found that these animals had a natural preference for alcohol and would readily drink alcohol solutions in concentrations up to 7%, independent of taste, smell, or caloric contents. Furthermore, the 7% solutions (equivalent to the alcohol concentration in some fermented fruits) were sufficient to produce behavioral indices of intoxication including ataxia and aggressive displays. Interestingly, when the elephants were experimentally stressed, as when herd density was increased or range area was decreased, the consumption of alcohol increased significantly.

There have been other field observations of alcohol addiction to fruits or beverages among a wide variety of animals including: birds, rats, racoons, pigs, goats, cows, sheep, horses, cats, bears, lemurs, monkeys, baboons, and chimpanzees.

4. Mushrooms

Both the reindeer and primitive peoples of the Asian forest and tundra regions share another type of natural addiction:

> Reindeer manifest two addictions, two passions, one to urine, especially human urine, and the other to mushrooms including the fly-agaric (the hallucinogenic *Amanita muscaria*). When human urine or mushrooms are in the vicinity, the half-domesticated beasts become unmanageable. All reindeer folk know of these two addictions. . . . Reindeer, like men, suffer (or enjoy) profound mental disturbances from eating the fly-agaric [Wasson, 1968, pp. 75–76].

The natural diet of the reindeer is composed almost exclusively of lichens. Nonetheless, Wasson (1968) summarizes evidence that suggests that reindeer develop special preferences for fly-agaric mushrooms or human urine that contains the active metabolites of fly-agaric. The native Chukchi people self-administer fly-agaric, and other native groups (e.g., the Karyaks) will drink their own urine for additional intoxications when the supply of mushrooms is exhausted. Such intoxications are marked by elation, sedation, colored visions, and hallucinations and are presumably caused by the active principle, muscimol (Waser, 1967; Wasson, 1967). Several observational reports indicate that the reindeer will repeatedly ingest these mushrooms or urine. The behavior of the reindeer appears similar to that of the people:

> The fluid [human urine] has the same effect on the reindeer as intoxicating drink has on people who have fallen victim to the drinking habit. The reindeer become just as drunk and have just as great a thirst. At night they are noisy and keep running around the tents in the expectation of being given the longed-for-fluid. And when some is spilled out into the snow, they start quarreling, tearing away from each other the clumps of snow moistened with it. Every Chukchi saves his urine in a sealskin container which is especially made for the purpose and from which he gives his reindeer to drink. Whenever he wants to round up his animals, he only has to set this container on the ground and slowly call out "Girach, Girach!", and they promptly come running toward him from afar [Wasson, 1968, p. 243].

Like elephants in search of fermented fruit, the reindeer have acute olfactory receptors which detect the human urine and attract them to human communities (Wasson, 1968). Indeed, one report stressed that the passion of the reindeer for human urine is so intense that "it is likely to make it dangerous to relieve oneself in the open when there are reindeer around [Wasson, 1968, p. 161]." Wasson recounts some scant evidence that the intoxicated reindeer isolate themselves from the herd. However, it is well known that other conditions, such as insect plagues and hunger, may cause individual animals to leave the herd groupings (Leeds, 1965). Indeed, when reindeer are afflicted with insects in their nostrils they are driven into a frenzy which appears behaviorally similar to that following mushroom ingestion. It is interesting to note in passing that the shamans of the Chukchi have come to believe that psychic disturbances are caused by insects, and they treat their patients with rituals based on ridding the head of these insects (Wasson, 1968).

There have been other field observations confirming similar "addictive" behaviors among cattle, dogs, deer, rats, and rabbits with respect to ingestion of *Amanita* and *Psilocybe* (containing the hallucinogens psilocybin and psilocin) mushrooms.

5. Locoweed and Other Range Forage

Numerous addictions to plant drugs have been observed among grazing cattle and horses. The criteria for labeling such behavior "addictive" is explained by British toxicologist Forsyth (1954):

> It is said that animals never become drug addicts, but this is hardly true. Once an animal acquires the taste for anything, good or bad, it will go to endless trouble to satisfy its craving. Most country veterinary surgeons and many stockowners can recall cases of animals which, having recovered from acute poisoning, have returned at the first opportunity to gorge again on the offending plants, often with more dire results than before. During early convalescence many animals will flatly refuse to eat normal foodstuffs, although they will hungrily devour the plant which poisoned them. In these instances, where the plant has not been identified, they will often lead one directly to it, if turned again into the same pasture [p. 3].

Accordingly, Forsyth documents addiction among cattle and horses to a wide variety of alkaloidal plants including buttercups, bryony, horseradish, woody nightshade, laurel, rhododendron, acorns, oak leaves, ash leaves, and rushes.

In his classic monograph on narcotic drugs, Lewin (1931) offers numerous examples of similar "addictions," "violent cravings," "eager ingestions," and "great preferences" whereby animals "ravenously consume and devour" psychoactive plants. For example, bees and rats are described as having a violent craving for opium poppies (p. 55). Grazing animals in Australia become addicted to the toxic *Swainsonia galegifolia* and: "The intoxicated animals, called in Australia indigo-eaters, keep aloof from the rest of the herd, exhibit disorders of the brain, troubles of vision, etc. They refuse to eat grass and only take this toxic herb. In this case also grave and deadly complication set in [p. 146]." Short-tailed sheep in Germany become addicted to common broom (*Sarothamnus scoparius*) and these "drunkards devour it ravenously and fall into a state of excitation succeeded by complete unconsciousness. In this state they are said to fall an easy prey to foxes or flocks of crows [p. 146]."

Lewin also describes the addiction of horses, cattle, and sheep to locoweed which includes *Astragalus* spp., *Aragallus* spp., *Oxytropis* spp., among other plants. The addicted animals

> behave in such a manner that we must conclude that a special state of mental disorder is present similar to the state of man under the influence of alcohol or other substances. This state lasts for months. During this time the animals refuse to take any other kind of food and greedily seek to procure their old fodder, like the morphinist his morphia. This phase of excitation is succeeded by physical decay to which the animals succumb. This is the cause of great losses in cattle-breeding [pp. 145-146].

Lewin observes that young grazing animals seem particularly prone to *Aragallus* addiction, and a single ingestion is enough "to render it an incurable slave to the passion as long as the plant is accessible [p. 146]." Lewin makes the interesting observation that one animal may induce others in the herd to ingest the plant (through modeling) and, accordingly, the younger animals are more susceptible to the craving than older ones.

Marsh (1909) has extended the list of animals addicted to locoweed to include mules, pigs, antelopes, and even some insects. He has observed accidental poisoning among wolves, birds, and other animals that can not tolerate such addictions. Marsh acknowledges that grazing animals are imitative and that loco eaters "are likely to teach others to do the same thing. Therefore, so far as possible, all animals that have acquired the habit of loco eating should be separated from the others (Marsh, 1924, p. 21]." While Marsh agrees that some range animals frequently acquire a specific taste for locoweeds, or other poisonous plants, and will eat nothing else even in the presence of other forage, he feels that such behavior is atypical of grazing animals in general. Indeed, he argues that all poisonous plants are distasteful to livestock and will be avoided under ordinary circumstances. The initial feeding on these plants "is almost invariably brought about by scarcity of food [Marsh, 1924, p. 32]" and it is this initial administration which triggers subsequent craving and addiction:

> It has long been known that loco eating is ordinarily commenced in the winter season or in the early spring when the loco plants are green and luscious, and before the grass has started. The loco plants at that time are the most prominent plants on the plains, and animals commence to eat them because of lack of other food. Many animals after feeding upon loco a short time acquire a liking for it and will continue to eat it even in the presence of an abundance of other food [Marsh, 1924, p. 32].

Such observations are consistent with those reported for mushroom poisoning in cattle (Piercy, Hargis, & Brown, 1944). As with locoweed, cattle will not eat toxic *Amanita* mushrooms unless forced to do so by a lack of other more palatable forage. But once tasted and ingested, cattle appear "to relish the fungi and were noted to seek them in preference to other range plants which were available [p. 206]."

6. Miscellaneous Animal Addictions

There are several other examples of animals addicted to plant drugs which lack identification of the active pharmacological principle and/or adequate behavioral studies. Nonetheless, a few examples are discussed below in order to illustrate the broad range of possible animal addictions in natural habitats.

A wide variety of field reports mention the ingestion of opium poppies by animals. While many such ingestions appear accidental, some animals have been observed to repeat the ingestion and subsequently become intoxicated and addicted. This occurs most frequently in cows, horses, and water buffalo, but even ants ingest poppies as a favorite food (Duke, 1973). Tortoises are also reported to develop a violent craving for opium poppies (Lagneau & Gallard, 1946). While controlled observations have not yet identified the extent of these phenomena, Cocteau's (1957) description is a romantic interpretation of these accounts:

> All animals are charmed by opium. Addicts in the colonies know the danger of this bait for wild beasts and reptiles. Flies gather round the tray and dream, the lizards with their little mittens swoon on the ceiling above the lamp and wait for the night, mice come close and nibble the dross. I do not speak of the dogs and monkeys who become addicted like their masters. At Marseilles, among the Annamites, where one smokes with im-

plements calculated to confuse the police, the cockroaches and spiders form a circle in ecstasy [p. 61].

A number of insects are reported to become addicted to unidentified psychoactive plant products. For example, Bell (1971) notes that the nectar of many of the Umbelliferae flowers is narcotic, especially to the *Bombus* bee and this functions to provide the plant with numerous captive pollinators:

> The drugged insects scurry frantically over the assemblage of primary, secondary and tertiary umbels—all of which are conveniently on the same horizontal plane by the time the flowers of the latter umbels open. Soon the insects fall into a stupor and drop to the ground, where they remain immobile for approximately $1\frac{1}{2}$ minutes. After some movement is evident another 15–30 seconds are required before the insects are air-borne again. They usually weave back to an umbel to start the cycle over [p. 103].

Still other insects are reported to become addicted to natural psychoactive substances produced by other animals. For example, certain varieties of ants live in symbiotic relationship with *Myrmecophilous pselaphid* beetles. Such beetles are referred to as *symphiles* or myrmoxenes ('true guests') and are accepted, to some extent, by their hosts as though they were members of the colony. Park (1964) describes cases in which worker ants licked the trichomes of adult beetles for long periods of time, after which they were "so overwhelmed by this trichome stimulant that they became temporarily disoriented and less sure of their footing [p. 133]." Wilson (1971) summarizes evidence relating to the narcotizing effect of symphilic substances in several different ants. *Hypoclinea biturberculata,* an abundant ant of Southeast Asia, licks an intoxicant attractant from trichome secretions of the bug *Ptilocerus ochraceus* and becomes overtaken by paralysis. Many such symphiles are repeatedly licked by their host ants, which self-administer the secretions and, in turn, provide regurgitated food for them. Indeed, Bejerot (1972) notes that in times of danger, the *Lasius flavus* ant, having become addicted to such secretions, tends to its symphile beetle larvae (*Lomechusa*) before it removes its own eggs to safety! Chauvin (1970) calls this "lomechusa-mania" among ants "the only known case of drug addiction among animals [p. 134]."

Honey is one of the oldest natural sugar supplies. According to folklore, it was discovered by early man observing a bear raiding the honey hoard of a wild bee colony. Subsequently, the man tried it and became addicted to its taste as did the bear (Lehner & Lehner, 1962). Since bees can absorb psychoactive substances through the ingestion of nectar and pass these substances along into their honey, there have been numerous reports of a wide variety of "honey addictions" in animals and man. Some bees that feed on the nectar of *Rhododendron ponticum* are apparently unaffected by the poison of this azalea, but their honey has a narcotic effect on humans. Indeed it is told that Heptakometes placed poisonous honey of this variety along the route traveled by Pompey's army. The soldiers ate the honey, became senseless, and were subsequently attacked and killed (Clausen, 1954, p. 98). Some insects seem less capable of tolerating psychoactive substances from the plants they feed on and display both intoxicated and addicted behaviors. For example, the Hercules beetles of the West Indies feed on fermenting sap of several indigenous trees, "drinking so deeply of the fermenting sap that they become inordinately drunk and reel and stagger about, or fall helpless to the earth like a crowd of tipsy sailors [Verrill, 1937, p. 92]." Carrighar (1965) describes a similar passion among hornets: "Hornets are fond of alcohol, and if they can get it, usually from fermenting fruit, they become drunk. They sip it until they fall into a stupor, and when they awake are so thirsty for more that they can't even be bothered to find the nest of another wasp in which to deposit their eggs [pp. 58-59]."

There are other stories of insect–plant interactions with little more than speculation as to the nature of the resulting behavior. For example, bees are naturally attracted to male *Cannabis* plants, and their honey, when collected and assayed, has been shown to contain traces of THC (Mendell, 1969). While some writers have speculated about "stoned bees" and "marijuana munching insects," there are no studies of individual bees demonstrating intoxicated behavior or even repeating the self-administration. Similarly, the bug *Orythris canabensis* is a natural enemy of *Cannabis* plants in Rumania but, again, there are no behavioral studies on this relationship (Addiction Research Foundation, 1972).

When bears are sick from ingesting plant toxins, they sometimes will eat ants as a laxative or emetic (Cowan, 1865, p. 163). Accordingly, this behavior was copied by man for treatment of a wide variety of illnesses including Mandrake poisoning. Similarly, early man used bee honey for treatment of snakebite as well as plant poisoning after watching bears do the same. According to an old Russian myth, bears are addicted to Mourveenue Maaslo or "ant butter," and Russian peasants have used the "ant butter" as a curative incense. The butter is actually resin collected by ants from juniper bushes and stored in the ant nests (*Formica ruf*). While the use of this resin by ants and bears is unknown, many peasant stories claim it is a narcotic drug because of special substances the ants add to it. Accordingly to some anthropologists, American Indians (e.g., the Kitanemuk in California) ingested ants both for laxative and psychoactive effects, and it has been suggested that these ants may have been ingested together with a narcotic resin. Alternatively, the psychoactive and hallucinogenic effects produced by this ingestion may have been induced by toxins in the ants which are similar in chemical structure to the hallucinogen nepetalactone.

III. Stimulus Control in Animal Addictions

A. BOTANICAL VARIABLES

Most of the animal addictions discussed here are based on the self-administration of plants by herbivores. Through such behavior, herbivores have come to exert strong evolutionary pressures on plant populations. Plants display a vast array of traits that give them some degree of protection from herbivores and these include evolutionary changes in chemistry (including nutrition), morphology, and escape in time and place (cf. Atsatt & O'Dowd, 1976). Some plants have simply evolved in ecological niches separate from potential herbivores. For example, catnip does not appear to grow wild in areas inhabited by cats that are sensitive to it. Some plants employ protective traits, such as spines, odors, tastes and shade, causing the herbivore to reject or fail to locate its normal prey. For example, henbane has a strongly nauseating odor and taste which is rapidly rejected by most animals. Spiny cacti are readily avoided by herbivores. The spineless peyote cactus escapes herbivore detection by growing close to ground level where it is browsed only rarely by deer and rodents.

Plants also produce a distinct set of defensive chemicals (called secondary compounds), and the psychoactive alkaloids constitute a major form of these substances. A few secondary compounds are lethal deterrents, but the majority function by influencing the feeding behavior of potential herbivores, causing the animal to exclude certain plants or plant parts from its optimal diet. Sometimes animals will respond to multiple plant defenses. For instance, the lethal spiny seed pod of *Datura* spp. is usually avoided by grazing animals, but the less toxic psychoactive leaves, stems, and flowers can be easily consumed. This ensures the survival of both plant and animal. Birds and rodents ingest *Cannabis* seeds because of strong preferences for the oils they contain, and only accidentally ingest psychoactive components of the plant while foraging for the seeds. The location of *Cannabis* seeds at the tops of the plants deters many rodents, while the birds help dispersal by ingesting and evacuating seeds.

A striking example of plant defense is wild tobacco. I have recorded the occasional eating of wild tobacco (*Nicotiana rustica*) by cattle and pigs on the Hawaiian Islands. This ingestion is usually the result of accidental browsing, but when wild tobacco is the only forage available in a given pasture area, animals have been observed to die from nicotine poisoning within 20 min following feeding. In Africa, *Nicotiana glauca* has caused the poisoning of cattle, ostrich, sheep, and rabbits: "the ostrich is particularly susceptible, the symptoms being staggering gait, spasmodic jerkings of the head, dullness and stupor. Death occurs within a few hours. . . . One seed is said to be certain death to a chick ostrich up to a month old [Watt & Breyer-Brandwijk, 1962, p. 985]." From such experiences, many grazing animals have undoubtedly learned to either avoid tobacco or lightly browse the plants. Indeed, "it is reported that poultry eat the leaf greedily when green-stuff is scarce and that the horse browses the plant, in both cases without injury [Watt & Breyer-Brandwijk, 1962, p. 986]." Other animals such as elephants also self-administer wild tobacco (Van Proosdy, 1960) but these cases are probably accidental.

In many instances both plants and herbivores have coevolved biochemically in response to evolutionary pressures. For example, many plants are rare or ephemeral and are simply hard to find by insect herbivores. The chemical defenses of such plants are usually diverse and "qualitative," posing evolutionary barriers to nonadapted insects but only minimal ecological barriers to adapted species (Feeny, 1975). Wild tobacco is such a plant and it secretes the alkaloid nicotine that is highly toxic to nonadapted insects like aphids but has no repellent value for the tobacco cutworms and other pests that feed on this plant. Conversely, plant species which are abundant or persistent or both are bound to be found by insects. These plants have evolved "quantitative" defenses, including tough leaves, low nutrient contents, and large amounts of tannins and alkaloids. For example, the ubiquitous tree *Daturas* has evolved considerable amounts of tannins in addition to abundant tropane alkaloids.

Concomitantly, the insect herbivores have coevolved mechanisms with which to detect and/or detoxify the secondary compounds produced by the plants. For example, beetle larvae feed on *Salvia divinorum* (containing hallucinogenic indole alkaloids) in Mexico and incorporate the alkaloids of the plant into their own chemical defenses against predators. Also the cinabar moth *Callimorpha jacobaea* and the tiger moth *Arctia caja,* which are unacceptable to a variety of potential predators, contain pyrrolizidine alkaloids derived from food plants of the genus *Senecio* (Levinson, 1976). Thus, the defensive plant alkaloids can act as repellents (phagorepellents) to herbivores and also signal food plants (phagostimulants) to herbivores. For example, the eucalyptus are rich with lethal amounts of prussic acid as well as other secondary compounds. Yet the eurymelid leafhopper has coevolved to exclusively favor this plant (Edmunds & Alstad, 1978). Southwood (1973) comments on this mechanism:

> When insects become resistant to secondary plant substances they frequently, to use a slightly misleading colloquial analogy, become "hooked" on them. Several of these secondary plant substances have been found to provide tokens for host plant recognition or for feeding, sometimes acting on their own, sometimes synergistically with nutrients. . . . Insects have gone further than simply using secondary plant substances as token stimuli, they may utilize these substances in their own defense mechanisms [p. 20].

Another plant variable that influences herbivory is explained by the concept of plant guild (Atsatt & O'Dowd, 1976). Plant guilds describe groups of plants that are in some way dependent on other neighboring plants with respect to their herbivores. Guild plant neighbors serve as insectary plants for herbivore predators and parasites and influence herbivore feeding by repelling, masking, attracting, and decoying. Consequently, the presence or absence of these guilds can greatly influence a herbivore's selection of food plants. In simple terms, guilds function to present some plants as more available, attractive and/or palatable to herbivores than others. For example, Atsatt and O'Dowd (1976) report that in pastures where highly palatable species are available, grazing animals will rarely ingest bracken fern (*Pteridium aquilinum*). In pastures with moderately palatable forage species available, cattle will consume up to 10 times their normal amount of bracken fern. With pastures containing many unpalatable species, bracken fern consumption jumps to lethal levels (100 times the normal amount). Thus, presence or absence of guilds may be a major variable underlying many animal addictions.

B. ANIMAL FEEDING VARIABLES

The effects of plant secondary compounds on the feeding traits of animals is another important factor in understanding the mechanisms of natural animal addictions. The discussion here is confined to mammals which are the largest group of plant drug eaters, but herbivorous birds, reptiles, fish, and insects should be amenable to analogous analysis.

The ubiquitous nature of plant secondary compounds would make herbivority impossible unless animals had mechanisms for degrading and excreting them, thereby avoiding either death or severe physiological impairment (cf. Freeland & Janzen, 1974). Even if an animal does not display symptoms of intoxication or poisoning, it still must cope with the problem of ridding itself of toxic compounds. As already discussed, most mammals avoid toxic effects by eating plants or plant parts that do not contain large amounts of secondary compounds. For example, laboratory rats, when presented with foods varying in concentration of selenium (the active principle in locoweed), will consistently eat the least toxic mixture (Franke & Potter, 1936). In natural habitats, mammals will also avoid especially toxic foods. Coyote will avoid the poisonous seeds of "coyotillo" plants (*Karwinskia humboldtiana*), but eat the surrounding pulp (Bourke, 1894). Deer and rats have specialized lower incisors that enable them to remove the hypersaline outer tissues of *Atriplex* leaves and consume the non-salty, starch-rich interior tissues (Freeland & Janzen, 1974, p. 271). However, it is probably more common to find mammals that eat plants known to contain toxic secondary substances. Indeed, the preferred foods of many mammals consist of extremely toxic plants, and the list includes many examples of what has been labeled animal addictions. For instance, camels in the Australian deserts feed on *Eucalyptus* leaves (rich in essential oils, phenols, and prussic acid); mountain viscachas in Peru feed mainly on *Senecio* (rich in pyrrolizidine alkaloids); rats on Eniwetok Atoll feed on morning glory vines (indole alkaloids); *Colobus* monkeys feed on *Rauwolfia* (reserpine); some rabbits feed on belladonna (tropane alkaloids). As Freeland and Janzen (1974) conclude:

> The importance of these toxic foods in the diet of the particular herbivore is highly variable, but the very fact that mammals can avoid toxic foods behaviorally suggests that these toxic plants are "knowingly" ingested. None of these mammals could survive on such diets unless they possess mechanisms that protect them from effects of toxins [p. 272].

These mechanisms include detoxification by microsomal (or drug) enzymes in the liver, kidneys, and other body parts; and degradation by enzymes in the stomach, small intestine, caecum, and colon. Many of these detoxification mechanisms occur as a normal part of mammalian digestion. For example, the alkaline stomachs of ruminating mammals degrade a wide variety of secondary plant compounds including pyrrolizidine alkaloids, *Digitalis* alkaloids, caffeic acid, oxalates, and cyanogenic glycosides. The extent to which a secondary compound is degraded depends in part on the experience the gut flora has had with the compounds (cf. Freeland & Janzen, 1974). Thus sheep that have experience with pyrrolizidine alkaloids can degrade them but inexperienced sheep cannot at first, although it may only take about 10 days for a rumen flora to become completely adapted to a new diet of secondary substances (Warner, 1962). Thus, in order to maximize food intake, and to be able to detoxify it, a herbivore is forced to take food from a variety of sources. But the continual consumption of novel foods puts intense and conflicting pressures on enzyme systems so that animals will usually introduce new foods very carefully.

There are also several subsidiary mechanisms that help herbivorous mammals handle plant drugs. For example, toxic compounds can interact in the gut to form insoluble nontoxic complexes. When tannins and alkaloids are ingested together, the alkaloid is usually precipitated as an insoluble tannate and this avoids toxic effects. However, the tannins also precipitate proteins, cause fecal loss of nitrogen, and produce marked weight loss. Many animals will then counter this tannic acid toxicity by seeking out and ingesting supplemental high-protein plants. Similarly, herbivores must feed on numerous specific nutrients in order to maintain efficient detoxification and degradation mechanisms.

Consuming plant secondary compounds is a potentially dangerous metabolically expensive behavior for herbivores. Consequently, the feeding strategies adopted by these animals to minimize drug effects are to (a) treat new foods with extreme caution; (b) learn to quickly ingest or reject specific foods based on sampling of minute quantities; (c) seek out and eat plants containing highly specific classes of nutrients; (d) indulge in a continuous food-sampling program while ingesting a number of different staple foods over a short period of time; (e) preferentially feed on familiar foods for as long as possible; (f) prefer foods with minor amounts of plant secondary compounds; and (g) to have searching strategies and a body size that allow for experimental eating (cf. Freeland & Janzen, 1974).

Despite the advantages of these feeding strategies, a number of animals appear to ingest plant secondary compounds more regularly and intentionally than would be expected from a simple searching strategy. The koala is considered a drug addict because of its exclusive preference for *Eucalyptus*, and the mountain viscacha can be termed an addict based on its restricted diet of *Senecio*. In these and related cases, principles of animal learning may play a major role in the addictive behaviors.

C. ANIMAL LEARNING VARIABLES

Many animals can learn to eat or reject a particular food-plant after a single trial that involves only a small amount of the new item. Such learning can take place even if the animal does not experience an immediate physiological or psychological stimulus and when the aversive or pleasurable stimulus occurs after delays of several hours or more (cf. Revusky & Garcia, 1970). Almost without exception, psychoactive drugs used by man have the interesting property of inducing learned gustatory taste aversions in laboratory rats (cf. Cappell & LeBlanc, 1977). The single exception is cocaine which probably has too short a duration of action to be an effective stimulus.

There is growing evidence in the food-aversion literature that suggests that many animals other than rats learn taste aversions based on psychoactive drugs or plant secondary compounds (see review by Barker, Best, & Domjan, 1977). However, prior exposure to a specific drug greatly attenuates a learned taste aversion to that drug. This may occur through habituation to the novelty of the drug itself or to actual physiological or behavioral tolerance. Thus, an aversion to a plant drug can be overshadowed or blocked by other learning variables. Consider the special case of the koala bear's addiction to *Eucalyptus* (cf. Garcia, Hankins, & Coil, 1977). The koala feeds exclusively on the pungent bitter leaves of five to seven species of *Eucalyptus*. The feeding is selective as the koala must avoid varieties with often lethal concentrations of prussic acid (also found in laurel leaves to which grazing animals become addicted). Based upon recent discoveries in the food-aversion literature, Garcia and his colleagues propose a solution to the problem faced by the developing koala infant that is raised on mother's milk and does not have the intestinal flora and fauna required to metabolize the bitter leaves into nutrients:

> First, the powerful oil of eucalyptus permeates the tissues of the koala bear, making its flesh unpalatable to man and other predators; thus, eating the bitter diet enhances survival of the species. The mother's milk must also be flavored by eucalyptus—we know that in the rat the mother's diet flavors her milk and predisposes her pups to select her diet after weaning. It is thus very likely that infantile nursing experience habituates the koala bear to eucalyptus. Second, the koala is a marsupial that raises its infants in a pouch which opens caudally near the mother's anus. At weaning time, the normal feces of the mother are purged from her gastrointestinal tract and she eliminates half-digested masses of eucalyptus pulp. Infant koala bears have been observed to feed on this eucalyptus pulp while in the pouch. The first samplings provide an opportunity for the infant to acquire the intestinal flora and fauna required to produce nutrients from the eucalyptus pulp. We know that the palatability of any substance is increased when it is followed by nutritious after effects. Thus, by the time it emerges from its mother's pouch, the koala infant has probably been conditioned to eat bitter eucalyptus leaves in a controlled setting directed by inherited structures. These structural constraints program the behavior of the developing koala bear so closely that, no matter how plastic its feeding behavior may be, this animal appears to be irrevocably fixed to a eucalyptus diet [Garcia, Hankins, & Coil, 1977, p. 196].

Nonetheless, even when ingestion of plant secondary compounds is associated with aversive stimuli to which habituation or tolerance does not develop, animals may still choose to self-administer those substances. Indeed, Mello (1978) has noted that under appropriate conditions animals will often self-administer stimuli with aversive consequences. Many animals will self-administer electric shock under certain schedules. Opiate-dependent monkeys will self-administer the narcotic antagonist nalorphine despite nalorphine-induced withdrawal effects including vomiting, coughing, salivation, tremors, and irritability. These and other data reviewed by Mello challenge common-sense assumptions about what constitutes a "positive" and an "aversive" event, and what types of events will be reinforcing. Mellow suggests that what is desired by such stimulus self-administration is a change in state of the organism. In other words, the animal desires to feel different, to change a state of arousal either by lowering it or by raising it. Indeed, the self-administration of some drugs like the hallucinogens is associated with both "stress seeking" and "stress reducing" motivations (Bogg, 1975; Siegel, 1973). Thus, the stimulus properties of the plant drugs—the ability to produce intoxication—may be more important than the specific qualities of the plants themselves (e.g., smells, odors, tastes, nutrients).

Animals can also learn to eat from observing the behavior of conspecifics. Observational learning and social communication of feeding behavior has been demonstrated to occur with edible foods in a wide variety of animal species. Although there is no hard evidence that learning to avoid distasteful or toxic foods by social cues occurs in natural forage situations (Fairbanks, 1975), there are abundant ethological observations suggesting that it might occur with certain species such as birds, fish, and domestic grazing animals (cf. Hafez, 1975; Marsh, 1924).

D. ANIMAL SOCIAL BEHAVIOR VARIABLES

The social behavior of herbivores can greatly influence the self-administration of plant secondary compounds. For example, there are abundant field observations suggesting that robins and cedar-waxwings intoxicate themselves on the fruit of *Pyracantha* spp. and *Cotoneaster* spp., becoming drunk, disoriented, and wander in front of cars, flying into cars and windows. In a series of field studies, I found that this behavior was not associated with the fermented berries or secondary compounds in the berries. Rather, the birds would mob the bushes which were near houses and highways and gorge themselves due to the competitive nature of feeding in large migratory flocks. Finally, gorged and weighted down with berries, startled by cars or humans, they would fly in confused and lowered altitudes into cars and windows. This mobbing behavior and confused startle reaction is characteristic of many birds, such as starlings, western bluebirds, and gray jays feeding on a variety of different seasonal fruits.

Social stress can also modify the intake of plant secondary compounds. This stress can be induced by group size and density, competition, and prey–predator pressure, among other factors. Cattle under "social stress" and high competition for food space tend to eat very rapidly, resulting in an increased consumption of nonpreferred toxic plants (Wood-Gush, Duncan, & Fraser, 1975). I have observed that increased herd density among grazing animals in the Hawaiian Islands results in an increased incidence of intoxications and deaths from *Daturas*. In laboratory studies, a number of investigators have induced cats and monkeys to prefer alcoholic solutions over nonalcoholic fluids as a result of experimentally induced stress (e.g., Masserman, 1957).

Indeed, although some animals have a natural preference for alcohol (e.g., hamsters and elephants) and others like chimpanzees can even become voluntarily addicted to it (Fitz-Gerald, 1972), social stress and conflict may influence the intake of this intoxicant. In a review of the experimental work on alcohol and conflict situations, Ahlfors (1969) concludes that there is a positive association between the self-administration of alcohol and the elimination of conflict. In addition, he summarizes work suggesting that other psychoactive drugs may be used by animals in similar ways. Thus, rats will increase their consumption of the tranquilizer reserpine, compared to water consumption, after induction of stress. In a comparison of wild and domesticated species, Richter (1957) found that only the stressed wild rats became alcoholic:

> The wild rats were under a great and constant stress; their normal intake is much greater than that of the domesticated rats, which would be expected to lead to a greater alcohol consumption when this was the only fluid available; and their livers were at least mildly cirrhotic as a result of their almost universal infestation with *Capillaria hepatica* [p. 140].

In a series of elegant studies, Ellison (1977) has extended these findings and suggested possible physiological mechanisms of action. Rats were initially made anxious by experimentally lowering their serotonin levels. Subsequent behavior in a familiar home environment was characterized as "aroused and exploratory," while behavior in a novel open-field environment was described as "frightened and paranoid." The animals always had free access to both water and alcohol, but the anxious (low-serotonin) rats immediately increased their consumption of alcohol. Conversely, rats with experimentally lowered norepinephrine levels became "driveless and withdrawn" in the familiar home environment and "fearless and nonvigilant" in the open field. These low-norepinephrine rats were thus depressed and lacked arousal, and they subsequently showed a decrease in alcohol consumption.

E. INTOXICATION AND CONSEQUENT VARIABLES

Clinical signs of intoxication or mild poisoning in animal addictions include a wide range of behaviors. A partial list of these behaviors together with common psychoactive plants that induce them are: loss or suppression of appetite (ergot); bloating (*Solanum* and *Datura*); diarrhea (*Nicotiana*); staggers (*Pteridium*, ergot); lameness (ergot); marked abnormal stance (all hallucinogens); hyperexcitability (ergot, *Datura*); "mad galloping" (many alkaloids); muscular spasms and/or convulsions (*Strychnos*, *Pteridium*); shivering or trembling (ergot, *Nicotiana*, *Duboisia*); depression and dullness (*Pteridium*, *Solanum*); among other symptoms. A characteristic sign is known as "walkabout" marked by isolation and dejection with periods of aimless, compulsive walking; this is seen in numerous states of alkaloidal intoxication (Gardner & Bennetts, 1956). Lagneau and Gallard (1946) describe opium poppy intoxication in cattle marked by some of these behaviors:

The onset is generally rapid, the first disturbances appear a few hours after ingestion of the plant and are essentially characterized by extreme lasting agitation, the animals constantly stamp from one rear leg to the other, while they paw the ground with their front legs . . . continual bellowing gives the scene an amazing aspect. . . . Out of doors the cattle turn in the same manner, without rest, at a real trot, around the pasture which . . . soon takes on the appearance of a race course [p. 311, translated by Ada Hirschman].

Sometimes the intoxication itself can lead to further abnormal ingestive behaviors. Siegmund (1973) describes a typical case of *Senecio* intoxication leading to pica behavior:

Some animals may become progressively weaker and rarely move while others wander aimlessly with an awkward gait, either stumbling against or actively pushing headlong into fences or other structures. Still others may become frenzied and dangerously aggressive. Pica may be observed in some individuals [p. 1004].

Pica is a curious behavior (cf. Humphries, 1965) that usually refers to the ingestion of substances not considered fit for food (e.g., plaster, clay, dirt). Traditionally, this behavior has been regarded as psychopathological, and studies have related pica to physiological needs for specific dietary supplements, usually iron. Nonetheless, in both animals and humans, pica can appear to be an addictive craving for specific substances. Pierquin (1839) describes several pica-addicted animals including a cat eating coal, a dog eating dirt and plaster, and cows eating wood. Sometimes the pica can lead to further intoxication and poisoning by minerals in these substances, and Siegmund (1973, pp. 935–936) describes a case of lead poisoning resulting from such behavior. In man, Garcia *et al.* (1977) note that such idiosyncratic behaviors are considered abnormal and the individual may be isolated socially, since common food habits are a primary group norm (p. 199). In animals, pica can also result in isolation from the social group, herd, or flock.

Intoxication itself can also result in social isolation. Animals suffering from locoweed disease or fly-agaric intoxication tend to isolate themselves from others. Similar observations have been made on "drunk" elephants (Carrington, 1959), sick eland and kudu (Davis, Karstad, & Trainer, 1970), sick reindeer (Davis & Anderson, 1971), and intoxicated sheep (Lewin, 1931), among others. In nearly all such cases, the sick or intoxicated animals behave in strange and socially inappropriate ways and either leave the herd or are segregated by the herd (Davis *et al.*, 1970). Much of this behavior is understandable in view of Ardrey's (1970) argument that a basic force of animal social structure is animal xenophobia, or the fear and avoidance of strangers. Ardrey argues that groups of animals or men reject the strange, whether strangely behaving or the actual stranger.

Elsewhere, Siegel (1973) has shown that intoxication in both animals and humans results in isolation from social groups and avoidance of social interactions. Whether sick, ill, intoxicated, poisoned, loco, stuporous, drunk, narcotized, or addicted, animals and humans tend to isolate themselves from social groups. This behavior may be related to states of central nervous system excitation and arousal and a tendency for social species to isolate themselves from further stimulation. The behavior may also be related to impaired perceptual–motor behavior necessary for maintaining normal social behaviors.

IV. Overview

Plants produce a vast array of secondary compounds as defensive mechanisms against herbivores. These secondary compounds, including the major classes of alkaloidal drugs, have a wide range of physiologic and psychologic activity. The inevitable ecological encounters of animal life with these plant drugs gave rise to many intoxications and poisonings. Some animals, like the dinosaurs, failed to evolve effective mechanisms with which to detect or to detoxify these compounds. They did not survive. Other animals, like the birds and mammals, developed acute sensory mechanisms to detect alkaloids and highly efficient livers for detoxifying them. Still others, like some insects, coevolved complex biochemical processes in order to neutralize and utilize the plant toxins. Grazing and foraging herbivores developed general feeding strategies to minimize intake of plant poisons and maximize nutrition. And through it all, many of these animals experienced the aversive and attractant stimulus properties of plant drugs and learned from that experience.

Man's folklore and mythology recount many tales of these animal–plant interactions. Much of early man's knowledge about plant drugs as medicines and intoxicants was based on observations of these animal behaviors. And early food gatherers must have engaged in similar accidental and purposeful ingestion in order to learn about plants as foods, drugs, medicine, and religious–magical agents.

Recent ethological observations have confirmed that, either by accident or design, numerous animals ingest plant drugs. Many of the examples cited in this review need further controlled study in order to identify the botanical, pharmacological, biological, and behavioral variables that reinforce and maintain these self-administrations. However, it is clear that many examples are intentional, repeated by individuals, intoxicating, satisfy little or no nutritional needs, and result in cravings and addictions.

Repeated drug-seeking and drug-taking behavior leads most observers to speak of motives and purposes for such behavior. For man there is an endless catalogue of motives, but the consequences of drugs may have nothing to do with initial intentions. Initial reactions to drugs are often aversive for man as well as for animals (cf. Blum, 1969, pp. 8–9). The intoxication that results from that experience may be the major factor in establishing drug addiction. As Blum (1969) puts it, the change in states of arousal experienced by intoxication becomes the "enhancing, invigorating, or driving action . . . when the person learns what the drug does for him, such as relieving his tension [p. 10].'' Similarly, some animals learn to self-administer fermented alcoholic fruit for the anxiety-reducing psychoactive effects. Even when ingestion of plant secondary compounds results in aversive stimuli, animals, like man, may continue to self-administer them in order to achieve a change in state (cf. Mello, 1978).

The direction of this change in arousal state of the organism, either up or down, may be of minor importance. What is important is that the organism experiences a subjective response to a drug-induced stimulus. The pharmacological properties may be less critical than the psychological properties of plant drugs acting as stimulus events with a resultant change in state. The coca-eating pack animals working in the difficult Peruvian mountains, the anxious elephants ingesting alcoholic fruit on the African savanah, the stressed cattle in dense herds on the Hawaiian Islands grazing on hallucinogenic jimsonweed, and contemporary human phencyclidine users who inject the drug to produce unconsciousness are all seeking stimulus change.

From the flowering of the angiosperms millions of years ago came the seeds of drug addiction. The seeds were sown throughout history, in the stomachs of poisoned dinosaurs, in birds who avidly devoured the seeds, and in the gardens of humans who cultivated them. From accident to addiction; from goats foraging on coffee beans and qat leaves, to humans drinking their daily stimulants; from rats and bees repeatedly revisiting opium poppies and marihuana plants with violent cravings, to humans getting their ''buzz'' from opiates and ''grass''; from the baboons of South Africa that crave tobacco in imitation of man, to the *Homo sapiens* who smoke cigarettes in order to be more like the Marlboro man; from elephants who seek out fermented fruit to alleviate stress, to stressed *Homo sapiens* who drink in order to see pink elephants; from the great herbals of the Middle Ages that described the inventiveness of animals in seeking natural cures for their ailments, to the speculative imagination of science fiction writers like Doris Buck (1964) who envisioned the use of a synthetic drug to escape the horrors of middle-age life in twenty-first century Washington, D.C. by mentally transporting the user to the Mexozoic Era and creating the illusion that she or he is a dinosaur, the history of drug addiction, like all history, repeats itself. Naturally.

REFERENCES

Abdo Abbasy, Ma. The habitual use of "qat." *Internationales Journal für Prophylaktische Medizin und Sozialhygiene*, 1957, *1*, 20–22.

Addiction Research Foundation. Insect warfare planned by U.N. *The Journal*, 1972, *1*, 15.

Ahlfors, U. G. *Alcohol and conflict*. Helsinki: The Finnish Foundation for Alcohol Studies, 1969, Vol. 16.

Anonymous. Fantasia. *This World*, February 15, 1976, p. 2.

Ardrey, R. *The social contract*. New York: Dell, 1970.

Arnold, H. L. *Poisonous plants of Hawaii*. Rutland, Vermont: Tuttle, 1944.

Atsatt, P. R., & O'Dowd, D. J. Plant defense guilds. *Science*, 1976, *193*, 24–29.

Barker, L. M., Best, M. R., & Domjan, M. (Eds.). *Learning mechanisms in food selection*. Houston: Baylor Univ. Press, 1977.

Bejerot, N. A theory of addiction as an artificially induced drive. *American Journal of Psychiatry,* 1972, *128,* 842–846.

Bell, C. R. Breeding systems and floral biology of the Umbelliferae or evidence for specialization in unspecialized flowers. In V. H. Heywood (Ed.), *The biology and chemistry of the Umbelliferae.* London: Academic Press, 1971. Pp. 93–107.

Bever, O. Why do plants produce drugs? Which is their function in the plants? *Quarterly Journal of Crude Drug Research,* 1970, *10,* 1541–1549.

Blum, R. H., & Associates. *Society and drugs.* San Francisco: Jossey-Bass, 1969.

Bogg, R. A. Stress-seeking and hallucinogenic drug usage. *Canadian Journal of Public Health,* 1975, *66,* 369–373.

Bourke, J. G. Popular medicine, customs, and superstitions of the Rio Grande. *The Journal of American Folk-Lore,* 1894, *24,* 119–146.

Brill, H. Introduction. In S. J. Mule & H. Brill (Eds.), *Chemical and biological aspects of drug dependence.* Cleveland: CRC Press, 1972. Pp. 3–9.

Buck, D. P. Come where my love lies dreaming. *Fantasy and Science Fiction,* 1964, *26*(2), 113–126.

Cappell, H., & LeBlanc, A. E. Gustatory avoidance conditioning by drugs of abuse. In N. W. Milgram, L. Krames, & T. M. Alloway (Eds.), *Food aversion learning.* New York: Plenum, 1977. Pp. 133–167.

Carrighar, S. *Wild heritage.* Boston: Houghton Mifflin, 1965.

Carrington, R. *Elephants.* New York: Basic Books, 1959.

Cassell. *Cassell's popular natural history* (Vol. 1). London: Cassell, Petter & Galpin, 1861.

Chauvin, R. *The world of ants.* (G. Ordish, trans.). London: Victor Gollancz, 1970.

Clausen, L. W. *Insect fact and folklore.* New York: Macmillan, 1954.

Cocteau, J. *Opium.* (M. Crosland & S. Road, trans.). London: Icon Books, 1957.

Cowan, F. *Curious facts in the history of insects; including spiders and scorpions.* Philadelphia: Lippincott, 1865.

Cowan, J. *The use of tobacco vs. purity, chastity and sound health.* New York: Cowan, 1870.

Crane, J. T. *Art of intoxication.* New York: Calton & Lanahan, 1871.

Darwin, C. *The descent of man and selection in relation to sex.* New York: A. L. Burt, 1874. (Originally published, 1871.)

Davis, J. W., & Anderson, R. C. *Parasitic diseases of wild mammals.* Ames: Iowa State Univ. Press, 1971.

Davis, J. W., Karstad, L. H, & Trainer, D. O. (Eds.). *Infectious diseases of wild mammals.* Ames: Iowa State Univ. Press, 1970.

Duke, J. A. Utilization of papaver. *Economic Botany,* 1973, *27,* 390–400.

Duke, J. A., Aulik, D., & Plowman, T. Nutritional value of coca. *Botanical Museum Leaflets, Harvard University,* 1975, *24*(6), 113–119.

Edmunds, G. F., & Alstad, D. N. Coevolution in insect herbivores and conifers. *Science,* 1978, *199,* 941–945.

Eisner, T., & Halpern, B. P. Taste distortion and plant palatability. *Science,* 1971, *172,* 1362.

Ellison, G. D. Animal models of psychopathology. *American Psychologist,* 1977, *32,* 1036–1045.

Esplin, D. W., & Zablocka-Esplin, B. Central nervous system stimulants. In L. S. Goodman & A. Gilman (Eds.), *The pharmacological basis of therapeutics* (4th ed.). London: Collier-Macmillan, 1970. Pp. 348–357.

Fairbanks, L. Communication of food quality in captive *Macaca nemestrina* and free-ranging *Ateles geoffroy. Primates,* 1975, *16,* 181–190.

Feeny, P. Biochemical coevolution between plants and their insect herbivores. In L. E. Gilbert & P. H. Raven (Eds.), *Coevolution of animals and plants.* Austin: Univ. of Texas Press, 1975. Pp. 3–15.

Fitz-Gerald, F. L. Voluntary alcohol consumption in apes. In B. Kissin & H. Begleiter (Eds.), *The biology of alcoholism. Vol. 2: Physiology and Behavior.* New York: Plenum, 1972. Pp. 169–192.

Folkard, R. *Plant lore, legends, and lyrics.* London: Sampson Low, Marston, Searle & Rivington, 1884.

Forsyth, A. A. *British poisonous plants.* (Bull. No. 161, Ministry of Agriculture and Fisheries.) London: Her Majesty's Stationary Office, 1954.

Franke, K. W., & Potter, V. R. The ability to discriminate between diets of varying degrees of toxicity. *Science,* 1936, *83,* 330–332.

Freeland, W. J., & Janzen, D. H. Strategies in herbivory by mammals: The role of plant secondary compounds. *The American Naturalist,* 1974, *108*(961), 269–289.

Furst, P. T. To find our life: peyote among the Huichol Indians of Mexico. In P. T. Furst (Ed.), *Flesh of the gods. The ritual use of hallucinogens.* New York: Praeger, 1972. Pp. 136–184.

Garcia, J., Hankins, W. G., & Coil, J. D. Koalas, men, and other conditioned gastronomes. In N. W. Milgram, L. Kramer, & T. M. Alloway (Eds.), *Food aversion learning.* New York: Plenum, 1977. Pp. 195–218.

Gardner, C. A., & Bennetts, H. W. *The toxic plants of western Australia.* Perth: West Australian Newspapers, 1956.

Gilges, W. *Some African poison plants and medicines of northern Rhodesia.* (Paper No. 11). Livingston: The Rhodes-Livingstone Museum, 1955.

Hafez, E. S. E. (Ed.). *The behavior of domestic animals* (3rd ed.). Baltimore: Williams & Wilkins, 1975.

Hatch, R. C. Effect of drugs on catnip (*Nepeta cataria*)—induced pleasure behavior in cats. *American Journal of Veterinary Research,* 1972, *33,* 143–155.

Hinton, H. E., & Dunn, A. M. S. *Mongooses.* London: Oliver & Boyd, 1967.

Humphries, B. *Bizarre.* New York: Bell, 1965.

Jackson, B., & Reed, A. Catnip and the alteration of consciousness. *Journal of the American Medical Association,* 1969, *207,* 1349–1350.

Janiger, O., & Dobkin de Rios, M. Suggestive hallucinogenic properties of tobacco. *Medical Anthropology Newsletter,* 1973, *4,* 6–11.

Janson, H. W. *Apes and ape lore in the middle ages and the renaissance.* Vienna: Brüder Rosenbaum, 1952.

La Barre, W. Anthropological perspectives on hallucination and hallucinogens. In R. K. Siegel & L. J. West (Eds.), *Hallucinations: Behavior, experience, and theory.* New York: Wiley, 1975. Pp. 9–52.

Lagneau, F., & Gallard, P. Intoxication des bovins par l'oeillette. *Recueil di Medicine Veterinaire,* 1946, *122*(1), 310–313.

Leeds, A. Reindeer herding and Chucki social institutions. In A. Leeds & A. P. Vayda (Eds.), *Man, culture, and animals.* Washington, D.C.: AAAS, 1965. Pp. 87–128.

Lehner, E., & Lehner, J. *Folklore & odysseys of food & medicinal plants.* New York: Farrar Straus Giroux, 1973. (Originally published, 1962.)

Levi, W. M. *The pigeon.* Sumter: Levi, 1957.

Levinson, H. Z. The defensive role of alkaloids in insects and plants. *Experientia,* 1976, *15,* 408–411.

Lewin, L. *Phantastica. Narcotic and stimulating drugs.* London: Kegan Paul, Trench, Trubner, 1931.

Lewinsohn, R. *Animals, men and myths.* New York: Harper, 1954.

Leyhausen, P. Addictive behavior in free ranging animals. In L. Goldberg & F. Hoffmeister (Eds.), *Psychic dependence.* (Bayer Symposium IV.) New York: Springer-Verlag, 1973. Pp. 58–64.

Lumholtz, C. *Unknown Mexico* (Vol. 1). New York: Scribner, 1902.

Marais, E. *The soul of the ape.* New York: Atheneum, 1969. (Originally published, 1936.)

Marsh, C. D. *The loco-weed disease of the plains.* (U.S. Department of Agriculture, Bureau of Animal Industry, Bulletin 112.) Washington, D.C.: U.S. Government Printing Office, 1909.

Marsh, C. D. *Stock-poisoning of the range.* (U.S. Department of Agriculture Bulletin 1245.) Washington, D.C.: U.S. Government Printing Office, 1924.

Masserman, J. H. Stress situations in animals and the nature of conflict. In H. A. Abramson (Ed.), *Neuropharmacology.* (Transactions of the Third Conference.) New York: The Josiah Macy, Jr. Foundation, 1957. Pp. 147–167.

Mathison, R. R. *The eternal search.* New York: Putnam, 1958.

Mello, N. K. Control of self-administration: the role of aversive consequences. In R. C. Petersen & R. C. Stillman (Eds.), *PCP. Phencyclidine Abuse: An Appraisal* (NIDA Research Monograph 21), 1978. Pp. 289–308.

Mendell, Y. Dr. Doorenbos cuts grass; says marihuana dangerous. *Reflector* (Mississippi State Univ.), 1969, *81*, 1.

Mességué, M. *Des hommes et des plantes.* Paris: Editions Robert Laffont, 1970.

Mortimer, W. G. *History of coca. The divine plant of the Incas.* San Francisco: And/Or Press, 1974. (Originally published, 1901.)

Murphy, J. M. Psychotherapeutic aspects of shamanism on St. Lawrence Islands, Alaska. In A. Kieve (Ed.), *Magic, faith, and healing.* New York: Free Press, 1954. Pp. 53–83.

Myerhoff, B. *Peyote hunt. The sacred journey of the Huichol Indians.* Ithaca: Cornell Univ. Press, 1974.

Northcote, R. *The book of herb lore.* New York: Dover, 1971. (Originally published, 1912.)

Palen, G. F., & Goddard, G. V. Catnip and oestrous behavior in the cat. *Animal Behavior,* 1966, *14*, 372–377.

Park, O. Observations upon the behavior of myrmecophilous pselaphid beetles. *Pedobiologia,* 1964, *4*, 129–137.

Penfold, A. R., & Willis, J. L. *The eucalypts.* London: Leonard Hill, 1961.

Piercy, P. L., Hargin, G., & Brown, C. A. Mushroom poisoning in cattle. *Journal of the American Veterinary Medical Association,* 1944, *105*, 206–208.

Pierquin, P. *Traité de la folie des animaux, de ses rapports avec celle de l'homme et les législatona actuelles.* Paris: Libraire de la Faculté de Médicine de Paris, Vol. 1, 1839.

Pope, H. G. *Tabernathe iboga:* An African narcotic plant of social importance. *Economic Botany,* 1969, *23*, 174–184.

Revusky, S., & Garcia, J. Learned associations over long delays. In G. H. Bower (Ed.), *The psychology of learning and motivation.* New York: Academic Press, 1970. Pp. 1–84.

Richter, C. P. Production and control of alcoholic craving in rats. In H. A. Abramson (Ed.), *Neuropharmacology.* (Transactions of the Third Conference.) New York: The Josiah Macy, Jr., Foundation, 1957. Pp. 39–146.

Ridley, H. N. *The dispersal of plants throughout the world.* Ashford, Kent: L. Reeve, 1930.

Schultes, R. E. Random thoughts and queries on the botany of cannabis. In C. R. B. Joyce & S. H. Curry (Eds.), *The botany and chemistry of cannabis.* London: J & A Churchill, 1970. Pp. 11–38.

Siegel, R. K. *The effects of LSD and alcohol on elephant behavior.* Unpublished manuscript.

Siegel, R. K. An ethologic search for self-administration of hallucinogens. *The International Journal of the Addictions,* 1973, *8*, 373–393.

Siegel, R. K., Collings, P. R., & Diaz, J. L. On the use of *Tagetes lucida* and *Nicotiana rustica* as a Huichol smoking mixture: the Aztec "yahutli" with suggestive hallucinogenic effects. *Economic Botany,* 1977, *31*, 16–23.

Siegmund, O. H. (Ed.). *The Merck veterinary manual* (4th ed.). Rahway, New Jersey: Merck, 1973.

Sikes, S. K. *The natural history of the African elephant.* London: Weidenfeld & Nicolson, 1971.

Southwood, T. R. E. The insect/plant relationship—an evolutionary perspective. In H. F. van Emden (Ed.), *Insect/plant relationships.* Oxford: Blackwell, 1973. Pp. 3–30.

Stevens, H. B. *The recovery of culture.* New York: Harper, 1949.

Swain, T. Cold-blooded murder in the Cretaceous. *Spectrum,* 1974, *120*, 10–12.

Taylor, N. *Plant drugs that changed the world.* New York: Dodd, Mead, 1965.

Todd, N. B. *The catnip response.* Unpublished doctoral dissertation. Harvard Univ., 1963.

Tolstoy, L. *Why do men stupefy themselves?* (A. Maude, trans.) Hankins, New York: Strength Books, 1975. (Originally published, 1890.)

Van Proosdy, C. *Smoking.* Amsterdam: Elsevier, 1960.

Verrill, A. H. *Strange insects and their stories.* Boston: L. C. Page, 1937.

Waller, G. R., Price, G. H., & Mitchell, E. D. Feline attractant, cis, trans-nepetalactone metabolism in the domestic cat. *Science,* 1969, *164*, 1281–1282.

Warner, A. C. I. Some factors influencing the rumen microbial population. *Journal of General Microbiology,* 1962, *28*, 129–146.

Waser, P. G. The pharmacology of *Amanita muscaria.* In D. H. Efron (Ed.), *Ethnopharmacological search for psychoactive drugs.* (U.S. Public Health Service Publication No. 1645.) Washington, D.C.: U.S. Government Printing Office, 1967. Pp. 419–439.

Wasson, R. G. Fly agaric and man. In D. H. Efron (Ed.), *Ethnopharmacologic search for psychoactive drugs*. (U.S. Public Health Service Publication No. 1645). Washington, D.C.: U.S. Government Printing Office, 1967. Pp. 405–414.

Wasson, R. C. *Soma. Divine mushroom of immortality*. New York: Harcourt, 1968.

Watt, J. M., & Breyer-Brandwijk, M. G. *The medicinal and poisonous plants of southern and eastern Africa*. London: E. & S. Livingstone, 1962.

Wilbert, J. Tobacco and shamanistic ecstasy among the Warao Indians of Venezuela. In P. T. Furst (Ed.), *Flesh of the gods. The ritual use of hallucinogens*. New York: Praeger, 1972. Pp. 55–83.

Wilson, E. O. *The insect societies*. Cambridge: Harvard Univ. Press, 1971.

Wolf, F. A. *Aromatic or oriental tobaccos*. Durham: Duke Univ. Press, 1962.

Wood-Gush, D. G. M., Duncan, I. J. H., & Fraser, D. Social stress and welfare problems in agricultural animals. In E. S. E. Hafez (Ed.), *The behavior of domestic animals* (3rd ed.). Baltimore: Williams & Wilkins, 1975. Pp. 182–200.

JOHN L. FULLER

Genetic Analysis of Deviant Behavior

3

I. Behavior–Genetic Analysis

Behavior–genetic analysis is a way of separating biological and experiential factors that are responsible for individual and group differences in behavior. Thus it must be concerned as much with environmental as with genetic sources of variability. Nevertheless, the emphasis of behavior–genetic analysis is directed at differences that are transmitted from parents to offspring through their gametes. The appearance (phenotype) of a breed of domestic animals is replicated, generation after generation, as long as mating is restricted to that breed. Mating across breeds produces hybrids with a mixture of the parental characteristics. The inheritance of physical phenotypes was recognized long before there was a science of genetics.

When we extend the concept of phenotype to behavior there are difficulties. Behavior is not a physical structure that can be, at least conceptually, traced backward to DNA's, their products and their interactions. Instead, behavior is a continuous process that begins at an early stage of development and persists until death. For description we can divide behavioral sequences into discrete units, but these are more arbitrary than the physical units of the chemist and anatomist. It is convenient, therefore, to divide phenotypes into two major classes: *somatophehes* that are characterized by their physical structure, and *psychophenes* that are defined by distinctive processes (Fuller & Wimer, 1973). The second

PSYCHOPATHOLOGY IN ANIMALS
Research and Clinical Implications

class can be further divided into *ostensible psychophenes,* acts that can be identified by all competent observers (e.g., number of avoidance responses in a shuttlebox), and *inferred psychophenes* that correspond to generalized behavioral tendencies (e.g., anxiety, intelligence).

In separating psychophenes from somatophenes there is no implication that behavior can be divorced from its physical substrate. Receptors, neural integrators, and effectors are essential for any behavior, and physiological behavior genetics is deeply concerned with tracing the pathways between genes and psychophenes through the maze of somatophenes. Although some progress has been made we are still a long way from understanding the pathways between genes and complex somatophenes, let alone extending this form of analysis to behavior. The problems are complex because a large proportion of the genome of higher organisms is devoted to regulating other genes, turning them on and off at particular stages of development. A genetic effect on behavior may be attributable to a gene that was activated (or inactivated) only for a brief period in infancy; the effects of its activity (or inactivity) may persist for life.

A. HERITABILITY

Genetic analysis of behavior is not restricted to a physiological approach. The contribution of genes to individual differences within a population can be investigated at a strictly behavioral level. The population approach leads to a consideration of the meaning of "heritability." The intense arguments over the heritability of human IQ are widely known. Unfortunately, some of the debaters displayed grave misconceptions of the meaning of this technical term. *Heritability* is the proportion of phenotypic variance attributable to genetic differences within a specified population. Although there are several methods of determining it, all essentially involve comparing similarity of a trait in relatives with that of individuals taken at random from the same population. If follows that heritability is a characteristic of a population, not of a trait. It will be higher in a genetically heterogeneous population and lower in a population whose members are exposed to a variety of different environments. Space permits only the briefest mention of the difference between broad and narrow heritability which is of critical importance in the application of genetics to animal breeding. In the broad sense, heritability incorporates *all* genetic influences upon the phenotype; in the narrow sense, it is more restrictive and describes the degree to which the phenotypes of offspring are predictable from those of their parents. Further explanation may be found in McClearn and DeFries (1973), Ehrman and Parsons (1976), and Fuller and Thompson (1978).

There is a paradox with respect to the concept of heritability. Animal research has shown that characteristics that are most critical for biological fitness tend to have lower heritabilities than characters of a more superficial nature. It follows that low heritability implies a more rigid genetic programming of the development of all members of a species than does high heritability. A species can enjoy the luxury of gene-based individuality in traits that have little influence on survival and reproduction; in traits of fundamental importance it is more efficient to rely on genetic preprogramming so that individuals respond correctly to common stimuli without the need for time-consuming learning. Such preprogramming does not always imply built-in stimulus–response sequences; it can refer to genetic coding of a uniform plan of neural organization which is essential if learning is to follow a predictable course.

B. PHENOSTABILITY

Heritability is a concept properly applied only to populations. There is need, however, for another term to refer to the developmental plasticity of an individual with a particular genotype. Consider, for example, a large group of individuals of identical genotype. (An inbred strain of fruitflies or mice would be an example.) As we look at such a group we observe that its members are not phenotypically identical. They may all have the same pigmentation but differ in size, rate of growth, and quickness to learn a new response. Coloration can be call *phenostable*; body size, growth rate, and learning ability, *phenolabile*. We designate the mean value of each labile trait as the *reaction norm*. We can also designate a *reaction range* spanning the distance between the highest and lowest observed values. The range can never be determined precisely since a new case may extend it. Given a sufficient sample size, however, useful estimates may be made.

Both the reaction norm and the reaction range are, of course, dependent upon the environment in which individuals of a particular genotype are placed. It should also be noted that their measurement is possible only when a genotype can be replicated accurately through inbreeding (or potentially by cloning). In humans, where such replication is found only in monozygotic twin pairs, empirical measurement is not possible. In our species, and probably in many natural populations, individuals are so genetically diverse that estimation of the plasiticity of any particular genotype is impossible. We can only guess as to how a specific organism might have developed given other circumstances. Still, all humans have much of their genotype in common, one that has been shaped by thousands of years of selection. It is unlikely that any radical environmental change could greatly alter the reaction range of our species, at least on the upper end, although it might shift the mean in either direction.

The concept of phenostability is central to the stress–diathesis theory that plays an important role in human psychiatric genetics. Essentially it postulates that genotypes differ in their ability to cope with stress during development. For some individuals no environment may be benign enough to forestall a severe behavioral disorder at some period of life; others cope successfully with any but the most devastating circumstances. Most individuals are closer to the reaction norm, and the probability that they will show deviant behavior is largely a function of the amount of stress that they encounter.

II. Why Animal Models in Genetic Research?

A tremendous amount of research has been published on the genetics of deviant behavior in humans. It varies greatly in quality, but it is fair to say that even the best work has left important issues in doubt. The truth is that humans are poor subjects for many kinds of genetic investigation. With animals we can control matings, establish inbred and selected lines, produce neurological and metabolic mutants in large numbers, and control the rearing, diet, and life experiences of our subjects from conception to death. Ethical restrictions on the experimental use of drugs, confinement, or pain are much less stringent with animals. Thus, we have enhanced ability to search for correlations between deviant behavior and brain anatomy, neurophysiology, and neurochemistry. Genetic control and genetic variation often facilitate the search for such correlations. The disadvantage of animal models is obvious. How equivalent are behavioral deviations in a rat or dog to those of our own species? We do not yet have a complete animal model of schizophrenic behavior, and only imperfect ones of drug addiction, that could be used as a perfect substitute for observations on humans. I doubt that such equivalence will ever be attained. Nevertheless, if we accept the idea that we are part of an orderly universe, some principles may be common to many species. In this chapter I shall review a number of research areas where principles related to deviant behavior may be emerging.

A. AUDIOGENIC SEIZURES

When Maier and Glazer (1940) demonstrated that rats confronted an insoluble discrimination problem in a Lashley jumping apparatus convulsed when forced by an air blast to jump toward a stimulus card, they believed that they had identified an experimental neurosis. However, by the time of Finger's (1947) review of convulsive behavior, there was general agreement that "neurosis" was a misleading term and that the response to intense sound was better called an "audiogenic seizure." If there is a homology of these seizures with any human disorder, it seems to be with grand mal epilepsy. Leaving aside the matter of phenotypic homology with human disorders, audiogenic seizures are an instructive example of genetic and environmental influences upon a dramatic form of behavior (Fuller & Collins, 1970). Although these seizures have been studied in several species I shall concentrate on work with the laboratory mouse, the mammal most used in genetic experiments.

In suspectible mice the seizure pattern is elicited by continued exposure for 5–60 sec to a high-pitched sound: An electric doorbell yielding 95 dB is excellent. Animals not seizing within a minute almost never do even if stimulation is prolonged. A complete seizure progresses in a fixed order of increasingly severe phases; however, it may terminate at any level. Conventionally, four phases are recognized: (a) wild running; (b) clonic convulsion is which the mouse falls on its side and flexes and extends its limbs rhythmically; (c) tonic extension of limbs and tail with muscle rigidity; and (d) death from asphyxiation due to the prolonged muscle spasm.

1. Strain Differences

Strains of mice differ markedly in their susceptibility to seizures (Hall, 1947; Ginsburg & Miller, 1963; Fuller & Sjursen, 1967). Thus, in a series of four weekly exposures to a bell beginning at 3 weeks of age, approximately 90% of DBA/2J mice had a fatal seizure. About 60% of BALB/cJ mice convulsed on at least one trial but none died. C57BL/6J mice had a lower seizure risk (about 25%) but half of those convulsing did not survive (Fuller & Sjursen, 1967). Seizure risk varies greatly with age; DBA/2J mice more than 6 weeks of age are generally resistant. The risk is also strongly influenced by prior exposure to sound. Henry (1967) showed that normally resistant C57BL/6J mice stimulated by bell ringing between 15–24 days of age became susceptible after a 2-day delay. This phenomenon of *priming* has been found in other "resistant strains," for example, in SJL/J (Fuller & Collins, 1968a). Thus it appears that susceptibility may connote a particular genotype (as in DBA/2J) or a particular life experience (as in C57BL/6J or SJL/J). Priming-induced seizures appear to be perfect replicas of spontaneous ones; in genetic terminology they are called *phenocopies*.

2. Mode of Inheritance

One might expect that it would be a relatively easy matter to determine the mode of inheritance of seizure susceptibility by making appropriate crosses between susceptible and resistant strains. Actually the task turns out to be complicated. Different investigators have advocated: (*a*) a single-locus model with susceptibility dominant; (*b*) a single-locus model with susceptibility recessive; (*c*) a two-locus model with a strong influence of background genotype; and (*d*) a polygenic system with multiple loci involved in determining the position of an individual, or a strain, on a quantitative scale of susceptibility. The last is a form of stress–diathesis model. Part of the disagreement among experimenters stems from the failure, in many instances, to distinguish between spontaneous and priming-induced seizures. When repeated exposures to the sound stimulus are given and a convulsion on any trial is the criterion of "susceptibility," the pattern of transmission appears quite different from that obtained when only one test is given. Considerable evidence favors a major recessive gene, *asp* (audiogenic seizure prone), producing susceptibility to spontaneous seizures with polygenic regulation of the incidence of priming-induced seizures (Collins & Fuller, 1968; Henry & Bowman, 1970). This model may not be valid for tests at all ages, or for all strains of mice, or for different conditions of testing.

3. Physiological Correlates

Considerable attention has been given to the physiological basis of spontaneous susceptibility to audiogenic seizures. Strain and mutant differences have been linked with variation in adenosine triphosphatase activity and in glutamic acid decarboxylase activity. Both enzymes are involved in the balance between excitation and inhibition in nerve cells (Ginsburg, Cowen, Maxson, & Sze, 1969). Both norepinephrin and serotonin are more abundant in the brains of resistant C57BL than in susceptible DBA mice. In the former strain, moderate doses of reserpine (a depleter of brain amines) increases seizure risk; increasing the level of brain amines by injecting monamine oxidase inhibitors protects DBAs against seizures (Schlesinger & Griek, 1970).

Priming-induced seizure susceptibility has been hypothesized to result from hypersensitization of portions of the auditory neural system following cochlear damage (Gates, Chen, & Bock, 1973; Henry & Saleh, 1973; Willott & Henry, 1974). Fuller and Collins (1968b) demonstrated that the priming effect can be localized on one side of the brain. This is achieved by blocking one ear during the priming exposure. If the originally open ear is blocked and the originally blocked ear left open during a test trial no convulsion occurs. If the same ear is open on both exposures a typical bilateral seizure is seen.

All of this evidence supports the idea that, as viewed by an observer, spontaneous and priming-induced seizures are phenotypically identical, but that the genes for spontaneous susceptibility do not produce the same internal state as priming does. Genetic studies have verified the separability of the two kinds of susceptibility. In families from a heterogeneous population of mice there was no significant correlation of the liabilities for the two kinds of seizures (Fuller, 1975). It is possible to select lines of mice that are either susceptible or resistant to priming. Mice selected for priming-susceptibility do not differ from unselected controls in the incidence of spontaneous seizures (Chen & Fuller. 1976; Deckhard, Tepper, & Schlesinger, 1976). Strain variability in priming and in spontaneous susceptibility must involve at least two distinct processes.

4. Summary

Audiogenic seizures in mice demonstrate the interplay of genotype, developmental age, physiological substrate, and prior experience. In this respect they are a model that is generally applicable to the behavior–genetic analysis of more complex and subtle behavioral deviations. This brief survey of research also conveys a sobering message. With all the advantages of genetic control, access to the brain, and an extremely well-defined phenotype we are still ignorant of many characteristics of the seizures. How much more difficult will be the task of genetic analysis of deviant behavior in humans where none of these three advantages is present.

B. EMOTIONAL INSTABILITY IN DOGS

Dog owners are often aware of striking differences in the emotional behavior of their pets. Some are sociable and responsive to commands; others appear "neurotic" or "spooky." Pavlov (1927) recognized individual differences in ease of salivary conditioning in his dogs and predicted that the use of his methods for analyzing higher nervous activity would "greatly assist the development of a strictly scientific experimental investigation of the hereditary transmission of different aspects of nervous activities in animals [p. 285]."

Pavlov himself did not move in this direction, but the research program at the University of Arkansas and the Veterans Administration Hospital in North Little Rock is a fulfillment of this prophecy.

The Arkansas program has concentrated on two lines of pointer dogs, an emotionally stable (A) and an emotionally unstable (E) line. These lines were originally derived from two pairs selected by breed specialists as representing the behavioral extremes among pointers. A number of simple tests differentiate the two lines (Murphree, Dykman, & Peters, 1967). Unstable E dogs are less active in an unfamiliar empty room; more of them freeze when a 122-dB klaxon is sounded. At 1 year of age, 80% of A dogs, but only about 25% of E dogs, approach a friendly human. A threatening man induces 60% of E dogs, but less than 20% of A dogs, to freeze. The lines also differ in their cardiac response to approach and petting by a human (Murphree, Peters, & Dykman, 1967). The basal heart rate of A dogs was 120/min; it decreased during petting. In E dogs the basal rate was lower (80/min) and did not vary during petting.

Murphree and Newton (1971a) looked for maternal effects on emotionality by making reciprocal crosses between the two lines. The hybrid offspring of either type of cross should be the same genetically. If maternal nongenetic influences are important the A-male × E-female cross should yield offspring more nervous than those from the E-male × A-female cross. Actually, there were no significant differences in motor activity or responses to humans between the offspring from the two types of crosses. Neither uterine environment nor nursing care seemed to influence emotional development. Both kinds of crossbreds were behaviorally similar to their E-line progenitors indicating dominance of high emotionality. An attempt to modify reactions of E dogs to a human by providing extra handling during infancy resulted in consistent, but small, improvement. There was no effect on the differences in heart rate.

A more innovative approach to rehabilitation of nervous dogs was an attempt to build upon their "instinct" to point toward the scent of quail (McBryde & Murphree, 1974). Five E dogs and three A-dog controls were systematically desensitized to open areas, live quail, gunshots, and humans. The animals were then rated on their performance in actual quail hunting. Nervous pointers scored as well as controls on this practical test; they obeyed commands and retrieved birds efficiently. However, the improvement was situation specific. No significant changes in the index of emotional instability were noted in any individuals as a result of field training. The data are consistent in supporting the hypothesis that nervousness in these dogs is an inherited characteristic that is not readily modified by experience.

1. Physiological Correlates

Considerable attention has been given to possible physiological correlates of nervous instability. In a sample of 67 E-line dogs the mean heart rate was 65/min; 70% of these animals showed at least one atrioventricular (AV) block in their electrocardiogram (EKG). In 52 A-line animals the mean heart rate was

110/min; only 15% had records with AV block (Newton, Murphree, & Dykman, 1970). Crossbred subjects were intermediate in circulatory functions just as they were in behavior. In a later study Newton, Chapin, and Murphree (1976) were able to judge with 75% accuracy the genetic status of a sample of 20 dogs solely from their EKG records. Correlations of an index of emotional instability with various circulatory measures were: with heart rate, -.62; with rate of blood pressure response to injected methylphenidate (Ritalin), -.81; and with the variability of the P–R wave interval in the EKG, .64.

Differences between the lines have also been found in the electroencephalogram (Lucas, Powell, & Murphree, 1974). In A-line dogs a diminution of the energy of hippocampal theta waves (4–8 Hz) is associated with orienting and avoiding. In E-line animals, hippocampal theta energy is low at all times. Apparently these dogs are, in a sense, continuously orienting to their surroundings and never adapting to them. During REM sleep, however, hippocampal theta waves are found in both lines.

2. Schizokinesis

Evidence of differences between these two lines in physiology as well as in behavior is clear. Murphree and Newton (1971b) have attempted to incorporate their observations into Gannt's theory of schizokinesis. Ten E- and 10 A-line dogs were trained to avoid an electric shock, administered through the animal's collar by radio control, by jumping a barrier in a small arena. A 3000-Hz tone was the conditioned stimulus (CS). Behavior was shaped by reinforcing successively closer approximations to the desired final pattern. Nine A dogs learned the barrier-jumping task. Five E dogs also learned, but they required much more time and special coaching. Six to 8 weeks after termination of training, a retention test was given with EKG monitoring. At the first tone the heart rate of most A dogs increased; that of E dogs decreased.

The schizokinetic interpretation of the difficulties of the E dogs goes as follows. When the tone is sounded these dogs, instead of behaving in a manner that permits the experimenter to reinforce selectively components of the desired final pattern, freeze and crouch in an awkward, unbalanced position. With no suitable behavior to be reinforced it is impossible to train them. The same animals, however, usually demonstrate classical, Pavlovian conditioning by flinching during presentation of the CS. Schizokinesis seems to be the obverse of Seligman's (1971) concept of *preparedness* which has attracted considerable attention from learning theorists. Genetic influence on the initial response to an alerting stimulus may have major effects upon adaptive learning. This point has been made by Bolles (1970) who postulates that animals have innate species-specific defense reactions, such as fleeing, freezing, and fighting. The extension of his concept to intraspecific genetic differences in the prepotency of various defense reactions is supported by a considerable body of research involving dogs, mice, and rats (Fuller & Thompson, 1978). It is not difficult to adapt this model to a refractory human in a behavior-modification setting. The laws of operant conditioning may be universal, but if behavior suitable for reinforcement does not occur there is no way to increase its frequency by reinforcement. The freezing response of an E dog may be reinforcing to the animal, but it is not to the psychologist trying to establish avoidance behavior. Thus, inherited neurophysiological characteristics could have important, indirect effects on the components of the behavioral repertoire that must be learned through involvement with the environment.

C. MATERNAL SEPARATION AND EXPERIENTIAL DEPRIVATION

1. Macaques

Separation of an infant from its mother is believed to play an important role in the etiology of some depressive reactions. The best known experimental studies of this phenomenon in animals are those of Harlow and his colleagues at the Wisconsin Primate Laboratory (McKinney, Suomi, & Harlow, 1973). However, in a review of genetics and deviant behavior Kaufman's (1973) study of the differences between the effects of maternal separation on laboratory-reared young of two species of macaques, *Macaca nemestrina* (pigtails) and *M. radiata* (bonnets), is of particular interest. Both species were maintained in groups of one adult male with four or five adult females. A pigtail youngster (19–24 weeks old) whose mother is removed from the group goes almost immediately into a state of acute distress and agitation that typically lasts about a day. This is followed by a week-long period of severe depression of activity, and withdrawal from social intercourse with other members of the group. Depression abates gradually, and by the fourth week most youngsters are close to normal. In bonnets, removal of the mother may be followed by a brief period of agitation in the orphan, but no instances of depressive reaction were noted. The maternal-deprived bonnet youngster strongly increases its interaction with other members of the group that seem to be an adequate substitute for the absent mother.

Kaufman believes that the difference in reaction to maternal deprivation has a genetic basis. Although the two species of macaques are closely related and have very similar social structures and modes of life there are subtle differences between them. Bonnets in a group keep close and often huddle; they sleep upright in physical contact. A bonnet female-with-infant remains close to other females in her group; she retrieves and protects her infant infrequently. Pigtails, in contrast, make physical contact with other group members only when fighting, mating, or grooming. A female-with-infant tends to stay apart from other members of her group. Pigtail infants play with objects more than bonnets do; the opposite is true of social play. The species difference in vulnerability to reactive depression seems to be correlated with these features of social behavior. Both systems work equally well in undisturbed groups, but under stress a bonnet orphan can draw on the resources of the group. A pigtail orphan must fend for itself and adapts only after a prolonged period of withdrawal. In nature, such a depression would likely be fatal.

There is no clear proof that the differences in social behavior of these two macaques are completely of genetic origin, or that they could not be modified by altering the environment. It would be extremely interesting to study mixed groups and try to discover the relative importance of the infant's own genetically programmed reactions and the social milieu in which separation occurs. Perhaps it would be possible to alter social behavior by reinforcing close contacts in pigtails and separation in bonnets. Such experiments would simulate the effects of cultural practices upon the emotional development of young animals, and perhaps give clues to the degree to which social organization is biologically determined.

2. Domestic Dogs

Breed differences in the reaction of dogs to an impoverished environment during a period of rapid physical and behavioral development have been reported in a series of papers by Fuller and Clark. In the initial phases of their work (Fuller, 1964) three objectives were stated:

1. How much experience suffices to stimulate normal behavioral development?
2. Is there a critical period for such experience?
3. Do breeds differ in their reaction to experiential deprivation?

Behavioral development was assayed in a 7.5-min arena test during which reactions to a human, to toys, and to another puppy of the same age and breed were recorded. Responses were categorized as avoidance, orientation, approach, investigation, and manipulation. Observations on posture and locomotor activity were also made. The basic isolation procedure was solitary confinement in a continuously lighted cage without physical or visual contact with humans or other dogs from the age of 21 days through 105 days. In some experiments, periodic breaks were made in isolation thus permitting varied doses of experience. In other instances specific forms of stimulation were provided within the home cages.

The effects of dosage of experience upon 10 beagles and 10 wire-haired fox terriers are shown in Table 3.1 The data were obtained in a series of 12 arena tests, 4 per week, during Weeks 16–19. Isolation of Group K was continuous from Weeks 4–15; isolation of individuals in Group N was interrupted four times per week by an arena test. The results are not particularly surprising. Isolates generally, but not always, were less responsive to the arena stimuli than were dogs of the same age who had 6 hours of arena experience spread over 12 weeks. The one unexpected result was that this modest amount of exposure produced dogs whose behavior was almost indistinguishable from that of animals reared in a spacious enclosure with extensive social contacts with humans and other dogs. Notable also was the greater activity of isolates compared with semi-isolates. Most relevant to the present discussion was the prevalence of significant differences between the two breeds. Terriers made more intense contacts with humans, showed greater social dominance, and were more active. There was a tendency for measures showing a treatment effect to show also a breed effect.

Table 3.1

Treatment and Breed Effects on Behavior at Nineteen Weeks[a]

Measure	Treatment effect total score			Breed effect total score		
	K[b]	N[b]	p[b]	B[c]	T[c]	p
All contacts—human	164	264	.05	589	596	ns
Strong contacts—human	47	215	.01	249	492	.01
Pendulum response	22	64	.05	103	92	ns
Ball response	41	55	ns	117	124	ns
Puppy response	54	61	ns	144	144	ns
Dominance	5	42	.05	39	119	.01
Locomotion	896	311	.01	1199	1844	.01

[a] Based on Fuller (1964).

[b] For simplicity, only data from the most extreme of the five groups are shown. Group K was completely isolated Weeks 4–15; four tests per week, Weeks 16–19. Group N, isolation interrupted four times weekly, Weeks 4–15; four tests per week, Weeks 16–19. p values based on ANOVA of all five groups.

[c] B = beagles; T = wire-haired fox terriers.

Consequently there was no basis for separating behavioral measures into a class whose variability is primarily genetic and another whose variability is attributable to differences in the opportunity to learn. Some kinds of behavior seem to be more malleable than others under either genetic or environmental influences.

The dogs in the experiment just described varied not only in the scheduling of their experiences but also in their amount of time spent in the arena. A second study compared the rates of acquiring adaptive responses in the arena when the same number of tests were distributed one per week over Weeks 4–19 or four per week over Weeks 16–19 (Fuller & Clark, 1966a). Puppies were brought from their home cages to the arena in a transport box from which they had to emerge in order to interact with the arena stimuli. In this experiment, also, terriers were much more reactive than beagles. However, almost all of the difference was shown to be due to the more rapid emergence of the terriers from their transport cage (Table 3.2). Once the beagles entered the arena their behavior was similar

Table 3.2

Mean Frequency of Nonemergence of Isolated Dogs[a]

Week	Beagles	Terriers
1	3.3	.9
2	2.3	.1
3	.9	.0
4	.4	.0
5	.2	.0

[a] Maximum weekly score = 4.

to that of the terriers. The two breeds appear to be potentially equally responsive, but beagles are more readily inhibited by new stimuli and situations.

In another experiment the same two breeds were reared in isolation and compared with pet-reared animals of the same age who had 2 hours daily of interaction with humans and other puppies in the laboratory, but not in the arena (Fuller & Clark, 1968). All were given four arena tests per week for 5 weeks beginning at Week 16. Treatment groups were: I, isolation-reared and matched with a similarly reared puppy in the arena; C, pair-isolated and matched with companion in the arena; I', isolation reared and matched with a pet-reared puppy in the arena; P, pet-reared as defined above. Separate indices for level of activity and for reactivity to specific stimuli were derived from the COFOD (code for observational data) system for recording (Fuller & Clark, 1966b). All groups of isolated beagles were less active that pet-reared beagles in early tests, but by the fifth week the differences were not significant. There was an indication that isolates paired with pets (Group I') adapted more quickly than isolates in pairs (Group I). In contrast all of the isolate groups of terriers were significantly hyperactive compared with pet-reared terriers. On the reactivity index all terrier groups were identical after the first week indicating that social and manipulative skills had not been permanently impaired by isolation. Beagle isolate groups remained less reactive than beagle pets for the full 5 weeks. Pet-reared beagles and terriers were equally reactive toward all classes of stimuli with the exception that more social dominance was shown by the terriers. In summary, this experiment found that two breeds responded in an opposite manner on the activity index scale, and were quantitatively different on the reactivity scale.

When beagles and terriers are reared in litters in spacious quarters under a uniform regimen they differ in many attributes (Scott & Fuller, 1965). In a general way, terriers may be characterized as more high-strung and aggressive than beagles. Apparently, these attributes protect them during isolation from the deleterious effects of a low level of stimulation. It may be emphasized here that the period of isolation in these experiments is one of the most rapid phases of development. By 16 weeks of age the standard reared dog has an adult behavioral repertory except for courtship, mating, and, for females, nursing. Even in these areas the beginnings of sexual play are sometimes evident.

Fuller (1967) interpreted the postisolation syndrome in terms of emergence stress. For the isolated, naive puppy, exposure to the arena produces a stimulus overload and elicits a withdrawal response that is incompatible with responding adaptively and receiving reinforcement. Learning ability, at least for simple tasks, is not impaired permanently by experiential deprivation of the degree used in these studies (Fuller, 1966). In fact little learning, if any, appears necessary for investigation and manipulation of objects and the initiation of social behavior. Amelioration of emergence shock by special handling and by administration of chlorpromazine had positive effects upon reactivity in the arena (Fuller & Clark, 1966a). This finding contrasts with the ineffectiveness of special handling in reducing emotionality in nervous pointers (Murphree & Newton, 1971a), but the procedures differ in many ways.

The most important conclusion from this series of experiments is that behavior–genetic analysis must incorporate a developmental point of view. The same type of early experience has quite different consequences in two breeds of dogs. We might ask ourselves if there are human analogues to beagles and terriers. I suspect that there are and that the influence of early experience upon personality may vary considerable in children of differing biological constitution.

D. ALCOHOL-RELATED BEHAVIOR

In humans, addiction to drugs is frequently highly maladaptive and may lead to neurotic or even psychotic behavior. Although the source of such deviant behavior is attributable to an external pharmacological agent, it is well known that people vary greatly in their ability to cope with potentially habit-forming substances, such as alcohol. Cultural beliefs related to alcohol usage are believed to play an important role in the incidence of alcoholism in different countries and social strata. However, within any group defined by sociological or ethnic criteria there are individuals who differ greatly in their consumption of and reaction to alcohol. Such variation could be the product of microenvironmental differences within a group; it could also reflect inherited biological differences in the effect of alcohol on the nervous system. Thus, it is of interest to review genetic studies of alcohol-related behavior in animals as possible models for understanding individual variability in our own species. Some attention will also be given to morphine, with particular attention to the question of whether addictability to one drug is prognostic of addictability to another with different chemistry and physiological effects.

Our species is not unique as a devotee of psychoactive compounds including alcohol (Siegel, Chapter 2 of this volume), though only humans have developed cultures that tend to promote or discourage the use of such substances. Although observations of apparent addictions in natural populations are interesting and suggestive, conclusions regarding genetic variability in addictability of individuals must necessarily be based upon laboratory experiments with genetically controlled subjects. Most genetic studies of alcohol- and morphine-related behavior have been done with rats and mice. These researches have dealt with the following issues: (*a*) genetic variation in free-choice alcohol intake; (*b*) differences in behavioral sensitivity to administered ethanol; and (*c*) the physiological and behavioral correlates of inherited differences in preference and in sensitivity.

1. Alcohol Intake

Interest in the genetics of free-choice alcohol intake is undoubtedly based on the hope that such studies may help to understand what McClearn (1968) has called the ethanol intake control system (EICS). It has proved easy to find strains of mice differing in free-choice alcohol intake. McClearn and Rodgers (1961) and Fuller (1964) using different techniques and sublines ranked four inbred strains as follows starting at the high end of the scale: C57BL, C3H, A, and

DBA. The consistency of ranking in related lines that had been separated for many generations and maintained in different laboratories indicates a stable genetically transmitted system of intake regulation.

Alcohol intake in rats has responded well to genetic selection. The *Alko alcohol* (AA) and *Alko nonalcohol* (ANA) lines from the Finnish Foundation for Alcohol Studies have been used in many research projects (Eriksson, 1968). Forcing alcohol consumption in young rats by providing it as the only source of fluid does not change ANA rats into alcohol acceptors (Eriksson, 1969a). Low-alcohol-preferring strains of mice increase alcohol intake when it is presented in a sweetened solution (Rodgers & McClearn, 1964). However, the relative ranking of the strains remains the same. In general, genotype outweighs experience as a factor influencing alcohol consumption. Environmental influences have been reported, though they do not negate this generalization. For example, Randall and Lester (1975) reported that DBA/2J mice reared with C57BL/6J foster parents increased their alcohol consumption as compared with controls.

The mode of inheritance of alcohol preference has been investigated by an analysis of rate of change under selection and the results of crosses between high and low-preference strains. Eriksson (1969b) estimated the heritability of alcohol consumption in his AA and ANA lines as .26 for males and .37 for females. In crosses between mouse strains, heritability estimates have varied considerably depending upon the strains used, the preference measure employed, and the method of computation (Whitney, McClearn, & DeFries, 1970). All studies, however, are consistent in showing that hybrids are intermediate to their parents in alcohol intake. Whitney *et al.* conclude that the most representative value for heritability of alcohol preference in laboratory rodents lies between .10 and .15.

Probably many genes are involved in the regulation of alcohol intake, though a few may be particularly important. Fuller and Collins (1972) found, for example, that a two-locus model gave a nearly perfect fit to data from a cross between C57BL/6J and DBA/2J. A brief report of a nonpreferring subline of C57BL/6 suggests that a mutation may have produced a significant change in preference behavior (Poley, 1972). Detection of specific genes is a first step in approaching the biochemical variations that presumably underlie differences in alcohol preference.

2. Behavioral Sensitivity

Mouse strains also vary in their sensitivity to the disruptive effects of alcohol upon behavior. Sleep time following injection of a standard dose of ethanol varied threefold in the alcohol-preferring C57BL strain (Mean = 38 min) and the alcohol-avoiding BALB strain (mean = 138 min) (Kakihana, Brown, McClearn, & Tabershaw, 1966). The difference was not simply a consequence of more rapid elimination of alcohol from C57BL mice. At waking, the mean brain concentration of alcohol in this strain was 430 mg/100 gm; in BALB mice it was 287mg/100gm. McClearn and Kakihana (1973) selected a long-sleep and short-sleep line from a heterogeneous population. Goldstein (1973) selected mice with high and low vulnerability to withdrawal reactions following prolonged exposure to alcohol vapor. It is clear that gene differences can produce variations in the psychopharmacological response to alcohol.

The relationship between neural sensitivity to alcohol and alcohol intake is somewhat complex. Ethanol is ingested less by long-sleep than by short-sleep mice, suggesting that the more sensitive strain avoids it (Church, Fuller, & Dann, 1979). However, C57BL/6J mice are more sensitive than DBA/2J mice to ethanol as measured by sleep time or by a locomotor coordination test (Belknap, Belknap, Berg, & Coleman, 1977).

3. Physiological Correlates

Even an alcohol-preferring mouse, such as C57BL/6J, does not ordinarily consume enough ethanol to become grossly intoxicated. This suggests that somewhere within an organism there is an ethanolostat that is set at different points—high for C57BL/6J and low for DBA/2J. There may, of course, be several such control mechanisms, each coming into play at different points. Two major categories of control processes have been postulated: (a) preabsorptive, including taste, odor, and irritability of mucous membranes; and (b) postabsorptive, including rate of metabolism, toxicity of its metabolic products (chiefly acetaldehyde), and neural sensitivity. These possibilities are discussed by Belknap et al. (1977) who compared the control of intake in C57BL/6J and DBA/2J mice. The latter, when water-deprived, avoided ethanol solutions long before enough of the substance had accumulated in the blood to trigger any conceivable postabsorptive control mechanism. Retroactive conditioned taste aversions to 15% sucrose and 2% alcohol were readily produced in DBAs by lithium chloride injections. The same procedure in C57BL produced aversion to sucrose but not to alcohol. Preabsorptive control is apparently absent in this strain. Sensitivity to the effects of injected ethanol was quantified by sleep time and by a motor coordination test. On both of these measures, strain C57BL was significantly more depressed than strain DBA. It appears that preabsorptive processes dominate in the latter, postabsorptive processes in the former. Humans may vary in a similar manner.

4. Psychological Correlates

A popular explanation of the use of alcohol by humans is that it reduces anxiety. If true, alcohol consumption could be an indirect measure of tension level. Adamson and Black (1959) predicted that consumption of alcohol in a free-choice situation would predict subsequent performance on conditioned avoidance. Their prediction that rats with intermediate levels of consumption would learn to avoid faster than either high or low imbibers was verified experimentally. In a more formal comparison of alcohol consumption in genetically selected lines of rats, Satinder (1972) found that Maudsley reactive subjects drank more than Maudsley nonreactives; Roman high avoiders more than Roman low avoiders. In both pairs of lines intake was higher in the presumably more stress-susceptible member.

Is high alcohol preference a predictor of high consumption of other drugs? It is well known that human drug abusers often, perhaps usually, partake of a variety of substances. In animals it is possible to test the hypothesis that there is an addiction-prone genotype that disposes to high intake of many behavior modifying drugs. In support of this idea, Nichols (1972) found that a morphine-addiction prone strain of rats was more disposed than a morphine-addiction resistant strain to consume alcohol. Contradicting this hypothesis are experiments on morphine preference of two sublines of C57BL, one of them an alcohol avoider (Whitney & Horowitz, 1978). The experimenters had previously shown that other C57BL strains were unique among mice in their high preference for morphine in a saccharin vehicle. When the alcohol-avoiding strain was tested with morphine it proved to be like other C57BL strains in morphine preference. The two preferences are genetically separable and must, therefore, depend upon different mechanisms. More research in this potentially important area is needed.

III. Summary and Evaluation

Even a brief survey provides evidence of important effects of heredity upon behavior of animals that is similar to deviant human behavior. At the very least, experimenters interested in testing hypotheses of the etiology and alleviation of deviant behavior in animal models should consider genetic variables in their choice of subjects. More important, the ubiquity of strain differences in many aspects of behavior is a caution to refrain from generalizations based on studies with a single strain or breed of animals. Standardization of subjects has many advantages, but premature standardization may prevent discovery of principles underlying individual differences, a major concern of both behavior–genetic analysis and clinical psychology.

One large class of deviant animal behavior, that related to inherited neurological defects, was omitted from this review. Most of these defects are inherited in classical Mendelian fashion; each is relatively uniform in its anatomical and biochemical features. These animal models are of greater interest to neurologists and developmental biologists than to psychologists. Genetic variability in the deviant behaviors discussed here seem, with the possible exception of the *asp* locus (audiogenic seizure prone), to involve polygenic mechanisms. This implies that individuals in a population are not separable into phenotypically distinct classes, each with a predictable liability to stressors. Instead, individuals high on a continuum are impaired by relatively minor stress, such as brief periods of isolation or low doses of alcohol; those low on the continuum are more resistant. In such a polygenic system, offspring will tend to resemble their parents, but will, on the average, regress toward the population mean. In the absence of selection the population mean will remain relatively constant. By selection it is possible to produce artificial populations that may differ widely from each other but be relatively homogeneous internally.

Animal studies are consistent in finding physiological and biochemical correlates of deviant behavior. However, much remains to be done before cause and effect relationships can be demonstrated. We are closer to such explanations for audiogeneic seizures and for alcohol preference than for other conditions discussed in this chapter. Even for these cases, our knowledge is incomplete. The biochemical–behavioral correlations have a temporal as well as a quantitative aspect. This is particularly well shown for audiogenic seizures, but it is probably a universal characteristic of such correlations. If any one area of behavior-genetic analysis of deviant behavior in animals is most promising it is the combination of genetic variables with developmental psychobiology. Such research programs require diverse skills and facilities; they yield results slowly, but the potential contributions to the understanding of the origins of maladaptive behavior are great.

REFERENCES

Adamson, R., & Black, R. Volitional drinking and avoidance learning in the white rat. *Journal of Comparative and Physiological Psychology*, 1959, *52*, 734–736.

Belknap, J. K., Belknap, N. D., Berg, J. H., & Coleman, R. Preabsorptive and postabsorptive control of ethanol intake in C57BL/6J mice. *Behavior Genetics*, 1972, *7*, 413–425.

Bolles, R. C. Species-specific defense reactions and avoidance learning. *Psychological Review*, 1970, *77*, 32–48.

Chen, C. S., & Fuller, J. L. Selection for spontaneous or priming-induced audiogenic seizure susceptibility in mice. *Journal of Comparative and Physiological Psychology*, 1976, *90*, 765–772.

Church, A. C., Fuller, J. L., & Dann, L. Alcohol intake: Importance of sex and genotype. *Journal of Comparative and Physiological Psychology* 1979, *93*, 242–246.

Collins, R. L., & Fuller, J. L. Audiogenic seizure prone (*asp*)—a gene affecting behavior in linkage group VIII of the mouse. *Science*, 1968, *162*, 1137–1139.

Deckhard, B. S., Tepper, J. M., & Schlesinger, K. Selective breeding for acoustic priming. *Behavior Genetics*, 1976, *6*, 375–381.

Ehrman, L. & Parsons, P. A. *The genetics of behavior.* Sunderland, Massachusetts, Sinauer, 1976.

Eriksson, K. Genetic selection for voluntary alcohol consumption in the albino rat. *Science*, 1968, *159*, 739–741.

Eriksson, K. Factors affecting voluntary alcohol consumption in the albino rat. *Annales Zoologica Fennici*, 1969, *6*, 227–265. (a)

Eriksson, K. The estimation of heritability for the self-selection of alcohol in the albino rat. *Annales Médicinae Experimentalis et Biologiae Fenniae*, 1969, *47*, 172–174. (b)

Finger, F. W. Convulsive behavior in the rat. *Psychological Bulletin*, 1947, *44*, 201–248.

Fuller, J. L. Effects of experiential deprivation upon behavior in animals. *Proceedings of the Third World Congress of Psychiatry, Montreal, 1961* (Vol. 3). Toronto: Univ. of Toronto Press, 1964, (Pp. 223–227). (a)

Fuller, J. L. Measurement of alcohol preference in genetic experiments *Journal of Comparative and Physiological Psychology*, 1964, *57*, 85–88. (b)

Fuller, J. L. Transitory effects of experiential deprivation upon reversal learning in dogs. *Psychonomic Science*, 1966, *4*, 273–274.

Fuller, J. L. Experiential deprivation and later behavior. *Science*, 1967, *158*, 1645–1652.

Fuller, J. L. Independence of inherited susceptibility to spontaneous and primed audiogenic seizures in mice. *Behavior Genetics,* 1975, *5,* 1-8.

Fuller, J. L., & Clark, L. D. Genetic and treatment factors modifying the postisolation syndrome in dogs. *Journal of Comparative and Physiological Psychology,* 1966, *61,* 251-257. (a)

Fuller, J. L., & Clark, L. D. Effects of rearing with specific stimuli upon postisolation behavior in dogs. *Journal of Comparative and Physiological Psychology,* 1966, *61,* 258-263. (b)

Fuller, J. L., & Clark, L. D. Genotype and behavioral vulnerability to isolation in dogs. *Journal of Comparative and Physiological Psychology,* 1968, *66,* 151-156.

Fuller, J. L., & Collins, R. L. Temporal parameters of sensitization for audiogenic seizures in SJL/J mice. *Developmental Psychobiology,* 1968, *1,* 185-188. (a)

Fuller, J. L., & Collins, R. L. Mice unilaterally sensitized for audiogenic seizures. *Science,* 1968, *162,* 1295. (b)

Fuller, J. L., & Collins, R. L. Genetics of audiogenic seizures in mice: A parable for psychiatrists. *Seminars in Psychiatry,* 1970, *2,* 75-88.

Fuller, J. L., & Collins, R. L. Ethanol consumption and preference in mice: A genetic analysis. *Annals of the New York Academy of Sciences,* 1972, *197,* 42-48.

Fuller, J. L., & Sjursen, F. H. Audiogenic seizures in eleven mouse strains. *Journal of Heredity,* 1967, *58,* 135-140.

Fuller, J. L., & Thompson, W. R. *Foundations of behavior genetics.* St. Louis: Mosby, 1978.

Fuller, J. L., & Wimer, R. E. Behavior genetics. In D. A. Dewsbury & D. A. Rethlingshafer (Eds.), *Comparative psychology.* New York: McGraw-Hill, 1973. Pp. 197-237.

Gates, G. R., Chen, C. S., & Bock, G. R. Effects of monaural and binaural auditory deprivation on audiogenic seizure susceptibility in BALB/c mice. *Experimental Neurology,* 1973, *38,* 488-493.

Ginsburg, B. E., Cowen, J. S., Maxson, S. C., & Sze, P. Y. Neurochemical effects of gene mutations associated with audiogenic seizures. In A. Barbeau & J. R. Brunette (Eds.), *Progress in neurogenetics.* New York: Excerpta Medica, 1969.

Ginsburg, B. E., & Miller, D. S. Genetic factors in audiogenic seizures. In *Psychophysiologie, neuropharmacologie et biochemie de la crise audiogene. Colloques Internationaux du Centre National de la Recherche Scientifique No. 112.* 1963. Pp. 217-225.

Goldstein, D. B. Inherited differences in intensity of alcohol withdrawal reactions in mice. *Nature,* 1973, *245,* 154-156.

Hall, C. S. Genetic differences in fatal audiogenic seizures between two inbred strains of house mice. *Journal of Heredity,* 1947, *38,* 2-6.

Henry, K. R. Audiogenic seizure susceptibility induced in C57BL/6J mice by prior auditory exposure. *Science,* 1967, *158,* 938-940.

Henry, K. R., & Bowman, R. E. Behavior-genetic analysis of the ontogeny of acoustically primed audiogenic seizures in mice. *Journal of Comparative and Physiological Psychology,* 1970, *70,* 235-241.

Henry, K. R., & Saleh, M. Recruitment deafness: Functional effect of priming-induced audiogenic seizures in mice. *Journal of Comparative and Physiological Psychology,* 1973, *84,* 430-435.

Kakihana, R. Y., Brown, D. R., McClearn, G. E., & Tabershaw, I. R. Brain sensitivity to alcohol in inbred mouse strains. *Science,* 1966, *154,* 1574-1575.

Kaufman, I. C., Mother-infant separation in monkeys: An experimental model. In J. P. Scott & E. C. Senay (Eds.) *Separation and depression.* Washington, D.C.: American Association for the Advancement of Science, (Publication 94), 1973. Pp. 33-52.

Lucas, E. A., Powell, E. W., & Murphree, O. D. Hippocampal theta in nervous pointer dogs. *Physiology and Behavior,* 1974, *12,* 609-613.

Maier, N. R. F., & Glazer, N. M. Studies of abnormal behavior in the rat. V. The inheritance of the "neurotic pattern." *Journal of Comparative Psychology* 1940, *30,* 413-418.

McBryde, W. C., & Murphree, O. D. The rehabilitation of genetically nervous dogs. *The Pavlovian Journal,* 1974, *9,* 76-84.

McClearn, G. E. Genetics and motivation of the mouse. In W. J. Arnold (Ed.), *Nebraska Symposium on Motivation.* Lincoln: Nebraska Univ. Press, 1968. Pp. 47–83.

McClearn, G. E., & DeFries, J. C. *Introduction to Behavioral Genetics.* San Francisco: Freeman, 1973.

McClearn, G. E., & Kakihana, R. Y. Selective breeding for ethanol sensitivity in mice. *Behavior Genetics,* 1973, *3,* 409–410.

McClearn, G. E., & Rodgers, D. A. Genetic factors in alcohol preference of laboratory mice. *Journal of Comparative and Physiological Psychology,* 1961, *54,* 116–119.

McKinney, W. T., Suomi, S. J., & Harlow, H. F. New models of separation and depression in rhesus monkeys. In J. P. Scott & E. C. Senay (Eds.), *Separation and depression, clinical and research aspects.* Washington, D.C.: American Association for the Advancement of Science, (Publication 94) 1973. Pp. 53–66.

Murphree, O. D., Dykman, R. A., & Peters, J. E. Genetically-determined abnormal behavior in dogs: Results of behavioral tests. *Conditional Reflex,* 1967, *2,* 199–205.

Murphree, O. D., & Newton, J. E. O. Crossbreeding and special handling of genetically nervous dogs. *Conditional Reflex,* 1971, *6,* 129–136. (a)

Murphree, O. D., & Newton, J. E. O. Schizokinesis: Fragmentation of performance in two strains of pointer dogs. *Conditional Reflex,* 1971, *6,* 91–100. (b)

Murphree, O. D., Peters, J. E., & Dykman, R. A. Effect of person on nervous, stable and crossbred pointer dogs. *Conditional Reflex,* 1967, *2,* 273–276.

Newton, J. E. O., Chapin, J. L., & Murphree, O. D. Correlations of normality and nervousness with cardiovascular functions in pointer dogs. *Pavlovian Journal of Biological Science,* 1976, *11,* 105–120.

Newton, J. E. O., Murphree, O. D., & Dykman, R. A. Sporadic transient atrioventricular block and slow heart rate in nervous pointer dogs. *Conditional Reflex,* 1970, *5,* 75–89.

Nichols, J. R. The children of addicts: What do they inherit? *Annals of the New York Academy of Sciences,* 1972, *197,* 60–65.

Pavlov, I. P. *Conditional reflexes. An investigation of the physiological activity of the cerebral cortex* (G. V. Anrep, Ed. and trans.). London: Oxford Univ. Press, 1927.

Poley, W. Alcohol-preferring and alcohol-avoiding C57BL mice. *Behavior Genetics,* 1972, *2,* 245–248.

Randall, C. L., & Lester, D. Social modification of alcohol consumption in inbred mice. *Science,* 1975, *189,* 149–151.

Rodgers, D. A., & McClearn, G. E. Sucrose versus ethanol appetite in inbred strains of mice. *Quarterly Journal of Studies in Alcohol,* 1964, *25,* 26–35.

Satinder, K. P. Behavior-genetic-dependent self-selection of alcohol in rats. *Journal of Comparative and Physiological Psychology,* 1972, *80,* 422–434.

Schlesinger, K., & Griek, B. J. The genetics and biochemistry of audiogenic seizures. In G. Lindzey & D. D. Thiessen (Eds.), *Contributions to behavior-genetic analysis: The mouse as a prototype.* New York: Appleton, 1970. Pp. 219–257.

Scott, J. P., & Fuller, J. L. *Genetics and the social behavior of the dog.* Chicago: Univ. of Chicago Press, 1965.

Seligman, M. E. P. Phobias and preparedness. *Behavior Therapy,* 1971, *2,* 307–320.

Whitney, G., & Horowitz, G. P. Morphine preference of alcohol-avoiding and alcohol-preferring C57BL mice. *Behavior Genetics,* 1978, *8,* 177–182.

Whitney, G., McClearn, G. E., & DeFries, J. C. Heritability of alcohol preference in laboratory mice and rats. *Journal of Heredity,* 1970, *61,* 165–169.

Willott, J. F., & Henry, K. R. Auditory evoked potentials: developmental changes of threshold and amplitude following early acoustic trauma. *Journal of Comparative and Physiological Psychology,* 1974, *86,* 1–7.

GAYLORD D. ELLISON

Animal Models of Psychopathology: Studies in Naturalistic Colony Environments

4

The development of convincing animal models of human psychopathology is a difficult task for a number of reasons. One primary difficulty is that of determining how to match symptomatology in humans and animals. Furthermore, there is a paucity of good normative data from human populations indicating what the fundamental symptoms are which accompany various psychopathological disorders. Humans are a highly evolved and differentiated species, and consequently what may be fundamentally the same emotional disorder is often expressed as different behaviors in different individuals. Then too, there is usually a focusing in the reports by the observing psychiatrist or psychologist on the cognitive and verbal behaviors of the patient, since these more evolved behaviors are often the ones in which treatment is effected, being the principal means of communicating with the patient (cf. Ferster, chap. 12). Yet in lower animals only more fundamental motor behaviors are observed and measured. More comparative studies of humans with different psychiatric diagnoses are needed, recording basic behaviors such as motor activity, sleep–wakefulness patterns, arousal levels, and even the initial emotional behaviors shown when the patient suddenly finds himself or herself in a novel environment, for these are the types of measures usually collected in animal studies. One good example of a basic description of such primary measures in human anxiety and depressive disorders is provided by Lader (1970). He points out some of the difficulties of symptom variance in humans: while the fundamental symptom of depression is

PSYCHOPATHOLOGY IN ANIMALS
Research and Clinical Implications

81

often supposed to be inertia, some depressives show constant purposeless motor activity. Whereas a lack of appetite is usually thought of as a symptom of depression, some depressives constantly overeat. Animal models must allow for these paradoxes.

A second major difficulty in the development of animal models is that of determining what are the comparable basic units of behavior between two species. At times, animals engage in behaviors that seem to be remarkable imitations of human behaviors. An often-cited example is what was probably one of the first alleged animal models of psychopathology: "experimental neurosis." Several investigators, including Pavlov (1927), Liddell (1938), and Masserman (1943), described the gradual evolution of compulsive, repetitive, and apparently purposeless stereotypes accompanied by abnormal physiological responses in animals exposed to conflict situations.[1] For example, a sheep trained to press a lever with the nose in order to obtain food but then shocked for leverpresses might spontaneously adopt the compulsive habit of repeatedly pawing at some irrelevant part of the experimental apparatus; or a rat trained to jump toward a black card in order to obtain food and avoid a white card, when faced with a difficult or insoluble discrimination, might adopt the habit of always jumping toward the card on the right side of the experimental apparatus, continuing this habit even though the left side of the apparatus is left open with food clearly visible.

The conclusion reached by most observers of such behaviors is that the animals are evidencing compulsive or fixated behaviors comparable, at some level, to the compulsive hand-washing of the human neurotic. Yet it is clear that the actual behaviors shown by these animals are quite different in topography, complexity, reinforcement history, and eliciting conditions from those seen in neurotic humans. The real problem here is how close the analogy must be in

---

[1] I became interested in the phenomenon of experimental neurosis early in my career when, while working on my Ph.D. thesis, one of the dogs I was training in a difficult discrimination developed a classical case. This dog had merely to stand in a conditioning platform and would receive a piece of dog candy 16 sec after presentation of a brief high tone but no candy following a brief low tone. He gradually refused to come to the experiment and had to be carried, even though dogs being shocked will readily follow the experimenter. He also developed trembling attacks and refused to eat candy dispensed from the feeder although he was quite hungry and would eat from the experimenter's hand (unless the piece of candy had previously been dispensed from the feeder!). His salivation became quite erratic, and he would stare fixedly at spots on the wall.

In conversations with Professors Fred Sheffield at Yale University and Jerzy Konorski in Warsaw, I came to realize the pecularities of experimental neurosis. Pavlov elicited experimental neurosis by producing a "clash in the nervous system between excitation and inhibition" by training a dog to expect food when a high tone was presented but no food or shock when a low tone was presented, then gradually making the two tones more and more similar. It is a difficult discrimination that produces an experimental neurosis. Yet the epitome of such a difficult discrimination, in some sense, is partial reinforcement, where the same tone is sometimes followed by food and sometimes not. Other dogs used for my thesis had identical training, yet none of them developed an experimental neurosis. It must be that an experimental neurosis develops when the animal "knows" that some discrimination is possible, and it is this frustrated problem-solving which leads to the abnormal behaviors. In partial reinforcement, the animal quickly learns merely that chance factors are involved, and experimental neuroses do not develop.

order to be useful, and how to assess the degree of closeness of the analogy. Partial models of psychopathology are, undoubtedly, more useful than having no model at all, but it is often difficult or impossible to arrive at an unbiased estimate of the degree of appropriateness or "goodness of fit" of an animal model. Too often the proponents of an animal model become highly involved with demonstrating that their particular animal model is a close fit to some human condition, and they can no longer evaluate the heuristic value of the model in an unbiased fashion.

A third difficulty is that of including social behaviors in an animal model. It can be convincingly argued that alterations in social behaviors are at the heart of human psychopathological disorders, for it is usually only when a human interferes with other humans that he or she is referred to the authorities, perhaps to be committed to an institution or sent before an authority in psychiatric diagnoses. Many psychopathological conditions (such as sociopathy) have abnormal social behaviors as the core symptoms. In other psychopathological conditions (such as schizophrenia or depression), abnormal social relations are one of several critical diagnostic criteria. Many of the other criteria, such as bizarre alterations in appearance or affect, are based on behaviors that are heavily socialized, such that the decision of whether or not criteria of abnormality are met are highly influenced by other members of the same species. It is probably safe to say that one cannot conclude that one has even a partial animal model without some testing of alterations in social behaviors.

Yet social behaviors are among the most difficult to study in a laboratory setting, and the majority of animal experiments involve the observation of caged, socially isolated animals. Such animals, when placed in artificial testing conditions with another animal of the same species, show highly abnormal social behaviors even in the absence of any experimental manipulation designed to produce a "psychopathological" animal. This serious drawback is multiplied many-fold when the experiment is designed so that the social behaviors which do occur are elicited by some strong and artificial stimulus. The classic example of such a test is shock-elicited aggression, in which two animals of the same species are placed together in a small cage and subjected to intense and painful electrical shocks. Fighting invariably occurs, but it is impossible to generalize from such pain-elicited aggression to more normal and spontaneous aggression, such as occasionally occurs in nature between pairs of animals of the same species and which can become pathological in certain cases.

The recognition of the importance of social behaviors have led a number of authors to attempt to study the social and other behaviors of animals housed in more naturalistic, social environments. The classic application of this type of study in rodent behavior was provided by Calhoun (1963), who studied the effects of such variables as overcrowding on social behaviors in rat colonies. Animals that have been highly domesticated, such as cats and most agricultural breeds, often have abnormal social behaviors and lend themselves less well to such social colony studies. However, the higher primates have been studied extensively in social colony environments, and such studies have yielded considerable data (e.g., Harlow, 1962). It seems likely that studies of animals housed in enriched and social environments are more generalizable to humans than are studies of individually caged animals, because humans live in social colonies. In the following sections I shall describe some experiments attempting to develop animal models of psychopathologies, such as affective disorders, alcoholism, and schizophrenia, that have been conducted in the complex rat colony environments my students and I have constructed at UCLA. For each of these three types of animal models of psychopathology, the colony-housed animal appears to manifest unique behaviors that approximate the human condition more closely than has been previously suspected.

I. Description of a Rat Colony Enclosure

Figure 4.1 is a drawing of one of the UCLA rat colony enclosures. It is a large (12 × 20 ft) structure with a room-sized behavioral arena in the center. On the straw-covered floor of this arena are several play objects, such as running wheels and tilt-boards. Rats can be observed on this floor engaging in a variety of social behaviors. A water tower in the center of the arena provides constant access to water and soon becomes a center for social interactions. There are also numerous ramps and ropes leading to high ledges, where rats can perch. On the left of this arena there are a number of holes which lead, through short tubes, to individual, straw-lined burrows. Typically, one to three rats adopt a given burrow. This burrows area is kept in constant dim red light, but the rats can be observed through overhead closed-circuit TV cameras with low-level illumination capabilities. The rest of the colony enclosure is kept on a reversed day–night

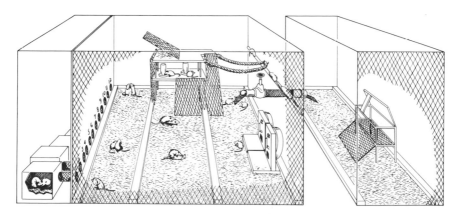

Figure 4.1. *An artist's conception of one of the University of California, Los Angeles rat colony environments. On the left is the burrows area, where separate straw-lined burrows can be reached through individual tubes. This area is kept in constant dim lighting. In the middle is the behavioral arena, where various social behaviors can be observed occuring on the straw-covered floor. On the right is the feeding area, connected to the behavioral arena by a large valve. [From Ellison, G. D. Animal models of psychopathology. The low-norepinephrine and low-serotonin rat. American Psychologist, 1977, 32, 1036–1045. Copyright 1977 by the American Psychological Association. Reprinted by permission.]*

lighting cycle, so that the rats are most active during the dim period. To accentuate this peak of activity, the rats are fed once daily in the middle of the dark cycle. We adopted this procedure because it is similar to the natural feeding habits of rats, which have principally become residents of the cities of man during the recent past, coming out at night to feed on garbage scraps. We feed our animals in the feeding arena on the right of Figure 4.1. Fresh food scraps are placed on the feeding platform, a bell is rung, and the valve connecting the feeding area to the behavioral arena is opened. Order through the connecting tube is recorded, and the first animals to feed are usually the most dominant.

Among the behaviors that can be observed are a variety of measures of activity, such as which animals run in the activity wheels and which animals spend the majority of their time out on the floor of the behavioral arena (as opposed to remaining back in the burrows or up on ledges). Most of the behaviors that can be observed are social behaviors. Several varieties of fighting bouts can be observed. "Stand and box" matches involve two animals standing on their hindlimbs, nose to nose, often pawing at each other. Such bouts are usually brief and end with one of the animals breaking off the encounter and running away. A second type of aggressive bout is what we call a "wrestling match." This involves two animals wrestling in the straw until one of the animals ends up being pinned to the floor by the other. This posture is briefly held, and then the two rats typically break off the encounter. At this moment we record the experimental group of the "top dog" and "bottom dog"; this becomes one of our chief measures of dominance standing. Other social behaviors, such as social grooming and mounting, are also observed and recorded.

We try to raise a colony of 24 rats together for 3 months before marking them with a fur dye and introducing experimental manipulations. During this time the colony gradually develops a dominance hierarchy and stable behavioral patterns. Certain rats develop distinctive behavioral patterns during this period. There is typically one "king rat," usually the largest animal, that is distinctive in his aggressive encounters, his adopting of a certain burrow, and his rank through the tube at feeding time. Some animals develop habits of frequently mounting other animals or hoarding food more than do the other animals. Colony animals become highly variable in their behavioral patterns, and their body weights and brain chemistry become much more variable than those of caged isolates. These colony animals are an ideal preparation for studying the gradual alterations in social and other behaviors which develop following various experimental manipulations. In our initial studies in these colony environments we studied animal models of affective disorders produced through biochemical manipulations.

II. The Low-Norepinephrine and Low-Serotonin Rat: Models of Anxiety and Depression

The field of psychiatry has become increasingly dominated by biochemical theories. This is due to the recent blossoming of biochemical techniques and information that has led to the development of a wide variety of pharmacological agents used in the treatment of many diverse psychiatric disorders. The pharmacological industry has produced increasingly more refined psychotherapeutic agents, and, in most cases, the principal mode of action, or neurochemical effect, of these agents has been extensively studied. It is probably no longer possible to develop a convincing animal model of psychopathology without including some kind of validation of this model using pharmacological agents, such as showing that the pathology can be reversed using the same pharmacological agents used to treat the symptoms in humans.

Many of the earliest pharmacological agents were developed from folk remedies using medicinal plants. One such drug is reserpine; it is derived from a plant used in India to treat mania and hypertension. Reserpine was frequently prescribed by physicians during the 1950s to treat hypertension, but it was found to have a number of undesirable side effects and is less widely used today. One of these undesirable side effects is that reserpine can induce a psychological depression in humans that is clinically indistinguishable from an endogeneous depression. These drug-induced depressions can become severe, and some patients for whom reserpine was prescribed became so depressed that they committed suicide. Once this fact was recognized, a number of similarities between the effects of reserpine on animal behavior and the symptoms of depression were noted: Reserpine sedates animals, decreases their appetite, causes a decrease in grooming behavior, and so forth (Bunney & Davis, 1965). When administered to monkeys, reserpine induces a withdrawn state characterized by irritability, weight loss, and social withdrawal (McKinney, Suomi, & Harlow, 1971). The "reserpine model of depression" came to be one of the dominant biochemical models of biological psychiatry.

Reserpine's major effect on the central nervous system is to cause a depletion of those central neurotransmitters called the monoamines: norepinephrine, dopamine, and serotonin. It does this by preventing the storage of these monoamines in synaptic vessicles, where they are normally protected from the degradative action of monoamine oxidase. When reserpine is injected into an animal, there is a brief arousal phase as the monoamines are released from synaptic vessicles, but then these monoamines are rapidly broken down by local enzymes and the concentrations of monoamines in the brain fall to levels considerably below normal. At this time the animal becomes inactive. However, even though reserpine can induce a model depression, it is not clear what the necessary and sufficient conditions for inducing this psychopathological state are. Reserpine depletes the brain of all three monoamines, and it is possible that a model depression could be induced by depletion of only one critical monoamine. Or, it could be that some other pharmacological property of reserpine unrelated to monoamine depletion was responsible. Questions such as these can only be answered by further analytical experiments, and such experiments of necessity involve the development of animal models of depression.

In a series of experiments, my students and I attempted to analyze the reserpine model of depression by studying the behavioral syndromes of animals depleted of either norepinephrine or of serotonin, or of both of these mono-amines. We chose to focus on these two monoamines for two reasons: (*a*) because there is a good evidence that antidepressants act to increase the levels of either or both of these monoamines, implying a correlation with affect; and (*b*) because they can both be manipulated by relatively selective pharmacological agents. One method for producing selective biochemical alterations involving either norepinephrine or serotonin is by injecting directly into the brains of animals the monoamine neurotoxins 6-hydroxydopamine (6-OHDA) or 5,6 di-hydroxytryptamine (5,6 DHT). These two chemicals are very similar struc-turally to either norepinephrine or serotonin, respectively (Figure 4.2). When injected into the lateral ventricles of rats 6-OHDA or 5,6 DHT diffuse throughout the brain and, because both norepinephrine and serotonin are characterized by a selective reuptake mechanism (whereby the neurotransmitter released at a nerve ending is later reabsorbed into the ending which released it, then to be restored for future reuse), these neurotoxins at low doses selectively enter only one or the other kind of monoamine cell ending. At brain pH and temperature, these compounds also have the chemical property of subsequently undergoing a spontaneous auto-oxidizing reaction such that they then degenerate into toxic compounds such as hydrogen peroxide. This results in selective damage to the terminals, axons, and at higher doses, even the cell bodies of either norepinephrine or serotonin cells (cf. Baumgarten, Bjorklund, Lachenmayer, Nobin, & Steneir, 1971; Kostrezewa & Jacobowitz, 1974). But

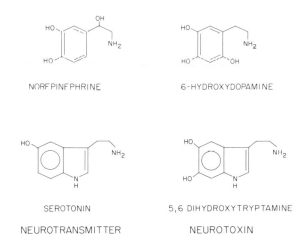

NOREPINEPHRINE   6-HYDROXYDOPAMINE

SEROTONIN   5,6 DIHYDROXYTRYPTAMINE

NEUROTRANSMITTER   NEUROTOXIN

Figure 4.2 *The neurotransmitters norepinephrine and serotonin (on the left) and the structurally similar neurotoxins (on the right). A third category could be added, that of psychoactive drugs. Amphetamine is similar in structure to norepinephrine, while LSD has similarities to serotonin. [From Ellison, G. D. Animal models of psychopathology. The low-norepinephrine and low-serotonin rat. American Psychologist, 1977, 32, 1036–1045. Copyright 1977 by the American Psychological Association. Reprinted by permission.]*

these neurotoxins will damage any brain cells they enter, so in order to use these properly we had to inject very small doses of these neurotoxins a number of times, one injection each day. It was also necessary to show that similar results could be obtained when selective monoamine depletions were produced by other means, such as with chronic injections of synthesis inhibitors (which block the production of a certain neurotransmitter) and also by making electrolytic lesions in the cell bodies which produce one or the other monoamine. Only when a variety of pharmacological manipulations all produce similar results on both behavior and on biochemistry can conclusions be drawn, for any one pharmacological agent may have other, unsuspected biochemical effects.

But if one must be cautious in using pharmacological agents, one must be even more cautious in the interpretation and design of behavioral experiments. How can one chose behavioral measures that convincingly identify a rat as depressed when so many varied behaviors accompany depression in humans? It seems clear that depression is a behavioral syndrome involving a variety of alterations, and so a variety of behavioral tests or measures must be made. Only after a cluster of interrelated, but distinct, alterations in behavior have been demonstrated can one begin to draw conclusions about an alteration in a behavioral state.

In our initial experimentation we had not yet developed our rat colony enclosures, so we attempted to model depression using a battery of relatively standard behavioral tests. We decided that the core symptoms of depression in humans are anergy (lack of energy), passivity, feelings of helplessness, and a shift in affect toward negativity. This last measure seemed most amenable to experimental manipulations, for an animal with a shift in emotional or affectual control toward negativity should be less responsive to positive reinforcers (rewards) and more reactive to negative reinforcers (aversive stimuli). This we proceeded to test by presenting each animal with a variety of positive and negative rewards in several modalities, such as in the gustatory modality (using dilute sucrose and quinine solutions) and in the visual modality (rats will work to turn on dim lights but will learn to escape from intense visual stimulation). We also observed our animals in an open-field test that proved to be one of the most revealing indications of alterations in emotional reactivity. A rat is placed into a novel environment consisting of a large round enclosure, and the rat's behavior during the next 5 min is then scored by trained observers, who record locomotion (by noting each time the rat crosses lines marked in a grid pattern on the floor of the field), rearing (standing up on the hind legs in an observing response), amount of time in the center of the round field, and grooming.

First we tested animals after extensive damage to the monoamines induced by multiple injections of neurotoxins or of synthesis inhibitors. We found that only the animals depleted of both norepinephrine and serotonin showed large behavioral disruptions and were underresponsive to all positive reinforcers while being overresponsive to all negative reinforcers (Ellison & Bresler, 1974). These doubly depleted animals increased their fluid intake the least of all groups when sucrose was added to their drinking water, but they decreased their intake the most when quinine was added. They were the most responsive of all the animals to electrical shocks, as measured by the amount of fighting induced in pairs of rats when shocked. These animals were also the most helpless in the open-field test. When suddenly thrust into a novel environment, the doubly depleted animals neither locomoted nor reared, but remained huddled near the walls and appeared helpless. We concluded that these animals depleted of both norepinephrine and serotonin best modeled reserprine-induced dysphoria.

Our experimental design also permitted us to compare the behaviors of animals depleted only of norepinephrine with those of animals depleted only of serotonin, so that we could discover which of these two monoamines was responsible. To our surprise, we found that neither of these animals showed the full syndrome of the doubly depleted animals, but rather behaved oppositely on most tasks, with the controls intermediate. The low-norepinephrine animals had hunger drive deficits (they underconsumed sucrose, even when food deprived), whereas the low-serotonin animals overconsumed sucrose, even when not food deprived. When tested for light aversion in a shuttlebox, the low-norepinephrine animals became progressively more lethargic with continued testing, whereas the low-serotonin animals became more agitated. Again, the best place to observe these animals was in the open-field test. The low-serotonin animals locomoted less than controls but reared more while staying near the walls of the enclosure. They appeared to be anxious, frightened animals: They froze and were hypervigilant. The low-norepinephrine animals behaved oppositely: They locomoted more than controls, reared less, and entered the center of the field frequently. They seemed to be inattentive and overconfident, walking all around the enclosure while making few observing responses. We concluded (Ellison & Bresler, 1974) that norepinephrine and serotonin have opposite effects on arousal, but when both are depleted the full reserpine syndrome can be seen.

These results from an attempted animal model of depression have more meaning when they are considered in the light of the many findings from the psychiatric clinic on the usefulness of various pharmacological agents in treating human emotional disorders. For example, it has been found that those tricylic antidepressants that best treat depressive cases involving lethargy and lack of drive selectively potentiate norepinephrine, whereas those that are more useful in cases when the core syndromes involve sleep loss and anxiety selectively potentiate serotonin (Carlsson, Corrodi, Fuze, & Hokfelt, 1969). It became clear to us that severe cases of dysphoria involve not only the retardation of emotion, thinking, and motor functions usually associated with depression, but also excessive worry and sleep loss. Thus, two normally opposed emotional states of imbalance can be recognized in humans—depression and anxiety. In the kind of severe unhappiness induced by reserpine, both of these primary negative emotions are simultaneously present.

We decided to pursue these findings further by studing our animals when they were housed in more natural environmental conditions involving social and enriched housing. The development of these free-behavior environments was, in part, a logical extension of our finding that it was the observations of animals' behavior in the open-field test that led to the clearest exposition of the emotional alterations produced by neurotoxin injections. But we also made this next step because it seemed likely to us that our animals would recover better from neurotoxins in a more enriched environment than the sterile and impoverished isolation cages which are used in most rat studies. Studying the process of recovery from neurotoxins was an important consideration because the ultimate goal of animal models should be not only to discover appropriate models, but then to study what are the stages of recovery and the optimal strategies for facilitating recovery from the model conditions, and thereby presumably from the psychopathological conditions.

Our findings from neurotoxin-injected rats studied in the enriched colony environment have been reviewed elsewhere (Ellison, 1977). One major finding was that there is a fundamental difference between the behaviors of animals observed in their home environment and those behaviors that appear when the same animals are observed in novel environments, such as the artificial testing situations. For example, just after the neurotoxin injections, the low-serotonin rats acted frightened in the novel environment of the open-field test, but in the colony environment these same animals seemed relatively fearless; they remained out in the open more than any other group, approaching the human observers and sniffing at them through the wire screening, whereas the low norepinephrine animals remained in their burrows more than any other group. These results were initially puzzling to us. Then we realized that they were consistent with the previous conclusion relating lowered levels of norepinephrine with depression and lowered levels of serotonin with anxiety, but that they emphasize the role of physical setting in determining the actual behaviors that result from these alterations in emotional set. The low-serotonin animal can be thought of as being in a state of general preparedness; a state that is appropriate for an animal out of its nest, in the periphery of its territory (Ellison, 1975). In the home environment, as studied in the colony environment, this meant the low-serotonin animals were hyperactive, slept little, and remained out in the arena. But in novel environments, these animals were frightened and overreactive to stimulation. Conversely, the low-norepinephrine rats were in a withdrawn state. In the colony they remained in the burrows, but in the novel environment they fearlessly ambulated about the enclosure.

Rats injected with neurotoxins recover better in the colony environment (Diaz, Ellison, & Masuoka, 1978), but their presence in the colony leads to gradually increasing social disruptions. By 25–30 days after neurotoxin injections, the nonlesioned controls had fallen to the bottom of the dominance heirarchy. An interesting question is how the recovery of biochemically imbalanced animals can be maximally facilitated by social colony environments while the deleterious effects on the remainder of the colony are minimized.

III. Alcohol Consumption in Seminaturalistic Colony Environments

Another area where animal models of psychopathology can be developed in colony environments is the study of alcohol consumption. It is usually assumed that because rats can be induced to consume appreciable quantities of alcohol only when they are forced to do so by hunger deprivation, water deprivation, or electrical shocks (Barry & Walgren, 1970), convincing animal models of human alcoholism cannot be developed. But it is also clear that when rats are given ad libitum food, water, and a distinctively flavored alcohol solution at near optimal preference (about 10% v/v), they consume the alcohol, although considerably less than they consume the water. However, it can be argued that a normal population of humans would probably show the same water preference. Some rats consume considerably more alcohol than others, but will generally not consume enough alcohol to have blood alcohol levels high enough to be considered intoxicated unless they are deprived of food, or given all of their water mixed with alcohol, or given frequent electrical shocks (Freed, 1968; Eriksson, 1969).

It can be argued, however, that these results do not necessarily imply that rats cannot serve as useful animal models of human alcoholism; they only mean that rats can only be partial models. It also seems likely that were rats housed in enriched social living conditions more like those in which humans live, their behavior would be more human-like than the behavior of rats kept in isolation cages.

To test this possibility, my student Frank Daniel and I conducted a colony experiment where we raised 24 young male rats with constant access to water and a 10% alcohol solution flavored with anise. These solutions were available in a "bar" we constructed in the middle of the behavioral arena, three spouts of either solution were available on opposites of the 2- × 3-ft enclosure. Photocells recorded when animals were at the spouts, and a closed circuit television camera in the ceiling permitted us to observe and photograph the animals. We gradually weaned the animals from a 1% to a 10% alcohol solution, let them establish stable baseline conditions over a 2-month period, and then began systematic observations.

One of our first observations was that there were different periods each day when the colony animals consumed water and alcohol solutions. This is shown in the solid black line in Figure 4.3. Water intake showed a typical diurnal rhythm: It began to increase at the onset of the dark cycle, gradually increased until the hour of feeding, and then peaked for the next 6 hours. It then rapidly dropped off as the animals returned to the burrows during the light phase. Alcohol intake showed a different pattern: It peaked during the hours just before feeding, sank to very low levels just after feeding, and again increased just before the onset of the light cycle. We called these two peak periods of alcohol intake the "cocktail" and "nightcap" effect. It is probable that the same rhythms of fluid consumption would be observed in a human colony, and this effect has never previously been reported in animals.

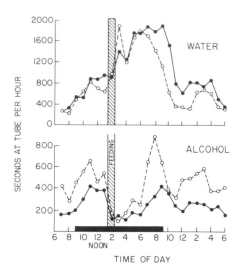

Figure 4.3 *Daily patterns of water and 10% alcohol intake by a colony of rats. The dark cycle, when the rats are most active, begins at 9 a.m. and continues until 9 p.m., and the rats are fed for 1 hour in the middle of this dark period. Water intake begins to increase at onset of the dark cycle, peaks just after feeding, and then gradually decreases. Alcohol intake shows a different pattern, with two peak periods; just before feeding ("cocktail period") and just before the onset of the sleep cycle ("nightcap"). The dark solid line is from a normal colony of animals, and the dotted line represents data collect 25–30 days following neurotoxin injections to two-thirds of the colony.*

We then captured the colony animals, marked them with a fur dye, and drilled holes in the skulls. After a 2-week recovery period in the colony, the animals were recaptured and injected in the lateral ventricles with the neurotoxins 6-OHDA, or 5,6 DHT, or control vehicle solutions, using the exact procedures employed in our previous studies. An equal number of animals were treated with the same, regimen and weaned to alcohol and water similarly, but were kept throughout their life in isolation cages.

Figure 4.4 shows the results. While alcohol and water intake gradually increased in the isolate animals considered as a whole, in the colony animals these measures showed fluctuations remarkably similar to the gradual social disruptions we have observed in colonies. Alcohol consumption gradually increased for 25 days, while water intake decreased. This led to a three-fold increase in the percentage of alcohol preference. We kept track of which animals were consuming alcohol by photographing the alcohol spouts every 15 sec they were interrupted. Just after lesioning, the 5,6 DHT animals consumed the most alcohol, and the 6-OHDA animals the least. This finding, in conjunction with our previous research, implies that alcoholism is more correlated with anxious than with depressive behaviors when transient biochemical imbalances are considered. This might partly explain why the pharmacological agent disulfiram (which depletes norepinephrine) is an effective drug in the treatment of some alcoholics.

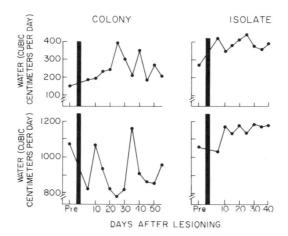

Figure 4.4 *Alcohol and water intake by colony and isolate rats following injections of the neurotoxins 6-OHDA, or 5, 6 DHT, or of control saline. In the colony animals alcohol intake gradually increases, peaking 25 days after neurotoxin injections. Water intake decreases during this same period, so that the proportion fluid intake which is alcohol trebles. No such delayed shift in preference toward alcohol is present in animals treated exactly the same but kept in isolation cages, demonstrating the social nature of these delayed increases in alcohol preference.*

But the gradual increase in alcohol consumption which then followed occurred in all three experimental groups, including the controls. Using such social models of psychopathology allowed us to demonstrate the effects of social disruptions on alcohol intake in normal, as well as in lesioned, animals. It should be possible in further research to study the social behaviors, or "personality traits," of those animals that spontaneously consume alcohol in rat colonies, and compare them with nonconsumers.

IV. An Animal Model of Paranoid Schizophrenia: Continuous Amphetamines

Schizophrenia is often considered as one of the most difficult of the psychopathologies to understand. Many of the symptoms are distinctively human, such as the alterations in cognitive styles and thought processes. Yet there are also a variety of primitive, or fundamental, symptoms in schizophrenics. It is these kinds of behaviors, which appear when the nervous system has regressed to lower levels of organization, that can be modeled in animals. Again, here is an example of a partial animal model of psychopathology. The extent to which this type of animal model can fruitfully advance our technology in the treatment or prevention of schizophrenia can only be determined by further experimentation.

In the case of schizophrenia, however, the type of modeling which can be conducted is even further removed from the human pathology because there are no agreed upon methods for inducing schizophrenic-like behaviors in animals, nor is there common agreement on what fundamental symptoms should be mimicked. Consequently, one of the most fruitfully heuristic strategies in the study of schizophrenia is the drug model. Thus, some aspects of schizophrenia can be modeled by the paranoid symptomatology that results from chronic amphetamine abuse in humans (Snyder, Banerjee, Yamamura, & Greenberg, 1974), while other aspects of schizophrenia are similar to the alterations in cognitive structure produced by hallucinogens (Bowers, 1972). The only avenue open to the animal researcher is to administer these drugs to animals, attempt to evoke a portion of the schizophrenic symptomatology, and then to study the behavioral and biochemical underpinnings of these alterations in cerebral functioning with the hope that these will shed light on the kinds of alterations present in human schizophrenics. It should be clear that these types of strategies are highly indirect; however, they are the best strategies presently available.

There have been a number of studies in which amphetamine psychosis has been evoked in human volunteers in controlled, hospital settings. In each case, a certain drug regimen has been used: The humans are administered small, frequent oral doses of amphetamines in order to achieve a continuous but low level of plasma amphetamines for up to 5 days (Griffith, Cavanaugh, Held, & Oates, 1972; Angrist, Sathananthan, Wilk, & Gershon, 1974). This regimen of amphetamine administration mimics the "speed binges" of human amphetamine addicts, and it is only after several days of continuous amphetamine intoxication that the paranoid syndrome typically develops in its full form, with ideas of reference, hallucinations of parasites under the skin, and delusions of persecution. Yet this continuous, low-level drug regimen is difficult to reproduce in animals because amphetamines are rapidly metabolized, and few researchers have the facilities essential for the administration of amphetamines every several hours to animals throughout the day and night. Such frequent injections would also surely be highly disruptive to the behavior of the experimental animals.

In order to overcome these difficulties, we developed a slow-release silicone pellet which can be implanted under the skin of animals and which slowly releases amphetamines continuously for up to 10 days (Huberman, Eison, Bryan, & Ellison, 1977). In a series of experiments on the behavioral and biochemical effects of amphetamine pellet implantation in rats, cats, and monkeys we have attempted to further develop an animal model of amphetamine psychosis. Table 4.1 shows the stages of alterations in behavior that follow amphetamine pellet implantation in rats. The implanted rats are initially quite exploratory: They remain out on the arena floor, where they walk about, pausing frequently to stand and sniff the air. They also come over to the screening enclosing the colony and sniff at the human observers. During this initial stage, which lasts for up to 6 hours, the implanted animals engage rarely in social behaviors with the control animals, but rather seem preoccupied with investigating.

The implanted animals then gradually enter motor stereotypies. The progression from exploratory behavior to motor stereotypy occurs as animals

Table 4.1
Stages of Behavior during Continuous Amphetamine Intoxication in Rats[a]

Stage	Description	Duration	Behavioral measures
1	Enhanced exploration and locomotion	0–6 hours	Head bob and sniff Enhanced locomotion Approach toward humans Out of burrows
2	Motor stereotypies	6 hours postimplant to Day 3	Surface sniffing Straw sifting Self-grooming
3	Crash period	Day 4 after implant	Back in burrows Startle responses
4	Social behaviors	Days 5–7	Stand and box Violent fighter Chased Pair-bonded aggression

[a] Rats were housed in enriched rat colony environments following implantation with slow-release *d*-amphetamine pellets.

become caught in increasingly more circumscribed paths of exploration. For example, an animal exploring a ledge will initially investigate one end of the ledge, locomote to the opposite end and explore, and then return. Progressively, the amount of space traversed becomes smaller and smaller, while long periods of time are spent sniffing one particular spot on the ledge. Finally, the animal enters a complete stereotypy whereby it never moves from a particular spot and spends all of its time sniffing the same surface, or grooming the same spot on the skin. These motor stereotypies remain basically uninterrupted for 2 full days (Ellison, Eison, & Huberman, 1978).

Then the amphetamine pellet implanted rats enter the third, or "crash" phase (Table 4.1). During the initial 3 days after pellet implantation the rats have been out in the behavioral arena almost continuously, and now they retreat to the burrows. At the same time they begin to show spontaneous startle responses which are often accompanied by spontaneous vocalizations. They now appear to be highly irritable and jumpy. Finally, on the fifth day after pellet implantation the rats enter the final, and social phase of continuous amphetamine intoxication. They now reappear on the arena floor and begin to fight among themselves and with the control animals. This marks the first time since pellet implantation that they have shown social behaviors, and these social interactions are characterized by excessive fighting, violent attacks on other animals, and a tendency for each individual amphetamine animal to latch onto one other rat as its archenemy. I had never before observed this remarkable tendency toward "pair-bonded aggression" in any previous study, and I believe that it represents at an animal model level a phenomenon analogous to the well-known fixation by paranoids on one other individual or organization as the focus of their delusional system.

This late stage of continuous amphetamine intoxication can serve as a useful animal model of amphetamine psychosis in humans, which, in turn, is a useful drug model of paranoid schizophrenia. This generalization can be made because of several facts. First of all, the drug regimen that produces the late stage and amphetamine psychosis are the same; daily injections of amphetamine, given once each day at the same time, do not suffice. Second, there are similarities in the stages of behavior shown by humans and rats when administered continuous amphetamines. Griffith *et al.* (1972) reported that humans given small, frequent doses of amphetamines were initially hyperaroused, but became irritable and depressed after several days of continued drug intake. They then withdrew to their rooms and isolated themselves; when they emerged they evidenced a paranoid delusion which had been formed during the isolation period. This is remarkably similar to the stages observed in rats, with the withdrawal period to the burrows just preceding the late, social phase, during which several paranoid-like behaviors appeared.

But an even more convincing argument that this late stage of continuous amphetamine intoxication achieved through implantation of slow-release silicone pellets can model amphetamine psychosis stems from the observation that when the amphetamine pellet is implanted into animals more highly evolved than rats, the behaviors evoked become even more suggestive of humanoid hallucinations. I refer here to the results we obtained in monkeys, which are admirably reviewed by Lyon and Nielsen in Chapter 5 in this volume. In the monkeys, as in the rats, there was a late stage of continuous amphetamine intoxication, but in these more evolved animals the hallucinatory behaviors were much more spectacular: The animals behaved as though seeing imaginary enemies and then fleeing, or experiencing bugs under the skin, or pouncing on objects that could not be detected by the human observers. It seems likely that one can construct a hierarchy of approximations to paranoid schizophrenia in humans using these types of experiments, with the results from lower animals providing only the most elemental aspects of the model. From these kinds of observations it becomes clear that an animal model will only be a partial model, but that it can also be a highly useful approximation.

But what is the ultimate goal of such animal modeling? It must be more than to merely demonstrate similarities between animal and human behavior. I believe that such animal models are useful only if one then uses the animal model to discover the underlying alterations in brain mechanisms that give rise to the pathological behavior, *and then to attempt to design novel methods for facilitating recovery in afflicted humans or discover new psychotherapeutic drugs.* Only when the results obtained can be said to have had an impact in the clinic can the fruitfulness of an animal model be demonstrated.

I would like to discuss how the continuous amphetamine model might be developed further with such a goal in mind. The most likely methodology for such further development is probably biochemical studies, for the pharmacological treatment of schizophrenia is presently the most evolved, and probably most successful, therapeutic mode. The phenothiazenes have played a central role in the treatment of schizophrenics for a number of years. These drugs have the interesting property of calming the agitated schizophrenic patient but also restoring spontaneous behavior in the withdrawn or catatonic patient, and they are often the only way of preventing the long-term downhill course of chronic schizophrenics which can result in the highly deteriorated, "burnt-out" schizophrenic.

Early studies by Randrup and Munkvaad (1965) and others demonstrated that a common characteristic of almost all phenothiazenes is that they block dopamine receptors in the brain, preventing the motor stereotypies which can be evoked by excessive dopaminergic stimulation. This common property was so striking that it led to the "dopamine theory of schizophrenia" (reviewed by Snyder *et al.*, 1974), which hypothesizes that excessive dopaminergic stimulation is an integral aspect of schizophrenic symptomatology. Although there are a few phenothiazene derivatives that are efficacious in the treatment of schizophrenia but which do not block dopamine receptors well, the dopamine theory has become one of the most influential forces in biochemical theorizing on the origins of schizophrenic symptomatology.

The continuous amphetamine animal should be a way of testing, or at least shedding some light on, the dopamine theory of schizophrenia. In order to investigate this, we began microscopic studies of dopamine and norepinephrine fibers in the brain of animals implanted with slow-release amphetamine pellets. We observed a remarkable correlation between the onset of the late phase of continuous amphetamine intoxication and the appearance of structural alterations in dopamine fibers in the caudate nucleus (Ellison *et al.*, 1978b). That is, at about the fifth day after pellet implantation, the catecholamine-fluorescing terminals in the caudate nucleus (which are almost exclusively dopaminergic) had largely disappeared, and swollen, enlarged axons with varicosities had become observable. This was a marked change from the appearance of a caudate nucleus in a control (nonamphetamine treated) rat, which had the diffuse, cloudy appearance reported by many other observers and which presumably reflects the presence of many extremely fine terminals. These structural alterations in the caudate dopaminergic terminals of amphetamine-pellet treated rats remained visible for several weeks after the pellet was removed at 7 days after implantation.

This observation led us to hypothesize that continuous amphetamines have a neurotoxic action on dopamine terminals in the caudate, and we tested this using an entirely different assay procedure: the measurement of tyrosine hydroxylase activity and catecholamine levels in various brain regions. We found that during the period of amphetamine pellet action the activity of tyrosine hydroxylase falls to extremely low levels in the caudate nucleus, much more than in several other brain regions, and that this decrease in caudate tyrosine hydroxylase activity is apparently permanent, inthat it can still be detected over 100 days after pellet removal. It is also apparently selective; the decreased tyrosine hydroxylase activity is not present long after pellet removal in a number of other brain regions, including some that contain other dopaminergic systems.

These results constitute a kind of independent varification of the dopamine theory of schizophrenia, for they indicate that the same exact regimen of drug administration that most closely produces a schizophrenic-like psychosis also selectively attacks dopamine terminals in the caudate nucleus. In addition, they may be a way of going far beyond the original dopamine theory, which merely states that schizophrenia is characterized by a hyperactive dopamine system. The results from the continuous amphetamine intoxication model indicate that while the initial stages of behavioral alterations are likely to be produced by excessive dopaminergic stimulation, the later phases, when actual hallucinatory behaviors occur, are more likely characterized by depletion of dopamine, damage to dopamine terminals, and an eruption of the motor stereotypies that are apparently mediated by excessive dopamine. When late stage amphetamine pellet animals are tested with injections of dopamine receptor stimulators, they are found to be subsensitive to dopaminergic stimulation. These facts all imply that the late and psychotic-like stage of continuous amphetamine intoxication is produced during a background of *decreased*, rather than increased, dopaminergic tone (Nelson & Ellison, 1978).

V. *Criteria for a Successful Animal Model of Psychopathology*

I have attempted to demonstrate three different ways in which animal models of psychopathology can be developed in the areas of effective disorders, alcohol intake, and paranoid schizophrenia. Discussions of animal models of psychopathology often rapidly develop into diatribes, with two opposing camps recognizable: "I have a perfect animal model of ____, "versus" ____ is distinctively a human condition and there can be no animal model of it." The heuristic values of partial animal models need to be recognized, for an animal model can serve in much the same way as a theory does in other sciences: It is a statement that can explain part of the data, but will surely either be modified or discarded as deductions from it are tested further. In this light, I would like to propose several criteria that should be met in any serious animal model of psychopathology:

1. *Face validity*. The model must be based on some clear and unique feature or precipitating event in the psychopathology. Examples are the roles of a lack of reinforcement conditions leading to learned helplessness and depression, or the role of fear conditioning in the production of neurotic-like behavior, avoidance behavior, or compulsive actions, or the way in which continuous amphetamine intoxication leads to delusions and parasitosis.

2. *Behavioral similarities*. The animal must show some of the same features of behavior shown by the psychopathological human. While this is usually the sole criteria by which behavioral models are measured, too often it is only the most salient features which are modeled, and these are reproduced only in limited testing conditions. I have tried to show in this chapter how studies of the behavior of animals housed in free-behavior, enriched environments can provide many details of behavior often overlooked in manipulative (as opposed to observational) studies. Alterations in social behaviors are probably one of the most distinctive features of most human psychopathologies. The modeling of these altered social behaviors can serve as a critical test of the animal model on the behavioral end.

3. *Biochemical similarities*. Biochemical and pharmacological knowledge has reached a degree of sophistication where it can no longer be ignored by the serious animal modeler. Any complete animal model should also demonstrate that at least some part of it is similar to the human psychopathology, whether at a biochemical level (for example, there are similar alterations in CSF constituents) or at a pharmacological level (for example, both the human and the animal can be treated successfully by the same drugs, such as by treating the animal model of depression with antidepressants).

4. *Predictive value for therapeutics*. The animal model must eventually suggest a new pharmacological treatment or some other kind of therapy, that is then validated in tests with humans. Until this has been accomplished, an animal model is just a statement of similarities; once this has occurred, the animal model becomes useful.

VI. A Theoretical Model of Schizophrenia

Humans undergoing a psychotic break often keep detailed diaries of their experiences as they enter a prolonged period of heightened arousal and insomonia, and as they begin to experience a heightened awareness that has been compared to the psychological alterations present in soldiers in combat. The stages of the psychotic break have been described by Bowers (1968) based on a study of the extensive diaries maintained during this period. Arising in many occasions from a crucial maturational step, the individual is faced with an inescapable but irresolvable conflict, and then begins to dwell on a problem. The self-centering that results eventuates in ideas of reference, in which randomly encountered strangers appear to have been sent to him to deliver a special message. During this stage, higher cognitive centers begin to attempt to explain everything about them in similar egocentric terms, and this leads to the next stage. Here the person experiences a loss of ego identity, which has attempted to expand so as to emcompass everything about it. It is only then that hallucinations arise. These are often self-reinforcing, since they can suddenly explain all of that which has occurred previously ("My real problem is that the CIA is against me and has been poisoning my food.").

During such prolonged crisis periods, it seems likely that stress-related alterations in neuromodulators and hormones are continuously produced. This is reproduced, in part, by continuous amphetamines, whether administered to humans or animals. The cumulative effects of such sympathomimetics eventually result in depletions, and even damage, to the neural circuitry on which they exert their maximal effects.

Many of the stages that appear in humans undergoing a psychotic break are seen in animals given continuous amphetamine doses, albeit in modified form. The ideational dwelling on a problem at a cognitive level is similar to the gradual development of intense, focused stereotypies at a motor level in animals. During this stage, both humans and animals become highly restricted in their behavior and attention. Dopaminergic terminals in the caudate nucleus are especially active during this period, but they then begin to deplete and to fail in their ability to drive caudate neurons in an highly organized fashion. This is both because some terminals are depleted or damaged when called upon to act, and also because there has been so much continuous hyperactivity that the terminals become less controlling over impulse flow due to the continued presence of dopamine in the synaptic cleft. Although the continued hyperactivity of dopaminergic systems continues (due to the continued presence of amphetamines or stress hormones), actual dopaminergic control over caudate neurons decreases as receptors become subsensitive and depletions continue.

The final, or late stage of continuous stress could be a result of several different phenomena at a biochemical level. One possibility is that damaged dopamine fibers begin to give off injury discharges, and the dopaminergic circuitry begins to "ring" in the manner characteristic of many partially damaged neuronal circuits. According to this model, the hallucinatory behaviors that appear during this stage would be correlated with transiently hyperactive dopamine circuits that cannot organize behavior well, but which can drive behavior to an exaggerated degree. Another possibility is that during this stage, dopamine fibers to the caudate nucleus are relatively quiet (due to damage and depletion), while those in the nucleus accumbens and frontal cortex become dominant. This produces the temporal lobe hyperactivity (and even mild seizures) that a number of investigators have long hypothesized to occur during hallucinatory episodes.

Deciding between these, and other possible models, can only be accomplished with further research. It is remarkable how the hypotheses that can be tested in current animal models of psychopathology have become so sophisticated and multidisciplinary in a relatively short period of time.

REFERENCES

Angrist, B., Sathananthan, G., Wilk, S., & Gershon, S. Amphetamine psychosis: Behavioral and biochemical aspects. *Journal of Psychiatric Research, 11,* 13.

Barry, H., & Wallgren, H. *Actions of alcohol,* 1970. Amsterdam: Elsevier.

Baumgarten, H., Bjorklund, A., Lachenmayer, L., Nobin, A., & Stenevi, U. Long-lasting selective depletion of brain serotonin by 5,6 dihydroxytryptamine. *Acta Physiologica Scandinavica,* 1971, Supplement 373.

Bowers, M. B., Jr. Pathogenesis of acute schizophrenic psychosis. *Archives of General Psychiatry,* 1968, *19,* 348–355.

Bowers, M. B., Jr. Acute psychosis induced by psychotomimetic drug abuse. *Archives of General Psychiatry,* 1972, *27,* 437–442.

Bunney, W., and Davis, J. Norepinephrine in depressive reactions: A review of supporting evidence. *Archives of General Psychiatry,* 1963, *13,* 483–497.

Calhoun, J. B. The ecology and sociology of the Norway Rat. U.S. Public Health Service Publ. No. 1008. Washington D.C.: U.S. Government Printing Office, 1963.

Carlsson, A., Corrodi, H., Fuxe, K., & Hokfelt, T. Effects of anti-depressant drugs on the depletion of brain catecholamine stores caused by 4-dimethylmetatyramine. *European Journal of Pharmacology,* 1969, *5,* 357–366.

Diaz, J., Ellison, G., & Masuoka, D. Stages of recovery from central norepinephrine lesions in enriched and impoverished environments: a behavioral and biochemical study. *Experimental Brain Research,* 1978, *31,* 117–130.

Ellison, G. Behavior and the balance between norepinephrine and serotonin. *Acta Neurobiologiae Experimentalis* (Warsaw), 1975, *35,* 499–515.

Ellison, G. Animal models of psychopathology: the low-norepinephrine and low-serotonin rat. *American Psychologist,* 1977, *32,* 1036–1045.

Ellison, G., & Bresler, D. Tests of emotional behavior in rats following depletion of norepinephrine, of serotonin, or of both. *Psychopharmacologia,* 1974, *34,* 275–299.

Ellison, G., Eison, M., & Huberman, H. Stages of constant amphetamine intoxication: Delayed appearance of abnormal social behaviors in rat colonies. *Psychopharmacology,* 1978, *56,* 293–299. (a)

Ellison, G., Eison, M., Huberman, H., & Daniel, F. Long-term changes in dopaminergic innervation of caudate nucleus after continuous amphetamine administration. *Science,* 1978, *201,* 276–278. (b)

Eriksson, K. Factors affecting voluntary alcohol consumption in the albino rat. *Ann. Zool. Fennici,* 1969, *6,* 227–265.

Freed, E. X. Effect of self-intoxication upon approach-avoidance conflict in the rat. *Quarterly Journal of Studies on Alcohol,* 1968, *29,* 323–329.

Griffith, J., Cavanaugh, J., Held, J., & Oates, J. Dextroamphetamine: Evaluation of psychomimetic properties in man. *Archives of General Psychiatry,* 1972, *26,* 97–100.

Harlow, H. The heterosexual affectional system in monkeys. *American Psychologist,* 1962, *17,* 1–9.

Huberman, H., Eison, M., Bryan, K., & Ellison, G. A slow-release silicone pellet for chronic amphetamine administration. *European Journal of Pharmacology,* 1977, *45,* 237–242

Kostrezewa, R., & Jacobowitz, D. Pharmacological actions of 6-hydroxydopamine. *Pharmacological Reviews,* 1974, *26,* 199–288.

Lader, M. Physical and physiological aspects of anxiety and depression. *British Journal of Clinical Practice,* 1970, *24,* 55–59.

Liddell, H. The experimental neurosis and the problem of mental disorder. *American Journal of Psychiatry,* 1938, *94,* 1035–1043.

Masserman, J. *Behavior and neurosis.* Chicago: Univ. of Chicago Press, 1943.

McKinney, W., Suomi, S., & Harlow, H. Effects of reserpine on social behavior of primates. *Diseases of the Nervous System,* 1971, *32,* 735–741.

Nelson, L., & Ellison, G. Enhanced stereotypies after repeated injections but not continuous amphetamines. *Neuropharmacology,* 1978, *17,* 1081–1084.

Pavlov, I. *Conditioned reflexes* (G. Anrep, trans.). London: Oxford Univ. Press, 1927.

Randrup, A., & Munkvad, I. Special antagonism of amphetamine-induced abnormal behavior. *Psychopharmacologia,* 1965, *7,* 416–422.

Snyder, S., Banerjee, S., Yamamura, H., & Greenberg, D. Drugs, neurotransmitters, and schizophrenia. *Science,* 1974, *184,* 1243–1253.

MELVIN LYON
ERIK BARDRUM NIELSEN

Psychosis and Drug-Induced Stereotypies[1]

5

Stereotyped behaviors have long been associated with psychopathology and, in particular, with schizophrenia. Bleuler (1950), in his classical descriptions of the pathogenesis of schizophrenia, writes:

> One of the most striking external manifestations of schizophrenia is the inclination to stereotypies. We find them in every sphere: that of movement, action, posture, speech, writing, drawing, in musical expressions, in the thinking and in the desires of the hallucinating patients. . . . Acts and behavior which per se need not be senseless are repeated incessantly, with an almost photographic sameness. The patient goes to bed always exactly in the same way, starting from exactly the same place, getting out of bed in exactly the same manner. In the garden he will run around the same circle or square, so that before long, he has dug tracks in the earth which have to be filled in. *Many years before his illness became manifest, a physician had made deep holes in the hardwood floor of his room because he always turned on his heels at exactly the same place on the floor* [pp. 185–186; emphasis added].

The latter observation has two important aspects. It confirms the presence of behavior that is extraordinarily stereotyped and it illustrates that this sort of behavior can go on, relatively unnoticed, for a long time before the more obvious symptoms of schizophrenia become apparent. Bleuler documents in

[1] Financial support for various parts of the work reported in this chapter was received from the Carlsberg Foundation, the Danish Medical Research Council (Grants No. 512–2542/512–8908) and the Medical Research Council for Greater Copenhagen, Faeroe Islands, and Greenland (Grant No. 75/76). Erik B. Nielsen also received the aid of a Gerda Lykfeldt grant.

PSYCHOPATHOLOGY IN ANIMALS
Research and Clinical Implications

many places that stereotyped behaviors are of paramount importance for the understanding of schizophrenia, and that they provide one of the most frequent signs accompanying and preceding the outbreak of mental disturbance.

Such clinical descriptions have been coupled more recently with the well-known effects of amphetamines in producing both stereotyped behaviors and symptoms that are not readily distinguishable from schizophrenia (Connell, 1958; Bell, 1965; Kalant, 1966).

In these drug-induced states, the stereotyped aspects of behavior are often most conspicuous during the first few hours after drug intake. Prolonged amphetamine intake, by repeated injections or ingestion with its accompanying loss of appetite and sleep, is marked by a developing tolerance to the drug and, in later stages, by more complicated and bizarre behavioral sequences than are seen in the early more obviously stereotyped stage. Furthermore, there are recorded instances where normal human subjects developed psychotic symptoms under amphetamine within 24 hours, at a time before sleep loss could play a major role (Griffth, Cavanaugh, Held, & Oates, 1970).

The possible relationship between schizophrenia and amphetamine psychosis was recognized many years ago, and in the late 1960s at least two groups of researchers proposed the so-called "dopamine hypothesis" of schizophrenia suggesting a definite biochemical basis for both conditions (Van Rossum, 1967; Fog, Randrup, & Pakkenberg, 1967; Randrup & Munkvad, 1968). More recently, Snyder (1973), Stevens (1973), Davison (1977), and Meltzer and Stahl (1976) have reviewed the evidence for this hypothesis and have confirmed that the earlier insights were indeed correct in many ways.

Although amphetamine psychosis does resemble strongly paranoid schizophrenia, some clinicians and others with great practical experience have pointed out some critical factors in the "dopamine hypothesis" of schizophrenia, upon which the validity of the relationship between amphetamine psychosis and schizophrenia appears to rest. The construction of a valid animal model for psychotic states requires examination of these critical points and, in particular, some defense of the implication in the present chapter title that stereotyped behavior, in some form, is broadly related to many or all forms of psychosis. Since stereotyped behavior is most evident with the central stimulant drugs, these must also be considered in particular.

I. Critical Issues for Central Stimulant Drug Models of Psychosis

The following points have been raised in criticism of a central stimulant (in particular, amphetamine) model of psychosis, even though paranoid schizophrenia is granted to show very close resemblance to certain symptoms of amphetamine intoxication. Each point is accompanied by some reference to evidence and counterevidence, and a brief mention of how this point might be treated in testing an animal model for psychosis.

1. Supposed failure of central stimulants to produce thought disorder and disturbance of affect.

While these are regarded as principal signs of schizophrenia (Bleuler, 1950), many clinicians are skeptical of their presence in amphetamine intoxication. These doubts may, in part, be the result of inadequate experience with amphetamine effects or of very short clinical observation times. There is evidence for thought disorder and changes in affect under amphetamine (Angrist & Gershon, 1970, 1971; Davis & Janowsky, 1973), and a closer perusal of the symptoms summarized by Kalant's earlier study (1966, Table IX) also indicates that such changes must be present. More importantly, studies of nonpsychotic human volunteers taking amphetamine (Bell, 1973; Griffith *et al.,* 1970; Griffith *et al.,* 1972) have illustrated that schizophrenic symptoms do occur, either within 24 hours following higher doses, or more slowly following repeated lesser doses. While it is true that the symptoms of paranoid schizophrenia are the most common, the other symptoms do occur. A recurring element in the symptomatology is stereotyped behavior, which is at first very rapid and continuous, but in later stages becomes disorganized and "fragmented."

An animal model for these symptoms must use the behaviors available. Thought disorders, failures in association, and changes in affect will be noticeable in animals while they are engaged in normal patterns of activity. Appearance of inappropriate behavior, "fragmented" or bizarre responses, in a known behavioral sequence such as grooming, feeding, or orienting to external stimuli can be made obvious by repeated close observations of behavior (Ellinwood & Kilbey, 1977). Likewise, the two symptoms described by Bleuler as a "predilection for fantasy rather than reality" and as a "tendency to divorce oneself from reality" can be tested indirectly, for instance in monkeys, by subjecting them occasionally to a series of evocative stimuli, such as approach, staring, and threat postures that always result in definite forms of reaction in normal monkeys. A failure to respond to these stimuli in the waking monkey under amphetamine can be interpreted as a temporary "loss of contact with reality," in the sense that sensory input seems to remain intact (McMillan & Morse, 1967), but responses now occur to internal changes which are not related closely to the external environment (sudden orienting, startle, hallucinatory reactions).

2. The reported failure of central stimulant drugs to produce manic or depressive types of psychotic symptoms.

If a drug effect were to act as a general model for psychotic reactions then it ought to produce some of these very common psychotic symptoms. Although it could be argued that central stimulants only produce certain types of schizophrenic symptoms, the relationship to other types is far from clear.

Robbins and Sahakian (1979), in reviewing possible animal models for mania, draw attention to the obvious behavioral parallels for hyperactivity, "elation" (or euphoria), and irritability which amphetamine stimulation provides. Not only is there a clearly parallel effect, but some evidence from animal studies, which they review, indicates that even "depression" may have some basic relationships with central stimulant drug action. The manic phase, which often clearly precedes the depressive phase in this syndrome, may be related to the extremely stereotyped hyperactivity, produced by amphetamine. Continued treatment with amphetamine in humans seems to produce a reduction in overt activity and social isolation which may initially resemble depression (Griffith *et al.*, 1970). This reduction in activity with social withdrawal has also been seen in rats treated with chronic amphetamine (Gambill & Kornetsky, 1976; Ellison, Eison, & Huberman, 1978), and is usually followed by an increase in what appear similar to paranoid psychotic reactions of a ''frightened–aggressive'' type. Robbins and Sahakian (1979) have presciently observed that possibly schizophrenia is a later and more severe developmental stage of the manic-depressive syndrome, and they cite the work of Carlson and Goodwin (1973) to support their suggestion. However, the central stimulant drugs, despite this perhaps ''pseudodepressive'' stage under the drug and the ''postamphetamine depression'' (Watson, Hartman, & Schildkraut, 1972) reported in humans, do not yet provide an acceptable model for severe depression.

An animal model could, however, by looking at these later stages of chronic-amphetamine treatment possibly indicate some reasons why the more obvious depression seems not to occur. It may be significant that lithium, which has a beneficial effect in treatment of mania seems to antagonize locomotor activity produced by amphetamine but does not appear to be effective against the amphetamine stereotypy (Robbins & Sahakian, 1979). Since the latter is a principal feature of schizophrenia, the apparent separation of hyperactivity and stereotypy may be important to the understanding of these various syndromes. Therefore, the animal models used should include some close analysis of behavioral details at all stages and of normal motor activity sequences versus clearly stereotyped patterns.

  3. Hallucinogenic effects of central stimulant drugs—problems of comparison.

  d- and *l-*amphetamine are not, in themselves, considered to be purely hallucinogenic drugs, although some of their derivative forms, such as paramethoxy-amphetamine, do have the property of inducing immediate and vivid hallucinations, without such a high degree of motor stimulation and stereotypy as the *d-* and *l-*forms produce (Beaton & Bradley, 1972; Loh, 1977). Other drugs, such as LSD and mescaline, are thought to produce more purely hallucinogenic effects which mimic those experienced in the early phases of schizophrenia. However, the latter drugs do not produce a general state of behavior that parallels that of schizophrenia, and the symptoms produced are relatively easy to distinguish, in their unusual context, from those produced by psychosis.

  However, the commonest amphetamine forms used by humans, (*d-, l-,* and methamphetamine) all produce frequent hallucinations that usually first appear after a period of hyperstimulation and lack of sleep. Thus the hallucinations appear, in this case, as a part of an evolving syndrome, which, in fact, is much closer to the typical development of schizophrenia then is the strong immediate elicitation of hallucinations produced by LSD and mescaline.

However, in order to make this comparison available in an animal model it is necessary to have some evidence of unequivocal hallucinatory experience. This is difficult to achieve but the following criteria may be suggested: *(a)* clear orienting to a stimulus that is not visible or audible to a human observer, preferably orienting to a point in space within the confines of the immediate observation situation; *(b)* clear signs of strong emotional reaction to this stimulus point (typical reactions include stiffening, piloerection, pupillary dilation, extreme palpebral opening, assumption of flight, or threat postures); *(c)* a definite coordinated sequence of responses oriented with respect to the given point in space (such as threatening actions, scratching, biting, striking, or fleeing from the point of initial orientation). Only when all three of these criteria are met is it possible to say that the probability of perceptual hallucination is very high. When possible, a close check of the point to which orientation was made should ensure that no stimulus of the appropriate type was, in fact, present.

Although there are reports of apparent hallucinations in cats (Ellinwood, Sudilovsky, & Nelson, 1973; Ellinwood & Kilbey, 1975) and of unexplained "hypervigilant" activity and rapid locomotion (flight?) in rats (Gambill & Kornetsky, 1976; Ellison *et al.,* 1978), there are few documented examples that meet all three of the above criteria. It is a prime aim of the present report to show that the use of amphetamine in animals can produce clear evidence of this important symptom development.

4. Unexplained differences in psychotic symptoms related to various stereotypy-inducing drugs.

Of the many drugs having some stereotypic effects related to a central stimulant action and dependent on changes in dopamine activity, the following are of special interest here: *(a)* d- and *l*-amphetamine; *(b)* methamphetamine; *(c)* methylphenidate (MPD); *(d)* phenylethylamine (PEA); *(e)* cocaine; *(f)* apomorphine and piribedil (ET-495). While all of these drugs can produce stereotypic reactions, they vary greatly in both their pharmacological mode of action (Braestrup, 1977; Braestrup & Scheel-Krüger, 1976; Braestrup & Randrup, 1978; Gessa & Tagliamonte, 1975; Costall, Kelly, & Naylor, 1975) and in their behavioral effects. An animal model based on stereotypy-inducing drugs must be capable of explaining and incorporating some of these differences.

Since the present chapter is not devoted especially to a comparison of drugs, special attention will be given to only three of these drugs: *d*-amphetamine (*d*-A) because of its powerful stereotypy and psychosis-inducing properties; methylphenidate (MPD) because of its different pharmacological action from *d*-A, its unusual potency for intensifying an ongoing psychosis and because of its widespread use against the hyperactivity syndrome in children; apomorphine (Apo) because of its very specific action on dopamine synapses, which is apparently different from both *d*-A and MPD, and because of the different nature of its stereotypy and behavioral effects as compared to *d*-A. Considered together, these three drugs present some of the most important issues for an animal model based on an increasing stereotypy of behavior.

d-Amphetamine can easily induce strong psychotic symptoms in humans (see previously cited references), and it is not necessary for the drug-taker to have any known familial or congenital disposition to psychosis (Angrist & Gershon, 1970; Griffith *et al.,* 1970). However, methylphenidate, while it is not a strong drug in initiating psychosis, is much stronger than *d*-A in exacerbating psychotic symptoms from an already existing psychosis. Furthermore, again in distinction from *d*-A, MPD does not tend to reinduce psychosis in schizophrenics who are in remission (Janowsky, Davis, & El-Yousef, 1974; Davis & Janowsky, 1973). On this basis, Davis (1974) proposed a two-factor theory of schizophrenia, in which the first factor was some, as yet unknown, but probably dopamine and/or noradrenalin related abnormal factor, such as endogenous PEA (Borison & Diamond, 1978). The second factor, which would be a sort of "gain control," would be related to dopamine hyperactivity and could easily be increased by drugs such as *d*-A. This theory would be consistent with the fact that *d*-A is much more active in noradrenergic metabolism than is MPD and that PEA is heavily dependent upon such a noradrenergic action for its stereotypic effects (Braestup & Randrup, 1978). It would also help to explain why *d*-A does not always induce psychosis despite high or chronic dosage (Griffith *et al.,* 1970; Kalant, 1966), since strong individual differences in predisposition to the first factor would be present.

The latter point implies that an animal model of schizophrenia based on this theory would need to expect some cases of strong individual resistance to the effect of *d*-A, so that exceptions to the induction of obvious psychotic symptoms in some animals would not be crucial evidence against the effect. Furthermore, such animals would be of special interest for analyzing their biochemical reactions during the drug challenge.

With regard to the amphetamine-based model for psychosis it may be noted that so far there has been great difficulty in documenting the presence of dopamine hyperactivity in schizophrenia (Matthysse, 1977b; van Praag, 1977), and there are occasional but persistent reports of improvement in long-standing psychosis following treatment with amphetamine (Arnold, Krebs, & Knopp, 1974; Nyman, 1975; Beckmann & Heinemann, 1976; Van Kammen, Bunney, Docherty, Jimerson, Post, Siris, Ebert, & Gillin, 1977).

Because amphetamine affects both noradrenergic and dopaminergic systems, apomorphine has some special interest as a relatively specific DA receptor agonist. Since apomorphine commonly produces nausea and vomiting it has seldom been a drug of abuse, but at least one study (Angrist, Thompson, Shopsin, & Gershon, 1975) showed that it can induce further deterioration in an ongoing schizophrenic state. Apomorphine was also found to produce a paranoid state especially marked by auditory hallucinations in two nonschizophrenics in the same study. None of the results were as strong, however, as those found with *d*-amphetamine, MPD, or *l*-dopa, but the induction of psychotic symptoms including hallucinations is of interest.

Methylphenidate also works by somewhat different biochemical interactions than *d*-amphetamine (Braestrup, 1977) and is of interest here because it is reported to exacerbate existing symptoms of schizophrenia, rather than to initiate a disturbance. Since the drug is widely used in lower doses in the hyperactive child syndrome, it is of value to know whether this drug does not cause any subtle disturbances in thinking or coordinated action that could be indicative of abnormal functioning. In this case, an animal model might be quite effective if it examined the low-dose reaction to complicated response sequences in order to expose possible incipient effects which are related to the very strong effect this drug has in psychosis.

In brief, the present chapter attempts to show how a combination of acute versus chronic treatment with several different central stimulant drugs, especially amphetamine, in various animals can illustrate the close relationship between the gradual development of stereotyped behavior and psychosis. Before it is possible to give a convincing picture of this relationship it is necessary to define the terms used and, in particular, to show that an obvious stereotypy often is the end result of a growing number of clearly recognizable symptomatic stages. The early recognition of these and the further recognition of a "late phase" lying beyond the more obvious stereotypy are major considerations for understanding why we feel that drug-induced stereotypies are of fundamental importance to the analysis of psychotic reactions.

II. Definition of Terms and Viewpoints

A great problem in discussing behavioral stereotypies is that the term "stereotyped behavior" has two common applications which are often confused. One usage is related to what might be called the naturally occurring or species-specific sequences of behavior that as the result of a unique bodily structure and physiology characterize a given species. For instance, rats have highly characteristic ways of grooming and drinking. These are readily identifiable, at least to gross observation, and yet they also reveal a more detailed structure and sequence when analyzed closely (Schiørring, 1971; Keehn, 1966). A definition of stereotypy based on these categories of behavior can be quite broad and has even been applied to categories such as "activity" and "exploration" (Keehn & Nobrega, 1978) which are highly affected by the environmental conditions and by early training. However, not all types of stereotypy fit such patterns, nor are stereotypies always species-specific behavior.

In the second and more general application, the term "stereotyped behavior" relates to a previously infrequent pattern of behavior, or even a newly learned pattern, not obviously important for survival or well-being, which is produced in a mechanical, repetitive fashion, such as lever-pressing obtained by operant conditioning. Such behaviors are both *repetitive,* in that they occur many times in the same form, and *perseverative,* in that once begun they are repeated for longer periods of time than normally. However, it is only when these behaviors are continuously produced without relevance to environmental consequences that they are regarded as abnormal. The final resulting stereotypy is typical of the high-dose effects of amphetamine during the first hours after treatment. Most descriptions of amphetamine effects concern this final stage of continuous stereotypy, which is clearly abnormal, but we wish to emphasize that behaviors under low-dose effects of amphetamines are often significantly changed in the direction of greater repetition and perseveration before any such gross abnormality in behavioral patterns is observable (Norton, 1969; Lyon & Robbins, 1975). Failure to realize this has led some experimenters to reject prematurely the possibility that effects related to stereotypy can be responsible for their observations of changed behaviors, since no obvious stereotypical responses were seen.

The main point here, and the gist of our conception of how stereotypies are related to psychopathology, is that in the beginning, normally occurring or previously trained behaviors gradually increase in both frequency and speed of execution under amphetamine-like drugs. Thus the initial action of the drugs is to accelerate and heighten the precision of some forms of behavior even though these activities remain generally normal in appearance. The altered behaviors, like the pacing of Bleuler's patient across the floor, are not obviously abnormal at this stage unless a more detailed sequential picture is obtained. But these initial changes are symptomatic, both in animals under amphetamine and in schizophrenics, of the coming severe disturbance. Therefore, in addition to general clinical observations, it is important to construct animal models with this in mind, and to analyze behavior in a detailed manner which is not limited to fixed patterns of species-specific responses.

Lyon and Robbins (1975) have described how this initial accelerative effect of amphetamines upon responding can result in the apparent predominance of certain behaviors and the loss of others as the drug effect increases. Essentially, they have built a complete theory around the postulate first presented by Lyon and Randrup (1972) that the increasing acceleration of behavioral initiation results in an increasing repetition within a decreasing number of response categories. The final effect is that some behaviors break down because they cannot be completed in sufficient detail to bring about changes in the environment (see also Grilly, 1977). Grooming movements in the air over the selected skin point and incomplete lever depressions in a Skinner box are thought to be examples of the same mechanism. While we cannot argue this point in detail here, the Lyon and Robbins viewpoint is taken here as a basis for further discussion. It is even central to the following explanation of the gradual losses in many stereotyped behaviors that occur with chronic amphetamine treatment.

Another major point for understanding amphetamine effects, and possibly also schizophrenia, is to distinguish between acute and chronic drug effects, since probably only the latter truly resemble a chronic state of schizophrenia. Acute single-dose drug treatment reveals much, but it cannot do more than act in a diagnostic way, since the few hours of drug effect are not usually sufficient to change the organism's behavior lastingly except in minor ways, probably related to the stimulation and signaling effect of amphetamines (Lyon, 1979). Single injections given at widely spaced intervals initiate a return to and even a strengthening of the stereotyped behavior seen after the first injections. However, there is another form of behavioral change, beyond this phase, that is only seen with more continuous treatment. If acute injections are given repeatedly and at closer and closer intervals, the effect begins to resemble that seen following continuous chronic treatment. Many examples of these types of effects have been reported by Ellinwood and his colleagues (Ellinwood, 1970; Ellinwood & Duarte Escalante, 1970; Ellinwood, Sudilovsky, & Nelson, 1972; Ellinwood & Kilbey, 1975).

Cats able to program their own self-injections of methamphetamine began to take the drug in such continuous fashion that their behavior exhibited another development than the simple stereotypies which regularly follow injections spaced at intervals of several days. The animals become hyperreactive and show a certain fragmentation in behavioral patterns, with frequent returns to the initial steps after only a partial act–sequence completion (Ellinwood & Kilbey, 1977). Furthermore, it appears that the stereotypies are particularly conditioned (Ellinwood, 1971) to the test situation. Fischman and Schuster (1974) gave monkeys regular IV injections of *d*-amphetamine every 3 hours around-the-clock. Some of the stereotypies which initially had interfered with conditioned leverpressing in the experimental box, began to disappear, but *only while the animals were under the experimental conditions*. Under home cage conditions, the stereotypies were still markedly evident. Furthermore, some activities, such as obtaining and eating food pellets that had been strongly reduced by the drug, increased as the animals adapted, until some monkeys were actually eating more pellets than they had initially under predrug control conditions.

Similarly, in the late stages of continuous amphetamine treatment in rats, Eison, Wilson, and Ellison (1978) reported that social contact, mounting, and aggression were at or above normal levels in frequency. The principal new features of these long-term treatment effects seem to be related to the constantly heightened activity, anorexia, and initial lack of sleep followed by hyperreactivity and a gradual failure to complete normal behavioral sequences (Ellinwood & Kilbey, 1977; Ellison, 1978). After a while, due to mechanisms not yet clearly understood, but often labeled either "physiological" or "behavioral" tolerance (Seiden, MacPhail, & Oglesby, 1975) the animals are able to recover certain forms of activity, beginning with responses such as leverpressing which can be fitted into the rapid, short-chain activities to which the drugged animals apparently are limited. Even when the recovery includes return to longer chains of activity, these are probably significantly different from the original chains and, in some cases, appear to be made up of disparate elements from several earlier chains (Ellinwood & Kilbey, 1975).

In summary, the present viewpoint is that stereotyped behaviors produced by a single high-dose injection of central stimulant drugs are usually the end product in a continuous alteration that begins with slight changes in repetition and perseveration patterns, sometimes initially indistinguishable from normal changes in response frequencies, but developing finally into an extremely localized form of stereotyped behavior that is almost totally limited and shows no regard for the consequences of the behavior. This change is illustrated (Figure 5.1) in three photographs of the alterations in leverpressing behavior to avoid shock in a rat under *d*-amphetamine. The end result is stereotyped sniffing and licking at the floor bars through which the animal now receives continuous shock. This is an excellent demonstration of the abnormal nature of the behavior produced by a single high dose injection of *d*-amphetamine. However, in this case the final stage of chronic amphetamine treatment is not present so that the "peak effect" is the stereotypy.

In developing animal models of psychopathology based on these initial observations, we will try to illustrate the continuum of change that exists between small single injections of central stimulants not even capable of producing a full-blown stereotypy and long-term chronic amphetamine intoxication, which we think resembles the schizophrenic process more closely than any other extant animal model. In attempting to do this we are fully aware of the large gap between this rather undifferentiated discussion of schizophrenia and the whole

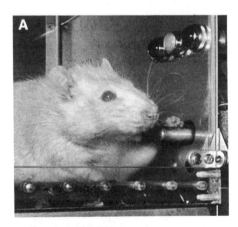
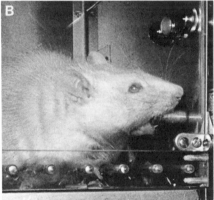

Figure 5.1. Three photographs showing the development of intense stereotypy under d-amphetamine in a rat leverpressing to avoid shock. (A) Normal holding of lever with paw, stereotyped sniffing and licking oriented above the lever. (B) Paw now leaving the lever, however biting and licking at the lever allow shock avoidance. (C) Licking and biting oriented at the grill floor, the animal receives continuous shock.

psychopathological process. However, in order to keep the door open for the widest possible discussion we have not distinguished between various types of psychopathology and psychosis, but have attempted to see these as various degrees of behavioral disturbance ranging from symptoms such as hyperactivity in disturbed children to the classical forms of schizophrenia. This working assumption should not be taken as a complete disavowal of the usual clinical distinctions between these conditions, but as a challenge to look at the more obvious behavioral similarities that seem to exist between these different syndromes. If there is, as there seems to be, an underlying behavioral and biochemical basis for these varying states, which can be revealed by looking more closely at the "amphetamine model" in animals, then our open-ended search may yield important advances. Furthermore, if the low-dose effects and early drug challenge effects do indeed mirror the later abnormal behavior then we may have, in the amphetamine model, an important diagnostic tool as well.

III. The Behavioral Analysis of Repetition, Perseveration, and Stereotypy

The general definitions outlined for repetition, perseveration, and stereotypy need to be specified more explicitly in the experimental situation before this model for psychopathology can be explored. Figure 5.2 is taken from Lyon (1979) and illustrates the nature of the changes that may occur in a lever-pressing task under the influence of *d*-amphetamine. The figure is diagrammatic, but represents with some accuracy the various changes which characterize the amphetamine effect on a fixed-ratio schedule maintained by a water reinforcement in deprived rats. The upper line, "no drug" condition, illustrates the highly "shaped" and, one might add, almost stereotyped, responses on the FR5 while the second line shows the response duration as the animal pokes its head into the dipper hole and drinks. This, too, normally has a rather fixed pattern and duration. If the animal is slightly affected by the *d*-amphetamine the early changes are seen in the "low dose" effect lines of Figure 5.2. The duration of lever depression (upward deflections in "lever" lines) is decreased, as is the interresponse time (IRT) within the ratio and even between the last two ratio "runoffs." The same acceleration effects are seen in the dipper-hole responses, but here there is a new feature, the repetition of entering the dipper hole, which results in an increase in total time spent at the dipper before the next ratio is run off. This feature illustrates the relationship between repetition and perseveration. The increasing repetition of entering the dipper hole is accompanied by an increase in perseveration of the dipper responding as a whole.

In the lower two lines of Figure 5.2 the high-dose effect shows increased acceleration, with responses occurring very rapidly, sometimes exceeding the FR5 requirement and sometimes, due to incomplete or too rapidly executed responses, not fulfilling the ratio requirement before the animal approaches the

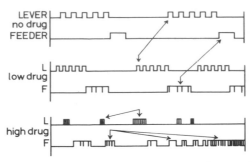

Figure 5.2. *Diagram showing lever and dipper-feeder orientation of a rat on FR 5 with water reinforcement. Responses to the lever or feeder and their duration are indicated by upward deflections. The upper two lines represent the control injection condition, whereas the middle two lines show the result of a moderate central stimulant drug effect, and the bottom two lines a high-dose effect. The upper two arrows indicate reductions in response duration and interresponse times for lever and feeder, respectively. The middle two arrows indicate too few (< FR 5) versus too many lever responses. The bottom three arrows mark bouts of perseverative feeder responses in the absence of water reinforcement. [From Lyon, 1979.]*

dipper. Both of these changes are atypical and seldom occur in deprived animals that are well trained on a FR schedule. The final limiting condition is seen in the lower line to the right in Figure 5.2 where the animal exclusively and in a stereotyped manner continues to reenter the hole and lick at the empty dipper. Any relationship to the production of reinforcement is now lost, and the behavior approaches what we would consider to be pathological in humans.

Figure 5.2 thus illustrates repetition, perseveration, and stereotypy, where the latter is the end result of the two initial processes. The particular choice of the final abnormal stereotype is probably dictated in part by its compatibility with the required speed of repetition (Lyon & Robbins, 1975; Grilly, 1977). This behavior is not abnormal because of its rapid or even faulty execution, but mainly because it: (*a*) is continuous; (*b*) blocks the occurrence of other behaviors except for occasional brief changes during intense and sudden stimulation; and (*c*) is unrelated to the prevailing reinforcement contingencies. These three features are almost never found simultaneously in normal waking organisms yet they are characteristic of many psychopathological conditions. Taken together, these three features are assumed here to represent one of the clear boundaries for psychotic behavior. But they are the extreme conditions, and we need to define the other phases preceding this state and, furthermore, the later phases which occur as the organism partially adapts to the continued presence of the drug and its induced stereotypy. The prestereotypy or *prephase* is considered to be the stage at which the behavioral patterns are significantly altered in their temporal qualities, where duration and repetition rate are changed. This prephase is seen both with single low doses of amphetamine or in the early stages of a deeper amphetamine intoxication. It is usually clearly visible before the behavior becomes perseverative enough to be called stereotyped, although some drugs (e.g., apomorphine) with central stimulant effects may produce only a very brief prephase before the fullblown stereotypy occurs.

The *stereotypy phase* itself appears after the prephase and can be produced both as the final stage before the *recovery phase* of a single large dose of amphetamine or as an intermediate stage in the effects produced by chronic amphetamine intoxication.

The poststereotypy, or *postphase,* is the stage at which alterations begin to appear in the stereotypy and the behavior once again appears to show more varied forms, even though these may still be severely limited. This postphase is seen only very weakly, if at all, before the *recovery phase* from a single large acute dose of amphetamine and only in the sense that behavior begins to return to normal through a series of altered response patterns (Schiørring, 1971). Following single injections of central stimulant drugs there is no real equivalent to the postphases seen with long-term closely spaced injections of amphetamine (Fischman & Schuster, 1974) or cocaine (Ellinwood & Kilbey, 1977), or with long-term chronic diffusion of amphetamine into the organism (Huberman *et al.,* 1977; Eison *et al.,* 1978).

There are two problems for animal models related to this postphase conception. The first problem is to demonstrate the possible relationship between low-dose effects and the later development of psychopathology. The second problem is to check whether the hallucinogenic-appearing activity in the postphase is comparable to human hallucinations. For these reasons we will concentrate here on a few experimental models that contrast acute and chronic drug treatment and which lay most emphasis upon the newer discoveries related to what we have called the postphase.

IV. Acute Single Treatment Stereotypies and Escape–Avoidance Behavior

As the result of the early observation (Verhave, 1958) that methamphetamine sometimes led to heightened responding in an avoidance situation, this is one of the most explored areas of amphetamine research with animal models. This extensive literature has been reviewed (see Kelleher & Morse, 1968), but some salient points deserve mention here. Teitelbaum and Derks (1958) demonstrated at a very early point the abnormal nature of the perseverative responding, in their case licking at a water tube, which allowed shock avoidance in rats under *d*-amphetamine. By altering the schedule requirements, they showed that responding became so rapid and perseverative that it far exceeded the practical requirements of the schedule and even continued long after the session was fully terminated. This abnormal pattern was more precisely explored by Lyon and Randrup (1972) who showed that the perseverative responding under amphetamine appeared to have beneficial effects only when the avoidance schedule parameters allowed the animals to pace their responding rapidly. A schedule requiring a leverpress–hold response was practically impossible to maintain under low doses of *d*-amphetamine, whereas at higher doses the bodily localizing due to increasing stereotypy allowed animals to remain on the lever for longer periods and to avoid shock more than with a lower dose. On the other hand, an active leverpress–release requirement in other animals benefitted from a low dose of *d*-amphetamine as the lever rate went up in parallel with the rapidity of all responses. At higher doses the "active" avoidance responding suffered more than the "holding" response because the localized stereotypy seemed to occur more frequently during the release (off-the-lever) phase. As mentioned earlier, the implications of these experiments are central to the general theory of amphetamine effects found in Lyon and Robbins (1975). Grilly (1976), partly on the basis of the same experiments, pointed out that the perseverative or stereotyped responding may "compete" with other responding and finally may occlude other classes of responding not compatible with the developing stereotypy.

Without going further into this area of research with acute injection effects upon trained behaviors, it can be stated unequivocally that animals under a high dose of amphetamine frequently perform in ways that are almost *never* seen with control injections, and which are difficult to replicate, even with high doses of other drugs such as barbiturates or analgesic drugs. For instance, Lyon and Randrup (1972) have reported cases in which rats take electric shock continuously for 30 minutes while actively licking and biting at the grid floor that is delivering shock. With a constant-current shock delivery apparatus it is difficult to imagine a more abnormal response, since the animal is not only passive, but acts to *increase* the shock contact. Yet, if the box is suddenly shaken or the animal is suddenly and rather roughly taken up, there is a brief return to the shock-avoidance lever and a few responses may occur before the animal lapses into the stereotypy again.

However, despite the abnormality of this response and its resemblance to the repetitive, seemingly irrelevant, activity seen in schizophrenics, the stereotypy is only temporary, and a few hours later the animal is apparently quite normal again in the most obvious respects. This acute treatment model thus has only certain elements of the longer-lasting and more debilitating psychotic states. However, it has been amply demonstrated that the reaction of schizophrenics and potential schizophrenics to a single dose of dopamine-related drugs such as *d*-amphetamine, methylphenidate, *l*-dopa, or apomorphine may provide important diagnostic parallels with the fully developed psychotic state characteristic of these individuals. (Davis & Janowsky, 1973; Angrist, Sathananthan, Wilk, & Gershon, 1974; Janowsky & Davis, 1974; Angrist *et al.*, 1975). Furthermore, if the initial changes in behavior at low doses of these drugs were better understood they might provide a diagnostic tool that would not require or risk the induction of an abnormal stereotyped phase. One of the major purposes of animal models ought to be the development of preventive diagnosis and treatment.

Whereas acute single treatment studies based on escape–avoidance procedures in animals have been among the first to show unequivocally the abnormal nature of the response changes induced by amphetamine, these schedules are not typical of human life situations. Both the drug state and the electric shock are introduced at intervals separated by long "safe" periods. Thus, although we can produce a severe disruption in the behavior of animals and humans from one hour to the next by a single infusion of amphetamine, this is not the typical course of events for schizophrenics, and, in particular, the use of powerful dose effects does not tell us very much about the events preceding a hospitalization.

V. Acute Low-Dose Methylphenidate and Problem-Solving in Monkeys

Partly as a result of the above reasoning concerning low doses of central stimulants as a possible diagnostic method, and partly because of its widespread use in the hyperactive child syndrome, methylphenidate is of special interest. MPD is reported to improve intellectual performance, including maze learning and associative learning in hyperactive children (Palkes, Stewart, & Kahana, 1968; Swanson & Kinsbourne, 1976). The reported effects are, however, mostly due to features common to low doses of central stimulant drugs, such as reduced latency of response and an increased reactivity to stimuli. The tasks on which performance improvement is shown are almost invariably those in which a *repetition of the same association* is the relevant feature (see, for instance, Kupletz & Balka, 1976; Swanson & Kinsbourne, 1976). When attempts are made to vary the task details such that repetition is not a major feature, no effect of MPD may be found (Wulbert & Dries, 1977). Mohs, Tinklenberg, Roth, and Kopell (1978) have also pinpointed this factor in studies of normal adult males under methamphetamine. They suggested that "methamphetamine can increase cognitive processing speed on tasks involving familiar cognitive operations but that an increase is not likely in tasks involving more complicated decision processes [p. 13]."

However, there is reason to believe that methamphetamine acts differently than does MPD upon dopamine systems (Scheel-Krüger, 1971; Ross, 1978), and it is not yet clear whether the same arguments can be applied to behavioral changes with both drugs.

If MPD is acting in the way suggested by Lyon and Robbins (1975), then the apparent improvements in hyperactive children are the result of an increasing repetition within more limited categories of response. This would reduce the grosser whole-body locomotion and increase the perseveration within the remaining response categories. Sahakian and Robbins (1977) have suggested that the result is an apparent "focusing" of attention, which will often result in improvement on tasks which require sustained attention, but would work in the opposite manner on tasks involving reversals or other sudden changes in cognitive strategy. If this assumption is correct, then the effects of MPD in hyperactive children are not "paradoxical" but are the early steps in a process that may have a direct relation to the psychotic changes mentioned earlier.

Sahakian and Robbins have supported this view with a number of references indicating the appearance of psychotic symptoms in hyperactive children being treated with MPD.

The following experiments, by one of us (M.L.) with monkeys performing a problem-solving task under low to moderate doses of MPD, were designed to investigate some of these issues. The immediate object was to see if the early low-dose effect of MPD did, indeed, produce improvements in manipulative problem-solving or whether any observed improvement in scores might be due to the same type of increased, but not always effective, behavior that had been demonstrated to occur in avoidance responding under amphetamine. Since the Lyon and Robbins (1975) theory has proposed that repetition and perseveration would begin to make their appearance early in the dose–response range, the various manipulative problems to be solved were constructed so that a number of points on each succeeding novel problem required the animals to shift their response ˉsequences or to develop an entirely new strategy with a different topography.

If the drug induced a tendency to repeat the same problem-solving movements even though they were ineffective with the novel problem, then longer solution times and more perseveration in specific response patterns could be expected.

Six adult male vervet monkeys (*Cercopithecus aethiops*) were used as subjects: They lived in individual metal cages, with a shelf and a moveable back wall which allowed restraining during injections. The room was temperature and humidity controlled and operated with a fixed day–night cycle. Animals were tested in their home cages by inserting the manipulative problem, on its rod, through an opening in the lower part of the cage front. The initial training problem is shown in Figure 5.3, and all animals were first adapted to this problem, while receiving NaCl injections, before drug tests began. The procedure on the subsequent typical drug test days began with injection of three animals with methylphenidate and of the remaining three with NaCl. After allowing time for the drug effect to reach a maximum, the animals were tested in the same sequence as they had been injected. Each animal received nine opportunities to solve the problem, but a limit of 3 min was set for each trial, unless the animal was actively engaged with the problem at the end of this time. In such rare cases, an additional several minutes (maximum of 3 min extra) was allowed before the problem was withdrawn. During the problem solution, two observers were usually present, one holding the problem rod and the other recording the sequence of responses, especially which paw was being used. and the times for: (*a*) opening the lid; and (*b*) consuming the grape used as a reinforcer. The observers stood in front of the cage and took precautions to remain quiet and make only the same necessary movements for each presentation. At the end of the trial they checked for agreement on the sequence of paw preference during solution and for other details of the monkey's behavior.

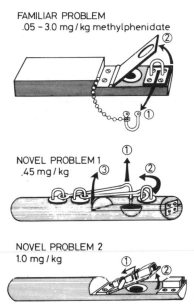

FAMILIAR PROBLEM
.05 – 3.0 mg / kg methylphenidate

NOVEL PROBLEM 1
.45 mg / kg

NOVEL PROBLEM 2
1.0 mg / kg

Figure 5.3. *Three manipulation problems presented to vervet monkeys under various doses of methylpheni-date. (A) The initial, "familiar" training problem, the single hasp; (B) Novel problem 1—the double hook; (C) Novel problem 2—the sliding bolt. During trials, half a sweet grape was placed in the hole under the latch or lid which was then slowly closed and latched in the animal's view.*

The general method of testing was to alternate each animal each week on Tuesdays and Fridays between the NaCl and the drug condition, so that all learning was counterbalanced for sequential effects. The same problem was presented on 3 days with drug and 3 days without, during a total of 3 weeks with no other delays. Three animals began each test sequence with drug and three without to control for effects due to specific weekdays. Testing on novel problems was carried out by the same general plan, after the solution to the initial (familiar) problem was well learned.

Detailed results of these investigations will be published elsewhere, but some general points may be summarized here. Figure 5.4 shows the time to solution for two animals during training on the familiar problem under NaCl with three dose levels of methylphenidate. Monkey No. 16 was very rapid in problem solution, whereas No. 19 was much more varied. Both animals show a general improvement over successive NaCl trials, but No. 19 appears to increase in solution time again at 1.0 mg/kg. Animals were tested at .05, .15, .25, .35, .45, .55, 1.0, 2.0, and 3.0 mg/kg methylphenidate, and, for most animals, obviously stereotyped behavior first appeared only at or above 1.0 mg/kg.

Novel problems 1 and 2, given in that sequence, are also shown in Figure 5.3. Note that these problems are not only different from each other but also require some movements opposite to those required for solving the preceding

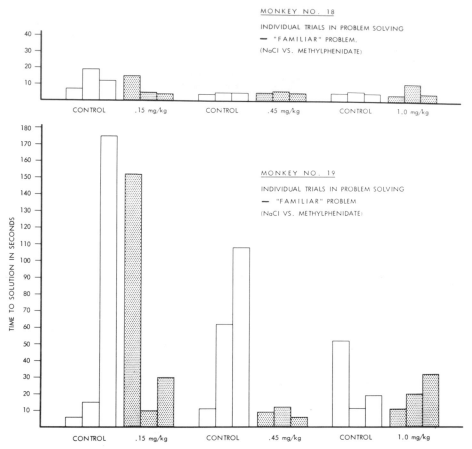

Figure 5.4.   *Time to solution for two monkeys on the ''familiar'' problem (see Figure 5.3A) under three different dose levels of methylphenidate.*

problem. For instance, novel problem 1 requires pulling out the hooks in the opposite direction to the locking hasp in the initial problem and the direction of opening the lid is also opposite to that in the familiar problem.

The general results for the novel problems are shown in Figure 5.5, which demonstrates that despite individual differences the group median times to problem solution are higher than the accompanying control times for all dose levels above .15 mg/kg. There is, thus, a small but general trend toward larger solution times even at dose levels where behavioral stereotypy is not evident and where individual animals sometimes exhibit their most rapid single trial solution times.

That this is not the only type of evidence indicating a more general deficit in performance despite single trials with improvements is illustrated in Table 5.1, which summarizes the number of times the novel problem was touched at all and the number of final solutions. On both points and at both dose levels it is

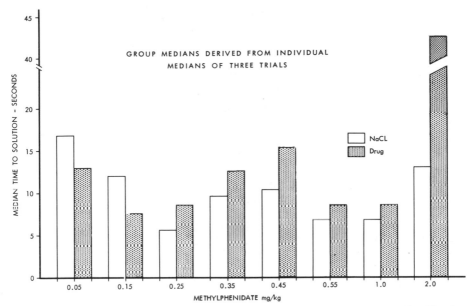

Figure 5.5. *Group medians of time to problem solution for all six monkeys on a "novel" problem (see Figure 5.3B under eight different dose levels of methylphenidate. The medians for NaCl control trials (white bars) and the drug trials (black bars) are, at each dose level, taken from the same days in order to control for variations in normal (NaCl) responding.*

apparent that the drug did not facilitate performance on the novel problem, but, in fact, hindered it.

The main point of this evidence on problem-solving under methylphenidate is that when a novel task is presented, deficits in performance are more characteristic than are improvements. As the theory of Lyon and Robbins (1975) predicts, when the task changes and new response topographies are required, the performance is often hindered by the repetitive and perseverative response

Table 5.1
Solutions with Novel Problems [a]

Monkey no.	Nine presentations of the novel problem 1 at .45 mg/kg MPD		Nine presentations of the novel problem 2 at 1.0 mg/kg MPD	
	Touching problem	Solutions	Touching problem	Solutions
16	3 times (9)	none (9)	none (9)	none (9)
17	1 time (8)	none (2)	none (8)	none (8)
18	9 times (9)	8 times (9)	8 times (9)	none (0)
19	9 times (9)	8 times (6)	1 time (7)	none (0)
20	9 times (9)	6 times (8)	none (9)	none (8)
21	3 times (9)	3 times (9)	1 time (9)	1 time (8)

[a] Numbers in parentheses are scores with NaCl.

qualities induced by the drug. Furthermore, this change occurs at dose levels before any obvious stereotypy is present, yet closer analysis of paw preference patterns and perseveration in ineffective attempts to solve the problem reveal the growing tendency to "lock-in" on specific patterns of behavior that is characteristic both of drug abuse with central stimulants (Rylander, 1966) and of schizophrenia (Matthysse, 1977a). Even in the low-dose ranges, the difference from normality begins to make itself apparent, sometimes aiding the response speed but equally often preventing the response entirely. These results also support the interpretation of Sahakian and Robbins (1977) and cast some doubt on the supposition that methylphenidate enhances problem-solving at any dose level when flexibility of response topography or cognitive strategy is necessary. As noted earlier, most of the tasks for which improvement in intellectual functioning under methylphenidate is reported, including certain uses of the Porteus Maze test, are based in large measure on repetition and association of fixed relationships between stimuli. Even with hyperactive children treated with MPD, the behavioral improvements reported by teachers and parents may be due mainly to an increase in certain aspects of the repetitive and perseverative behavior of these children and not to a general intellectual improvement. It is perhaps significant that Sheer (1976), Sahakian and Robbins (1977) and Kinsbourne, Swanson, and Kurland (1978) all mention problems in "focusing of attention" as a problem in children with learning disabilities. Such "focusing" could be beneficial in moderate amounts, but produce extreme stereotypy when present in excess. In summary, animal models using complex problem-solving and low doses of central stimulant drug appear to show results at a low-dose level consistent with narrowing of responses and gradual deterioration in flexibility of responding, which is often lost completely following high doses of central stimulants and in schizophrenia. The diagnostic potential of such low-dose testing both for children presumed to be hyperactive (see also Swanson & Kinsbourne, 1976) and potential schizophrenics (Davis & Janowsky, 1973) should not be overlooked.

VI. Chronic Treatment with Amphetamine

While the experiments with single injections of central stimulants illustrate a clear behavioral effect beginning at a very low dose level, the effects seen are restricted largely to a few hours after each injection. In order to make animal models more similar to the actual development of a human psychosis, it is probably necessary to develop chronic treatment techniques. The previous literature contains many reports of chronic treatment effects, which have been reviewed by Ellinwood and Kilbey (1977). It had been noted earlier by Yokel and Pickens (1973) that rats generally tended to give themselves less amphetamine on an intravenous free-access schedule if the injected solutions were potent, although it was not clear whether this was a protective mechanism or a side effect produced by the drug (Lyon & Robbins, 1975). Ellinwood and Kilbey (1975) did find cats which, by accident or design, self-administered lethal doses of the drug methamphetamine in a free-access situation. Although dogs (Risner & Jones, 1976) and rhesus monkeys (Estrada, 1978) have been shown to exercise some contraints in their self-administration behavior, Johanson, Balster, and Bonese (1976) found that rhesus monkeys with unlimited access to *d*-amphetamine, cocaine, or *d*-methamphetamine all died within less than 3 weeks due to excessive drug intake. That this was due to a loss of control over responding rather than to drug levels alone is suggested by the very high doses that could be attained gradually by the use of a paced automatic intravenous injection as used by Fischman and Schuster (1974). The latter technique yielded a strong stereotypy with increasing dosages, but the stereotypy could be replaced by effective leverpressing and pellet-feeding after the monkeys adapted to the drug. Even in the home cage without the lever–food schedule, stereotyped behaviors became less obvious after prolonged treatment.

Several researchers have tried giving amphetamine orally to rats in the drinking water (Magour, Coper, & Fähndrich, 1974, 1976; Banerjee, 1974). Results with this constant mode of administration are different from those seen in human drug abuse, with continuous period of high drug levels followed by a pause. Even amphetamine in the drinking water or fixed sequences of injections do not resemble the gradual unbroken development of a psychotic state. For this purpose it would be best to have a constant internal state, such as that produced by constant diffusion of the drug.

For the reasons cited earlier we have chosen to compare here two different techniques of the chronic type, one with self-administered amphetamine in the drinking water (Magour *et al.,* 1974) and one with the continuous diffusion of amphetamine from capsules implanted under the skin after the method of Huberman *et al.* (1978). Both techniques and their preliminary results deserve to be discussed here since they indicate what happens when amphetamine stereotypies and high-dose excitement and stimulation are carried beyond the first few days of continuous treatment. It is this range into which chronic psychosis presumably forces its victims, where excessive stimulation, lack of sleep, and compelling stereotypies of behavior finally result in behavior that is ineffective, hallucinatory, and full of changing but frequently incomplete and unrecognizable patterns of responding. These chronic-treatment animal models may help to explain how this transition occurs and where the search for treatment should begin.

VII. *Chronic Amphetamine in the Drinking Water of Rats*

Magour *et al.* (1974) demonstrated that rats could be forced to drink amphetamine solutions, although they prefer plain water if it is available. Such animals lose weight initially and become hyperactive and stereotyped, in some cases, depending on how much they drink. One of the salient features of amphetamine stereotypies is that licking behavior is still present and may even be stimulated at higher-dose levels (Teitelbaum & Derks, 1958). If such drinking results in greater amphetamine intake we might expect to see a serious behavioral effect, in which the animals give themselves a very high dose of amphetamine with corresponding stereotypy and behavioral abnormality. This model, where the animal is initially free to decide on its dosage level, is similar to free-access self-administration models using implanted IV catheters (Yokel & Pickens, 1973; Ellinwood & Kilbey, 1975; Johanson *et al.*, 1976) and to human drug abuse with "trips" which may result in amphetamine psychosis (Rylander, 1966; Kalant, 1966; Ellinwood, 1976).

Such models are of importance in research on psychopathology, since they can indicate whether or not the organism can remain in control of the dosing, and if not, what happens when the restraining tendency is lost. It is characteristic of many psychotics, when they are in a phase allowing them to review their experiences—and sometimes even during their psychotic episodes—to feel that they have "lost control." The possibility that this "loss of control" represents changes in the same neurotransmitter systems that are artificially disrupted by amphetamine treatment deserves careful attention. The present experiments were limited to two questions:

1. Would the animals show any tendency to lose control over their drinking behavior especially when they are forced to drink an amphetamine solution which is distinctly nonpreferred to water under normal circumstances?

2. Would such animals receive sufficient drug to interrupt their responding on a simple shock-avoidance task designed to be response compatible with low- but not high-dose amphetamine effects?

If control were maintained by taste preference one would expect these animals to drink only the minimum amount of the amphetamine—water solution necessary to maintain life and this would, in turn, allow them to maintain responding on the avoidance task.

These tests were carried out on 16 adult male Wistar rats, divided into eight "yoked" pairs, where one control animal in each pair received a daily water ration based on the amount of amphetamine solution drunk on the previous day by its partner. This allowed some control over the fluid intake limitations and weight loss that frequently accompanied forced drinking of amphetamine. After adapting the animals to a special drinking tube of Richter type with graduated scale, animals were paired according to average daily water intake. One animal from each pair received a solution of .2 mg/ml *d*-amphetamine, while its partner received plain water. Daily observations of water intake, body weight, and general activity were made, except on weekends when averages were determined for the 2 days. This regimen continued during a 4-month treatment period. Twice a week during the last 5 weeks, all animals were tested for 15 min on a nonsignaled shock avoidance task, and the number of avoidance and escape reactions, as well as the total shock-time were automatically recorded. The shock schedule was nonsignaled with a 4-sec shock interval if the animal did not respond and a 20 sec response–shock interval if it did. The shock pulses were 350 msec in length at an intensity of 90 V from a constant voltage type shock scrambler. The required response was to move a rod with a metal disk on its end, which was attached to a multidirectional microswitch, and hung from the top center of the cage. This response was desirable because of its simplicity and because rearing activity which would aid such responding is specifically increased by the low, but not the high, dose effects of amphetamine (Schiørring, 1971; Norton, 1969, 1973). Since very few undrugged animals ever fail to respond to this task, very poor responding would more likely be attributable to a high-dose amphetamine effect rather than to any other single cause.

The fluid intake results for two rather different animals are shown in Figure 5.6. These rats showed initially stable, depressed intake with much greater variance over the final treatment period. Not shown in the figure is the most typical effect, extremely variable water intake, but almost always higher than the control animals intake even on the days where, because of the yoked fluid volume control, the control animal had much more water available than it

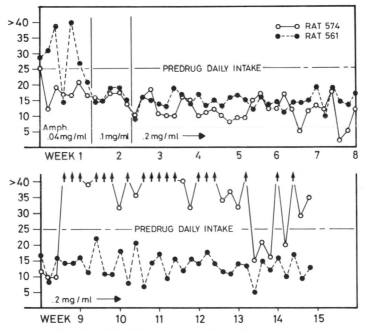

Figure 5.6. *The daily fluid intake in ml over a 6-week period for two experimental rats. Arrows indicate days where fluid intake exceeded 40 ml.*

drank. Control animals characteristically were stable and moderate in their water intake from the Richter tubes, whereas amphetamine animals were highly variable or, as in the other case shown in Figure 5.6 (574), showed stereotyped drinking activity. Animal 574 began to drink excessive amounts of the amphetamine solution on Day 17 and continued for more than 3 weeks to show highly stereotyped drinking activity, which included licking and biting at the edge of the drinking reservoir. This activity was so continuous for the first several days that the animal almost constantly was engaged in it, even during the night, when automatic videotape recordings at hourly intervals revealed only this activity. After a time, as is the case with other chronic treatment procedures (Eison *et al.*, 1978; Fischman & Schuster, 1974; see also Section VIII on chronic amphetamine in monkeys), the stereotypy became extremely rapid, then began to be incomplete, and finally changed into other patterns, frequently containing misplaced components of the original behavior. In this particular case, the licking became more and more ineffective as a means of obtaining fluid, and the licking and biting were oriented to the edge of the drinking reservoir which resulted in a great deal of spillage.

However, even during this poststereotypy, this animal was receiving a high dose of amphetamine as judged by its complete failure to avoid or even escape shock in the test situation. This failure continued throughout the 6-week testing period, yet was immediately altered to active escape responding on the very first postdrug escape test, 2 *months* after the end of drug treatment.

The general results on the shock-avoidance task given after the 2-month waiting period for all animals are summarized in Figure 5.7 which shows the averages and ranges for the 6 weeks of drug or control sessions for shock-time in seconds and total avoidance responses. The partial extinction test procedure, which was given after the drug treatment stopped, was unusual in that it only removed the effectiveness of avoidance responses (extra responses in the response–shock interval) but maintained the normal "escape" response (i.e., the first response in shock–shock condition). Since the avoidance responses had no effect in delaying the next shock, it was expected that they would gradually extinguish, whereas responses in the presence of the 4-sec shock–shock condition would demonstrate whether the animals still were responding to the shock at all. This partial extinction method thus has some advantage over no-shock or continuous-shock extinction procedures, where high responding or very low responding, particularly as a consequence of drug treatment, do not allow the animal to "sample" the contingencies adequately (Lyon, 1971).

Figure 5.7 also shows that all amphetamine animals were clearly different from their control partners in both excessive shock-time and in low numbers of avoidance response during the 6-week drug treatment. The partial extinction procedure reveals some further differences after drug treatment stopped. In shock-time allowed, the experimental animals dropped immediately down to the control range, but by the fourth extinction session they were allowing average shock-time increases that were in excess of the control range and approached

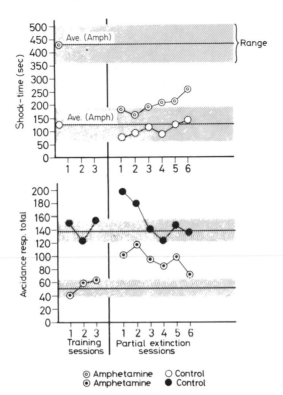

Figure 5.7. *Averages and ranges for a non-signaled shock-avoidance task of shock time in seconds and total avoidance responses for rats exposed to chronic drinking of a d-amphetamine solution (0.2 mg/ml) or equivalent amounts of tap water. Shock-shock interval = 4 sec; response-shock interval = 20 sec. During "partial extinction" only the first response during a shock period produced a 20 sec interval.*

their drug range values. Control animals climbed somewhat in shock-time under the partial extinction, but never came close to exceeding their normal range.

The avoidance response totals are also interesting, but without quite so clear import. Both control and experimental animals initially raised the number of avoidance responses, which is to be expected during extinction. The experimental animals kept their avoidance response total averages above their "training" (drug) range for more than twice as long as did control animals. However, this result may be an artifact of the response totaling procedure in that experimental animals are perhaps leveling off in response totals as they approach the minimum number of escape responses necessary to keep the shock off most of the time (approximately 45 responses).

Perhaps the most important feature of the avoidance findings is that animals appear to allow a greater absolute amount of shock to occur earlier in the partial extinction procedure if their previous drug experience included even higher shock times. One possible interpretation is that the effect of exposure to a highly abnormal state may increase the tendency to return to that state when new and somewhat uncertain conditions exist. The partial extinction procedure used here is an unusual schedule which necessarily produces some uncertainty initially. Responses that are made during the response–shock period are now inexorably followed by shock at intervals of less than 20 sec and ranging down to zero. Thus "late" responses in the response–shock interval are now punished by shock presentation while "early" responses have nearly the same consequences as originally. When this new uncertainty is introduced, it appears that the formerly drugged animals allow the shock-time to increase much more readily than their control partners. Enduring a chronic state of amphetamine intoxication which, although *nominally* self-administered, was partly by virtue of the licking stereotypy beyond the animal's own control (Lyon & Robbins, 1975), may produce changes that increase the tendency to return to the same abnormal state in time of uncertainty and stress (Lyon, 1979). The possible biochemical basis for this more permanent change is still unclear, but an effect that outlasts drug treatment by more than 2 months is not likely to be attributable to some simple residual drug effect. It is conceivable that the learning of inappropriate patterns of response, in the face of shock initially made unavoidable by the drug-induced behavior, is the essential change, but it should be explainable on a neurotransmitter basis as well. Weiss, Glazer, and Pohorecky (1976) suggest a noradrenergic deficit as the major change. Since it is known, in this connection, that psychomotor stimulant drugs can produce what appears to be a "reward-enhancing" effect in addition to the gradually increasing stereotypy, it has been suggested that the reward–enhancement feature can assist and strengthen the blending of the stereotyped activity with learned sequences of responses (Robbins, 1976; Lyon, 1979; Sahakian & Koob, 1978). The result may be a relatively lasting, even though slight, advantage in response strength for those responses that were performed under the drug influence. Furthermore, it has been demonstrated that giving the drug again in single low doses or sometimes merely presenting some of the stimuli previously associated with intake of amphetamines can temporarily restore the behavior elicited under the drug (Ellinwood, 1971a; Stretch & Gerber, 1973). All these bits of evidence support the conjecture that learning is taking place under the drug and that this learning may include some aspect of the stereotyped responding.

The immediate relevance of this point is that if such learning also takes place in schizophrenic patients while they are seriously disturbed, it could also have a stronger tendency to reappear later when stimulus conditions were similar to those during the original appearance of symptoms. Thus this sort of abnormal response could remain dormant in an otherwise normal former patient and if its brief reappearance led the patient to fear a further loss of control, which it might well do, then a rapid deterioration might occur. Such a possibility deserves closer investigation since even our simple animal models suggest the presence of a serious behavioral problem during the posttreatment (remission) period, not necessarily associated directly with the genesis of the original disturbance.

response to it. These responses were recorded on a crude point scale and any peculiarities were noted separately.

The general results are summarized in Figures 5.9 and 5.10 which show the total incidence of rated behaviors in two different monkeys over the treatment days. Figure 5.9 shows the general changes in five categories of behavior for

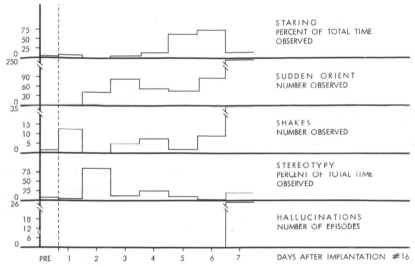

Figure 5.9. *Behavioral scoring from cumulative 24-hour videotape monitoring records (1 min/30 min) for monkey No. 16. (Responses selected here are described in Table 5.2.)*

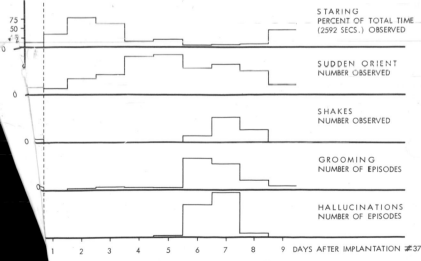

10. *Behavioral scoring from cumulative 24 hour-videotape monitoring records (1 min/30 min) 37. (Responses selected here are described in Table 5.2.)*

VIII. Chronic Amphetamine Treatment via Implanted Capsules in Monkeys

Even though the self-administration model is an excellent one for many purposes, it is not clear whether the human psychotic can directly control the early development of his or her own disturbances in any simple way. While we need the self-administration model to test the possibility that the subject still could use some control mechanisms if they were available, we need a chronic unremitting treatment with amphetamine to test the consequences of a real loss of control over dosage.

For all of the following experiments we owe a great debt to Gaylord Ellison, who stimulated our interest in this type of model and assisted us during the initial use of this technique with monkeys. On the basis of the development at his laboratory of a constantly diffusing capsule filled with amphetamine base for use in rats (Huberman *et al.*, 1977), Ellison became interested in the possibility of testing monkeys with the same technique. The result was an ongoing cooperative research endeavor initiated by him and incorporating further collaborative experiments in progress at our laboratory and at Cambridge University in England and under the guidance of Susan D. Iversen. Summarized here are the results of the first experiments with these monkeys at our laboratory. A preliminary report on the project as a whole is in preparation.

Although others have reported use of an implanted amphetamine capsule (Hitzemann, Loh, Craves, & Domino, 1973), the present method is one of the first to allow a relatively continuous amphetamine intoxication for periods up to 10 days or more without the use of chronic in-dwelling catheters and restraining chairs. The use of fully active monkeys is a distinct advantage in trying to assess any parallels with human patients. Furthermore, the initial use of these capsules in rats (Huberman *et al.*, 1977) revealed that there were several apparent stages, including hyperactivity, stereotyped behavior, irritability, and misplaced aggression as well as abnormal periods of isolation from the social group. Both the appearance of these types of change and their sequence seemed to run parallel to the sequence of activities reported by Griffith *et al.* (1972) following repeated small oral doses of amphetamine in humans over a 5-day period, and to the reports of social and behavioral changes seen in drug addicts under amphetamine at high dose levels (Rylander, 1966; Ellinwood, 1972) As noted earlier, such chronic dosage results in an entirely different final post stereotypy phase, which contains hallucinations and bizarre behavior not seen in the prephase or during stereotypy following acute dosage. For the exploration of this postphase and its importance for severe psychotic disturbance, the implanted capsule method is probably a great methodological improvement.

Experiments in our laboratory are being carried out on eight vervet monkeys (*Cercopithecus aethiops*), which are housed in pairs of individual cages set side-by-side and with a window in their common side. Two monkeys can thus be observed and videotaped with sound tracks, simultaneously. The cages have a plastic front door set in a wide grill frame and are equipped with a back shelf and movable back wall for use during injections or other treatment. The cages were monitored on videotape for approximately 1 min every half hour, around the clock during experiments. During the dark part of the regular day–night cycle, red overhead lamps were used to obtain sufficient light for the TV cameras. Animals were fed daily during experiments, and regular weight checks were made. In some cases it was necessary to supplement the diet temporarily with fruit during the maximum amphetamine stereotypy effect, and all animals continued to eat the fruit readily even though some did not eat dry food or drink much water from the water tube. Perhaps the most surprising thing was, in fact, the readiness with which most animals adapted to feeding and drinking under the drug, an effect also noted by Fischman and Schuster (1974).

The typical experimental procedure was as follows: Prior to implantation, the paired cages were placed in a separate room under TV surveillance, and while the monkeys adapted to the new cage position their behavior was recorded for at least 3 days prior to implantation. During the first few experiments, animals were implanted in pairs, with one animal receiving amphetamine base mixed with polyethylene glycol in the capsule and the other receiving only the polyethylene glycol. This provided a control for implantation procedures and, in addition, a normal partner which the drugged animal could observe through the common window.

Implantation of capsules took place under pentobarbital anesthesia supplemented in some cases by nitrous oxide. The capsules were made up in advance (see Figure 5.8) slightly modified from the method described by Huberman *et al.* (1977) and were filled with drug and/or vehicle immediately before implantation. Each capsule contained a given quantity of amphetamine base (initial dosages were 31 mg/kg) mixed with polyethylene glycol 300. In order to increase the diffusion surface and lessen the chance of blockage by surrounding tissue, the total dose was divided between two capsules implanted subcuta-

neously, under sterile conditions, in the back just beneath the shoul[...] animal. All animals received a single dose of a long-acting antibiot[...] dopene® 2 ml i.m.) and were allowed to recover in their home cages. [...] ing began immediately postoperatively. Usually the capsules were remo[...] 8–10 days, under anesthesia, and videotaping then continued for at lea[...] in the postcapsule period.

Scoring of the videotapes was done by trained observers using a vi[...] recorder with a slow-motion control for doubtful cases. The scoring she[...] tained the behavior items shown in Table 5.2.

As may be seen, most of the items were chosen to delineate the abnor[...] stereotyped behaviors that were expected on the basis of previously report[...] periments (see, for instance, Ellinwood & Kilbey, 1977). Control animals [...] rated on the same scales and during the same time periods. Twice daily [...] called "physical check" was made of each animal's response to (*a*) approac[...] of the cage, at 2 meters distance and then with face close to the cage, eyes o[...] monkey; (*b*) slow circular movement of a hand close to the cage; (*c*) "thr[...] approach" with hands raised and teeth bared, again first 2 meters away and t[...] close to cage; and (*d*) cessation of the threat–approach and subsequent los[...]

Table 5.2
Scoring Items—Monkey Amphetamine Capsule Experiments

Item	Brief description
Time recorded	From digital clock on the videotape—(hours, minutes, seconds)
Position in cage	Cage divided for scoring into four equal quarters
Activity (0–4)	Rating scale from none to extremely frequent movement
Staring	Focused looking at one point in space for more than 5 sec
Stereotypy	Continuously repeated, fixed sequences of behavior performed without res[...] to immediate environmental cues
Grooming	Cleaning fur, licking, or nibbling at the body
Shakes	Sudden, whole body shaking (similar to "wet-dog" shakes)
Eating	Ingestion of any food
Drinking	Licking at the drinking tube
Vocalization	Any noises; chattering, grunting, "barking"
Startle	A hyperreactive response, sometimes with spatial orientation to ap[...]
Visual tracking	Focusing of the eyes on, and appearing to follow the movements [...] space such as a fly
Sudden orienting	Clear and sudden head and body orientation to a point in [...] body—not quite like startle
Pouncing	Sudden striking out or grasping as if to capture; may be di[...] elsewhere
Hallucination	A consistent sequence of activity oriented toward an [...] stimulus. Typical patterns of behavior: sudden orie[...] flight + chatters + looking over shoulders; explosi[...] reactions; grasping in the air + putting "things" [...] and lip-smacking

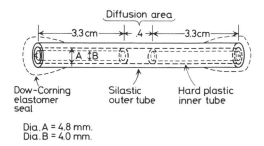

Figure 5.8. *Capsules to be filled with amphetamine base mixed with polyethyleneglycol 300 for subcutaneous implantation in the monkey. The inner, diffusion-limiting, tubes are made from plastic syringe barrels cut to size. The outer tubing is of Silastic® material and is sealed at each end with a special Dow-Corning cement (see Huberman et al., 1977).*

animal No. 16 which was the first monkey tested. All videotapes for this animal were scanned shortly after recording by several observers who all corroborated the general picture shown in Figure 5.9. It was found that scoring the full time base of 2592 sec/day (54 sec per observation every 30 min) frequently yielded repetitive observations, and analysis of the full sample at intervals for less than 60 min was not necessary. In Figure 5.9 the data from Day 1 are brief because the animals were recovering from the operation, and on Day 2 some data were lost by a technical error before the final scoring was made. However, even here the analyzed data and the original scanning by several independent observers showed that there was a pronounced increase in a particular stereotyped behavior for this animal. As is typical for human amphetamine addicts, there is always an individual pattern of stereotypy with a certain uniqueness. Animal No. 16 fingered in a clearly stereotyped manner an inoperative socket that had been surgically attached to its skull in a previous operation. It then sniffed and licked its fingers and repeated the movement. During the first 2 days the touching of the socket gradually became incomplete and after an upward movement toward the top of the head the animal developed a closer contact between fingers and mouth which finally culminated in a thumb-sucking activity in which the wrist was simultaneously rotated and the thumb moved about in the half-open mouth. This, too, was performed repeatedly in a very stereotyped manner.

Meanwhile, it is important to emphasize that the wakeful condition continued day and night for almost the entire 7 days of testing. In combination with this sleepless condition, some changes began to occur that are typical of extended chronic amphetamine intoxication (Ellinwood & Kilbey, 1977) but are rarely seen with spaced injections. The animal dropped off in its frequency of stereotyped socket-fingering and thumb sucking, although these appeared at intervals, but there was a sharp increase in sudden orienting, staring at a fixed point in space, and in whole-body shakes similar to the "wet-dog" shakes reported during morphine abstinence in rats. The sudden orienting resembles a startle reaction with visual orienting toward a point away from or behind the animal and is accompanied by muscular tension indicative of preparedness for immediate reaction. The tail of the monkey may be raised, and pilo-erection may also occur. However, relative to its initial strength the reaction disappears rather quickly at first, only to reappear shortly afterward. During the pauses, the animal may stare into space or at the wall, often at a particular spot or with a fixed orientation for many seconds, with the eyes seemingly focused but no head or body movements. Some dyskinesias appeared and limbs could be seen held in awkward positions for longer periods. Tremor, lip smacking, and chewing movements were also occasionally observed. The rise in body "shakes" in Figure 5.9 in intriguing since these movements are also typically induced by hallucinogens, but not by many other drugs (Siegel, Brewster, & Jarvik, 1974).

On Day 4 the animal began to give a "chuttering" vocalization described by Struhsaker (1966) as indicative of aggressive threat and solicitation of aid in vervet monkeys. This vocalization was first heard during the second daily physical check during which the animal's reactions to movements and "threat approach" by human observers were observed. On this occasion, after giving this vocal response sporadically during the close approach, the animal later continued to repeat it with an increasing frequency which developed until it went on incessantly for hours into the night, after the laboratory personnel were gone and after neighboring monkeys had ceased their more occasional but intense chuttering and barking, some of which was in response to this call. Some drugged monkeys also give a short, low, barking noise and occasionally show their teeth at irregular intervals in connection with sudden orienting or flight reactions. Undrugged monkeys kept in cages can also exhibit behaviors such as "chuttering," staring, or even briefly maintaining awkward limb postures, but never in our experience, as continuously or with such fixed visual orientation as in these drugged monkeys. It may be added that scoring and closer observation of the control monkeys in our experiments never yielded any really significant scores on any of the measures reported here. The control monkeys occasionally stared for many seconds and occasionally showed a startle, but almost always in response to a visual or auditory stimulus recognizable to the human observer. Shakes, stereotyped behavior of any consequence, and other more abnormal signs were never seen in control monkeys.

On Day 7 in Figure 5.9 there is a sudden rise in what we have labeled "hallucinations." We are well aware of the danger in attributing sensory perceptions to animals on the basis of their overt behavior, but despite our skepticism we are now convinced that the evidence warrants this labeling. Responses were attributed to "hallucinatory" stimuli without qualification *only* when well-coordinated and oriented startle, attack, or flight responses occurred in the absence of any obvious relevant stimulus to the human observer. Two other types of behaviors, "visual tracking" and very sudden oriented biting or scratching at the body, were considered as possibly related to hallucinations but were not so scored because of the difficulty of objective checking. However, the sudden, sometimes rather violent scratching, biting, or close investigation of a point on the body has good orienting and is a coordinated sequence closely related to normal grooming. It could easily be related to the rather common hallucinatory parasitosis reported in amphetamine psychosis (Stachelin, 1941; Kalant, 1966) and in the syndrome called "monosymptomatic hypochondriacal psychosis" with delusions of parasitosis (Gould & Gragg, 1976). The finding by Riding and Munro (1975) that the latter symptoms, which occur in individuals who are otherwise perfectly healthy and without a history of psychosis, can be treated successfully with Pimozide, a DA receptor-blocker, is also consistent with the present theoretical orientation. Whether scored or not recorded instances of potentially hallucinatory episodes were checked by direct observation in the cage and corroborated there and on videotape by several observers, if possible.

In monkey No. 16 some possible tactile hallucinatory episodes involved repeated, sudden scratching, picking, and investigation of spots on the skin. No gross skin abnormalities or evidence of parasites could be seen during pellet implantation or removal. This reaction thus corresponds rather exactly to the reports of "feeling" body parasites.

However, as potentially hallucinatory episodes, it was more impressive to see the sudden flight reactions that occurred without any obvious external stimulus and which during direct observation sometimes were seen to include stiffening, widening of the eyes, piloerection, and rapid movement away from the direction of visual orientation. In monkeys where the apparent stimulus seems to have been behind the animal, the resemblance to paranoid states is striking.

The most convincing signs of hallucinatory episodes in monkey No. 16 were sudden attacks upon nonvisible stimuli. The monkey would orient suddenly to a bare spot on the cage shelf upon which it sat, and would then withdraw with eyes widened and muscles tensed as if to flee. On several occasions, it then attacked the bare shelf with a strong striking movement of its paw, quickly withdrawing again after the attack while keeping its eyes on the same spot. There seems little doubt that this was a true hallucination, since the shelf was completely clean and had a dull, flat, sheet-metal surface with no protuberances or sharp edges.

At the end of the 7-day period the animal still did not sleep but the hallucinatory episodes were decreasing, and it was decided to terminate the experiment by removing the capsules. Observation of behavior after removal revealed much sleep and drowsiness and a return to more normal eating and drinking. Occasionally, even weeks after this experience, the monkey showed occasional responses reminiscent of the original socket-fingering stereotypy and some unusual head-twitching responses, including a sudden swinging back of the head with rotation of the neck. However, the latter movement may also be part of a normal "threat posture" sequence. In any case, these unusual responses, for this monkey, were never as perseverative or stereotyped for long periods as behavior was under the drug.

Figure 5.10 shows the course of behavioral change for a second monkey (No. 37), which illustrates the individual character of the developing stereotypies and hallucinatory episodes. This monkey was much quieter physically during the stereotyped phase, showing mainly staring at fixed points for long periods. During this staring the animal did not respond in any way to, or focus upon, a hand extended close in front of its face, a failure of response never seen in our normal monkeys. The resemblance to the "withdrawn" psychotic patient and to "absence of reality testing" was common in the late drug phase.

During the Days 3–5 there was a gradual increase in sudden orienting and at Day 6 "body shakes" began to appear and this animal's particular form of hallucinatory episodes appeared rather suddenly, just as in the first monkey and at about the same time. In monkey No. 37 the apparent hallucinatory episodes included a sudden orienting followed by startle and flight away from the point of visual fixation; grasping at invisible stimuli in the the air and then focusing on or sniffing at the retracted hand as if it might hold something; and finally, sudden looking over the shoulder sometimes followed by startle and flight. This latter

observation may be important if it indicates the occurrence of auditory hallucinations, which are less frequently associated with amphetamine, but are often
found in paranoid psychosis. There were also large numbers of sudden grooming or picking reactions at points on the legs or lower abdomen, which looked as
if the animal had been bitten or was reacting strongly to sudden stimulation at
these points. These resembled the fewer instances of the same behavior seen in
monkey No. 16.

We are still recording and analyzing data from these experiments, but
several things now seem clear:

1. The poststereotypy phase in the monkey resembles very closely, symp-
   tomatically, the picture seen clinically in many psychotic patients. There
   are clear parallels to loss of reaction to the external environment, and its
   consequences, increasing hyperexcitability to minimal stimulation and,
   finally, hallucinatory episodes of various types.
2. Lack of sleep may play an important role in the development of the
   hallucinatory episodes. There is evidence indicating that extreme
   deprivation of REM sleep may result in brief episodes of hallucinatory
   nature in humans, and the early return of sleep was associated in some
   of our other monkeys with failure to display clear hallucinatory episodes.
3. Not all monkeys show a clear development of the poststereotypy phase,
   even though all tend to go through some type of stereotypy. One of our
   monkeys has been implanted three times with increasing doses, but remains free of the poststereotypy phase development. A quicker recovery
   from the stereotyped phase and the earlier reappearance of normal
   eating and sleeping accompany this resistance to the amphetamine effect. This finding may fit with the common observation that although
   prolonged stress is a frequent accompanying factor in the development of
   psychosis, it is not, in itself, sufficient to bring about a psychotic
   breakdown.

Finally, it is reasonable to urge some caution in the tendency to dismiss
nonstereotyped or only commonly stereotyped behavior in animals as a failure to
show correlation with human psychosis. It is virtually certain that, just as human
patients do, animals under the effect of central stimulant drugs adjust or
"blend" their behavior to fit the necessities of their reduced behavioral
capacities (Lyon & Randrup, 1972; Lyon & Robbins, 1975). Thus animals may
not continue indefinitely to show *overt* signs of hallucinatory activity, just as
many patients are bothered by, but do not overtly react to, the "voices" that
they hear. A second possible reason why behavior of this type may not continue
to be overtly observable is that as the dose level (or the psychosis) is heightened,
the behavior may become so limited in many ways that gross whole-body
responses are no longer present—as may be the case, for instance, in various
forms of catatonia or "withdrawal" in schizophrenia and with monkeys given
very high doses of central stimulant drugs (Fischman & Schuster, 1974).

There is some evidence that one or both of these factors also can be present in the amphetamine-capsule model as presented here. In our latest experiments, which will be reported in detail elsewhere, we have reimplanted capsules in some of our previously tested monkeys. The result in animal No. 37 is especially interesting in that the implantation of capsules containing a dose nearly twice that used in the first experiments, did not result in more than some stereotypy, especially of the "hypervigilant" type mentioned often by Ellinwood and Kilbey (1977), and only a few clear instances of apparent hallucinations. The animal sat relatively still for long periods and, although alert and never sleeping, did not show the type of constant *overt* hallucinatory reactions as before. A second reimplant with fresh capsules at the same high dose level on Day 7 after the first implant still did not produce any significant alteration, even on Day 13 of continuous amphetamine intoxication. As is the case with many human amphetamine addicts and with psychotic patients, this monkey and its neighboring cage mate, which received the same drug treatment, both began to show brief signs of clear reaction to the outside environment ("threat" gestures, etc.) even though they were definitely within the time limits of the *poststereotypy phase,* where bizarre behavior and lack of contact with the environment had characterized their original drug treatment.

Further studies with be necessary to determine whether this change in response is due to dose level, adaptive behavior, or some alternation or tolerance to the drug itself. Even though it is reasonable to suppose that this development is simply a parallel to the varying strength of overt symptoms in humans, it is a more difficult problem for an animal model because it removes some of the obvious criteria for acceptance of the hallucinogenic effect in animals. If the monkey "sees" a hallucinatory object but does not respond overtly to it we must develop a more sensitive method of testing for the continued presence of the hallucination. This will be the next step in the use of this particular animal model.

IX. Summary and Conclusions

An attempt has been made, using the Lyon and Robbins (1975) theory of central stimulant drug action, to assess the value of this type of drug effect as a model for psychotic disturbances.

Four general experimental procedures were described: the effect of single acute doses of *d*-amphetamine upon escape–avoidance behavior in rats; the effect of low doses of methylphenidate upon problem-solving in monkeys; the effect of chronic intake of amphetamine in the drinking water by rats; the effect of chronic amphetamine intoxication by diffusions from subcutaneously implanted capsules of amphetamine base in monkeys.

It was concluded that the two, low-dose, acute methods could have diagnostic value on account of their clear production of response-limiting effects at relatively low dosages. The increased "focusing" of behavior and decreasing tendency to solve problems as the MPD dose increased suggest a questionable benefit from using these drugs in treating hyperactive children.

The chronic drinking of amphetamine solutions in rats demonstrated the loss of behavioral control which may occur in a "free access" situation. The postdrug effects on avoidance extinction also suggested a tendency to return too quickly to the unfavorable behavior that had been present under the drug.

The final model, using amphetamine-base subcutaneous capsules in monkeys, demonstrated the full parallel to human psychosis that can be obtained with certain animal models. It was demonstrated that this technique can produce not only hypervigilance and stereotypy, but also, in a postphase period, genuine hallucinations that were identifiable as sequences of behavior oriented to invisible stimuli. Some possible evidence of tactile hallucinations was also discussed. Repetition of treatment with doubling of dosage level did not always yield any clear hallucinatory effect even in monkeys that had demonstrated this during the original experiments. New methods for testing the presence of hallucinations in the absence of overt reactions are needed both for human and animal testing of this symptom.

It was concluded that the amphetamine intoxication model for schizophrenia is even better than had been originally supposed when slow-diffusion capsules are used and animals are free to move about. This model warrants further investigation and use.

ACKNOWLEDGMENTS

We are grateful for the theoretical inspiration and practical assistance of Gaylord Ellison with the implanted amphetamine capsule technique. The excellent technical assistance of Birgit Bager, Eva Holm, Grethe Jensen, Rigmor Jensen, and Birthe Lehmann was of great value to these projects.

REFERENCES

Angrist, B. M., & Gershon, S. The phenomenology of experimentally induced amphetamine psychosis—preliminary observations. *American Journal of Psychiatry*, 1970, *126*, 95–107.

Angrist, B. M., & Gershon, S. Some recent studies on amphetamine psychosis—unresolved issues. In E. H. Ellinwood *et. al.* (Eds.), *Current concepts on amphetamine abuse*. National Institute of Mental Health, 1972. Rockville, Maryland. Pp. 193–204.

Angrist, B. M., Sathananthan, G., Wilk, S., & Gershon, S. Amphetamine psychosis: Behavioral and biochemical aspects. *Journal of Psychiatric. Research*, 1974, *11*, 13–23.

Angrist, B. M., Shopsin, B., & Gershon, S. Comparative psychotomimetic effects of stereoisomers of amphetamine. *Nature*, 1971, *234*, 152–153.

Angrist, B. M., Thompson, H., Shopsin, B., & Gershon, S. Clinical studies with dopamine-receptor stimulants. *Psychopharmacologia*, 1975, *44*, 273–280.

Arnold, L. E., Krebs, G., & Knopp, W. Amphetamine treatment of paranoid obsessions. Case report and biochemical implications. *Pharmakopsychiatrie Neuro-Psychopharmakologie* (Stuttgart), 1974, *35*, 322–327.

Banerjee, U. Programmed self-administration of potentially addictive drugs in young rats and its effects on learning. *Psychopharmacologia,* 1974, *38,* 111–124.

Beaton, J. M., & Bradley, R. J. The behavioral effects of some hallucinogenic derivatives of amphetamine. *British Journal of Psychiatry,* 1972, *111,* 701–707.

Beckmann, H., & Heinemann, H. D-Amphetamin beim manischen Syndrom. *Arzneimittel-Forschung,* 1976, *26,* 1185–1186.

Bell, D. S. Comparison of amphetamine psychosis and schizophrenia. *British Journal of Psychiatry,* 1965, *111,* 701–707.

Bell, D. S. The experimental reproduction of amphetamine psychosis. *Archives of General Psychiatry,* 1973, *29,* 35–41.

Bleuler, E. *Dementia praecox.* New York: International Univ. Press, 1950.

Borison, R. L., & Diamond, B. I. A new animal model for schizophrenia: Interactions with adrenergic mechanisms. *Biological Psychiatry,* 1978, *13,* 217–225.

Bræstrup, C. Biochemical differentiation of amphetamine contra methylphenidate and nomifensine in rats. *Journal of Pharmacy and Pharmacology,* 1977, *29,* 463–470.

Bræstrup, C., & Randrup, A. Stereotyped behaviour in rats induced by phenylethylamine, dependence on dopamine and noradrenaline and possible relation to psychoses? In A. D. Mosnaim & M. Wolf (Eds.), *Phenylethylamine,* Dekker, Inc. New York. Pp. 245–261.

Bræstrup, C., & Scheel-Krüger, J. Methylphenidate-like effects of the new antidepressant drug nomifensine (HOE 984). *European Journal of Pharmacology,* 1976, *38,* 305–312.

Carlson, C., & Goodwin, F. K. The stages of mania: A longitudinal analysis of the manic episode. *Archives of General Psychiatry,* 1973, *28,* 221–228.

Connell, P. H. *Amphetamine psychosis* (Maudsley monographs No. 5.). London: Chapman Hall, 1958.

Costall, B., Kelly, D. M., & Naylor, R. J. Nomifensine: A potent dopaminergic agonist of antiparkinson potential. *Psychopharmacologia* (Berl.), 1975, *41,* 153–164.

Davis, J. M. A two factor theory of schizophrenia. *Journal of Psychiatric Research,* 1974, *11,* 25–29.

Davis, J. M., & Janowsky, D. Amphetamine psychosis. *Life Sciences,* 1973, *13,* 25–26.

Davison, K. Drug-induced psychoses and their relationship to schizophrenia. *Schizophrenia Today,* 1977, *3,* 105–133.

Eison, M. S., Wilson, W. J., & Ellison, G. A refillable system for continuous amphetamine administration: Effects upon social behavior in rat colonies. *Communications in Psychopharmacology,* 1978, *2,* 151–157.

Ellinwood, E. H. "Accidental conditioning" with chronic methamphetamine intoxication: Implication for a theory of drug habituation. *Psychopharmacologia* (Berl.), 1971, *21,* 131–138. (a)

Ellinwood, E. H. Comparative methamphetamine intoxication in experimental animals. *Pharmakopsychiatrie Neuro-Psychopharmakologie* (Stuttgart), 1971, *4,* 351–361. (b)

Ellinwood, E. H. Amphetamine psychosis: Individuals, settings and sequences. In E. H. Ellinwood & S. Cohen (Eds.), *Current concepts in amphetamine abuse.* Rockville, Maryland: DHEW Publication No. (HSM) 72-9085, 1972. Pp. 143–158.

Ellinwood, E. H., & Duarte Escalante, O. D. Chronic amphetamine effect on the olfactory forebrain. *Biological Psychiatry,* 1970, *2,* 189–203.

Ellinwood, E. H., & Kilbey, M. M. Amphetamine stereotypy: The influence of environmental factors and prepotent behavioral patterns on its topography and development. *Biological Psychiatry,* 1975, *10,* 3–16.

Ellinwood, E. H., & Kilbey, M. M. Chronic stimulant intoxication models of psychosis. In I. Hanin & E. Usdin (Eds.), *Animal models in psychiatry and neurology.* 1977. Pp. 61–74.

Ellinwood, E. H., Sudilovsky, A., & Nelson, L. M. Evolving behavior in the clinical and experimental amphetamine (model) psychosis. *American Journal of Psychiatry,* 1973, *130,* 1088–1093.

Ellison, G. D. Animal models of psychopathology. The low-norepinephrine and low-serotonin rat. *American Psychologist,* 1978, *32,* 1036–1045.

Ellison, G., Eison, M. S., & Huberman, H. S. Stages of constant amphetamine intoxication: Delayed appearance of paranoid-like behaviors in rat colonies. *Psychopharmacology,* 1978, *56,* 293–299.

Estrada, U. Self-injection of anorectics in Rhesus monkeys. In S. Garattini & R. Samanin (Eds.), *Central mechanisms of anorectic drugs.* New York: Raven Press, 1978.Pp. 357–364.

Fischman, M. W., & Schuster, C. R. Tolerance development to chronic methamphetamine intoxication in the rhesus monkey. *Pharmacology, Biochemistry and Behavior,* 1974, *2,* 503–508.

Fog, R., Randrup, A., & Pakkenberg, H. Amines in the corpus striatum associated with the effects of both amphetamine and antipsychotic drugs. Amsterdam: Excerpta Medica, International Congress Series No. 150, 1967. Pp. 2580–2582.

Gambill, J., & Kornetsky, C. Effects of chronic d-amphetamine on social behavior of the rat: Implications for an animal model of paranoid schizophrenia. *Psychopharmacology,* 1976, *50,* 215–223.

Gessa, G. L., & Tagliamonte, A. Effect of methadone and dextromoramide on dopamine metabolism: Comparison with haloperidol and amphetamine. *Neuropharmacology* 1975, *14,* 913–920.

Gould, W. M., & Gragg, T. M. Delusions of parasitosis: An approach to the problem. *Archives of Dermatology,* 1976, *112,* 1745–1748.

Griffith, J. D., Cavanaugh, J. H., Held, J., & Oates, J. Experimental psychosis induced by the administration of d-amphetamine. In E. Costa & S. Garattini (Eds.), *Amphetamines and related compounds* New York: Raven Press, 1970 Pp. 897–904.

Griffith, J. D., Fann, W. E., & Oates, J. A. The amphetamine psychosis: Experimental manifestations. In E. H. Ellinwood & S. Cohen (Eds.), *Current concepts on amphetamine abuse,* 1972. Pp. 185–191. DHEW Publication No. (HSM) 72–9085, Rockville, Md.

Grilly, D. M. Rate-dependent effects of amphetamine resulting from behavioral competition. *Biobehavioral Reviews,* 1977, *1,* 87–93.

Hitzemann, R. J., Loh, H. H., Craves, F. B., & Domino, E. F. The use of *d*-amphetamine pellet implantation as a model for *d*-amphetamine tolerance in the mouse. *Psychopharmacologia* (Berl.), 1973, *30,* 227–240.

Huberman, H. S., Eison, M. S., Bryan, K. S., & Ellison, G. A slow-release silicone pellet for chronic amphetamine administration. *European Journal of Pharmacology,* 1977, *45,* 237–242.

Janowsky, D. S., & Davis, J. M. Dopamine, psychomotor stimulants, and schizophrenia: Effects of methylphenidate and the stereoisomers of amphetamine in schizophrenics. In E. Usdin (Ed.), *Neuropsychopharmacology of monoamines and their regulatory enzymes.* New York: Raven Press, 1974. Pp. 317–323.

Janowsky, D. S., Davis, J. M., & El-Yousef, M. K. Effects of intravenous d-amphetamine, l-amphetamine and methylphenidate in schizophrenics. *Psychopharmacology Bulletin,* 1974, *10,* 15–24.

Johanson, C. E., Balster, R. L., & Bonese, K. Self-administration of psychomotor stimulant drugs: The effects of unlimited access. *Pharmacology, Biochemistry and Behavior,* 1976, *4,* 45–51.

Kalant, O. J. *The amphetamines: Toxicity and addiction.* Toronto: Univ. of Toronto Press, 1966.

Keehn, J. D. Licking rates of albino rats. *Science,* 1960, *132,* 739–741.

Keehn, J. D., & Nobrega, J. Stereotyped behaviors during acquisition and extinction in rats. *The Psychological Record,* 1978, *28,* 245–251.

Kelleher, R. T., & Morse, W. H. Determinants of the specificity of behavioral effects of drugs. *Reviews of Physiology, Biochemistry and Experimental Pharmacology,* 1968, *60,* 1–56.

Kinsbourne, M., Swanson, J., & Kurland, L. Stimulant effects on the hyperactive child paired-associate learning: Time x dose response analysis. In American Psychological Association. 86th annual convention, Toronto, Canada, 1978. Pp. 99.

Kupietz, S. S., & Balka, E. B. Alterations in the vigilance performance of children receiving amitriptyline and methylphenidate pharmacotherapy. *Psychopharmacology,* 1976, *50,* 29–33.

Loh, H. H. Studies of acute and chronic amphetamine actions. *Psychopharmacology Bulletin,* 1977, *13,* 62–63.

Lyon, M. The effect of no-shock or continuous shock upon avoidance behavior in rats under *d*-amphetamine. *Activitas nervosa superior* 1971, *13,* 78–81.

Lyon, M. Central stimulant drugs and the nature of reinforcement. In P.-O. Sjödén, S. Bates, & W. S. Dockens, III (Eds.), *Trends in behavior therapy.* New York: Academic Press, 1979.

Lyon, M., & Randrup, A. The dose–response effect of amphetamine upon avoidance behavior in the rat, seen as a function of increasing stereotypy. *Psychopharmacologia,* 1972, *23,* 334–347.

Lyon, M., & Robbins, T. W. The action of central nervous system stimulant drugs: A general theory concerning amphetamine effects. In W. Essman & L. Valzelli (Eds.), *Current developments in psychopharmacology* (Vol. 2.) New York: Spectrum Press, 1975. Pp. 89-163.

McMillan, D. E., & Morse, W. H. Schedules using noxious stimuli: II. Low intensity electric shock as a discriminative stimulus. *Journal of the Experimental Analysis of Behavior,* 1967, *10,* 109-118.

Magour, S., Coper, H., & Fähndrich, Ch. The effects of chronic treatment with *d*-amphetamine on food intake, body weight, locomotor activity and subcellular distribution of the drug in rat brain. *Psychopharmacologia* (Berl.), 1974, *34,* 45-54.

Magour, S., Coper, H., & Fähndrich, Ch. The effect of chronic self-administration of d-amphetamine on food intake, locomotor activity, and C^{14}-leucine incorporation into cerebral cortex protein. *Psychopharmacologia,* 1976, *45,* 267-270.

Matthysse, S. (1977a). Animal models of human cognitive processes. In I. Hanin & E. Usdin (Eds.), *Animal models in psychiatry and neurology* Oxford-New York: Pergamon, 1977. Pp. 75-82. (a)

Matthysse, S. Central catecholamine metabolism in psychosis. In H. M. van Praag & J. Bruinvels (Eds.), *Neurotransmission and disturbed behavior,* Utrecht: Bohn, Scheltema & Holema, 1977. Pp. 60-72. (b)

Meltzer, H. Y., & Stahl, S. M. The dopamine hypothesis of schizophrenia: A review. *Schizophrenia Bulletin,* 1976, *2,* 19-76.

Mohs, R. C., Tinklenberg, J. R., Roth, W. T., & Kopell, B. S. Methamphetamine and diphenhydramine effects on the rate of cognitive processing. *Psychopharmacology,* 1978, *59,* 13-19.

Norton, S. The effects of psychoactive drugs on cat behavior. In E. Tobach (Ed.), *Experimental approaches to the study of emotional behavior.* New York: New York Academy of Science, 1969, Pp. 915-927.

Norton, S. Amphetamine as a model for hyperactivity in the rat. *Physiology and Behavior,* 1973, *11,* 181-186.

Nyman, A. K. Influence of amphetamine treatment on subjective symptoms and working ability in schizophrenic patients. *IRCS Medical Science; Clinical Pharmacology and Therapeutics; Psychiatry and Clinical Psychology, 3,* 510.

Palkes, H., Stewart, M., & Kahana, B. Porteus maze performance of hyperactive boys after training in self-directed verbal commands. *Child Development,* 1968, *39,* 817-826.

Randrup, A., & Munkvad, I. Stereotyped activities produced by amphetamine in several animal species and man. *Psychopharmacologia,* 1967, *11,* 300-310.

Randrup, A., & Munkvad, I. Behavioural stereotypies induced by pharmacological agents. *Pharmakosychiatrie Neuro-Psychopharmakologie* (Stuttgart), 1968, *1,* 18-26.

Riding, J., & Munro, A. Pimozide in the treatment of monosymtomatic hypochondriacal psychosis. *Lancet,* 1975, *1,* 400.

Risner, M. E., & Jones, B. E. Characteristics of unlimited access to self-administered stimulant infusions in dogs *Biological Psychiatry,* 1976, *11,* 625-634.

Robbins, T. Relationship between reward-enhancing and stereotypical effects of psychomotor stimulant drugs. *Nature* (Lond.), 1976, *264,* 57-59.

Robbins, T., & Sahakian, B. J. Animal models of mania. In R. Belmaker & H. Van Praag (Eds.), *Mania: An evolving concept.* New York: Spectrum, 1979.

Ross, S. B. Antagonism by methylphenidate of the stereotyped behaviour produced by (+)-amphetamine in reserpinized rats. *Journal of Pharmacy and Pharmacology,* 1978, *30,* 253-254.

Rylander, G. Addiction to preludin intravenously injected. In J. J. Lopez-Ibor (Ed.), *Proceedings, Fourth World Congress of Psychiatry, Madrid.* Int. Congr. Ser. 150 (3). Amsterdam: Excerpta Medica, 1966.

Rylander, G. Psychoses and the punding and choreiform syndromes in addiction to central stimulant drugs. *Folia psychiatrica, neurologica et neurochirurgica neerlandica,* 1972, *75,* 203-212.

Sahakian, B. J., & Koob, G. F. The relationship between pipradrol-induced responding for electrical brainstimulation, stereotyped behaviour and locomotor activity. *Neuropharmacology,* 1978, *17,* 363-366.

Sahakian, B. J., & Robbins, T. W. Are the effects of psychomotor stimulant drugs on hyperactive children really paradoxical? *Medical Hypotheses,* 1977, *3,* No. 4

Scheel-Krüger, J. Comparative studies of various amphetamine analogues demonstrating different interaction with the metabolism of the catecholamines in the brain. *European Journal of Pharmacology,* 1971, *14,* 47–59.

Schiørring, E. Amphetamine induced selective stimulation of certain behaviour items with concurrent inhibition of others in an open-field test with rats. *Behaviour,* 1971, *34,* 1–17.

Schiørring, E. Changes in individual and social behavior induced by amphetamine and related compounds in monkeys and man. In E. H. Ellinwood & M. M. Kilbey (Eds.), *Cocaine and other stimulants.* New York: Plenum, 1977. Pp. 481–522.

Seiden, L. S., MacPhail, R. C., & Oglesby, M. V. Catecholamines and drug-behavior interactions. *Federation Proceedings,* 1975, *34,* 1823–1829.

Sheer, D. E. Focused arousal and 40-Hz EEG. In R. M. Knights & D. J. Bakker (Eds.), *The neuropsychology of learning disorders.* London: Univ. Park Press, 1976. Pp. 71–87.

Siegel, R. K., Brewster, J. M., & Jarvik, M. E. An observational study of hallucinogen-induced behavior in unrestrained Macaca Mulatta. *Psychopharmacology,* 1974, *40,* 211–223.

Staehelin, J. E. Pervitin-Psychose. *Zeitschrift für gesamte Neurologie und Psychiatrie,* 1941, *173,* 598–620.

Snyder, S. H. Amphetamine psychosis: A "model" schizophrenia mediated by catecholamines. *American Journal of Psychiatry,* 1973, *130,* 61–67.

Snyder, S. H. & Banerjee, S. P. (1973). Amines in schizophrenia. In E. Usdin & S. H. Snyder (Eds.), *Frontiers in catecholamine research,* New York: Pergamon, 1973. Pp. 1133–1138.

Stevens, J. R. Anatomy of schizophrenia. *Archives of General Psychiatry,* 1973, *29,* 177–189.

Stretch, R., & Gerber, G. J. Drug-induced reinstatement of amphetamine self-administration behavior in monkeys. *Canadian Journal of Psychology,* 1973, *27,* 168–177.

Struhsaker, T. T. Auditory communication among vervet monkeys (Cercopithecus aethiops). In S. A. Altman (Ed.), *Social communication among primates* Chicago: Univ. of Chicago Press, 1966. Pp. 281–284.

Swanson, J., & Kinsbourne, M. Stimulant-related state-dependent learning in hyperactive children. *Science,* 1976, *192,* 1354–1356.

Teitelbaum, P., & Derks, P. The effect of amphetamine on forced drinking in the rat. *Journal of Comparative and Physiological Psychology,* 1958, *51,* 801–810.

Van Kammen, D. P., Bunney, W. E., Docherty, J. P., Jimerson, D. C., Post, R. M., Siris, S., Ebert, M., & Gillin, J. C. Amphetamine-induced catecholamine activation in schizophrenia and depression: Behavioral and physiological effects. In E. Costa & G. L. Gessa (Eds.), *Advances in biochemical psychopharmacology,* New York: Raven Press, 1977. Pp. 655–659.

Van Praag, H. M. The significance of dopamine for the mode of action of neuroleptics and the pathogenesis of schizophrenia. In A. R. Cools *et al.* (Eds.), *Psychobiology of the striatum.* Amsterdam: North Holland, 1977.

Van Rossum, J. The significance of dopamine receptor blockade for the action of neuroleptic drugs. In H. Brill (Ed.), *Neuropsychopharmacology* (Vol. 5). Int. Congr. Ser. 129. Amsterdam: Excerpta Medica, 1967. Pp. 321–323.

Verhave, T. The effect of methamphetamine on operant level and avoidance behavior. *Journal of the Experimental Analysis of Behavior,* 1958, *1,* 207–219.

Watson, R., Hartman, E., & Schildkraut, J. Amphetamine withdrawal, affective state, sleep patterns and MPHPG excretion. *American Journal of Psychiatry,* 1972, *129,* 263–269.

Weiss, J. M., Glazer, H. I., & Pohorecky, L. A. Coping behavior and neurochemical changes. An alternative explanation for the original "learned helplessness" experiments. In G. Serban & A. Kling (Eds.), *Animal models in human psychobiology.* New York: Plenum, 1976. Pp. 141–173.

Wulbert, M., & Dries, R. The relative efficacy of methylphenidate (ritalin) and behavior-modification techniques in the treatment of a hyperactive child. *Journal of Applied Behavior Analysis,* 1977, *10,* 21–31.

Yokel, R. A., & Pickens, R. Self-administration of optical isomers of amphetamine and methylamphetamine by rats. *Journal of Pharmacology and Experimental Therapeutics,* 1973, *187,* 27–33.

SHEPARD SIEGEL

The Role of Conditioning in Drug Tolerance and Addiction[1]

6

I. What Is Addiction?

There are a variety of drugs that are categorized as "addictive." That is, if these substances are administered for some period of time, termination of administration is frequently followed by withdrawal symptoms and craving for the substance. This craving and withdrawal discomfort is often sufficiently intense so that the individual relapses to drug use to ameliorate the withdrawal effects. Such relapse occurs even if the acquisition of the drug entails considerable expense and personal risk. The individual is then said to be dependent upon, or addicted to, the drug.

Most, but not all, drug addictions are characterized as psychopathology (American Psychiatric Association, 1968). Addictions to some drugs are not so classified because their habitual use is sanctioned by social custom (see Inglis, 1975). Examples of such drugs in our own culture are caffeine and nicotine.[2] For

[1]Research summarized in this chapter was supported by Research Grants DA–01200 from the United States National Institute on Drug Abuse, APA–0298 from the National Research Council of Canada, and MT–3577 from the Medical Research Council of Canada.

[2]Although nicotine addiction is specifically excluded from drug-dependence disorders in the most recent (2nd.) edition of the *Diagnostic and Statistical Manual of Mental Disorders* of the American Psychiatric Association (1968), it is likely that "tobacco dependence" will be a recognized diagnostic category in the next edition of this manual (American Psychiatric Association, 1976).

discussions of caffeine and nicotine as drugs of abuse, see Gilbert (1976) and Russell (1976), respectively.

Closely associated with drug addiction is the phenomenon of "tolerance." *Tolerance* refers to the decreasing effect of a drug over the course of repeated administrations (or, similarly, the necessity for increasing the amount of the drug on successive occasions in order to maintain the initial level of drug effect): The analgesic effect of morphine is generally much more pronounced following the first few administrations than it is following subsequent administrations, and the experienced drinker requires more alcohol to become drunk than does the inexperienced drinker. Both are examples of drug tolerance. It has frequently been noted that drug tolerance and drug dependence are highly correlated, and most recent theoretical treatments of addiction have attempted to present a unitary explanation for both tolerance and dependence (see Goldstein, Arnow, & Kalman, 1974, Chap. 9).

This chapter describes a model of drug tolerance and dependence and summarizes the evidence in support of this model. For simplicity, the focus of the chapter is limited to opiate addiction, but the principles discussed may well be relevant to addiction to other categories of drugs.

II. Addiction and Tolerance in Animals

The phenomena of opiate tolerance and addiction may be seen readily in animals. Tolerance is illustrated by the decrease in many of the effects of the drug over the course of repeated administrations. For example, after their first injection of a moderate dose of morphine (e.g., 5 mg/kg), rats are very slow to respond reflexively to nociceptive stimulation, such as heat or electric shock (demonstrating the analgesic effect of morphine), and their body temperature increases (demonstrating the hyperthermic effect of morphine). However, as these rats continue to receive morphine, they respond more rapidly to the nociceptive stimulation and the hyperthermia becomes less pronounced, indicating the development of tolerance to the analgesic and hyperthermic effects of the drug.

Rats with a history of opiate administration, like humans, display signs of withdrawal distress when the pharmacological stimulation is terminated: Body temperature decreases, they lose weight, become hyperactive and aggressive, and exhibit muscle spasms, writhing movements, and other bizzare motor behaviors. As in the case of human withdrawal symptoms, different components of the syndrome persist for various periods of time (from days to months) following termination of drug administration, and these symptoms are promptly relieved by opiate administration (see Gianutsos, Drawbaugh, Hynes, & Lal, 1975).

Rats administered morphine not only display tolerance to many of the effects of the drug, and withdrawal symptoms when drug administration is terminated, but they also appear highly motivated to self administer the drug. They will drink bitter-tasting morphine-adulterated water in preference to plain water (e.g., Thompson & Ostlund, 1965), and they rapidly learn to press a lever to obtain the drug (e.g., Weeks, 1962).

If opiate addiction is considered a form of psychopathology, it is probably the form of psychopathology that is most readily and unambiguously demonstrable in animals. This characteristic of addiction makes the disorder especially appropriate for investigation in the animal laboratory.

The model of opiate tolerance and dependence described in this chapter is based primarily on animal research.

III. Opiate Tolerance: Evidence Implicating Learning

In contrast with most theories of tolerance, which stress the physiological consequences of repeated pharmacological stimulation, the approach to tolerance described here emphasizes the associative characteristics of the usual drug administration prodecure. Such a view follows from the work of a number of researchers, but primarily from Wikler (1953, 1968, 1973), who stressed the importance of pharmacological learning in pharmacological effects.

The results of a number of experiments, from many different laboratories, all suggest that the acquisition of tolerance shares similarities with memory or learning processes: Both tolerance and learning are retained over long periods of time, and both are similarly disrupted by electroconvulsive shock, frontal cortical stimulation, and metabolic inhibtors (and both are facilitated by antagonists of metabolic inhibitors).

A. RETENTION OF TOLERANCE

Evidence suggesting that associative processes may be involved in tolerance is provided by experiments indicating that tolerance dissipates little with the passage of time (see Cochin & Kornetsky, 1964; Kayan & Mitchell, 1972). Indeed, it has been reported that former opiate addicts display profound tolerance to the analgesic effect of morphine for as as long as 8 years after their last experience with the drug (Andrews, 1943). Such persistence of tolerance, in the absence of any experience with the opiate, is not interpretable by many systemic theories of tolerance (e.g., Cochin, 1970). However, this great retention of tolerance would be expected on the basis of a learning analysis of tolerance, since learned responses are very resistant to decrement merely as a result of the passage of time (see Kimble, 1961, p. 281). Indeed, Cochin (1972) suggested that since tolerance occurs with very long intervals between drug administrations, "a reaction analogous to memory [p. 265]" may be important in the phenomenon.

B. METABOLIC INTERVENTION AND TOLERANCE

There is evidence that a variety of suppressors of protein synthesis, such as puromycin and cycloheximide, retard the acquisition of certain learned responses (see review by Nakajima, 1976). These drugs also retard the development of morphine tolerance (see review by Ginsburg & Cox, 1972). Cohen, Keats, Krivoy, and Ungar (1965) suggested that there may be a parallel between learning and tolerance since metabolic inhibitors have similar effects on both processes.

It has been reported that the ability of metabolic inhibitors to retard learning is antagonized by the pituitary peptide, desglycinamide[9]-lysine vasopressin (e.g., Lande, Flexner, & Flexner, 1972). Futhermore, this vasopressin facilitates some types of learning (e.g., Lande, Witter, & DeWied, 1971). Krivoy, Zimmermann, and Lande (1974) demonstrated that desglycinamide[9]-lysine vasopressin facilitated the acquisition of morphine analgesic tolerance, again demonstrating a similarity in the effect of metabolic agents on learning and tolerance.

C. CONSOLIDATION AND TOLERANCE

Learning can be retarded by a variety of cerebrally insulting events presented shortly after the learning experience, such as electroconvulsive shock (ECS) or electrical stimulation of certain brain regions—such as the frontal cortex (see Jarvik, 1970; McGaugh & Herz, 1972). Results from two laboratories, obtained in experiments specifically designed to examine the analogy between tolerance and learning, both reported that ECS retards the development of tolerance to the analgesic effect of morphine (Stolerman, Bunker, Johnson, Jarvik, Krivoy, & Zimmermann, 1976; Kesner, Priano, & DeWitt, 1976). Similarly, Kesner *et al.* (1976) further demonstrated that stimulation of the frontal cortex following each morphine administration disrupts the acquisition of tolerance and they concluded. . . . "The data from both the ECS and discrete brain stimulation experiments provide additional support for a possible parallel between conventional learning and tolerance to drugs [p. 1081]."

IV. *A Pavlovian-Conditioning Model of Tolerance*

A model of tolerance, which is consistent with the previously presented evidence implicating learning in tolerance, emphasizes Pavlovian conditioning principles.

A. THE PAVLOVIAN-CONDITIONING SITUATION

In the course of his Nobel prize-winning research on the digestive activity in dogs, Pavlov noted the phenomenon of "psychic secretion"—gastric secretion in response to environmental signals of food elicited before the food actually stimulates receptors in the stomach (Pavlov, 1910). Pavlov realized that "psychic secretion" was not merely a laboratory curiosity, but rather an important aspect of normal digestive functioning. Gastrointestinal activity is more efficient when food is presented subsequent to cues, which, in the past, have been reliable predictors of food presentation, compared to the situation in which food delivery is unheralded: The dog learns the association between prefeeding cues and food and adaptively evidences digestive responses in anticipation of feeding; such learned responses summating with the reflexively elicited digestive responses.

In about 1902, Pavlov committed himself to the systematic study of the psychic-secretion phenomenon, that is, responses conditional upon the past history of the organism. The general paradigm used by Pavlov to study these conditional responses (CRs) involves the use of two cues. The first, the conditional stimulus (CS), is said to be "neutral"; it elicits little relevant activity prior to its pairing with the second stimulus, the unconditional stimulus (UCS). As the name implies, the UCS is selected because it elicits relevant activities from the outset—unconditionally—prior to any pairings. These UCS-elicited responses are called unconditional responses (UCRs). In Pavlov's original observations, the CS consisted of preparations for feeding and the UCS consisted of the ingested food. In Pavlov's later, and better known, conditioning work, the CS was some conveniently manipulated exteroceptive stimulus (bell, light, etc.), and the UCS was food, which elicited a conveniently measured salivary response (Pavlov, 1927).

B. DRUG ADMINISTRATION AS A CONDITIONING PROCEDURE

Pavlov was the first to suggest that the usual drug administration procedure satisfied the requirements of the conditioning paradigm (Pavlov, 1927, pp. 35–37). The CS consists of those procedures, rituals, or other environmental cues that reliably precede the systemic stimulation produced by the drug, with the actual central effects of the drug constituting the UCS. The development of the association between the environmental CS and pharmacological UCS may be revealed if the subject, following a history of drug administration, is presented with the usual drug administration procedure not followed by the usual pharmacological stimulation; rather, for such a CR test session, a placebo is administered.

C. THE COMPENSATORY CONDITIONAL
PHARMACOLOGICAL RESPONSE

Following Pavlov's demonstration that responses to drugs can be subject to conditioning, there has been a considerable amount of research concerning such pharmacological learning (see review by Siegel, 1977a). Although many forms of drug CRs can be conceptualized, and have been reported, an especially common type of CR is opposite in direction to many of the effects of the pharmacological UCS. Table 6.1 summarizes a number of investigations that have reported such CRs opposite in direction to the unconditional effect of the drug.

D. THE DRUG-COMPENSATORY CONDITIONAL RESPONSE AND TOLERANCE

Since organisms frequently evidence CRs opposite to the effects of the drug when confronted by the usual administration cues without the usual pharmacological stimulation (see Table 6.1), it would be expected that when the drug *is* presented in conjunction with the usual predrug cues the effect of the drug would be attenuated by these anticipatory compensatory responses. As the association between the drug administration procedure and the systemic effect of the drug is strengthened by repeated pairings, the effect of the drug would be expected to become increasingly cancelled as the compensatory CR increases in magnitude.

Table 6.1

Compensatory Conditional Pharmacological Responses

Unconditional stimulus	Unconditional response	Conditional response	Reference
epinephrine	tachycardia	bradycardia	Russek & Piña (1962); Subkov & Zilov (1937)
epinephrine	↓ gastric secretion	↑ gastric secretion	Guha *et al.* (1974)
epinephrine	hyperglycemia	hypoglycemia	Russek & Piña (1962)
glucose	hyperglycemia	hypoglycemia	Mityushov (1954); Deutsch (1974); LeMagnen (1975)
insulin	hypoglycemia	hyperglycemia	Siegel (1972a, 1975a)
nicotine	hyperglycemia	hypoglycemia	Lundberg & Thyselius-Lundberg (1931)
atropine	antisialosis	hypersalivation	Korol, Sletter, & Brown (1966); Lang, Brown, Gershon, & Korol (1966); Lang, Rush, & Pearson (1969); Mulinos & Lieb (1929); Wikler (1948)
chlorpromazine	↓ activity	↑ activity	Pihl & Altman (1971)
amphetamine	↑ O_2 consumption	↓ O_2 consumption	Obál (1966)
dinitrophenol	↑ O_2 consumption, hyperthermia	↓ O_2 consumption, hypothermia	Obál (1966)
histamine	hypothermia	hyperthermia	Obál, Vicasay, & Madarász (1965)
methyl dopa	↓ blood pressure	↑ blood pressure	Korol & McLaughlin (1976)
lithium chloride	↓ drinking	↑ drinking	Domjan & Gillan (1977)
nalorphine	tachycardia	bradycardia	Goldberg & Schuster (1967, 1970)
morphine	bradycardia	tachycardia	Rush, Pearson, & Lang (1970)
morphine	hyperthermia	hypothermia	Siegel (1979)
morphine	analgesia	hyperalgesia	Siegel (1975b)

Such a decreased effect of a drug, as a function of successive experiences with the drug, defines tolerance.

This conditioning model of tolerance is illustrated in Figure 6.1. The drug UCR is represented as an increase from baseline level of an arbitrary response (+ change), and the drug-compensatory CR is represented as a decrease from baseline level (− change). The net effect of the drug, according to the conditioning analysis, depends on the results of the interaction between these two opposing responses.

Figure 6.1A illustrates the time-effect curve of a drug on one of the first occasions that it is administered. The drug has not yet become associated with predrug environmental cues, thus the drug effect depicted in Figure 6.1A is not yet modulated by any anticipatory responding. The effect of the drug increases and decays following administration in accordance with the pharmacokinetics of the drug. However, as the drug is administered with increasing frequency in the context of the same environmental cues, the drug administration situation is followed not only by the pharmacological UCR, but also by the drug-compensatory CR. This is illustrated in Figure 6.1B; the net drug effect is smaller than it was initially because the drug UCR is somewhat attenuated by the drug

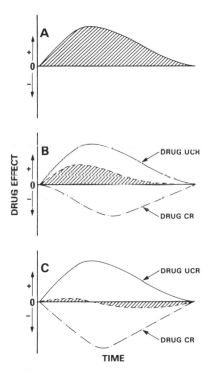

Figure 6.1. *Time course of the net drug effect (hatched area) resulting from the interaction between the pharmacological UCR and drug-compensatory CR during successive stages in tolerance development.*

CR. Figure 6.1C illustrates the interaction between the drug UCR and the drug-preparatory CR in the subject who has received the drug many times. As shown in Figure 6.1, the CR is large, and the net result of the interaction between this CR and the direct drug effect is a very small net drug effect—the subject is highly tolerant to the drug. The net drug effect depicted in Figure 6.1C is biphasic. That is, although there is a small net drug effect in the expected direction shortly after drug administration, this is followed by a net drug effect *opposite* in direction to the pharmacological UCR. Such paradoxical responding to a drug is a frequent finding in subjects with an extensive history of opiate administration. For example, animals given a constant dose of morphine on many occasions become tolerant to the analgesic effect of the drug, and, if morphine administration is continued, actually become hyperalgesic in response to further opiate administrations (e.g., Kayan, Woods, & Mitchell, 1971; Mulé, Clements, Layson, & Haertzen, 1968). A similar finding in humans has been reported by Andrews (1943). As illustrated in Figure 6.1C, such paradoxical responding to a drug results from an asynchrony between the UCR elicited by the drug and the CR elicited by drug-associated cues.

E. COMPARISON WITH NONASSOCIATIVE INTERPRETATIONS OF TOLERANCE

The conditioning interpretation of tolerance may be contrasted with formulations of the phenomenon that do not acknowledge a role for associative processes. These alternative theories usually postulate physiological changes, induced by early drug administrations, which functionally reduce the effect of later drug administrations. Such systemic alterations may involve opiate receptors in the brain (e.g., Synder & Matthysse, 1975), or peripheral changes which hinder the drug from gaining access to central receptors (e.g., Cochin, 1971; Mulé & Woods, 1969). These physiological theories have been extensively reviewed elsewhere (see Hug, 1972; Kuschinsky, 1977).

Some nonassociative theories of tolerance, like the conditioning theory, stress the role of counteradjustments to the pharmacological stimulation. As the drug is repeatedly administered, these "autonomic hyperreactions" (Himmelsbach, 1943) or "opponent processes" (Solomon & Corbit, 1974) elicited by the drug become stronger as they are repeatedly exercised, acting to increasingly cancel the effect of the drug. In these models, the growth of such counteradjustment has typically not been attributed to learning, but, with some modifications, these counteradjustment models and the conditioning model may become compatible (Siegel, 1978b; Solomon, 1977).

V. *Evidence for the Conditioning Model of Tolerance*

Results of a number of recent experiments appear inexplicable by traditional interpretations of tolerance, which stress only the effects of repeated pharmacological stimulation and ignore the importance of environmental cues present at the time of such stimulation. However, these findings, summarized in this section, are to be expected on the basis of the conditioning account of tolerance.

A. PREDRUG CUES AND TOLERANCE

According to the conditioning model of tolerance, tolerance results because environmental cues regularly paired with the drug come to elicit a compensatory CR that attenuates the unconditional effect of the narcotic. Thus, on the basis of this model, environmental cues consistently predicting the systemic effect of the drug should be crucial to the development of tolerance because they enable the subject to make timely compensatory CRs in anticipation of the pharmacological UCR.

The results of many experiments do demonstrate the important role of predrug cues in tolerance. That is, tolerance does *not* result simply from the organisms experiencing repeated pharmacological stimulation. Rather it *does* result from repeated administration of the drug in the context of environmental cues that reliably signal the impending pharamacological stimulation. All these experiments incorporated two groups, both receiving morphine a sufficient number of times for tolerance to develop during the initial "tolerance development" phase of the experiment. The effects of the drug were then evaluated during a subsequent "tolerance test" phase. For one of the two groups, this tolerance test was conducted following the same cues that signaled the drug during the tolerance development phase (same tested). For the other group, the tolerance test was conducted following different cues than those that signaled the drug during the tolerance development phase (different tested). Although there were many procedural differences between the experiments, the designs may be conveniently categorized into three classes. These designs are summarized in Figure 6.2, and will be discussed separately.

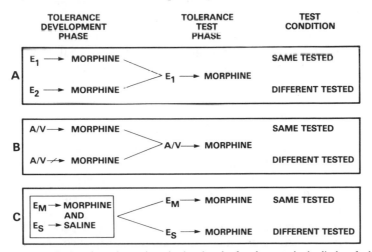

Figure 6.2. *Design of experiments investigating the role of predrug cues in the display of tolerance.*

1. The Environmental Specificity Design

Figure 6.2A illustrates the most frequently used design of experiments demonstrating the importance of drug-associated cues in tolerance. During the tolerance development phase of the experiment, one group of rats receives a number of morphine injections in one environment, designated as E_1 in Figure 6.2A (e.g., E_1 might be a room with distinctive visual and olfactory cues). A second group receives their injections in an alternative environment, E_2 (e.g., the animals' colony room). During the tolerance test phase of the experiment, the effect of the drug is assessed for all animals following administration in E_1. Thus, same-tested subjects receive their tolerance test following the same environmental cues that signaled the drug during tolerance development, and different-tested subjects receive their tolerance test following cues that have not, in the past, signaled the drug. It should be emphasized that, prior to the tolerance test, both groups receive the same dose of morphine, equally as often, and at the same intervals. On the basis of any of the nonassociative theories of tolerance, it would be expected that both groups should display equivalent levels of tolerance on the tolerance test. However, on the basis of the conditioning model of tolerance, it would be expected that same-tested subjects should be more tolerant than different-tested subjects. This prediction of the conditioning model of tolerance has been confirmed in a number of experiments by Mitchell and his colleagues (e.g., Adams, Yeh, Woods, & Mitchell, 1969; Kayan, Woods, & Mitchell, 1969; for a complete review, see Siegel, 1978a). These results concerning the situation-specificity of tolerance have been replicated and extended (Siegel, 1975b), and it has been further demonstrated (Siegel, 1976) that even if rats are demonstrably morphine tolerant in one environment (previously associated with the drug), they evidence a relatively nontolerant response when the drug is administered in a different environment (not previously associated with the drug).

2. Signaled versus Unsignaled Drugs and Tolerance

Figure 6.2B illustrates a second experimental design that has been used to assess the role of drug-predictive cues in tolerance. During the tolerance development phase of the experiment, two groups of rats have equivalent experience with an arbitrary audiovisual cue and with morphine. The cue and drug are always paired for one group (A/V → morphine). For the second group the cue and morphine are never paired during tolerance development (A/V ⇸ morphine). In the tolerance test phase, subjects in both groups are administered the drug in conjunction with the cue, and the effect of the drug is assessed. Thus, again, one group is tested for the effects of morphine following the same environmental stimuli which, in the past, signaled the drug (same tested), and a second group is tested following a cue not previously experienced in conjunction with the drug (different-tested). Prior to this test, the groups do not differ in pharmacological history.

The results of an experiment designed in the manner depicted in Figure 6.2B demonstrated that although same-tested subjects displayed tolerance to the analgesic effect of morphine, different-tested subjects displayed no evidence of tolerance on the tolerance test (Siegel, Hinson, & Krank, 1978). Despite their extensive pretest experience with morphine, different-tested rats responded on the tolerance test with the completely nontolerant response that would be expected in animals receiving the drug for the very first time.

3.   Discriminative Control of Tolerance

Figure 6.2C illustrates another experimental design demonstrating the importance of predrug cues in tolerance. During tolerance development, all animals receive a number of injections of morphine and a number of injections of an inert substance, physiological saline. Different environmental cues are associated with each substance, such that all morphine injections take place in environmental E_M, and all saline injections take place in environment E_S. Thus, on some days the rat is injected with the opiate in one environment, and on other days it is injected with saline in the alternative environment. Finally, the effect of morphine is tested for all subjects, with half the rats receiving this tolerance test in the morphine-associated environment, E_M (same tested), and half the rats receiving this morphine tolerance test in the saline-associated environment, E_S (different tested).

The results of an experiment which used this discrimination design (Siegel, 1978b) demonstrated that same-tested rats, but not different-tested rats, displayed tolerance to morphine. Again, despite their extensive pretest experience with morphine, different-tested rats responded to the drug in the context of nondrug cues as did animals that had never received morphine before. Such results, although predicted by the conditioning model of tolerance, are not expected on the basis of alternative formulations.

B.   RETARDATION OF TOLERANCE

There are several manipulations that are effective in retarding the acquisition of CRs in a wide variety of Pavlovian-conditioning preparations. If morphine tolerance is a manifestation of a conditioning process, it would be expected that such manipulations would similarly retard the acquisition of morphine tolerance. Results of experiments which have investigated two such acquisition-retardation procedures, CS habituation and partial reinforcement, demonstrated that these procedures do, indeed, retard the development of tolerance to morphine.

1.   CS Habituation and Tolerance

Animals and humans are generally slower to display CRs to familiar CSs than to novel CSs. That is, simply be presenting the subject with the CS alone a number of times, prior to the pairing of that CS with a UCS, the acquisition of CRs is retarded (compared to the situation in which the subject has little or no experience with the CS prior to acquisition). This phenomenon, sometimes termed "latent inhibition" (Lubow & Moore, 1959), has been extensively reviewed elsewhere (Cantor, 1969; Lubow, 1973; Siegel, 1972b; Weiss & Brown, 1974). According to the conditioning model of tolerance, which attributes tolerance to an association between the predrug CS and the pharmacological UCS, the development of tolerance should be affected by the relative novelty of the predrug cues. Thus, according to this model, animals exposed to the administration procedure prior to the pairing of this procedure with morphine should be slower to become tolerant to the drug than animals with minimal prior experience with these environmental cues, despite the fact that both groups suffer the systemic effects of the same dose of morphine, given the same number of times, at the same intervals. In other words, a series of morphine injections should induce less tolerance if these injections are preceded by a series of placebo injections than if the morphine injections do not follow such predrug experience with the drug administration procedure. This prediction of the conditioning model of tolerance has been confirmed in an experiment by Siegel (1977b, Experiment 3).

The finding that morphine tolerance is retarded by an initial series of placebo administrations supports a unique prediction of the conditioning interpretation of tolerance. Like the previously described findings concerning the role of predrug cues in tolerance, it is not readily interpretable by theories of tolerance that do not incorporate any learning mechanism.

2. Partial Reinforcement of Tolerance

Partial reinforcement refers to the procedure of pairing only a fraction of the presentations of the CS with the UCS. It may be contrasted with the *continuous-reinforcement* procedure, in which every presentation of the CS is paired with the UCS. In a wide variety of Pavlovian-conditioning situations, it has been reported that CR acquisition is slower with a partial reinforcement procedure than with a continuous reinforcement procedure (see Beecroft, 1966, pp. 126–129).

The implication of this partial reinforcement literature for the conditioning theory of tolerance is clear. A group in which only a portion of the presentations of the drug administration cues are actually followed by morphine should be slower to develop tolerance than a group that is never exposed to the drug administration cues without actually receiving the drug.

Two recent experiments were designed to investigate the effects of partial reinforcement on the acquistion of tolerance to the analgesic (Siegel, 1977b, Experiment 4) and hyperthermic (Siegel, 1978b, Experiment 3) effects of morphine in rats. In both experiments, the animals were administered morphine a sufficient number of times for tolerance to be evidenced, with the interval between morphine administrations irregularly varied. In each experiment, one group of rats was continuously reinforced; all presentations of the drug administration procedure were accompanied by the drug, with these subjects being left undisturbed during the intervals between morphine injections. A second group in each experiment was partially reinforced. Subjects in the partially reinforced groups received the drug at the same times as subjects in the continuously rein-forced groups, but they were also given placebo sessions between drug sessions. Thus, for partially reinforced subjects, only a portion of the presentations of predrug cues were actually followed by the drug.

The results of the two experiments were clear (Siegel, 1977b, Experiment 4; Siegel, 1978b, Experiment 3). The partially and continuously reinforced groups differed markedly in the speed of acquisition of tolerance, despite the fact that they did not differ with respect to pharmacological history. The partial reinforce-ment procedure retarded the acquisition of morphine tolerance, just as it retards acquisition in more traditional conditioning situations. The experiments demonstrate clearly that the development of tolerance can be affected by the manipulation of the reliability of environmental cues as signals for morphine. The findings, although not explicable by any interpretation of tolerance which ignores these cues, are predictable on the basis of the conditioning model of tolerance.

C. EXTINCTION OF TOLERANCE

If a CR has been acquired, presenting the CS without the UCS causes a diminution in the CR. This phenomenom is termed *extinction*. If morphine tolerance results because the predrug CS elicits a drug-compensatory CR, tolerance should be subject to extinction. In other words, it would be expected that placebo sessions would attenuate established tolerance.

The results of a number of experiments have, in fact, demonstrated that morphine tolerance in rats can be extinguished (Siegel, 1975b, Experiment 3; Siegel, 1977b, Experiments 1 and 2; Siegel, 1978b, Experiment 2). Although there were numerous procedural differences between the experiments, all incor-porated two groups, both of which received a series of morphine injections suffi-cient to induce pronounced tolerance. These sessions constituted the tolerance development phase of the experiment. Some days later, all animals received at least one further injection of morphine. This final drug injection constituted the tolerance-test phase of the experiment. The two groups differed only with respect to their treatment during the interval between the tolerance acquisition phase and the tolerance-test phase. One group received daily placebo sessions, that is they were treated in the same manner as on morphine sessions, except that physiological saline rather than the drug was injected. The response of this extinction group to the drug during the tolerance test indicated the effects of repeated presentations of the morphine administration procedure, in the absence of the drug, on tolerance acquired during the tolerance-acquisition phase. Rats in the second group were simply left undisturbed in their home cages during the period between tolerance acquisition and tolerance testing. The response of sub-jects in this control group during the tolerance test provided a measure of any alteration in tolerance attributable simply to the intervening interval between the tolerance development and tolerance test phases of the experiment.

In all experiments, it was found that the placebo sessions promoted the recovery of tolerance; extinction group subjects evidenced significantly greater responding to the analgesic (Siegel, 1975b, Experiment 3; Siegel, 1977b, Experiments 1 and 2) and hyperthermic (Siegel, 1978b, Experiment 2) effects of morphine during the tolerance test than did control group rats, despite the fact that the two groups did not differ in any way with respect to their experience with morphine prior to the tolerance test. Indeed, in one experiment, the extinction procedure completely obliterated tolerance; extinction group rats responded on the tolerance test with the completely nontolerant response seen in rats receiving the drug for the very first time (Siegel, 1978b, Experiment 2).

It would appear to be well established that tolerance can be extinguished. Indeed, under some circumstances, repeated presentations of the drug administration environment in the absence of the drug to the tolerant subject can completely abolish tolerance. Evidence for such extinction of tolerance is robust, having been demonstrated in many experiments encompassing a range of procedural differences and parametric manipulations. These findings that tolerance is subject to extinction appear inexplicable by traditional interpretations of tolerance, which stress only the systemic effects of repeated pharmacological stimulation and ignore the importance of environmental cues present at the time of such stimulation. However, the finding that tolerance can be extinguished is readily interpretable by the conditioning analysis of tolerance.

VI. The Conditioning Theory of Tolerance: Implications for Drug Dependence

As indicated previously, following a sufficient number of opiate administrations for tolerance to become pronounced, if drug administration is terminated, humans and animals usually suffer withdrawal symptoms and display evidence of craving for the drug. The organism is then said to be dependent upon the drug. Since drug tolerance and dependence are highly correlated, "A satisfactory theory should offer a unitary explanation of the fact that tolerance and dependence apparently develop, persist, and disappear together, as though they were reflections of the same underlying biologic change [Goldstein *et al.,* 1974, p. 510]." The conditioning theory of tolerance does offer such a unitary mechanism for tolerance and dependence—the compensatory conditional pharmacological response.

A. DRUG-COMPENSATORY CONDITIONAL RESPONSES AND DEPENDENCE

According to the conditioning theory of tolerance, if the organism "expects" the drug because it is confronted with cues that have previously signaled the drug—for example, time of usual administration might serve as an effective cue (Dmitriev & Kochigina, 1959)—it evidences drug-compensatory conditional responses that act to cancel the effect of the drug, thereby producing tolerance. If, however, these usual predrug cues are *not* followed by the usual pharmacological consequences, the organism should display a syndrome consisting of drug-compensatory responses that achieve full expression because they are unmodulated by the drug. It may be useful to consider this syndrome, evidence in these circumstances, as a major basis for withdrawal symptoms. These drug-preparatory responses elicited by stimuli which, in the past, have predicted the drug, are presumably uncomfortable, and may be an important aspect of "craving."

If the symptoms of opiate withdrawal are, in fact, learned compensatory responses that would attenuate the effects of the drug, were the drug administered, it would be expected that these symptoms would be opposite in direction to those induced by the opiate. This expectation is in agreement with the observations of several investigators (e.g., see Marx, 1976). To substantiate these observations, the effects of opiate administration and the effects of opiate withdrawal were tabulated from the relevant chapters of a major pharmacology textbook (Goodman & Gilman, 1975, Chaps. 15 and 16, respectively). When these effects are aligned, as is done in Table 6.2, it is apparent that many of the characteristic symptoms of opiate withdrawal are, in fact, opposite to the effects noted when the drug is administered.

According to the conditioning theory of tolerance, as extended to incorporate phenomena of dependence, the display of withdrawal symptoms should (to a great extent) be under the control of environmental signals that have become associated with the opiate. There are considerable data indicating that this is indeed the case.

Table 6.2
Effects of Opiate Administration and Opiate Withdrawal

Opiate administration[a]	Opiate withdrawal[b]
hypothermia	hyperthermia
decrease in blood pressure	increase in blood pressure
peripheral vasodialation, skin flushed and warm	piloerection (gooseflesh), chilliness
miosis	mydriasis
drying of secretions	lacrimation, rhinorrhea
constipation	diarrhea
respiratory depression	yawning, panting
decreased urinary 17-Ketosteroid levels	increased urinary 17-Ketosteroid levels
antitussive	sneezing
decreased sex drive	spontaneous ejaculations and orgasms
relaxation	restlessness, insomnia
analgesia	pain and irritability
euphoria	depression

[a] Data are from Jaffe and Martin (1975).
[b] Data are from Jaffe (1975).

B. EVIDENCE THAT DRUG-ASSOCIATED CUES
   ELICIT SYMPTOMS OF WITHDRAWAL

One way to determine if environmental stimuli previously associated with
the drug are expecially effective in eliciting symptoms of withdrawal is simply to
ask former addicts. O'Brien (1976) did just this, and presented an illustrative
ranking of stimuli, in order of potency, that one patient reported was still
capable of eliciting "sickness and craving." This hierarchy is reproduced in
Table 6.3. The situations inducing discomfort in this former addict are those
which either were closely associated with the central effects of the opiate, or those
which would be expected to generalize from these primary signals for the drug.

Further evidence of the role of drug-related conditional stimuli in causing
drug-related responses comes from observations made while addict patients were
undergoing therapy. Teasdale (1973) reported that during behavior therapy,
"subjects found that viewing the syringe, tourniquet, etc., used in the aversion
therapy procedure evoked craving, and imagining themselves injecting drugs in
their customary setting often evoked quite powerful craving [p. 277]." Similarly, O'Brien (1976) reported observing withdrawal symptoms (yawning and
lacrimation, see Table 6.2) in some patients when drugs were discussed during
group therapy sessions.

The ability of environmental cues uniquely present at the time of heroin
self-administration to provoke withdrawal distress is illustrated clearly by
Teasdale's (1973) description of the effects of a drug-signaling olfactory stimulus
to elicit craving in some addicts: "A number had been accustomed to inject
themselves in public lavatories and reported that the smell as they passed one of
these could evoke craving [p. 277]." Also, it has been reported that drug-free
former addicts displayed clear signs of narcotic withdrawal when they performed

Table 6.3
Hierarchy[a] of Stimuli Provoking "Sickness" and/or "Craving"[b]

---

1. Being offered a "taste" by an old copping buddy.
2. Seeing a friend in the act of "shooting up."
3. Talking about drugs on copping corner.
4. Standing on copping corner.
5. Seeing a successful pusher—making lots of money, envy.
6. Socially awkward situation: job interview, family criticism,
      feeling like an outsider at a party.
7. Talking about drugs in group therapy.
8. Seeing a few bags of heroin.
9. Seeing someone's "works."
10. Seeing pictures of drugs and "works."
11. Seeing antidrug poster with "good veins" and somebody "shooting up."

---

   [a] Ranked from the most potent to the least potent.
   [b] From O'Brien, C. P. Experimental analysis of conditioning factors in human narcotic addiction. *Pharmacological Review*, 1976, 27, 533–543. Copyright 1976 by Williams & Wilkins Co., Baltimore. Reprinted by permission.

their usual "cooking up" ritual in the laboratory while various physiological indices were being monitored (O'Brien, Testa, O'Brien, & Greenstein, 1976).

Finally, in an experiment specifically designed to examine effects of drug-
associated cues, Teasdale (1973) showed addict–patients slides, some illustrating
drug-related material (e.g., scenes of inserting a syringe into a vein), and others
illustrating nondrug-related material (e.g., scenes of a hand holding a coffee
mug). On the basis of a variety of psychometric measures, he concluded that the
drug-related slides induced more emotional responding and evidence of
withdrawal distress than the nondrug-related slides.

In summary, several investigators have reported anecdotal observations
and results from laboratory studies attesting to the ability of environmental
stimuli, which subjects have previously experienced in conjunction with narcotic
self-administration, to elicit evidence of drug withdrawal—both subjective
reports of craving and observable withdrawal symptoms. There is, however, a
more persuasive case that can be made for the importance of drug-associated environmental cues in provoking withdrawal distress and drug craving. This case
is based on the inevitable conclusion to be reached from a mass of data assem-
bled since 1935, which was the year that the first public hospital for the treatment of addiction was opened in Lexington, Kentucky. With a relative handful
of exceptions, addicts detoxified in an environment other than that in which they
were addicted relapse when they are released and return to the environment in
which they previously used drugs.

VII.   Relapse to Addiction: Evidence for the
Role of Drug-Associated Environmental
Cues in Drug Dependence

According to the conditioning analysis of dependence, compensatory CRs
are the basis of both tolerance (when the anticipated drug is administered) and
withdrawal symptoms (when the anticipated drug is not administered). These
drug preparatory responses, in common with other CRs, would be expected to
dissipate little simply with the passage of time (see Section III,A). Although
there do not appear to have been any studies specifically designed to assess the
retention of pharmacological CRs, Siegel (1975b, Experiment 2B) reported a
morphine-compensatory CR in rats (hyperalgesia) 2 weeks after their last morphine administration. Moreover, as has been discussed previously (Section
III,A), it has been demonstrated that opiate tolerance, which is hypothesized to
be a manifestation of drug-compensatory CRs, is retained over very long
periods.

One implication of this evidence indicating such extensive retention of
pharmacological learning is that mere drug abstinence, in the context of environmental cues other than those associated with the drug, should not be an
effective procedure for the treatment of drug dependence. If the dependent in-

dividual is one who displays drug-compensatory CRs in response to drug-associated environmental stimuli, mere removal from these environmental stimuli for a period of "detoxification" should not substantially affect the capacity of these stimuli to elicit drug-compensatory CRs. Following such treatment, when the individual returns to environmental situations previously associated with the opiate, he or she should again display opiate-compensatory CRs. Such CRs, or symptoms of withdrawal, would be ameliorated by the drug, thus the individual should relapse.

An illustration of the potent effect of drug-related environmental stimuli in relapse following detoxofication has been presented by O'Brien (1976). He described the case of an addict who, after the first 4 or 5 days of a 6-month prison sentence, no longer displayed any symptoms of withdrawal, and soon reported no longer craving narcotics: "He gained weight, felt like a new man, and decided that he was finished with drugs [p. 533]." On the day that he was released from prison, he took the subway home and evidenced withdrawal symptoms as soon as he approached his old neighborhood. He quickly relapsed. A large number of follow-up studies of former patients of narcotic treatment facilities indicate that this scenario is the rule, rather than the exception.

A. PREVALENCE OF RELAPSE

A general finding among researchers in the area of drug dependence is that virtually all forms of treatment are equally ineffective in achieving a permanent cure for addiction. Following a period of detoxification, either as a result of incarceration or of forced or voluntary treatment, the patients' return to the environment in which they previously received drugs is usually followed by withdrawal symptoms, craving, and relapse to addiction. The poor record of achievement in the treatment of drug addiction has been summarized elsewhere (e.g., Brecher, 1972, Chap. 10; Hunt, Barnett, & Branch, 1971). Briefly, of those addicts who enter treatment programs, approximately 90% relapse within 1 year; of those addicts who successfuly complete a treatment program, approximately 80% relapse within 1 year. It should be noted that some treatment programs may be effective in achieving a variety of desirable goals, other than abstinence, which improve the functioning of the treated addict and reduce the cost of addiction to society (see McGlothlin, Anglin, & Wilson, 1975/76). However, the vast majority of alumni of all evaluated programs relapse following treatment, and the various treatment procedures that have been attempted have been characterized as an "uninterupted series of failures [Brecher, 1972, p. 83]."

According to the conditioning model of addiction, posttreatment relapse occurs because individuals evidence drug-compensatory CRs when they return to situations that previously signaled the effects of the narcotic. According to this model, if patients did *not* return to the drug-associated environment following treatment, such a high return to addiction would not be expected. There are obvious problems in doing the appropriate experiment to assess whether there is such environmental-specificity of relapse to addiction following a period of enforced abstinence. However, epidemiological data supporting the conditioning model of drug dependence may be found in a follow-up investigation of a large population of detoxified addicts who, after treatment, were returned to an environment other than that which they had associated with drugs—addicted Vietnam veterans.

B. THE VIETNAM DRUG ADDICTION EXPERIENCE

During the Vietnam military action, a large number of American soldiers became, by most definitions, addicted to heroin. The drug was readily available, high in pharmacological quality, and very inexpensive. A study of a sample of army enlisted men departing Vietnam in September, 1971 indicated that approximately 20% of them were addicted to heroin while in Vietnam (Robins, Davis, & Goodwin, 1974). An enormous social problem was anticipated. Although the soldiers were treated for their addiction before release, following discharge this large population of former addicts would descend on America. Since there were about 13,760 enlisted men who left Vietnam in September, 1971 (Robins et al., 1974), it could be estimated that about 2750 detoxified addicts would be returned to the civilian population during this one month alone. Considering the high rate of relapse to addiction following all known forms of treatment, a substantial social problem appeared inevitable. Testimony before the Senate Subcommittee to Investigate Juvenile Delinquency (1972) indicated the magnitude of the anticipated problem:

> Unlike the United States, in Vietnam a man can afford to just sniff heroin. He can get large quantities very cheaply. This will obviously lead to crime and other problems with law enforcement when he brings his addiction home. . . . There are many problems which will be experienced when these men return to the States. They will be unable to cut off this drug use . . . I speak from experience from having treated drug addicts in the States who have returned from Vietnam. These men who use drugs only sporadically for relief get in the habit, a habit that continues in the States [Senate Testimony, 1972, pp. 481-482].

On the basis of a conditioning analysis of drug dependence, it might be expected that these prophesies concerning the impending increase in the population of addicts in the United States to be overly pessimistic. If relapse to addiction results from environmental cues associated with the drug eliciting drug-preparatory responses, relapse should not be expected to be substantial in this group of Vietnam-addicted veterans; following treatment and discharge, they were returned to an environment very different from that in which they used opiates. The relapse data of this group supported the conditioning model of relapse; 1 year after discharge, the relapse rate of this population was not the usual 80-90% (Brecher, 1972; Hunt et al., 1971), but only about 7% (Robins et al., 1974).

In summary, the epidemiological data concerning relapse is consistent with the conditioning account of drug dependence. According to this analysis, drug-associated environmental cues elicit symptoms of withdrawal, thus patients returning to the environment that they had associated with opiates revert to drug use. However, such relapse need not be the inevitable aftermath of treatment for drug dependence. As indicated by the Vietnam experience, and expected on the basis of the conditioning model of dependence, the problem of relapse to addiction is relatively trivial if the former addict returns to an environment other than that associated with the drug. Although these data are congenial with the view of withdrawal symptoms as drug-compensatory conditional responses, they are obviously subject to alternative interpretations. For example, the differences in relapse rate between Vietnam veteran and civilian addicts may be attributable to any of the many differences that would be expected to distinguish these two populations, rather than simply to the degree of similarity between the environment in which they were addicted and the environment to which they were released following treatment. In addition, it may be that relapse almost invariably follows postdetoxification return to the addiction environment because the culture of the addiction environment encourages and rewards drug use (see Agar, 1973), rather than because the drug-associated environment elicits drug-compensatory CRs.

Obviously, the conditioning interpretation of the role of environmental cues in relapse would be strengthened by an experiment specifically designed to assess relapse tendency in groups for which addicting, withdrawal, and postwithdrawal environments were systematically manipulated. To obviate any interpretation of the results based on cultural or personality factors, this study should examine the relapse–environment interaction with infrahuman subjects. Fortunately, the experiment has been done.

C. RELAPSE TO ADDICTION IN ANIMALS

In an experiment by Thompson and Ostlund (1965), rats were orally addicted in their "home" environment by ad libitum access to a morphine solution as their only available fluid for 60 days. Following addiction, all subjects were withdrawn from the drug for 30 days by having water, rather than morphine solution, as the only available fluid. For half the subjects, this withdrawal phase of the experiment was conducted in the initial addiction environment, and for the remaining subjects it was conducted in an alternative environment (which differed from the home environment along several dimensions, such as ambient temperature, cage size, and constancy of background illumination intensity). The third and final phase of the experiment involved readdiction to morphine. This readdiction occurred either in the initial addiction environment or the alternative environment (half the subjects withdrawn in each of the two environments were assigned to each readdiction environment).

According to the conditioning analysis of addiction, relapse, to a great extent, results because the addiction environment elicits drug-preparatory CRs. On this basis, relapse would be expected to be more pronounced when, following withdrawal, subjects were given access to morphine in their "home" environment (the one in which they were originally addicted), than if the drug were available in another environment. This was found to be the case: Rats displayed a greater postwithdrawal preference for morphine when readdiction occurred in the environment where original addiction occurred than when readdiction occurred in the alternative environment (this was the case for groups withdrawn in either of the two environments).

In summary, the results of this experiment with animal subjects are in agreement with the data concerning relapse in human addicts. Thompson and Ostlund (1965) demonstrated that postwithdrawal return of rats to the addiction environment favors relapse to a greater extent than does return to a different environment. The findings are remarkably parallel to the epidemiological data from humans: Relapse to addiction is far more pronounced following post-detoxification return to the addiction environment (civilian addicts) than return to different environment (Vietnam addicts). Furthermore, the data from the animal experiment are not readily attributable to population or cultural differences between the groups showing high and low relapse tendencies. Thus, the results of this experimental study with animal subjects encourages the application of the conditioning model of tolerance and dependence to the relapse phenomenon in humans.

VIII. Summary and Conclusions

The purposes of this chapter have been to outline a Pavlovian-conditioning model of opiate tolerance and to indicate the implications of this model of tolerance for opiate dependence.

A. CONDITIONING AND TOLERANCE

The results of many experiments have suggested parallels between learning and morphine tolerance: Both processes exhibit great retention, both are disrupted by electroconvulsive shock and frontal cortical stimulation, both are retarded by inhibitors of protein synthesis, and both are facilitated by antagonists of these metabolic inhibitors. A Pavlovian-conditioning model of tolerance is consistent with this evidence implicating a learning process in tolerance. It has been demonstrated that many CRs to a variety of drugs are opposite in direction to the unconditional effects of the drug, and the conditioning analysis of morphine tolerance emphasizes the fact that subjects with a history of morphine administration display morphine-compensatory CRs when confronted with the usual administration procedure but without the drug. Thus, when the drug *is* presented in the context of the usual administration cues, these conditional morphine-compensatory responses would be expected to attenuate the drug-induced UCRs, thereby decreasing the observed response to the drug.

Research has been summarized that supports this compensatory-conditioning model of tolerance by demonstrating that rats with a history of morphine administration display morphine tolerance only if the drug is administered in conjunction with environmental cues that have previously signaled the drug, but not if the drug is administered in conjunction with cues that have not previously signaled the drug. Further evidence supporting the conditioning theory of tolerance has been provided by studies establishing that CS habituation and partial reinforcement–nonpharmacological manipulations known to be effective in retarding the development of a variety of CRs, similarly retard the development of morphine tolerance. Finally, an extinction procedure, which generally attenuates the strength of established CRs, also attenuates established morphine tolerance.

Because of the intimate relationship between drug tolerance and drug dependence, it was thought appropriate to attempt to extend the compensatory-CR interpretation of opiate tolerance to opiate dependence.

B. CONDITIONING AND ADDICTION

It is suggested that the symptoms of drug dependence are displayed when circumstances are such that the usual predrug cues are not followed by the drug. Consider the situation in which no drug is available, but the subject is in an environment where he or she has frequently used opiates, or it is the time of day when the drug is typically administered, or it is the usual number of hours since the last drug administration, or any of a variety of other drug-associated stimuli are available (see Table 6.3). The drug-compensatory CRs elicited by these signals of pharmacological stimulation are displayed clearly (much as they are in a placebo test session), for they are unaltered by any drug effects and may be the basis of withdrawal symptoms and subjective reports of craving.

In support of this extrapolation of the drug-compensatory conditional response model of tolerance to addiction, it was noted that: (*a*) opiate withdrawal symptoms are, to a great extent, opposite in direction to the effects of the drug; (*b*) environmental stimuli that would be expected to have become associated with the drug in human addicts elicit both observable withdrawal symptoms and subjective reports of craving; (*c*) following a period of withdrawal, when addicts return to the environment in which they have previously used drugs, they frequently evidence withdrawal symptoms, report craving, and (with very few exceptions) relapse; (*d*) following a period of withdrawal, when addicts return to an environment *other* than that in which they previously used drugs, they report little discomfort and (with very few exceptions) do *not* relapse; and (*e*) addicted rats, like opiate-dependent humans, evidence more pronounced postwithdrawal relapse if the readdiction environment is the same as the original addiction environment than if the readdiction environment is different.

C. CONDITIONING AND PHARMACOLOGY

For purposes of exposition, a conditioning interpretation of tolerance and addiction has been distinguished from more traditional, nonassociative theories.

In fact, both associative mechanisms and systemic processes unrelated to associative mechanisms are, undoubtedly, involved in tolerance and addiction (see Siegel, 1978b). The purpose of this chapter is to summarize findings indicating the important role that learning plays in an organism's response to drugs. Based on the material presented in this chapter, it seems clear that further studies of learning and memory will help in understanding drug tolerance and dependence. It is interesting to note that the equivalent position has been stated from a pharmacological perspective too: ''Perhaps understanding the processes of dependence will go hand in hand with understanding the possibly analogous processes of memory [Collier, 1972, p. 129].''

REFERENCES

Adams, W. H., Yeh, S. Y., Woods, L. A., & Mitchell, C. L. Drug–test interaction as a factor in the development of tolerance to the analgesic effect of morphine. *Journal of Pharmacology and Experimental Therapeutics*, 1969, *168*, 251–257.

Agar, M. *Ripping and running: A formal ethnography of urban heroin addicts.* New York: Seminar Press, 1973.

American Psychiatric Association. *Diagnostic and statistical manual of mental disorders* (2nd ed.). Washington, D.C.: American Psychiatric Association, 1968.

American Psychiatric Association. *Draft of DSM–II classification, as of November 10, 1976* New York: Author, Task Force on Nomenclature and Statistics, 1976.

Andrews, H. L. The effect of opiates on the pain threshold in post-addicts. *Journal of Clinical Investigation*, 1943, *22*, 511–516.

Beecroft, R. S. *Classical conditioning.* Goleta, California: Psychonomic Press, 1966.

Brecher, E. M. *Licit and illicit drugs.* Boston: Little, Brown, 1972.

Cantor, G. N. Stimulus familiarization effect and the change effect in children's motor task behavior. *Psychological Bulletin*, 1969, *71*, 144–160.

Cochin, J. Possible mechanisms in development of tolerance. *Federation Proceedings*, 1970, *29*, 19–27.

Cochin, J. Role of possible immune mechanisms in the development of tolerance. In D. H. Clouet (Ed.), *Narcotic drugs: Biochemical pharmacology.* New York: Plenum, 1971.

Cochin, J. Some aspects of tolerance to the narcotic analgesics. In J. M. Singh, L. Miller, & H. Lal (Eds.), *Drug addiction.1: Experimental pharmacology.* New York: Futura, 1972.

Cochin, J., & Kornetsky, C. Development and loss of tolerance to morphine in the rat after single and multiple injections. *Journal of Pharmacology and Experimental Therapeutics*, 1964, *145*, 1–10.

Cohen, M., Keats, A. S., Krivoy, W., & Ungar, G. Effect of actinomycin D on morphine tolerance. *Proceedings of the Society for Experimental Biology and Medicine*, 1965, *119*, 381–384.

Collier, H. O. J. The experimental analysis of drug-dependence. *Endeavour*, 1972, *31*, 123–129.

Deutsch, R. Conditioned hypoglycemia: A mechanism for saccharin-induced sensitivity to insulin in the rat. *Journal of Comparative and Physiological Psychology*, 1974, *86*, 350–358.

Dmitriev, A. S., & Kochigina, A. M. The importance of time as stimulus of conditioned reflex activity. *Psychological Bulletin*, 1959, *56*, 106–132.

Domjan, M., & Gillan, D. J. After-effects of lithium-conditioned stimuli on consummatory behavior. *Journal of Experimental Psychology: Animal Behavior Processes*, 1977, *3*, 322–334.

Gianutsos, G., Drawbaugh, R., Hynes, M., & Lal, H. The narcotic withdrawal syndrome in the rat. In S. Ehrenpreis & A. Neidle (Eds.), *Methods in narcotics research.* New York: Dekker, 1975.

Gilbert, R. M. Caffeine as a drug of abuse. In R. J. Gibbins, Y. Israel, H. Kalant, R. E. Popham, W. Schmidt, & R. G. Smart (Eds.), *Research advances in alcohol and drug problems* (Vol. 3). New York: Wiley, 1976.

Ginsburg, M., & Cox, B. M. Proteins and nucleic acids. In S. J. Mule & H. Brill (Eds.), *Chemical and biological aspects of drug dependence.* Cleveland: CRC Press, 1972.

Goldberg, S. R., & Schuster, C. R. Conditioned suppression by a stimulus associated with nalorphine in morphine-dependent monkeys. *Journal of the Experimental Analysis of Behavior,* 1967, *10,* 235–242.

Goldberg, S. R., & Schuster, C. R. Conditioned nalorphine-induced abstinence changes: Persistence in post morphine-dependent monkeys. *Journal of the Experimental Analysis of Behavior,* 1970, *14,* 33–46.

Goldstein, A., Arnow, L., & Kalman, S. M. *Principles of drug action: The basis of pharmacology* (2nd ed.). New York: Wiley, 1974.

Goodman, L. S., & Gilman, A. (Eds.). *The pharmacological basis of therapeutics* (5th ed.). New York: Macmillan, 1975.

Guha, D., Dutta, S. N., & Pradhan, S. N. Conditioning of gastric secretion by epinephrine in rats. *Proceedings of the Society for Experimental Biology and Medicine,* 1974, *147,* 817–819.

Himmelsbach, C. K. Symposium: Can the euphoric, analgetic and physical dependence effects of drugs be separated? IV. With reference to physical dependence. *Federation Proceedings,* 1943, *2,* 201–203.

Hug, C. C. Characteristics and theories related to acute and chronic tolerance development. In S. J. Mulé & H. Brill (Eds.), *Chemical and biological aspects of drug dependence.* Cleveland: CRC Press, 1972

Hunt, W. A., Barnett, L. W., & Branch, L. G. Relapse rates in addiction programs. *Journal of Clinical Psychology,* 1971, *27,* 455–456.

Inglis, B. *The forbidden game: A social history of drugs.* London, England: Hodder and Stoughton, 1975.

Jaffe, J. H. Drug addiction and drug abuse. In L. S. Goodman & A. Gilman (Eds.), *The pharmacological basis of therapeutics* (5th ed.). New York: Macmillan, 1975.

Jaffe, J. H., & Martin, W. R. Narcotic analgesics and antagonists. In L. S. Goodman & A. Gilman (Eds.), *The pharmacological basis of therapeutics* (5th ed.). New York: Macmillan, 1975.

Jarvik, M. E. The role of consolidation in memory. In W. L. Byrne (Ed.), *Molecular approaches to learning and memory.* New York: Academic Press, 1970. Pp. 15–25.

Kayan, S., & Mitchell, C. L. Studies on tolerance development to morphine: Effect of the dose-interval on the development of single dose tolerance. *Archives Internationales de Pharmacodynamie et de Thérapie,* 1972, *199,* 407–414.

Kayan, S., Woods, L. A., & Mitchell, C. L. Experience as a factor in the development of tolerance to the analgesic effect of morphine. *European Journal of Pharmacology,* 1969, *6,* 333–339.

Kayan, S., Woods, L. A., & Mitchell, C. L. Morphine-induced hyperalgesia in rats tested on the hot plate. *Journal of Pharmacology and Experimental Therapeutics,* 1971, *177,* 509–513.

Kesner, R. P., Priano, D. J., & DeWitt, J. R. Time-dependent disruption of morphine tolerance by electroconvulsive shock and frontal cortical stimulation. *Science,* 1976, *194,* 1079–1081.

Kimble, G. *Hilgard and Marquis' conditioning and learning.* New York: Appleton, 1961.

Korol, B., & McLaughlin, L. J. A homeostatic adaptive response to alpha-methyl-dopa in conscious dogs. *Pavlovian Journal of Biological Science,* 1976, *11,* 67–75.

Korol, B., Sletten, I. W., & Brown, M. L. Conditioned physiological adaption to anticholinergic drugs. *American Journal of Physiology,* 1966, *211,* 911–914.

Krivoy, W. A., & Zimmermann, E., & Lande, S. Facilitation of development of resistance to morphine analgesia by Desglycinamide[9]-Lysine Vasopressin. *Proceedings of the National Academy of Science,* 1974, *71,* 1852–1856.

Kuschinsky, K. Opiate dependence. *Progress in Pharmacology,* 1977, *1,* (Whole No. 2).

Lande, S., Flexner, J. B., & Flexner, L. B. Effect of corticotropin and desglycinamide[9]-lysine vasopressin on suppression of memory by puromycin. *Proceedings of the National Academy of Science,* 1972, *69,* 558–560.

Lande, S., Witter, A., & DeWied, D. Pituitary peptides, an octapeptide that stimulates conditioned avoidance acquisition in hypophysectomized rats. *Journal of Biological Chemistry,* 1971, *246,* 2058–2062.

Lang, W. J., Brown, M. L., Gershon, S., & Korol, B. Classical and physiologic adaptive conditioned responses to anticholinergic drugs in conscious dogs. *International Journal of Neuropharmacology,* 1966, *5,* 311–315.

Lang, W. J., Rush, M. L., & Pearson, L. Pharmacological investigation of the mechanism of conditional salivation in dogs induced by atropine and morphine. *European Journal of Pharmacology,* 1969, *5,* 191–195.

Le Magnen, J. Olfactory–endocrine interaction and regulatory behaviours. In D. A. Denton & J. P. Coghlan (Eds.), *Olfaction and taste V.* New York: Academic Press, 1975.

Lubow, R. E. Latent inhibition. *Psychological Bulletin,* 1973, *79,* 398–407.

Lubow, R. E., & Moore, A. U. Latent inhibition: The effect of nonreinforced pre-exposure to the conditional stimulus. *Journal of Comparative and Physiological Psychology,* 1959, *52,* 415–419.

Lundberg, E., & Thyselius-Lundberg, S. Betrag zur Kenntnis des innersckretorischen Gleichgewichtsmech-anismus: Die Einwirkung des Tabakrauchens auf den Blutzucker. *Acta Medica Scandinavica,* 1931, Supplement 38.

Marx, J. L. Research news, neurobiology: Researchers high on endogenous opiates. *Science,* 1976, *193,* 1227–1229.

McGaugh, J. L., & Herz, M. J. *Memory consolidation.* San Francisco: Albion, 1972.

McGlothlin, W. H., Anglin, M. D., & Wilson, B. D. Outcome of the California civil addict commitments: 1961–1972. *Drug and Alcohol Dependence,* 1975/76, *1,* 165–181.

Mityushov, M. I. The conditional-reflex incretion of insulin. *Journal of Higher Nervous Activity* (Uslovnorleflektornaya inkretsiya insula. *Zhurnal Vysshei Nervnoi Deigtel*), 1954, *4,* 206–212. (Read in translation prepared by L. J. Shein, Department of Russian, McMaster Univ.)

Mulé, S. J., Clements, T. H., Layson, R. C., & Haertzen, C. A. Analgesia in guinea pigs: A measure of tolerance development. *Archives Internationales de Pharmacodynamie et de Thérapie,* 1968, *173,* 201–212.

Mulé, S. J., & Woods, L. A. Distribution of N-C^{14} methyl labeled morphine. I. In central nervous system of nontolerant and tolerant dogs. *Journal of Pharmacology and Experimental Therapeutics,* 1962, *136,* 232–241.

Mulinos, M. G., & Lieb, C. C. Pharmacology of learning. *American Journal of Physiology,* 1929, *90,* 456–457. (Abstract)

Nakajima, S. Cycloheximide: Mechanisms of its amnesic effect. *Current Developments in Psychopharmacology,* 1976, *3,* 26–53.

Obál, F. The fundamentals of the central nervous control of vegetative homeostasis. *Acta Physiologica Academiae Scientiarum Hungaricae,* 1966, *30,* 15–29.

Obál, F., Vicasay, M., & Madarász, I. Role of a central nervous mechanism in the acquired tolerance to the temperature decreasing effect of histamine. *Acta Physiological Academiae Scientiarum Hungaricae,* 1965, *28,* 65–76.

O'Brien, C. P. Experimental analysis of conditioning factors in human narcotic addiction. *Pharmacological Review,* 1976, *27,* 533–543.

O'Brien, C. P., Testa, T., O'Brien, T. J., & Greenstein, R. Conditioning in human opiate addicts. *Paulonian Journal of Biological Science,* 1976, *4,* 195–202.

Pavlov, I. P. *The work of the digestive glands* (W. H. Thompson, trans.). London: Griffin and Company, 1910.

Pavlov, I. P. *Conditioned reflexes* (G. V. Anrep, trans.). London: Oxford Univ. Press, 1927.

Pihl, R. O., & Altman, J. An experimental analysis of the placebo effect. *Journal of Clinical Pharmacology,* 1971, *11,* 91–95.

Robins, L. N., Davis, D. H., & Goodwin, D. W. Drug use by U.S. Army enlisted men in Vietnam: A follow-up on their return home. *American Journal of Epidemiology,* 1974, *99,* 235–249.

Rush, M. L., Pearson, L., & Lang, W. J. Conditional autonomic responses induced in dogs by atropine and morphine. *European Journal of Pharmacology,* 1970, *11,* 22–28.

Russek, M., & Piña, S. Conditioning of adrenalin anorexia. *Nature,* 1962, *193,* 1296–1297.

Russell, M. A. H. Tobacco smoking and nicotine dependence. In R. J. Gibbins, Y. Israel, H. Kalant, R. E. Popham, W. Schmidt, & R. G. Smart (Eds.), *Research advances in alcohol and drug problems* (Vol. 3). New York: Wiley, 1976.

Senate Testimony. *Hearings before the subcommittee to investigate juvenile delinquency of the Committee on the Judiciary, United States Senate, Ninety-Second Congress.* Washington, D.C.: U.S. Government Printing Office, 1972.

Siegel, S. Conditioning of insulin-induced glycemia. *Journal of Comparative and Physiological Psychology,* 1972, *78,* 233–241. (a)

Siegel, S. Latent inhibition and eyelid conditioning. In A. H. Black & W. F. Prokasy (Eds.), *Classical conditioning II.* New York: Appleton, 1972. Pp. 231–247. (b)

Siegel, S. Conditioning insulin effects. *Journal of Comparative and Physiological Psychology,* 1975, *89,* 189–199. (a)

Siegel, S. Evidence from rats that morphine tolerance is a learned response. *Journal of Comparative and Physiological Psychology,* 1975, *89,* 498–506. (b)

Siegel, S. Morphine analgesic tolerance: Its situation specificity supports a Pavlovian conditioning model. *Science,* 1976, *193,* 323–325.

Siegel, S. Learning and psychopharmacology. In M. E. Jarvik (Ed.), *Psychopharmacology in the practice of medicine.* New York: Appleton, 1977. (a)

Siegel, S. Morphine tolerance acquisition as an associative process. *Journal of Experimental Psychology: Animal Behavior Processes,* 1977, *3,* 1–13. (b)

Siegel, S. A Pavlovian conditioning analysis of morphine tolerance. In N. A. Krasnegor (Ed.), *Behavioral tolerance: Research and treatment implications* (National Institute on Drug Abuse Research Monograph No. 18; U.S. Department of Health, Education, and Welfare Publication No. [ADM] 78-551). Washington, D.C.: U.S. Government Printing Office, 1978. (a)

Siegel, S. Tolerance to the hyperthermic effect of morphine in the rat is a learned response. *Journal of Comparative and Physiological Psychology,* 1978, *92,* 1137–1149. (b)

Siegel, S., Hinson, R. E., & Krank, M. D. The role of predrug signals in morphine analgesic tolerance: Support for a Pavlovian conditioning model of tolerance. *Journal of Experimental Psychology: Animal Behavior Processes,* 1978, *4,* 188–196.

Synder, S. H., & Matthysse, S. *Opiate receptor mechanisms.* Cambridge, Massachusetts: MIT Press, 1975.

Solomon, R. L. *An opponent-process theory of acquired motivation: The affective dynamics of addiction.* In J. D. Maser & M. E. P. Seligman (Eds.), *Psychopathology: Experimental models.* San Francisco: Freeman, 1977.

Solomon, R. L., & Corbit, J. D. An opponent-process theory of motivation. *Psychological Review,* 1974, *81,* 119–145.

Stolerman, I. P., Bunker, P., Johnson, C. A., Jarvik, M. E., Krivoy, W., & Zimmermann, E. Attenuation of morphine tolerance development by electroconvulsive shock in mice. *Neuropharmacology,* 1976, *15,* 309–313.

Subkov, A. A., & Zilov, G. N. The role of conditioned reflex adaptation in the origin of hyperergic reactions. *Bulletin de Biologie et de Medécine Expérimentale,* 1937, *4,* 294–296.

Teasdale, J. D. Conditioned abstinence in narcotic addicts. *International Journal of the Addictions,* 1973, *8,* 273–292.

Thompson, T., & Ostlund, W. Jr. Susceptibility to readdiction as a function of the addiction and withdrawal environments. *Journal of Comparative and Physiological Psychology,* 1965, *60,* 388–392.

Weeks, J. R. Experimental morphine addiction: Method for automatic injections in unrestrained rats. *Science,* 1962, *138,* 143–144.

Weiss, K. R., & Brown, B. L. Latent inhibition: A review and a new hypothesis. *Acta Neurobiologiae Experimentalis,* 1974, *34,* 301–316.

Wikler, A. Recent progress in research on the neurophysiologic basis of morphine addiction. *American Journal of Psychiatry,* 1948, *105,* 329–338.

Wikler, A. *Opiate addiction: Psychological and neurophysiological aspects in relation to clinical problems.* Springfield, Illinois: Thomas, 1953.

Wikler, A. Interaction of physical dependence and classical and operant conditioning in the genesis of relapse. In A. H. Wikler (Ed.), *The addictive states.* Baltimore: Williams & Wilkins, 1968.

Wikler, A. Conditioning of successive adaptive responses to the initial effects of drugs. *Conditional Reflex,* 1973, *8,* 193–210.

JOHN GAITO

The Kindling Effect: An Experimental Model of Epilepsy?[1]

7

I. Introduction

Many scientists are involved in the attempt to control and/or reverse various psychopathologies. Unfortunately, an understanding of psychopathology using human cases is limited because the psychopathology must be taken as it is. On the other hand, experimental production of psychopathologic conditions in animals provides the scientist with great flexibility in that he or she may produce, and study, many conditions. Epilepsy is one psychopathology that has afflicted humans for centuries and for which procedures have been developed that can produce a condition in animals that appears to be similar to that found in humans.

There are a number of procedures for experimentally producing seizures similar to those found in human epilepsy. These experimental procedures provide an opportunity for *controlled investigation* of an epileptic-type condition and have certain advantages over the condition in humans.

1. There is the potential for determining the brain features that accompany the seizure state. In this case the emphasis can be on:

[1] Parts of this chapter are an updating of an article, The kindling effect as a model of epilepsy, published previously by the author in the *Psychological Bulletin,* 1976, *83,* 1097–1109. Copyright 1976 by the American Psychological Association. Reprinted by permission.

(a) Chemical aspects—for example, quantitative and/or qualitative changes in so-called inhibitory chemicals, such as gamma-aminobutryic acid (GABA), or taurine or in other chemicals.
(b) Neurological features—for example, a determination of cortical or sub-cortical foci that give rise to seizures, and synaptic events which are involved.

2. There is the capacity for evaluating potential therapeutic agents.

(a) *Anticonvulsant chemicals.* These agents are the ones which have been evaluated most frequently. It is a simple task to administer specific chemicals to animals that have shown seizure states. Thus this practical aspect is mainly responsible for the popularity of this procedure.
(b) *Brain electrical stimulation.* Because brain activity has electrical components, it seems logical that some type of electrical stimulation of a nonconvulsive nature might be beneficial. Although this procedure has been used infrequently (Valenstein, 1973), it may offer some therapeutic promise (see following discussion).
(c) *Surgical extirpation of ''epileptic'' tissue.* Removal of tissue that shows seizure activity is a possible therapeutic procedure with human epilepsy (Penfield & Roberts, 1959), but it has not been employed in animal studies.

Woodbury (1972) has indicated that there are two criteria for a potentially useful experimental model of human epilepsy:

1. Electrographic studies should show the presence of epileptic-like activity in the EEG.
2. Behavioral seizure-like activity must be manifested.

Many methods meet these criteria. Some of these are more natural than others, for example, audiogenic seizures (usually in mice)[2] and photogenic seizures in baboons, which require only a slight modification of normal environmental conditions. Other methods use a drastic modification of the organism; these latter methods usually involve electrical or pharmacological stimulation of the organism. There are many methods of this nature to produce seizure conditions in the organism. Most of them produce convulsions lasting for short periods of time (acute), but some, for example, alumina cream on brain tissue, are more long lasting (chronic) in their effect. Most of these methods are described in detail in Purpura, Penry, Woodbury, Tower, and Walter (1972).

One recent experimental procedure for simulating the epileptic condition uses repeated electrical stimulation of specific brain structures. If the brain of a rat is electrically stimulated unilaterally at a low intensity (e.g., in the amygdala), the rat will continue to explore its environment as it would normally do. However, after a number of trials with the same intensity of stimulation, the rat will rear up on its hind paws and the forelimbs will begin to convulse. Appar-

---

[2] See Chapter 3 of this volume for a number of specific details about audiogenic seizures.

ently, the brain conditions are being modified, and the animal's susceptibility to convulsing is being increased. This procedure, in which an animal's behavior is being modified slowly over a period of trials in response to an invariant stimulus, has been called the *kindling effect* (Goddard, McIntyre, & Leech, 1969). In recent years this paradigm has been used by a number of researchers with interesting results. This chapter is concerned with a discussion and evaluation of the kindling effect as a useful procedure for the production of an epileptic-type condition in animals so as to gain some understanding of human epilepsy and to suggest possible therapies for seizure conditions.

II. Epilepsy

Epilepsy is a general term for a diverse group of convulsive disorders. These disorders are characterized by spontaneous, paroxysmal firing of neurons that produce peculiar electroencephalogram (EEG) patterns (spike and wave) and seizure behavior in humans. Differentiation of the various types of epilepsy is frequently based on characteristic behavioral symptoms, especially by psychologists. A prominent classification of symptoms is the following (Coleman, 1956; Millon, 1969):

1. Grand mal—the outstanding features are loss of consciousness and convulsive motor activity.

2. Petit mal—a diminution rather than a complete loss of consciousness. The person stops what he or she is doing, stares vacantly, and then resumes his or her previous activity within a few seconds. There may be rhythmic twitching of eyelids or eyebrows.

3. Jacksonian (focal)—the attack begins at a focal point from one region of the body with a muscle twitching or spasm or with a sensory disturbance such as burning, tingling, or numbness. These disturbances then pass over the entire side of the body from which they originated. The person may remain conscious during the initial stage of the attack but usually loses consciousness as the attack spreads. In most cases the attacks terminate in generalized convulsive seizures. Presumably the attack arises from involvement of brain areas controlling the movements of sensory functions in which the symptoms first appear, and then the involved brain areas become more general.

4. Psychomotor—the distinguishing feature of this condition is the loss of consciousness along with ongoing activity, which may last for a few seconds or minutes to several days in some cases. During this period, the person may perform routine tasks or some unusual or antisocial acts. Behavior at this time is automatic; the person is unaware of his or her activity.

Another prominent classification is described by McNaughton and Rasmussen (1975). They divide epilepsies into (*a*) the partial (or focal) forms, with varied etiology; and (*b*) the generalized forms, based on clinical and EEG findings. The generalized forms are subdivided into those of unknown cause (primary generalized epilepsies, also referred to as "idiopathic"), those caused by diffuse or multifocal cerebral lesions (secondary generalized epilepsies), and those of "undetermined generalized epilepsies." The primary generalized epilepsies constitute a large group, and genetic factors appear to be of great importance.

Epileptic conditions are found in a sizable proportion of human beings. However, it is difficult to determine the exact incidence. Many epileptics appear normal, and the disclosure of epilepsy still has serious social and economic consequences such that reticence is considered appropriate (Pryse-Phillips, 1969). In many cases, serious emotional problems may result.

Epilepsy has the longest medical history of any disease. In early times, it was considered to be "the sacred disease," because it was assumed to be the result of divine visitation. Although Hippocrates in 460 B.C. suggested that the disease was no more sacred than any other ailment but was based on brain malfunction, the idea that the supernatural was involved still persists to the present time (Pryse-Phillips, 1969; Tower, 1960). Traces of this attitude are still encountered in some individuals today, but with increased study and improved surgical and chemical methods of dealing with epilepsy in recent years, its true nature is becoming clearer.

Although our understanding of epilepsy has increased because of the study of humans with this condition, such procedure has some obvious limitations. Thus, it would be valuable to have an experimental procedure by which a relatively permanent epileptic-type condition could be produced in animals so that brain aspects could be determined. Having developed such a procedure, one then could ascertain any changes in neurological and biochemical aspects of the brain and evaluate the ability of specific agents in moderating these convulsive effects. The kindling effect provides a potential procedure for this purpose. It shows itself at behavioral, electrophysiological, neurological, and chemical levels, at least.

III. The Kindling Effect

A. BEHAVIORAL

Goddard *et al.* (1969) reported a three-stage process during kindling with rats, cats, and monkeys. For example, unilateral electrical stimulation to the amygdala produced clonic convulsions on the average in about 15 trials with Wistar rats. The initial stimulations had little effect on the animal's behavior (Stage 1—normal exploratory behavior). With a few repetitions, automatic behavioral activity (e.g., eye closure, chewing, salivation) could be observed (Stage 2—behavioral automatisms), and with further stimulations these automatisms culminated in a complete convulsion (Stage 3—clonic convulsions). The rat stood on its hind paws, and bilateral clonic convulsions developed. These convulsions continued after the electrical stimulation was terminated. Stimulation of both amygdalae (or other bilateral structures) hasten the onset of convulsions (Racine, Okujava, & Chipashvili, 1972). This pattern of behavior develops in a similar pattern and rate for normal rats, split-brain rats (McIntyre, 1975), and for adrenalectomized rats (McIntyre & Wann, 1978). However, in split-brain rats the convulsion was lateralized to the contralateral side.

Some researchers have reported that a faster rate of kindling occurs with split-brain rats (Nobrega & Gaito, 1978) and cats (Wada & Sato, 1975). No significant differences in rate of kindling were found for three small groups of split-brain rats that were compared separately with a normal control group (Mc-Caughran, Corcoran, & Wada, 1976). However, the mean number of sessions to kindle were lower for each of the three groups; the tendency for split-brain rats to kindle faster than normals seems to be suggested by the data.

For a few minutes after the termination of a Stage 3 clonic convulsion, rats are hyperactive, difficult to handle, and have strong tendencies to bite. On some occasions a few rats have jumped out of our observation box, which is about 1 ft. in height. These same rats appear calm and are easy to handle approximately 1 hour later when they are stimulated again in our laboratory. However, apparent calmness may be misleading; Pinel, Treit, and Rovner (1977) reported that rats kindled in either the amygdala or hippocampus were more aggressive than rats stimulated in the caudate nucleus or than nonstimulated controls. Level of aggression was determined by reactivity to a pencil tap to the base of the tail and by resistance to capture; these behavioral assessments were conducted after a 24-hour stimulation free period.

It is possible to partition the first and second stages into finer segments. Thus, Racine (1972) reported three specific stages for Stage 2 and two for Stage 3, determined by specific behaviors, whereas Wada and Sato (1974) had four for Stage 2 and two for Stage 3.

Goddard *et al.* (1969) reported that a 60–Hz current with a 24-hour interval between stimulations provided the fastest rate of kindling. Kindling was induced also with intervals of 7 days and with shorter intervals (12, 8, 1, and 1/3 hours). Intervals of 10 min or less resulted in adaptation; some automatic behavior could be initiated, but it would not persist. Mucha and Pinel (1977) found similar results as had Goddard *et al.* with interstimulation intervals below 20 min. They also reported that duration of motor seizures and brain electrical afterdischarges were shorter for interstimulation intervals up to 45 min than for a 90-min interval.

Racine, Burnham, Gartner, and Levitan (1973) stimulated rats with a 1-sec train of 400 μA diphasic square wave pulses (1 msec) at 60 Hz with 24, 2, 1, and .5-hour intertrial intervals. There were no statistically significant differences in kindling between the three longest intervals, but the .5-hour interval resulted in slower kindling. Racine *et al.* found also that Wistar rats required a significantly greater number of stimulations to develop seizures than did Sprague–Dawley or Royal Victoria Hooded strains.

Goddard *et al.* (1969) found that effective kindling was produced also by other frequencies than 60 Hz, for example, 25 and 150 Hz. A frequency of 3 Hz was ineffective—it provided neither the characteristic behavioral nor electrophysiological changes (Fried & McIntyre, 1973; Goddard *et al.*, 1969). In research underway in our laboratory at the present time, we have stimulated many rats each with 24 trials of 3-Hz sine wave stimulation to the amygdala and have seldom observed a single definite behavioral automatism or clonic convulsion, unless the intensity was extremely high (Gaito, 1979b).

The duration of stimulation required to produce kindled seizures has been as low as 1 sec (Corcoran, McCaughran, & Wada, 1973; Racine *et al.*, 1973), although longer periods of time, for example, 5, 15, or 30 sec, are used by most investigators. The intensity of stimulation has usually been in microamperes (e.g., 50 or 100 μA), although some researchers have used milliamperes (e.g., Corcoran *et al.*, 1973). Pinel, Phillips, and Deol (1974) showed that the intensity of the current had an effect in kindling development, with higher intensities (500 μA) facilitating kindling more so than near-threshold intensities. They indicated also that the initial clonic convulsions were more intense if the current intensities were high. Similar results have been observed in our laboratory (Gaito, 1977a). These results seem to be at variance with those of Goddard *et al.* (1969), who maintain that intensity had little effect on the kindling process as long as the intensity is above threshold for the subject. However, the intensities used by Pinel *et al.* and by Gaito were much greater than those used by Goddard *et al.*

The kindled seizures are precipitated by the electrical stimulation, although once initiated these seizures may persist for many seconds after the termination of the current; they rarely begin spontaneously. This lack of spontaneous convulsions is common for most researchers in this area. However, two groups (Pinel, Mucha, & Phillips, 1975; Wada *et al.*, 1974) reported spontaneous seizures in a few rats and cats following many stimulations after the development of seizure activity.

Although behavior appears normal between trials, electrical afterdischarges or unusual spiking patterns may occur, which usually disappear in the rat within 2 or 3 days after the last convulsive trial (Goddard & Douglas, 1975; Racine, 1972). However, in the cat the presence of afterdischarges between trials may be a permanent event (Goddard & Douglas, 1975). Thus, one would expect that spontaneous convulsions would appear occasionally, with the probability of such an event being greater for cats than for rats.

Pinel and Rovner (1978a) extended stimulation sessions of the amygdala of rats to about 300 over a 134-day period. Spontaneous seizures were observed in 16 of the 18 kindled subjects. Presumably the failure of other researchers to note spontaneous seizures is based on the short-term nature of their research effort. Pinel and Rovner (1978b) further noted that stimulation of three other sites (caudate, hippocampus, entorhinal cortex) for extended periods produced spontaneous seizures in rats. These seizures persisted over a 35-day test period following the cessation of stimulation.

An unique aspect of the kindling phenomenon is the relative permanency of the effect (Goddard et al., 1969; Wada et al., 1974). The convulsions occur either on the first trial or within a few trials, even after a 3-month interval of no stimulation (Gaito, 1976g; Goddard et al., 1969; McIntyre & Goddard, 1973), 6 months (Gaito, 1976g), or 12 months (Wada et al., 1974). Over long intervals, several trials are usually required for convulsions to occur. Thus, there is the suggestion of some loss of strength of the tendency over periods of nonstimulation. Goddard et al. (1969) reported about a 10% loss in rekindling after a 3-month period. Wada et al. (1974) reported the persistence of the effect in two cats for more than 12 months, but an elevated intensity was required to elicit seizure activity. We have observed also that an increased intensity or greater number of trials are required after 6 months of rest in most rats (Gaito, 1976g). However, an interval of 14–30 days produced no significant increase in the number of trials to reach criterion (Gaito, 1976c, 1976g; McIntyre & Goddard, 1973). Even though there is no change in the number of trials to reach a specific number of convulsions following short periods of no stimulation, we have found consistently an increase of 10–20 sec in the duration of convulsions (Gaito, 1976c, 1976g). The longest convulsion we have observed was for about 5 min with a rat that had been rested for 30 days (Gaito, 1976g).

Recent research has suggested that the paradoxical sleep periods with associated rapid eye movements (REM) are involved in the mechanisms of memory consolidation (Drucker-Colin & McGaugh, 1977). Thus, it is interesting to note that Smith and Miskinian (1975) reported an increase in paradoxical sleep in response to daily, mild amygdaloid stimulation to rats prior to any evidence of Stage 2 or 3 behavior.

B. ELECTROPHYSIOLOGICAL

A number of investigators have reported electrical changes during the kindling process (Goddard, 1972; Goddard et al., 1969; McIntyre & Goddard, 1973; Racine, 1972). Racine (1972) described a sequence of changes in the amygdala. First there was the normal electrical pattern. With repeated stimulation, the threshold for an afterdischarge was decreased. Soon the afterdischarge appeared; it was a simple spike and wave form, 1 cycle per second, with a duration of about 6–50 sec and a mean amplitude of 702 μV. The first afterdischarge appeared before behavioral automatisms were observed. With further stimulation, the wave form became more complex, and increases occurred in frequency, duration, and amplitude. Then an afterdischarge was induced in the contralateral amygdala. At first the amplitude of this wave was lower than the afterdischarge in the ipsilateral amygdala. When the two were approximately equal in amplitude, clonic convulsions ensued.

Racine, Newberry, and Burnham (1975) found that kindling of the amygdala was facilitated by repeated tetanic stimulation of this structure prior to the onset of kindling. The tetanic stimulation characteristics partially mimicked the cellular discharge parameters during an afterdischarge.

Tanaka (1972) found somewhat similar electrical events with rabbits, as had Racine (1972), and indicated that the amygdaloid afterdischarge spread not only to the contralateral amygdala but to other parts of the brain as well, usually in an orderly sequence (namely, to the hippocampus first, then to the occipital cortex, and finally to the frontal cortex). (Tanaka recorded only from the amygdala, hippocampus, and frontal and occipital cortices.) The propagated afterdischarge usually disappeared concomitantly with or earlier than that of the original after-discharge in the amygdala, although the hippocampus afterdischarge continued longer in some cases. Convulsive behavior coincided with the brain wave changes in the frontal cortex.

Burnham (1975) did a thorough analysis of afterdischarges in ipsilateral and contralateral structures during kindling with four structures: amygdala, septal area, ventral hippocampus, and dorsal hippocampus. During unilateral stimulation of each structure, progressive growth of afterdischarge occurred in each, similar to that noted by Goddard et al. (1969) and Racine (1972). However, this afterdischarge growth took place in sudden, large increments rather than in a gradual manner, especially in the amygdala and septal area. Afterdischarges were induced in each of the three other contralateral structures during ipsilateral stimulation of the amygdala and septal area. However, stimulation of each of the hippocampal areas produced afterdischarges only in the contralateral amygdala and septal area.

Upon stimulation of contralateral structures after kindling in ipsilateral sites, the afterdischarges were relatively mature from the start, averaging longer durations and showing more mature amplitudes and spike patterns than in the initial ipsilateral stimulation. This afterdischarge maturity was most pronounced in the amygdala and septal areas.

By very careful measurement and analysis of synaptic fiber potentials in the squirrel monkey and rat hippocampus during kindling, Douglas and Goddard (1975) and Goddard and Douglas (1975) indicated that a potentiation of evoked potentials resulted, which was of relatively permanent nature. They could not indicate whether the potentiation of excitatory synapses was based on presynaptic or postsynaptic membrane events.

Adamec (1975) found that afterdischarge threshold varied directly with attack tendencies in cats and inversely with withdrawal tendencies. Periodic stimulation of the amygdala of rat-killing cats lowered their afterdischarge threshold to within the range of non-rat-killing cats and inhibited their tendency to kill rats. These changes appeared abruptly and lasted as long as the cats were kept alive (up to 3 months with some cats).

C. NEUROLOGICAL

By careful analysis using sine wave electrical stimulation, Goddard et al. (1969) indicated that the behavioral changes were not due to a pathological brain process but were a function of the stimulating parameters. Kindling was not caused by metallic ions deposited by the electrode during stimulation or to lesions produced by the electrical activity. In fact, a lesion placed at the site to be stimulated eliminated the behavioral changes. Examination of this kindled site with the light or electron microscope revealed no abnormality that could not be observed at the tip of an electrode in animals that were not kindled or did not receive electrical stimulation (Goddard & Douglas, 1975). Tress and Herberg (1972) also reported that the effect was produced by electrical stimulation and was not the result erosion of metallic particles from the electrodes or of transient and reversible changes taking place at the electrode tips.

Many brain regions are not responsive, for example, the majority of the neocortex, the thalamus, and the brainstem. Those that were responsive to electrical stimulation extended from the olfactory bulbs to the entorhinal cortex, including the septal region and the hippocampus. Almost all points in this olfactory–limbic system gave positive effects. The amygdala was the most responsive; all amygdaloid nuclei appeared to be equally responsive. There was a tendency for the number of trials to the first clonic convulsion to correspond roughly with the extent of anatomical connections with the amygdaloid complex. The responsive areas with the number of trials to first convulsion with Wistar rats were (60Hz sine waves, 50 μA for 60 sec): amygdala, 15; globus pallidus, 22; pyriform cortex, 24; olfactory area, 29; anterior limbic field, 29; entorhinal cortex, 37; olfactory bulb, 44; septal area, 55; preoptic area, 63; caudate putamen, 74; hippocampus, 77. These areas fall roughly into two systems—the anterior limbic and the olfactory limbic. Stimulation of the first system produced tonic–clonic convulsions; convulsions from the second were clonic–clonic in nature.

A number of other researchers also indicated that stimulation of the amygdala provides the fastest kindling (Burnham, 1975; Racine, 1975). With the Royal Victoria Hooded strain (which usually kindles faster than Wistar strains) and a greater intensity of stimulation, Burnham (1975) reported the mean number of afterdischarges to first convulsion as follows: amygdala, 11; septal area, 17; ventral hippocampus, 21; dorsal hippocampus, 37. With the intensity that Burnham used, afterdischarges occurred on the first trial or within a few trials.

Racine, Rose, and Burnham (1977) found some results similar to those of Burnham (1975). Electrodes were implanted into the dorsal hippocampus (CA1), ventral CA1, dorsal dentate gyrus, or ventral dentate gyrus. The dorsal areas required a greater number of stimulations prior to convulsions than the ventral areas, but the afterdischarge thresholds were lower.

Racine (1975) was able to differentiate three cortical areas according to afterdischarge responses and behavior following repeated electrical stimulation. Paleocortical areas (pyriform cortex, entorhinal cortex, cingulate cortex, and frontal pole) were similar to subcortical sites in the gradual development of afterdischarge and behavioral seizure activity. Anterior neocortical stimulation provided afterdischarges and seizure activity from the first trial. At first the behavior was mild but it increased in intensity with repeated stimulation. However, little change resulted in the afterdischarge. Posterior neocortical areas yielded afterdischarge activity similar to that of the anterior neocortex, but convulsive behavior did not develop.

Gaito (1979a) found a pattern unique to the dorsal caudate putamen, which was quite different from that of the amygdala. The three stages for stimulation of the later are: exploratory behavior, behavioral automatisms, and clonic convulsions. The caudate putamen (CP) reaction pattern was different in each of the three stages, but especially in Stage 1. For most rats the immediate reaction to stimulation was a sharp pull of the head to the ipsilateral side, a slight or extreme roll in the ipsilateral direction, and spastic jerks of the forepaws. These behaviors terminated with the offset of stimulation. The CP reaction pattern appeared to decrease in duration and intensity as kindling proceeded during the first few stimulation trials, but with many rats it was present initially during the trials in which behavioral automatisms or clonic convulsions occurred. The CP reaction pattern, in full or modified form, also was present after the rat had convulsed many times. In many cases the CP reaction would blend into the onset of the CC. Thus, in each of the three stages there was a part or full CP reaction pattern with the onset of current; this behavior was partially or completely displaced by the behavioral automatisms or clonic convulsions during Stages 2 and 3, respectively. It appears that as kindling proceeds with associated underlying brain changes, these changes bring about a partial displacement or modification of the brain events that are responsible for the CP reaction. We see that an acquired reaction (kindling) is displacing or modifying a natural involuntary reaction (CP reaction). This result is another aspect of kindling that is similar to that during the learning process (Gaito, 1974).

Both positive and negative intraanimal transfer effects are possible (Goddard *et al.,* 1969). Kindling one amygdala (primary site) reduced the number of trials required to kindle the second amygdala (secondary site), although increased latency to convulsion resulted. This reduction in number of trials to convulsions in the secondary site was present even when the primary site was ablated or lesioned after kindling (McIntyre & Goddard, 1973; Racine *et al.,* 1972). However, having kindled the secondary site, interference resulted when rekindling the primary site with normal or split-brain rats (McIntyre, 1975; McIntyre & Goddard, 1973). These results suggested that brainstem structures were important for transfer aspects. The negative transfer was directly proportional to the number of convulsions, and spontaneously dissipated over time; complete dissipation occurred after a 2-week rest period (McIntyre & Goddard, 1973). Positive transfer resulted not only from amygdala to amygdala, but from amygdala to some other brain structure, such as the septal region (Goddard *et al.,* 1969).

Burnham (1975) found results similar to those of McIntyre and Goddard. Positive transfer occurred at the secondary site with four limbic structures, namely, amygdala, septal area, dorsal hippocampus, and ventral hippocampus.

The afterdischarge in the secondary site was mature from the onset of the kindling trials in this site. Negative transfer during rekindling of the primary site occurred in significant amounts only when the kindled secondary site was the amygdala.

During the occurrence of positive transfer in the kindling of the secondary site, Burnham noted that the duration of seizures at the onset was similar to that seen during the last kindling trial with the primary site but that latencies,[3] although greater at the onset of secondary site kindling than at the onset of primary site kindling, slowly decreased. This discrepancy in duration and latency data suggested that two mechanisms might be involved: (*a*) a convulsive mechanism that is fully developed during primary kindling, with duration as an indicator; and (*b*) a triggering mechanism that is only partially developed during primary kindling, with latency as its indicator. Results in our laboratory with latency data are consistent with those of Burnham, but we found that duration values slowly increase over the first three convulsions in a set of six convulsions in the secondary site and in further stimulation of the primary site (Gaito & Gaito, 1979). However, we used three stimulations per day whereas Burnham had a single trial each day.

It has been assumed that transsynaptic circuitry changes occur during the kindling process (Goddard *et al.*, 1969; Goddard, 1972). In this process, the modified neural circuits could be limbic–limbic or limbic–motor in nature. Research by Racine *et al.* (1972) suggested that this development resulted from increased strength of limbic–limbic connections rather than the strengthening of limbic-motor connections.

Goddard *et al.* (1969) discussed possible neural circuitry changes. To account for the slow change in behavior culminating in convulsions, and for the intraanimal positive and negative transfer results, they suggested that two specific, but widespread, neural circuits were established. One was developed during stimulation of the primary site. During kindling of the secondary site, the second circuit utilizes and ties into response elements of the first circuit and triggers convulsions in fewer trials than were required with stimulation of the primary site. As a result of this utilization, however, the circuits are changed to correspond with the activity of the second region and lose some of their correspondence with the first. A few trials are necessary to reestablish the original connection with the first circuit. The results by Goddard and Douglas (1975) and Douglas and Goddard (1975) showing potentiation of evoked potentials at the synapse are consistent with the notion of neural circuitry change, possibly of a transsynaptic facilitation nature.

D. CHEMICAL

With changes in behavior, electrophysiology, and neurological aspects, one would assume that chemical changes were occurring also. Gaito, Hopkins, and

---

[3] Time between onset of current to onset of convulsions.

Pelletier (1973) found the same electrophoretic pattern of prealbumin region acidic proteins for amygdaloid-kindled rats as for nonstimulated controls and for rats subjected to stimulation for varying periods prior to convulsion. An intraperitoneal injection of homogenate supernatant from convulsed rats resulted in a retardation in the kindling process with naive recipients, if the injection contained the equivalent of 1, 2, 2.5, or 3 brain amounts when the interval between injection and stimulation was 24 hours (Gaito, 1975, 1976a; Gaito & Gaito, 1974).

Gaito (1976b) reported that the amino acid, taurine, produced a retardation effect on rats that had not reached the behavioral automatism or clonic convulsion stages. However, no effect occurred when rats had progressed to these advanced stages in the kindling process to be discussed later.

Other chemicals that retard the kindling rate are atropine (Arnold, Racine, & Wise, 1973), Δ^9-tetrahydrocannabinol (Fried & McIntyre, 1973), phenobarbitol (Arnold et al., 1973; Wise & Chinerman, 1974), and diazepam (Wise & Chinerman, 1974). The kindling rate is facilitated by reserpine, 6-hydroxydopamine, and handling, possibly by reducing stress and lowering the norepinephrine levels (Arnold et al., 1973; Corcoran, Fibiger, McCaughran, & Wada, 1974). Facilitation with pentetrazol was also reported by Tanaka (1972).

Chemicals that are able to suppress or moderate the intensity of convulsions are diazepam and phenobarbitol (Tanaka, 1972; Wise & Chinerman, 1974), Δ^9-tetrahydrocannabinol (Corcoran et al., 1973; Fried & McIntyre, 1973), and acetazolamide, lidocaine, and mephamphetamine (Tanaka, 1972). Shock to the feet of rats, administered just prior to brain stimulation, was able to shorten or completely block both motor seizures and afterdischarges (Pinel, Phillips, & MacNeill, 1973). The authors suggested that the effect of the footshock may have increased levels of norepinephrine at the synapse.

A convenient manner in which to determine the effects of chemicals on the kindling process is to utilize the two mechanisms of Burnham (1975). Table 7.1 provides a descriptive summary of the chemical data. Presumably, those chemicals that suppress convulsions affect the triggering mechanism, whereas those that affect the kindling rate of development probably influence the development of the convulsive mechanism. However, some chemicals affect both mechanisms.

Chemicals may produce a "kindling type" development. Vosu and Wise (1975) produced behavioral seizure activity with injections of carbachol (a cholingergic agonist) into brain areas of the rat. The behavior developed in similar fashion to that in response to electrical stimulation. Chemical stimulation of the amygdala produced faster kindling-type development than did stimulation of either the caudate or the hippocampus.

Likewise, kindling-type effects have been produced by subconvulsive levels of metrazol or other convulsive chemicals administered periodically (Pinel & Van Oot, 1975). Therefore, for the lower part of Table 7.1, it is probable that convulsion-producing chemicals (sub- or supraconvulsive levels), such as metrazol, would potentiate the kindling effect if administered prior to the kindling attempt.

Table 7.1
Kindling Mechanisms and Chemicals That Affect Each [a]

Mechanism	Chemical effect
Convulsive mechanism	Effect on rate of development
Retard	Interanimal retardation factor
	Taurine
	Atropine
	Δ^9-tetrahydrocannabinol
	Phenobarbitol
	Diazepam
Facilitate	Reserpine
	6-hydroxydopamine
	Handling (reducing stress and lowering
	level of norepinephrine?)
Triggering mechanism	Effect on trigger
Suppress	Δ^9-tetrahydrocannabinol
	Phenobarbitol
	Diazepam
	Acetazolamide
	Lidocaine
	Mephamphetamine
	Footshock (increase levels of
	norepinephrine?)
Potentiate	Convulsion producing chemicals
	(e.g., metrazol)

[a] From Gaito, J. The kindling effect as a model of epilepsy. *Psychological Bulletin*, 1976, *83*, 1097–1109. Copyright 1976 by the American Psychological Association. Reprinted by permission.

Kindling may have an effect on the behavior of an organism that has been receiving certain chemicals which are later withheld. As indicated earlier, rats that have been stimulated to the behavioral automatism stage or beyond appear to be hypersensitive. For example, an animal after completing a clonic convulsion is extremely difficult to handle. Thus, it is not surprising that Pinel and Van Oot (1975) and Pinel, Van Oot, and Mucha (1975) found that repeated stimulation of the amygdala of rats potentiated the effects of subsequent alcohol withdrawal.

E. OTHER ASPECTS

In the course of investigating kindling phenomena in our laboratory, we found results that were of an unusual nature. McIntyre and Goddard (1973) and Burnham (1975) were concerned with sequential alternation of unilateral stimulation for three phases (primary–secondary–primary). Gaito (1976c) extended the number of alternating phases to 10 (5 for primary site—5 for secondary site) and found unexpected results. Behavior stablized in criterion values (number of trials to six convulsions) by Phases 3 and 4, with many rats showing a convulsion on every trial. However, in latency data the difference in values for primary and secondary sites tended to persist. Most rats showed a successive low–high pattern for latencies over the 10 phases. If the mean latency for each set of six clonic convulsions for individual rats or groups of rats were plotted over the 10 phases, a sawtooth oscillation type curve appeared. Thus, this result has been called the *oscillation effect*. The predominant type of oscillation pattern is primary oscillation (primary sites have low values); however, secondary oscillation (secondary sites have low values) occurs also.

This sequential alternation procedure has been carried up to 50 phases (six convulsions per phase). Some rats showed an oscillation pattern over the entire 50 phases (Gaito, 1978).

Oscillation is not disrupted by a number of experimental variables. In latency data, simultaneous bilateral stimulation prior to, or after, the development of oscillation had no disruptive effect on the oscillation tendency (Gaito, 1976d). The tendency persisted with 1, 3, or 6 trials per day (Gaito, 1976e), and 1, 6, and 12 convulsions per phase (Gaito, 1976f). Oscillation was as prominent in old rats (420–475 days of age) as in younger ones (135–200 days) (Gaito & Nobrega, 1977). Rest intervals of 1, 3, and 6 months interspersed between two sets of 10 sequential alternation phases had no deleterious effect (Gaito, 1976g). The tendency was unaffected by intensities of 100 and 280 μA, but 560 μA intensity had a slight disruptive effect (Gaito, 1977a). Thus, it appears that the oscillation effect is an extremely robust event for latency data.

A set of statistical analyses with the data from these experimental variables was performed by Gaito, Gaito, & Nobrega (1977). With data from 139 rats over 10 phases, one common factor was obtained in a factor analysis for duration to convulsion data, but two common factors appeared in latency to convulsion and criterion data. The two factors were a Primary Site Stimulation factor and a Secondary Site Stimulation factor. The two common factors were moderately correlated in the former data but not in the latter measure. The presence of two interrelated factors in these statistical analyses is consistent with the Goddard *et al.* (1969) notion of interrelated neural aspects in the primary and secondary sites.

In other statistical analyses, Gaito, Nobrega, and Gaito (1978) reported that primary oscillation predominated in overall numbers in three measures (latency, criterion, duration) but only in latency data was the ninth regression component a significant one in an orthogonal polynomials trend analysis. The regression equation using this component provided a low–high sequence of values as a sawtooth oscillation type curve.

The oscillation effect occurs even when the brain is split in rats (Nobrega & Gaito, 1978). Presumably, the brainstem is important in any interaction between the two hemispheres during kindling and oscillation events (McIntyre, 1975; Nobrega & Gaito, 1978; Wada & Sato, 1975).

The exact basis for the oscillation effect is unknown at this time. However, a number of possible bases for it have been eliminated (Gaito *et al.,* 1978). This effect is not due to chance. The probability of a sequence of "lows" and "highs" meeting our criterion of "oscillation" based on chance is .17.[4] In every experiment conducted so far the proportion of oscillators has been significantly greater than that expected based on a *p* of .17. Furthermore, stimulation of a single side over 10 phases indicated that the proportion of oscillators observed was approximately .17 (Gaito & Nobrega, 1978).

The effect is not due to differential thresholds for the two sides or on differential effectiveness of the two electrodes for the effect occurs when the same intensities are used for both sides or when intensities just above threshold are employed (Gaito, 1977b).

The effect is not based on differential placement of the two electrodes (as long as one or both electrodes are in the amygdala or in nearby tissue, according to histological analyses) (Gaito, 1979a), or on a differential natural reactivity of the two brain sites. This last possibility appeared to be eliminated because specific behavior observed seems to suggest the operation of an active inhibitory process (Gaito, 1976c, 1976d, 1977a, 1977b; Gaito & Nobrega, 1977). Although a rat may rear upon its hind paws immediately with stimulation of either side, the convulsion tends to occur quickly for one side but appears to be actively inhibited with stimulation of the other side. On this latter side, the rat's forepaws may begin to move slightly (incomplete convulsion) but then will stop for 5–10 sec before a complete convulsion occurs. These incomplete convulsions tended to be more frequent on the high latency side.

Transfer and interference effects between primary and secondary sites are presumed to be responsible for the results found by McIntyre (1975) and McIntyre and Goddard (1973) over three phases of unilateral stimulation with normal and split-brain rats. Thus, we assume that some type of interaction between the two brain sites is occurring over the 10 or more phases involved in our sequential alternation research.

Presumably there are some inhibitory and/or facilitatory effects from the primary site to the secondary site, and vice versa, to produce the oscillation effect (Nobrega & Gaito, 1978). A pattern appears to be set up, either primary oscillation or secondary oscillation, during Phases 1 and 2, or by Phases 3 and 4, and most rats continue with this pattern for the remainder of the 10 phases. In one experiment in which rats were stimulated through 50 phases, some rats showed a consistent pattern of oscillation for the 50 phases (Gaito, 1978).

Irrespective of the basis for the oscillation effect, the unilateral sequential alternation procedure and the resulting oscillation effect appear to be useful for obtaining information on some aspects of the events underlying the kindling

[4] To be designated as an "oscillator," a rat has to show a "low-high" or "high-low" pattern for 8 or 10 of the 10 phases of stimulation. This criterion gives 8, 9, or 10 runs with the one sample runs test (Hoel, 1954) to provide a probability of .17 (Gaito, Nobrega, & Gaito, 1978).

effect, for example, possible differential electrical synaptic patterns related to the difference in latency values for the primary and secondary sites. Because kindling shows many parallels to learning and to epilepsy, and can be considered as a model of consistent behavioral changes in response to an invariant stimulus, experimentation with the oscillation effect may have the potential for providing information relevant to brian function in general.

IV. The Kindling Effect as a Suitable Procedure for Simulating Epileptic Conditions

It is interesting to note the possible relationship of Stages 2 and 3 behavior to some types of epilepsy. Stage 2, with the behavioral automatisms such as short arrest reaction and eye closure, appears to be similar to the momentary lapses present during the petit mal condition in humans. The convulsive behavior present during Stage 3 resembles the grand mal state. Thus, it would appear that this brain stimulation procedure would be a useful addition to those available in the experimental study of epilepsy (Purpura *et al.*, 1972). Kindling is unique because it shows the slow development of a process leading to convulsions. Thus, one can stop the process at any point to evaluate brain conditions. Also, the effects of potential anticonvulsants can be evaluated at different points in the kindling process.

Although the kindling effect may appear to be an excellent model of epileptic events, there may be important differences. One is that the mechanisms underlying the two conditions may be dissimilar. To account for the various events involved in kindling, Goddard and his colleagues suggested the involvement of the following two effects: (*a*) a long-term effect of positive nature, due to modified neural circuitry (Goddard *et al.*, 1969); and (*b*) a short-term aftereffect of negative nature (McIntyre & Goddard, 1973). The former involved the establishment of two specific but widespread neural circuits, as discussed earlier. The results by Douglas and Goddard (1975) and Goddard and Douglas (1975), indicating a potentiation of evoked responses of relatively permanent nature, are consistent with this possibility.

The exact nature and mechanism of the aftereffect are not known. The aftereffect is able to suppress seizure activity in different parts of the nervous system, is proportional to the number of convulsions, and spontaneously dissipates over time; complete dissipation occurs in 2 weeks (McIntyre & Goddard, 1973).

The convulsive and triggering mechanisms of Burnham (1975) appear to be related to these two effects. Presumably, the convulsive mechanism would be based on modified neural circuitry, and the short-term aftereffect might involve a retardation of the operation of the triggering mechanism.

Logically, because there are many types of epilepsy, one would expect that the mechanisms underlying the kindling seizures would not be the same as those for some epilepsies. Thus, under the assumption that in the kindling process gradual changes occur in neural circuitry, these changes would seem to be different from the mechanisms involved in some types of epilepsy, that is, those in which seizures presumably develop in response to hyperactive or hypersensitive brain cells (i.e., it is only the triggering mechanism that is of concern because the convulsive mechanism is already available to be triggered).

It is possible to evaluate the adequacy of the kindling process as a useful model of epilepsy by testing if chemicals that have shown anticonvulsant properties with epileptic patients moderate the convulsions induced by kindling. If the chemical is successful as an anticonvulsant with human epilepsy and with kindling convulsions, this result would suggest (but not verify) that the mechanism underlying the convulsions may be the same for both conditions. If the chemical is effective with one but not the other, the suggestion is that the mechanisms are different. Recently, we have made such an evaluation with taurine. Likewise, we have evaluated another agent, low frequency stimulation as a potential therapy with epilepsy. First, let me discuss some of the characteristics of taurine and then note its capability as a therapeutic agent in kindling events. Then I will consider brain stimulation therapy.

A. BIOCHEMICAL THERAPY: TAURINE

Taurine appears to have a moderating effect on convulsions produced by some experimental methods and in some human cases; however, it is not clear that taurine would have the same effect with convulsions resulting from amygdaloid stimulation, because the mechanism underlying the kindling effect may be quite different from that in the human cases and that produced by other experimental methods of seizure production.

In recent years there has been a tremendous interest in the amino acid taurine from basic and applied viewpoints. Taurine (2-aminoethanesulphonic acid) is a sulfur-containing amino acid that is found in nearly all tissues investigated (Gaitonde, 1970). It is interesting to note that taurine is structurally similar to gamma-aminobutryic acid (GABA), an amino acid that is assumed to be in inhibitory neurotransmitter (Kaczmarek & Adey, 1974).

The release of taurine from cells appears to be related to activity level. Jasper and Koyama (1969) found that such release was higher during arousal than during sleep. The most striking condition for change of taurine is during convulsive behavior. When seizures are produced via a number of methods (e.g., cobalt, ouabain, penicillin, zinc) in cats, rats, or mice, the concentrations of taurine decrease in and around the focal point, and the amounts released increase (Barbeau & Donaldson, 1974; Craig & Hartmann, 1973; Kaczmarek & Adey, 1974; Koyama, 1972; Van Gelder, 1972). With administration of taurine, the seizures were suppressed or reduced in severity and the amounts of taurine approached the preconvulsive levels (Barbeau & Donaldson, 1974; Kaczmarek & Adey, 1974: Van Gelder, 1972). Similar results occurred in some human epileptic conditions (Barbeau & Donaldson, 1974; Bergamini, Mutani, Delsedime, & Durelli, 1974). Other amino acid levels changed also—a decrease in GABA, glutamic acid, and aspartic acid and an increase in glycine (Van Gelder & Courtois, 1972; Van Gelder, Sherwin, & Rasmussen, 1972).

Although the exact role of taurine in the nervous system is unknown, a number of functions have been suggested in recent years. The most intriguing role for taurine that has been offered is that affecting synaptic events, either as an inhibitory neurotransmitter or as a synaptic modulator. Although the idea that taurine is an inhibitory neurotransmitter has much supportive evidence (Haas & Hosli, 1973; Hosli, Haas, & Hosli, 1973), it is possible that it is acting as a synaptic modulator. For example, taurine may interact with one or more transmitters (inhibitory and/or excitatory) or other chemical agents to produce a moderating effect at the synapse. Much of the evidence cited for transmitter function is not inconsistent with the modulator role. It is difficult to differentiate between these two roles.

Because it seems that taurine is most sensitive during increased nerve activity (Kaczmarek & Adey, 1974), it is possible that taurine is a "stabilizer of membrane excitability" (Barbeau & Donaldson, 1974). When sufficient intensity of a specific stimulus is provided to brain tissue, seizure activity will occur. A seizure pattern is not solely a pathological manifestation but an inherent property of neurons; it is increased nervous activity characterized by the spontaneous, paroxysmal firing of neurons (Tower, 1960). Thus, it would seem imperative that the central nervous system contain some type of defensive mechanism to keep seizure patterns to a minimum. If taurine's function is as a "stabilizer of membrane excitability," then we would assume that taurine may function to decrease seizure activity. Recent research tends to support this possibility.

Barbeau and Donaldson (1974) suggested that seizure patterns are produced by a deficit in zinc metabolism. This deficit brings about a disturbance in zinc–adenosinetriphosphate (ATP)–GABA complexes with the storage of GABA or interference with ATPase uptake mechanisms of GABA and a decrease in taurine levels. Low brain concentrations of GABA would cause increased excitability to stimuli. Decreased levels of taurine would result in a disturbance of the sodium–potassium–ATPase activity. The overall effect would be membrane instability. Increasing the levels of taurine by external administration was suggested to reverse this pattern.

Although it appears that taurine performs some important intercellular role, the exact function is conjectural at this time. However, research performed in our laboratory on taurine is important relative to our concern that there are different mechanisms underlying the kindling effect and some types of epilepsy. The results of nine experiments reported by Gaito (1976b), undertaken to evaluate the effect of taurine on rats during various stages of the kindling process, were quite clear.

1. The administration of taurine to Wistar rats at Stage 3 had no effect on the latency or duration of the clonic convulsions, nor was there a moderation or suppression of the convulsions. This result occurred over a number of dosages (50, 100, 200, 400 mg/kg body weight), a number of intervals between injection and stimulation (5, 30, and 60 min), and a number of injections (6 and 12).
2. Similar results occurred when rats were injected upon achieving Stage 2.
3. The administration of taurine to rats at Stage 1 retarded the onset of clonic convulsions.

These results are consistent with those obtained by other researchers (Wada, Osawa, Wake, & Corcoran, 1975; Burnham *et al.*, 1975) for animals at the clonic convulsion stage. However, Burnham *et al.* found no differences at the exploratory stage. In any event, it seems clear that if taurine is to have an effect, it will be early in the kindling process. It appears that as soon as electrophysiological and neurological changes occur during stimulation (Goddard *et al*, 1969; McIntyre & Goddard, 1973; Racine, 1972), taurine is ineffective in suppressing or moderating behavioral effects.

This lack of anticonvulsant effect of taurine is in sharp contrast to that with some human epilepsy cases and in other experimentally induced convulsive events (Barbeau & Donaldson, 1974; Bergamini *et al.*, 1974; Mutani, Bergamini, Delsedime, & Durelli, 1974a; Mutani, Bergamini, Fabriello, & Delsedime, 1974b; Izumi, Donaldson, Minnich, & Barbeau, 1973; Van Gelder, 1972), but is consistent with the failure of taurine to attenuate audiogenic seizures in rats with intraperitoneal administration (Laird & Huxtable, 1976). Taurine had attenuating action with intraventricular administration but produced marked behavioral depression. Laird and Huxtable maintained that the attenuating effect of taurine involved a nonspecific central nervous system depression rather than that of a selective anticonvulsant effect.

The experimental methods of inducing convulsions for which taurine has been a successful anticonvulsant are those using cobalt in cats and mice (Van Gelder, 1972), a combination of sodium penicillin, conjugated estrogens, and strychnine with cats (Mutani *et al.*, 1974b), ouabain with rats (Izumi *et al.*, 1973), and alumina cream with cats (Mutani *et al.*, 1974a). The human epileptic cases for which taurine was effective were primary generalized epilepsy, secondary generalized epilepsy, and partial seizures (Bergamini *et al.*, 1974a).

After 10 days of daily treatment with taurine 13 of 15 patients had no seizures. Taurine was administered weekly over 50 more days. Only 4 of the subjects were seizure free and showed normal EEG records at the end of this period. Barbeau and Donaldson (1974) also reported that taurine had antiseizure effects with focal epilepsy patients.

The difference in the methods showing success and failure may be based on different mechanisms underlying each event. It appears that neural circuitry changes occur during kindling (Goddard *et al.,* 1969; McIntyre & Goddard, 1973; Racine, 1972), whereas in some human epilepsy or other induced seizures, such drastic changes may not be produced. Presumably, in the latter case, hypersensitive or hyperactive cells, but no circuitry changes, are involved. Therefore, although the kindling process has been suggested as an excellent model of epilepsy (Gaito, 1974; Goddard *et al.,* 1969; Pinel *et al.,* 1973; Tanaka, 1972; Wada *et al.,* 1974), the results with taurine suggest that the similarity between the two may be only at the behavioral level and that different mechanisms may underlie the two conditions, at least in some cases.

B. BRAIN STIMULATION THERAPY: LOW FREQUENCIES

The most obvious use of a method such as kindling is to evaluate the effectiveness of potential chemical anticonvulsants. However, another possibility is that of inducing kindled seizures by 60-Hz stimulation and then to use other frequencies which do not produce seizures (e.g., 3 Hz) in an attempt to reverse the seizure state. Thus, 60-Hz brain stimulation would be competing with 3-Hz stimulation, either in a successive or simultaneous fashion. Both successive and simultaneous 60–3-Hz brain stimulation competition methods have been used in our laboratory with similar results. *The 3-Hz stimulation obscured the effect of 60-Hz brain stimulation with some rats under some conditions.*

In one experiment, one group of rats was stimulated bilaterally in the amygdalae with 60-Hz sine waves of low intensity. A second group was stimulated with 60 Hz in one amygdala and by 3 Hz in the other one. The presence of 3-Hz stimulation to one amygadala retarded the development of Stages 2 and 3 behavior (Gaito, 1979b). In the first group, Stage 2 behavior was achieved in 4.7 trials (mean), whereas the second group required a mean of 22.2 trials to attain this stage. The mean number of convulsions in 20 trials was 5.2 for the first group and .4 for the group receiving 3-Hz stimulation on one side.

In a number of experiments, 3-Hz stimulation following the achievement of convulsions with 60-Hz brain stimulation brought some rats back to Stage 1 (exploration). In these experiments, all rats were brought to a criterion of 6, 36, 48, 60, or 100 clonic convulsions. The rats were split into two types of groups: One received 24–100 convulsive trials of 60-Hz stimulation (controls); the other group was stimulated with 3-Hz sine waves for 24 or 36 trials at the same or double the intensity of stimulation that was used with the previous 60-Hz stimulation (experimentals). Both groups then were stimulated again by 60-Hz sine waves over 6 or more trials and their behavior noted. The rats that had been subjected only to 60 Hz stimulation continued to convulse on each trial. Some rats in the 3-Hz group, however, showed exploratory behavior during the early trials; with some rats this behavior persisted over many trials. The behavior of this group indicated three important points (Table 7.2):

1. 3-Hz stimulation completely reversed the 60-Hz effect, that is, 14 of 23 rats were brought back to Stage 1 or 2 behavior.

Table 7.2
Aspects of 14 Rats Which Showed Reversal Effect during Test Trials

Rat No.	Conditions[a]	Test trial of first CC	Number of CC	Increase (μA) in ETI[b]
15	48CC-24-double	8	4 in 12	0
20	48CC-24-double	10	6 in 15	70
24	48CC-36-same	10	6 in 15	84
16	48CC-36-same	10	6 in 15	70
13	60CC-24-same	4	8 in 12	0
9	60CC-24-double	10	7 in 18	140
14	60CC-24-double	13	6 in 18	140
4	60CC-36-same	8	6 in 13	56
23	60CC-36-same	10	6 in 15	56
1	60CC-36-same	10	6 in 15	140
3	98CC-36-double	7	6 in 12	0
21	102CC-36-double	12	6 in 17	84
8	102CC-36-double	6	6 in 11	0
18	100CC-36-double	4	6 in 9	0

[a] The first part refers to the number of clonic convulsions (CC) trials with 60-Hz stimulation. The second portion indicates the number of treatment trials with 3-Hz stimulation. The last part specifies the intensity of the 3 Hz compared to the intensity of the previous 60 Hz used.
[b] ETI = effective threshold intensity, 15 μA above threshold.

2. To bring these rats to the convulsive stage during further stimulation trials with 60 Hz required a greater intensity of stimulation than had been the case with the previous 60-Hz stimulation procedures for 9 of the 14, that is, their convulsion threshold had been increased by the interpolated 3-Hz stimulation, from 56–140 μA. The average increase over the 14 rats was 60 μA, a substantial increment.

3. The conditions which appeared most favorable for precipitating the reversal effect were 48, 60, or 100 convulsion trials coupled with 24 trials of 3-Hz stimulation at double intensity or 36 trials of 3-Hz stimulation at the same intensity as that used with the prior 60-Hz stimulation.

Histological analyses of brain tissue slices were conducted on all rats. There was no evidence of any tissue damage around the electrode tips in the rats subjected to 3-Hz stimulation. Thus, the apparent competition effect of 3-Hz stimulation appeared not to be due to brain damage. The results of Douglas and Goddard (1975) and Goddard and Douglas (1975) suggested that 60-Hz stimulation brings about the convulsive stages by synaptic changes. Possibly, the 3-Hz stimulation altered these synaptic modifications.

This "reversal effect" has been substantiated in more recent research. In one experiment, rats were given 60 convulsion trials and then 36 trials of stimulation with 3 Hz. Not a single rat convulsed on the first test trial. Most of these animals convulsed on Trial 10 when intensity of stimulation was increased above previously used levels. In another experiment the effect was obtained also with bilateral stimulation of the amygdalae. In other experiments the presence daily of one or two trials of 3-Hz stimulation preceding, and one or two trials following, stimulation with 60 Hz partially or completely prevented the occurrence of convulsions in most rats; increased levels of stimulation were required to attain the convulsion stage with these animals.

Further research is underway in our laboratory using these procedures with 3-Hz sine waves, and other frequencies, in an effort to elucidate the events underlying these effects.

These results suggest the possibility that low-frequency brain stimulation might prove beneficial to some cases of human epilepsy. However, it should be recognized that both the inducer of convulsions (60 Hz) and the reverser (3 Hz) have frequency aspects in common and this commonness may be responsible for the success of 3 Hz in reversing the 60-Hz effect. Unfortunately, in epilepsy cases the inducer of the seizure condition is seldom known. Thus, 3-Hz stimulation may not have anything in common with the basis for the epilepsy condition. However, the potential benefit of this method with humans does warrant its further evaluation.

Obviously, further research with these methods with animals are required, to indicate the reproducibility of the results, and especially to indicate that other processes (e.g., learning and other intellectual capabilities) are not affected adversely, before applying them to humans. However, these results do indicate that animal research with the kindling effect has been, and should continue to be, a useful method in simulating a human pathologic condition.

V. Conclusions

In evaluating the usefulness of the kindling effect as a model of epilepsy we can use two aspects that I have considered above.

A. MECHANISMS

1. Results Using Taurine (Biochemical Therapy)

The results in some laboratories indicate strongly that taurine may be a useful chemical in alleviating the condition of some epileptic persons. However, the results using taurine with the kindling process suggest that the latter does not provide a model that completely parallels epileptic conditions. Thus, although the union of the kindling procedures (to initiate epileptic type conditions) and taurine (as an anticonvulsant to moderate or reverse the kindled states) appeared, at first, to provide a valuable set of procedures for applied purposes, the results may seem to question such possibility. The inability of taurine to affect rats at Stages 2 or 3 in the kindling process, and the reversal or moderation of some epileptic seizures in humans by taurine suggest that different mechanisms may be involved in the two conditions.

Thus there appears to be a lack of complete parallelism between the kindling process and epileptic conditions. However, this is to be expected. Each of the experimental methods to produce seizures is different and possesses only one or a few of the properties of human epilepsy (Purpura *et al.*, 1972). Presumably, the kindling effect does not differ in this respect from the other models.

2. Results Using Low Frequency Stimulation (Brain Stimulation Therapy)

The kindling effect was reversed completely in some rats under some conditions by 3 Hz brain stimulation. However, this type of therapy has not been used yet with humans with an epileptic condition. Thus, at this time we can not draw any conclusions concerning mechanisms underlying the kindling effect and epilepsy based on these results.

B. BEHAVIORAL CONGRUITY

I have indicated earlier in this chapter the remarkable similarity of behavior of rats at Stage 2 with the petit mal state, and also Stage 3 with grand mal seizures. One can add also the occurrence of spontaneous seizures in rats stimulated for long periods of time (Pinel & Rovner, 1978a, b). Therefore, the behavioral aspects of the kindling effect indicate an adequate representation of the behavior during seizure activity in epilepsy. If one uses this aspect of behavioral congruity, the kindling effect could be considered useful for some purposes.

From these considerations it seems appropriate to conclude that the kindling effect is probably a limited model of epilepsy. However, even though the model is a limited one, it can be useful in setting up and evaluating hypotheses relative to brain aspects and in screening potential therapeutic agents.

Furthermore, one should recognize that the classification of epilepsy encompasses a number of diverse conditions. Therefore, it is possible that the kindling effect may not represent a completely adequate model of some types of epilepsy, whereas it may be analogous to other epileptic conditions (e.g., one of the conditions persisting from infancy in which hereditary and "faulty" circuits may be involved, possibly some of the primary generalized epilepsies discussed by McNaughton & Rasmussen, 1975).

Finally, the potential usefulness of an experimental procedure with animals should be restated. All of the procedures or models provide advantages relevant to human epilepsy (Purpura *et al.*, 1972). Obviously, because human epilepsies comprise a myriad of conditions with different underlying bases, no single experimental model should be expected to be a model of all epilepsies. The kindling effect would appear to have a few advantages over most of the other methods. These advantages are:

1. The parameters of electrical stimulation can be controlled with great precision.
2. The point of the stimulation can be precisely localized and its effect restricted somewhat.
3. The convulsions produced are of a relatively permanent nature and can be precipitated when desired.
4. The development of the process proceeding to the convulsive state can be stopped at any point for study, and potential anticonvulsants can be evaluated. This appears to be a major advantage.

At this time the full potential of the kindling effect as a model of epilepsy has not been utilized. Presumably, its potential efficacy should become clearer over the next few years.

REFERENCES

Adamec, R. Behavioral and epileptic determinants of predatory attack behavior in the cat. *The Canadian Journal of Neurological Sciences*, 1975, *2*, 457–466.

Arnold, P. S., Racine, R. J., & Wise, R A. Effects of atropine, reserpine, 6-hydroxydopamine, and handling on seizure development in the rat. *Experimental Neurology*, 1973, *40*, 457–470.

Barbeau, A., & Donaldson, J. Zinc, taurine, and epilepsy. *Archives of Neurology*, 1974, *30*, 52–58.

Bergamini, L., Mutani, R., Delsedime, M., & Durelli, L. First clinical experience on the antiepileptic action of taurine. *European Neurology*, 1974, *11*, 261–269.

Burnham, W. M. Primary and "transfer" seizure development in the kindled rat. *The Canadian Journal of Neurological Sciences*, 1975, *2*, 417–428.

Burnham, W. M., Arnold, P., & Racine, R. J. *Effects of taurine on "kindled" seizures: A preliminary survey.* Paper presented at the meeting of the Clinical Research Society, Toronto, April 5, 1975.

Coleman, J. C. *Abnormal psychology and modern life.* Chicago: Scott, Foresman, 1956.

Corcoran, M. E., Fibiger, H. C., McCaughran, J. A., Jr., & Wada, J. A. Potentiation of amygdaloid kindling and metrazol-induced seizures by 6-hydroxydopamine in rats. *Experimental Neurology*, 1974, *45*, 118–133.

Corcoran, M. E., McCaughran, J. A., Jr., & Wada, J. A. Acute antiepileptic of Δ^9-tetrahydrocannabinol in rats with kindled seizures. *Experimental Neurology*, 1973, *40*, 471–483.

Craig, C. R., & Hartmann, E. R. Concentration of amino acids on the brain of cobalt-epileptic rat. *Epilepsia*, 1973, *14*, 409–414.

Douglas, R. M., & Goddard, G. V. Long term potentiation of the perforant path–granule cell synapse in the rat hippocampus. *Brain Research*, 1975, *86*, 205–215.

Drucker-Colin, R. R., & McGaugh, J. L. (Eds.) *Neurobiology of sleep and memory.* New York: Academic Press, 1977.

Fried, P. A., & McIntyre, D. C. Electrical and behavioral attenuation of the anti-convulsant properties of Δ^9-THC following chronic administration. *Psychopharmacologia*, 1973, *31*, 215–227.

Gaito, J. The kindling effect. *Physiological Psychology*, 1974, *2*, 45–50.

Gaito, J. Further results obtained with pairing of the "kindling effect" and the "transfer experiment." *Physiological Psychology*, 1975, *3*, 237–239.

Gaito, J. Pairing of the transfer experiment with the kindling paradigm: A summary of results. *Bulletin of Psychonomic Society*, 1976, *1*, 50–52. (a)

Gaito, J. The effects of taurine on various stages of the kindling process: A summary of results. *Bulletin of Psychonomic Society,* 1976, *4,* 397–400. (b)

Gaito, J. An oscillation effect during sequential alternations of unilateral amygdaloid stimulations within the kindling paradigm. *Physiological Psychology,* 1976, *4,* 303–306. (c)

Gaito, J. The effect of bilateral stimulation during sequential alternation of unilateral amygdaloid stimulation. *Bulletin of the Psychonomic Society,* 1976, *4,* 355–357. (d)

Gaito, J. The effect of number of trials per day during sequential alternation of unilateral amygaloid stimulation. *Bulletin of the Psychonomic Society,* 1976, *4,* 403–404. (e)

Gaito, J. The effect of number of convulsions per phase on the oscillation tendency. *Bulletin of the Psychonomic Society,* 1976, *8,* 392–394. (f)

Gaito, J. The effect of varying rest intervals following the development of oscillation during unilateral amygdaloid stimulation. *Bulletin of the Psychonomic Society,* 1976, *8,* 457–458. (g)

Gaito, J. The kindling effect as a model of epilepsy. *Psychological Bulletin,* 1976, *83,* 1097–1109. (h)

Gaito, J. The effect of intensity during sequential alternation of unilateral amygdaloid stimulation. *Bulletin of the Psychonomic Society,* 1977, *9,* 64–66. (a)

Gaito, J. The oscillation effect at near threshold intensities. *Bulletin of the Psychonomic Society,* 1977, *10,* 145–148. (b)

Gaito, J. The oscillation effect over long term periods. *Bulletin of the Psychonomic Society,* 1978, *11,* 9–12.

Gaito, J. An experimental evaluation of the differential natural reactivity as a basis for the oscillation effect. *Bulletin of the Psychonomic Society,* 1979, *13,* 53–54. (a)

Gaito, J. Three Hz brain stimulation interferes with various aspects of the kindling effect. *Bulletin of the Psychonomic Society,* 1979, *13,* 67–70. (b)

Gaito, J., & Gaito, S. T. Interanimal negative transfer of the kindling effect. *Physiological Psychology,* 1974, *2,* 379–382.

Gaito, J., & Gaito, S. T. *Factor analysis of oscillation effect data.* Manuscript in preparation, 1979.

Gaito, J., Gaito, S. T., & Nobrega, J. N. A factor analysis of data from 10 phases of sequential alternation of amygdaloid stimulation within the kindling paradigm. *Physiological Psychology,* 1977, *5,* 300–310.

Gaito, J., Hopkins, R. W., & Pelletier, W. Interanimal transfer and chemical events underlying the kindling effect. *Bulletin of the Psychonomic Society,* 1973, *1,* 319–321.

Gaito, J., & Nobrega, J. The oscillation effect during sequential alternation of amygdaloid stimulation with aged rats. *Bulletin of the Psychonomic Society,* 1977, *9,* 151–154.

Gaito, J., & Nobrega, J. N. Random oscillation patterns with stimulation of a single brain site. *Bulletin of the Psychonomic Society,* 1978, *11,* 65–67.

Gaito, J., Nobrega, J. N., & Gaito, S. T. Statistical analysis of several aspects of the oscillation effect. *Physiological Psychology,* 1978, *6,* 209–214.

Gaitonde, M. K. Sulfur amino acids. In A Lajtha (Ed.), *Handbook of neurochemistry* (Vol. 3). New York: Plenum, 1970.

Goddard, G. V. Long term alteration following amygdaloid stimulation. In B. E. Eleftheriou (Ed.), *The neurobiology of the amygdala.* New York: Plenum, 1972.

Goddard, G. V., & Douglas, R. M. Does the engram of kindling model the engram of long term memory? *The Canadian Journal of Neurological Sciences,* 1975, *2,* 385–394.

Goddard, G. V., McIntyre, D. C., & Leech, C. K. A permanent change in brain function resulting from daily electrical stimulation. *Experimental Neurology,* 1969, *25,* 395–330.

Haas, H. L., & Hosli, L. The depression of brain stem neurones by taurine and its interaction with strychine and bicuculline. *Brain Research,* 1973, *52,* 339–402.

Hoel, P. G. *Introduction to mathematical statistics.* New York: Wiley, 1954.

Hosli, L., Haas, H. L., & Hosli, E. Taurine—a possible transmitter in mammalian central nervous system. *Experientia,* 1973, *29,* 743–744.

Izumi, K., Donaldson, J., Minnich, J. L., & Barbeau, A. Ouabain-induced seizures in rats: Suppressive effects of taurine and g-aminobutryic acid. *Canadian Journal of Physiology and Pharmacology,* 1973, *51,* 885–889.

Jasper, H. H., & Koyama, I. Rate of release of amino acids from the cerebral cortex in the cat as effected by brainstem and thalamic stimulation. *Canadian Journal of Physiology and Pharmacology,* 1969, *47,* 889–905.

Kaczmarek, L. K., & Adey, W. R. Factors affecting the release of (^{14}C)-taurine from cat brain: The electrical effects of taurine on normal and seizure prone cortex. *Brain Research,* 1974, *76,* 83–94.

Koyama, I. Amino acids in the cobalt-induced epileptogenic and non-epileptogenic cat's cortex. *Canadian Journal of Physiology and Pharmacology,* 1972, *50,* 740–752.

Laird, H. E., & Huxtable, R. Effect of taurine on audiogenic seizure response in rats. In R. Huxtable and A. Barbeau (Eds.), *Taurine.* New York: Raven, 1976.

McCaughran, J. A., Jr., Corcoran, M. E., & Wada, J. A. Development of kindled amygdaloid seizures after section of the forebrain commissures in rats. *Folia Psychiatrica et Neurologica Japonica,* 1976, *30,* 65–71.

McIntyre, D. C. Split-brain rat: Transfer and interference of kindled amygdala convulsions. *The Canadian Journal of Neurological Sciences,* 1975, *2,* 429–437.

McIntyre, D. C., & Goddard, G. V. Transfer, interference and spontaneous recovery of convulsions kindled from the rat amygdala. *Electro-encephalography and Clinical Neurophysiology,* 1973, *35,* 533–543.

McIntyre, D. C. & Wann, P. D. Adrenalectomy: Protection from kindled convulsion induced dissociation in rats. *Physiology and Behavior,* 1978, *20,* 469–474.

McNaughton, F. L., & Rasmussen, T. Criteria for selection of patients for neurosurgical treatment. In D. P. Purpura, J. K. Penry, & R. D. Walter (Eds.), *Advances in neurology* (Vol. 8). New York: Raven, 1975.

Millon, T. *Modern psychopathology.* Philadelphia: Saunders, 1969.

Mucha, R. F., & Pinel, J. P. J. Postseizure inhibition of kindled seizures. *Experimental Neurology,* 1977, *54,* 266–282.

Mutani, R., Bergamini, L., Delsedime, M., & Durelli, L. Effects of taurine in chronic experimental epilepsy. *Brain Research,* 1974, *79,* 330–332. (a)

Mutani, R., Bergamini, L., Fabriello, R., & Delsedime, M. Effects of taurine on cortical acute epileptic foci. *Brain Research,* 1974, *70,* 170–173. (b)

Nobrega, J. N., & Gaito, J. Long term induction of kindled seizures in rats: Interhemispheric factors. *The Canadian Journal of Neurological Sciences,* 1978, *5,* 223–230.

Penfield, W., & Roberts, L. *Speech and brain mechanisms.* Princeton, New Jersey: Princeton Univ. Press, 1959.

Pinel, J. P. J., Mucha, R. F., & Phillips, A. G. Spontaneous seizures generated in rats by kindling: A preliminary report. *Physiological Psychology,* 1975, *3,* 127–129.

Pinel, J. P. J., Phillips, A. G., & Deol, G. Effects of current intensity on kindled motor seizure activity in rats. *Behavior Biology,* 1974, *11,* 59–68.

Pinel, J. P. J., Phillips, A. G., & MacNeill, B. Blockage of highly-stable "kindled" seizures in rats by antecedent foot shock. *Epilepsia,* 1973, *14,* 29–37.

Pinel, J. P. J., & Rovner, L. I. Experimental epileptogenesis: Kindling-induced epilepsy in rats. *Experimental Neurology,* 1978, *58,* 190–202. (a)

Pinel, J. P. J., & Rovner, L. I. Electrode placement and kindling-induced experimental epilepsy. *Experimental Neurology,* 1978, *58,* 335–346. (b)

Pinel, J. P. J., Treit, D., & Rovner, L. D. Temporal lobe aggression in rats. *Science,* 1977, *197,* 1088–1089.

Pinel, J. P. J., & Van Oot, P. H. Generality of the kindling phenomenon: Some clinical implications. *The Canadian Journal of Neurological Sciences,* 1975, *2,* 467–475.

Pinel, J. P. J., & Van Oot, P. H. Intensification of the alcohol withdrawal syndrome following periodic electroconvulsive shocks. *Biological Psychiatry,* 1977, *12,* 479–486.

Pinel, J. P. J., Van Oot, P. H., & Mucha, R. F. Intensification of the alcohol withdrawal syndrome by repeated brain stimulation. *Nature,* 1975, *254,* 510–511.

Pryse-Phillips, W. *Epilepsy.* Bristol: John Wright and Sons, 1969.

Purpura, D. P., Penry, J. K., Woodbury, D. M., Tower, D. B., & Walter, R. D. (Eds.). *Experimental models of epilepsy—A manual for the laboratory worker.* New York: Raven, 1972.

Racine, R. J. Modification of seizure activity by electrical stimulation: II. Motor seizure. *Electroencephalography and Clinical Neurophysiology,* 1972, *32,* 281–294.

Racine, R. J. Modification of seizure activity by electrical stimulation: Cortical areas. *Electroencephalography and Clinical Neurophysiology,* 1975, *38,* 1–12.

Racine, R. J., Burnham, W. M., Gartner, J. G., & Levitan, D. Rates of motor seizure development in rats subjected to electrical brain stimulation: Strain and inter-stimulation interval effects. *Electroencephalography and Clinical Neurophysiology,* 1973, *35,* 553–556.

Racine, R., Newberry, F., & Burnham, W. M. Postactivation potentiation and the kindling phenomenon. *Electroencephalography and Clinical Neurophysiology,* 1975, *39,* 261–271.

Racine, R., Okujava, V., & Chipashvili, S. Modification of seizure activity by electrical stimulation: III. Mechanisms. *Electroencephalography and Clinical Neurophysiology,* 1972, *32,* 295–299.

Racine, R., Rose, P. A., & Burnham, W. M. Afterdischarge thresholds and kindling rates in dorsal and ventral hippocampus and dentate gyrus. *The Canadian Journal of Neurological Sciences,* 1977, *4,* 273–278.

Smith, C. T., & Miskinian, D. E. Increases in paradoxical sleep as a result of amygdaloid stimulation. *Physiology and Behavior,* 1975, *15,* 17–19.

Tanaka, A. Progressive changes of behavioral and electroencephalographic responses to daily amygdaloid stimulation in rabbits. *Fukuoka Acta Medica,* 1972, *63,* 152–164.

Tower, D. B. *Neurochemistry of epilepsy.* Springfield, Illinois: Thomas, 1960.

Tress, K., & Herberg, L. J. Permanent reduction in seizure threshold resulting from repeated electrical stimulation. *Experimental Neurology,* 1972, *37,* 347–359.

Valenstein, E. S. *Brain control. A critical examination of brain stimulation and psychosurgery.* New York: Wiley, 1973.

Van Gelder, N. M. Antagonism by taurine of cobalt induced epilepsy in cat and mouse. *Brain Research,* 1972, *47,* 157–165.

Van Gelder, N. M., & Courtois, A. Close correlation between changing content of specific amino acids in epileptogenic cortex of cats, and severity of epilepsy. *Brain Research,* 1972, *43,* 477–484.

Van Gelder, N. M., Sherwin, A. M., & Rasmussen, T. Amino acid content of epileptogenic human brain: Focal versus surrounding regions. *Brain Research,* 1972, *40,* 385–393.

Vosu, H., & Wise, R. A. Cholinergic seizure kindling in the rat: Comparison of caudate, amygdala and hippocampus. *Behavioral Biology,* 1975, *13,* 491–495.

Wada, J. A., Osawa, T., Wake, A., & Corcoran, M. E. Effects of taurine on kindled amygdaloid seizures in rats, cats, and photosensitive baboons. *Epilepsia,* 1975, *16,* 229–234.

Wada, J. A., & Sato, M. Generalized convulsive seizures induced by daily electrical stimulation of the amygdala in cats. *Neurology,* 1974, *24,* 565–574.

Wada, J., & Sato, M. The generalized convulsive seizure state induced by daily electrical stimulation of the amygdala in split brain cats. *Epilepsia,* 1975, *16,* 417–430.

Wada, J. A., Sato, M., & Corcoran, M. E. Persistent seizure susceptibility and recurrent spontaneous seizures in kindled cats. *Epilepsia,* 1974, *15,* 465–478.

Wise, R. A., & Chinerman, J. Effects of diazepam and phenobarbitol on electrically-induced amygdaloid seizures and seizure development. *Experimental Neurology,* 1974, *45,* 355–363.

Woodbury, D. M. Applications to drug evaluation. In D. P. Purpura, J. K. Penry, D. M. Woodbury, D. B. Tower, & R. D. Walter (Eds.). *Experimental models of epilepsy—A manual for the laboratory worker.* New York: Raven, 1972.

HANK DAVIS

Behavioral Anomalies in Aversive Situations[1]

8

As the title implies, the focus of this chapter will be upon anomalous behavior that occurs in aversive situations. What the title does not suggest is the problematic nature of the term "anomaly." To view behavior as anomalous, one must first have an expectancy of the form behavior should take and subsequently have this expectancy violated. Obviously, if our preconception is inaccurate, then much "normal" or reasonable behavior is likely to be seen as "anomalous." With the wisdom of hindsight, it is clear that the experimental literature on animal learning is replete with such instances. Typically, they are born of our ignorance; most commonly stemming from an incomplete knowledge of the subject's predispositions (i.e., species-specific tendencies), or from a limited view of the environment that produced the so-called anomalous behavior.

I. On Anomalies and Abnormalities

Without suggesting anything as radical as the possibility that all behavioral anomalies can be reduced to misjudged normal behavior, it is worth considering the relationship between anomalous and abnormal behavior. There are two im-

[1]Preparation of this chapter was supported, in part, by Grant No. A0673 from the National Research Council of Canada.

portant dimensions to "normalcy": *frequency* and *lawfulness*. Although a strictly
statistical definition of normalcy may be appropriate for the insurance industry,
it is arguably of insufficient value to a psychologist. For instance, Sidman (1960)
has proposed that if uncommon behavior can be reliably replicated under similar
environmental conditions, then its lawfulness suggests that it is not abnormal,
despite its low frequency. In fact, in these circumstances, the label "uncommon" may be better applied to the stimulus environment than to the
behavior which follows.

This conclusion is not restricted to the external environment. Anatomical or
neurological damage may similarly result in bizarre behavior, but it is arguably
the damage which is abnormal (in a statistical sense), and not the behavior. In
fact, the resultant behavior may be entirely lawful given the physical state of the
organism.

This determinist position can be elaborated further. In its ultimate form, it
holds that behavior must be analyzed not only in terms of its immediate
stimulus environment (external and internal), but also in light of its entire conditioning history (Skinner, 1971). Given the range of experience this holds for
most organisms, it is hard to imagine behavior that is not "normal"—infrequent, bizarre, maladaptive, perhaps, but invariably lawful in terms of its
stimulus antecedents. Whether or not the criterion of lawfulness trivializes the
notion of normalcy is a matter of continuing debate.

II. Anomalous Effects of Aversive Control Procedures

As I shall argue at the conclusion, the search for anomalies is productive in
its own right. If it does nothing else, it clarifies the processes of normal behavior.
To this end I shall survey several anomalous behaviors that result from a variety
of aversive control procedures. In each case, the presumption will be made that
the behavioral results might have been otherwise. In some sense, these violated
expectancies are "straw men." There is little point in clinging to them; the
behavioral outcomes are now a matter of record, and our violated expectancies
merely underscore our ignorance and set the stage for the following discussion of
anomalies.

A. CONDITIONED SUPPRESSION

Nearly 40 years ago, Estes and Skinner (1941) demonstrated that an ongoing behavioral baseline could be suppressed by superimposing a signal that had
been paired with unavoidable shock. The effects of this procedure, known as
conditioned suppression, have been surveyed (Davis, 1968), as well as replicated
extensively. Although literally hundreds of experiments have convinced even the
most skeptical observer that conditioned suppression "works," the question of
how or *why* still remains a mystery. Although proclamations about motivational

or response incompatibility are often made (e.g., Rescorla & Solomon, 1967), no one has elucidated the exact manner in which an aversive Pavlovian CS–US produces changes in the rate of an appetitive operant baseline.

In one sense the basic demonstration of conditioned suppression itself is somewhat unexpected, and, had it not been replicated so widely, might have been considered anomalous. Consider the following: A hungry animal is placed in a situation in which barpressing may produce the major portion of its daily food supply. The suppression of responding that occurs during the CS may ultimately cost the animal considerable nutrition. There is no "reason" to cease responding, at least insofar as both signal and shock deliveries are programmed independently of the animal's behavior. Nevertheless, animals do stop responding and earning food during the CS that precedes shock. The typical outcome of a conditioned-suppression procedure appears even more paradoxical when one considers that comparable results have been reported when food rather than shock is superimposed upon responding (Azrin & Hake, 1969). These authors report a suppression of appetitively maintained responding—not during threat of shock, but rather during the presence of a prefood or prewater signal. Thus, whatever explanation one calls forth to account for the typical results of a conditioned-suppression procedure must ultimately accommodate these anomalous findings of Azrin and Hake.

One might assume that a signal that is potent enough to suppress a food-reinforced operant must be highly aversive. However, there is a large body of evidence to suggest that in situations involving the unavoidable delivery of shock, subjects actually prefer to receive just such a signal prior to shock delivery (Harsh, 1978). This evidence, gathered from a variety of "preference testing" procedures (e.g., Lockard, 1963; Perkins, Levis, & Seymann, 1963), not only suggests that rats prefer warning to no warning, but also indicates that subjects will take stronger or more frequent shock in order to receive warning (Badia, Culbertson, & Harsh, 1973). Attempts to deal with the question of why warning is preferred in such situations have reached formal status (e.g., the "safety-signal hypothesis," Seligman & Binik, 1977). Because these are the same signals that have been hypothesized to reinforce shock-avoidance behavior by their termination (cf. Herrnstein, 1969; Miller, 1951), the preference for warning signals would seem less anomalous if one could demonstrate the exact use to which an animal puts such signals. To date no one has done so.

The preference for warning is further surprising if one considers the results of an experiment by Orme-Johnson (1967). In this study, pigeons were trained to keypeck for grain on a variable-interval (VI) reinforcement schedule. Once responding had stabilized, a mild shock was made contingent upon each response. Because the intensity of shock was relatively low, the rate of baseline punished responding stabilized at approximately 80% of the prepunished rate. It was upon this baseline, on which every response was punished, that a conditioned-suppression procedure was superimposed. The CS–US presentations suppressed the punished baseline entirely, a result that might not be surprising were it not for the fact that the intensity of the shock–US was identical to that of the punisher. In other words, when shock was response contingent, it had only a mild suppressive effect on responding. However, a signal that preceded unavoidable delivery of this shock was sufficiently aversive to eliminate baseline responding.

B. LEVERPRESS ESCAPE

It is not unreasonable to view leverpress escape as the simplest of all aversive control procedures. The sheer economy of its requirement, a single leverpress to terminate shock, suggests that all subjects should perform efficiently and reach criterion rapidly.

These expectancies are not unwarranted. Most demonstrations of leverpress escape have reported extremely rapid acquisition and relatively stable performance. The anomalous aspect of leverpress escape is that from its earliest demonstration (Keller, 1941), subjects have given *more* than what was formally required by the procedure. The "something extra" which occurs is known as *leverholding*. Typically, subjects leverpress almost immediately after shock occurs. But rather than making a single response and emitting other behaviors during the shock-free intertrial interval, most rats remain situated on the lever, keeping it depressed until the occurrence of the next shock (see Figure 8.1).

Figure 8.1.   *Illustrative photographs of leverholding during leverpress shock escape procedure. Note atypical use of rear paw on lever in lower right photograph.*

Leverholding during escape has been considered anomalous since its earliest appearance. It has been viewed with gentle amusement, mild curiosity, outright annoyance, and ultimately with the reverence due any persistent enigma. It has moved from being of peripheral to central concern in the treatment of leverpress escape behavior (cf., Dinsmoor & Hughes, 1956; Davis & Burton, 1974). Various attempts have been made to explain it. It has been described as *preparatory* (i.e., functionally and topographically related to making low-latency responses), and *perseverative* (i.e., a spillover or continuation of behavior that was previously reinforced) (cf. Campbell, 1962: Keehn, 1967b). Concerted efforts have been made to eliminate it, regardless of its reason for being (Migler, 1963).

In 1968, Bolles and McGillis reconsidered the simplicity of the leverpress-escape procedure. The results of this procedure were attained so readily that perhaps it was inappropriate to view leverpress escape as a conventional operant response. Could a subject reasonably be expected to emit an operant escape response to terminate shock with latencies between .05 and .10 sec? Unlikely, they argued. Instead, Bolles and McGillis proposed that despite the opportunity for operant reinforcement (i.e., shock termination), leverpress escape actually was derived from species-specific and reflexive behaviors. Specifically, they suggested that rats were likely to freeze at the moment of shock offset, a naturally occurring defensive behavior. This, of necessity, would locate the animal on the lever. The subject then remained motionless in this position throughout the intershock interval until the next shock occurred. At shock onset, the rat made a "reflexive lurch" from and return to the lever, thereby terminating shock and simulating a very low-latency leverpress response.

This rather heretical proposal intrigued us. Beginning in 1971, my laboratory began a series of experiments to explore leverpress escape. An early concern was that traditional response measures might be insensitive to the behavior described by Bolles and McGillis; that is, simply counting the number of escape responses might fail to detect species-specific or reflexive elements. We performed some pilot studies in which subjects were videotaped and the duration of lever depressions were continuously assessed. Our findings supported the analysis proposed by Bolles and McGillis and suggested that further work should concentrate on the properties of leverholding, per se. We reasoned that information beyond response duration would be helpful. To this end we devised a method for measuring the force of all lever contact. Conventional response measurement in escape is borrowed from techniques used with food reinforcement; thus, it not only ignores lever contact beyond the initial 50 msec, but also excludes all lever contact that does not exceed the arbitrary response force criterion (e.g., 15 gm). As we later learned (Davis & Burton, 1974), it can also generate a highly inaccurate picture of on-lever behavior.

Our initial technique continuously monitored lever contact by transducing lever depressions from 0–150 gm to voltage change and, ultimately, to pen deflections on a physiograph (see Davis & Burton, 1974 for procedural details).

Adjustments to paper speed gave us ample opportunity to analyze the stability of the force of lever contact, as well as to look for general changes in the pattern of force that occurred within and across trials. Our findings again supported the hypothesis put forth by Bolles and McGillis regarding the importance of species-specific and reflexive behaviors. Subjects did, in fact, appear to "freeze on the lever." The properties of lever contact are illustrated in Figure 8.2. Leverholding appeared as remarkably stable lever contact; for example, force fluctuations were often less than 3 gm over 25 sec. The reflexive lurch from the lever, which appeared regularly on our videotape records, also appeared in characteristic form on our physiograph records as a brief surge in peak force (as the subject pushed off from the lever), followed rapidly by a period of zero force and return to the lever. After approximately 5 sec of instability, the force of lever contact settled down to the typically stable intershock pattern. At no point did our subjects approach the lever and emit a discrete leverpress response in order to terminate shock.

Leverpress escape was clearly not what we expected it to be. Its dynamics were actually quite simple, but considerably different from our initial expectancies (many of which were based on behavior generated by positive reinforcement). Two other studies from the escape program in our laboratory are worth commenting upon briefly. Prior to our response force work, we performed an experiment in which pairs of rats were exposed to leverpress escape (Davis & Hirschorn, 1973). The presence of a second (untrained) animal in the chamber was tremendously disruptive to a pretrained escape animal. Had we believed that our pretrained subjects had learned a discrete operant response to escape shock, then our results would have, indeed, appeared anomalous. Such a view

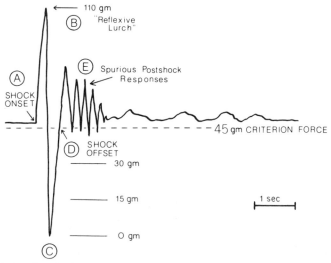

Figure 8.2. *Essential features of level contact during initial portion of leverpress escape trial. See text for explanation.* [From Favis & Burton, 1974. Reprinted by permission.]

would have led us to expect that social behaviors might be initially disruptive, but that the subject would eventually retain mastery over the escape situation. This was clearly not the case. When shock occurred, both subjects thrashed about the chamber until shock was terminated by "accidental" contact with the lever. Most often, subjects froze in their tracks when shock went off. This resulted in freezing occurring in a variety of inappropriate places, including the back of the other rat. The lever appeared to have minimal valence, and the notion of a discrete operant response appeared alien to any of the subjects.

In contrast to our previous "social" experiments with food-reinforced subjects, the escape procedure yielded behavior that was more readily disrupted in the presence of a second subject (cf. Davis & Wheeler, 1966). In fact, had pretrained subjects not been dye-marked, a naive observer would not have been able to tell which subject actually "knew" how to escape. These results further suggested that leverpress escape is not solely under control by operant reinforcement. We had, in a sense, used a social anomaly to reflect upon the sources of control of individual behavior.

Subjects had learned far less about escape than we expected; in fact, a virtually untrained animal might perform competently by simply "doing what came naturally." On one occasion we placed a deeply anesthetized rat in the escape chamber, taking care to place him upon the lever in a typical leverholding posture. The subject was incapable of skeletal movement, but the pattern of intertrial leverholding we recorded on the physiograph was virtually indistinguishable from our "normal" records. When shock occurred, the rat made a brief reflexive twitch and fell back upon the lever, thereby terminating shock efficiently. Unfortunately, the subject continued to slide down the front wall of the cage and onto the floor and had to be propped up again before another successful trial could proceed. Nevertheless, we had our first demonstration of leverpress escape in a clinically unconscious subject (Davis, 1979).

A subsequent study (Davis & Kenney, 1975) again suggested the rather precarious nature of leverpress escape. Without realizing it, we had been providing a highly supportive environment for successful escape performance. Our subjects were typically tested in LeHigh Valley operant chambers. When subjects were exposed to cages manufactured by a different company, the dynamics of escape behavior changed radically. Campden Instruments manufacture two-lever chambers that, because of the location of the levers, do not allow the subject to brace itself comfortably during leverholding. As a consequence, shock onset often threw our subjects off the lever, and did not support the leverholding–reflexive lurch pattern. When tested in Campden chambers, subjects began by trying to leverhold. This strategy was eventually abandoned by all subjects in favor of a pattern of waiting for shock onset, and then moving forward rapidly and emitting a single leverpress response. The movement forward typically consisted of a leap or chaotic scramble for the lever. Although escape latencies were stable, they were not as brief as those we had reliably obtained under the leverholding-response topography.

These findings are somewhat ironic in light of a recently completed study in our laboratory (Herrmann, Davis, & Woods, 1978). In this experiment, escape-trained subjects received bilateral septal lesions. Whereas subjects had initially escaped shock via the leverholding–reflexive lurch pattern, the postsurgery strategy did not typically involve leverholding. Instead, subjects waited near the lever for shock onset and then emitted a leverpress as rapidly as possible (see Figure 8.3). This change likely resulted from a septal deficit in the ability to rear up, an integral component of the reflexive lurch pattern. It is worth noting, however, that the septal-lesioned subjects, like the Campden chamber subjects in

Figure 8.3.   *Illustrative photographic sequence of nonleverholding escape response pattern that occurred in septal-lesioned subjects. Like exposure to the Campden Instruments test chamber, septal surgery altered the leverholding–reflexive lurch pattern to one in which subjects waited and quite literally flew at the lever when shock occurred.*

our previous experiment, actually gave us behavior that resembles the discrete, discriminated operant response we initially expected. The irony, of course, is that the only way to obtain such "normal" or nonanomalous behavior was to introduce some abnormal feature into the situation—either in terms of features of the external environment or, via surgery, into the internal environment.

C. CONDITIONED AVOIDANCE RESPONSES

If the postponement of an aversive event is made contingent upon a particular response, the probability of that response should increase. This is a simple definition of avoidance conditioning, and its effects have been widely documented across a variety of species, aversive events, and response requirements (Hoffman, 1966; Sidman, 1966). Given the historic success of this procedure, one might view the *failure* to produce avoidance behavior as something of an anomaly.

Interestingly, such failures to condition within the avoidance literature have only come into prominence during the past two decades. This is possibly due to a more sympathetic theoretical climate which has made it increasingly easy to publish such seemingly negative results.

It is worth considering several demonstrations of conditioning failures and difficulties. Following Meyer, Cho, and Wesemann's (1960) discussion of the difficulty in conditioning discriminated leverpress avoidance, Feldman and Bremner (1963) suggested that leverpress-avoidance conditioning with rats was often hampered by the animal's remaining on the lever between shock deliveries, rather than emitting a discrete leverpress-avoidance response. They suggested that if one wanted a rat to leverpress in order to avoid shock delivery, it might first be necessary to "break up" leverholding. To this end they surveyed some less than orthodox procedures, including prodding the subject off the lever with a pencil.

A number of similar reports began to appear in the avoidance literature in the late 1960s. Both Hurwitz (1967) and Keehn (1967a) reemphasized the pervasive nature of leverholding. There is a subtle shift in the emphasis of these latter papers. Like previously surveyed work in leverpress escape, both of these investigators dealt directly with leverholding rather than dismissing it as an annoyance or obstacle to "true" responding.

Collectively, the implications of these studies did not fit the conventional model of avoidance conditioning that suggested that any response that avoided an aversive event or terminated a signal preceding such an event could be reinforced. This rather simple view, an outgrowth of what Seligman (1970) has called the "equipotentiality premise," has been further taken to task by Bolles (1970). In his seminal paper, Bolles offered a new set of expectancies for avoidance conditioning that made results such as those of Hurwitz, Keehn, or Meyer *et al.*, appear far less anomalous. Bolles argued that a narrow range of behaviors, known as species-specific defense reactions (SSDRs), were most likely to occur in aversive situations. Conditoning procedures, such as avoidance, must therefore contend directly with these behaviors (e.g., fleeing, freezing, fighting). Simply put, the more closely the topography of an avoidance response resembles an SSDR, the more readily it will be conditioned. In fact, some responses, because of their similarity to species-specific reactions, will be conditioned with such a minimum of effort that one might question whether, in fact, anything has been learned. Furthermore, certain responses might be virtually impossible to condition, at least until all SSDR-related behaviors have been suppressed.

In light of the SSDR model of avoidance, the ubiquity of leverholding, a direct outgrowth of freezing, is not hard to understand. What is perhaps a more meaningful question is how leverholding facilitates or impedes successful avoidance behavior. We have already argued that the leverpress-escape response so closely resembles an SSDR that effective escape behavior may be readily acquired, but is extremely vulnerable to environmental change. The case of leverpress avoidance may not be as simple. Free-operant avoidance (Sidman, 1953) requires a fairly stable rate of responding. Extensive leverholding, which is fundamental to successful escape, may, as Feldman and Bremner (1963) suggest, have to be "broken up" before discrete avoidance responses can occur.

It is obvious that an investigation of this question cannot proceed along the lines of conventional response measurement. Although response rate may be adequate to describe steady-state avoidance responding, it is insensitive to the properties of leverholding, per se. In our work with avoidance, we employed the continuous measurement technique previously described in conjunction with our escape research. In one study (Davis & Porter, 1976), rats were exposed to a free-operant shock avoidance procedure in which each response avoided shock for 15 sec. If no response was made brief shocks continued to occur every 5 secs until a response was made. We arbitrarily set a response-force criterion of 15 gm; that is, any lever contact that excceeded 15 gm was sufficient to activate programming equipment and avoid shock. In addition to response force recordings, we employed a cumulative-response recorder so that direct comparision could be made between lever contact records and traditional discrete response measurement.

A number of surprising results emerged. First, we obtained little evidence that subjects ever avoided shock by making discrete leverpress responses. Rather, our subjects remained in contact with the lever almost continuously throughout the session as they had during escape conditioning. There were some clear changes produced by the avoidance procedure, however. As performance improved, we noted a shift in the mean force and stability of lever contact. These changes are shown in Figure 8.4. Their response rate counterpart appears in the cumulative records shown in Figure 8.5. It is notable that the rate increase clearly evident in Segment B of the cumulative record does not result from an increase in so called "discrete responding." Instead, it derives, perhaps artifactually, from changes in sustained lever contact which occurred during each

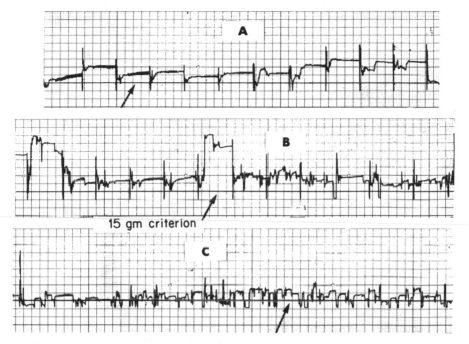

15 gm criterion

Figure 8.4. *Transition in the form of lever contact observed during three segments of a shock-avoidance session. Record A shows the characteristic warm-up effect observed at the start of the session. Note the relative stability in the force of lever contact between the regular occurrences of shock-induced "reflexive lurch" from the lever. During the midpoint of the session (Record B), the shock rate is essentially unchanged and shock termination still occurs as a consequence of the reflexive lurch, although the force of lever contact between shock deliveries has become less stable. Because response force fluctuations later in the session occur near the criterion force value, a fairly high response rate is recorded in Record C and shock rate is reduced, despite the fact that "discrete" avoidance responses rarely occur. The heavy horizontal ruling at the arrow indicates the 15-gm response force criterion.*

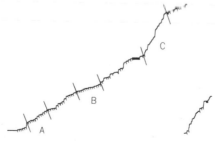

Figure 8.5. *Cumulative response record obtained during the same shock avoidance session shown in Figure 8.4. Segments A, B, and C correspond to response force records A, B, and C in Figure 8.4 Blips below the record indicate the delivery of shock.*

session. This is not to suggest that avoidance behavior is not learned or outcome
sensitive, but rather that the extensive lever contact that occurs during avoidance
situations need not be disrupted or broken up for successful avoidance to occur.

A second result worth noting is that virtually all avoidance sessions began
with a period of highly stable leverholding; in fact, performance during this segment of the session was virtually indistinguishable from leverpress escape
behavior. It is widely known that avoidance sessions begin with a warm-up
phase, and our data suggest that warm-up may consist of unadulterated escape
behavior. Thus, rather than failing to respond during warm-up, subjects may
actually be in continuous contact with the lever. This lends credence to the
possibility that subjects may be *too* motivated for effective avoidance early in the
session (cf. R. W. Powell, 1972).

D. PUNISHMENT AND RESPONSE-INDEPENDENT SHOCK

A number of additional findings related to shock delivery deserve notice in
our survey of anomalies. Perhaps the most "classic" of all of these is known as
vicious circle behavior, reviewed by Brown (1969). Mowrer (1947) reported that
rats that had been trained to avoid shock persisted in making responses during
avoidance extinction despite, or perhaps because of, the fact that these responses
were now punished. Under the extinction condition the simplest "solution" was
for the animal to cease responding and thereby experience no further shock.
Paradoxically, however, subjects continued to respond, actually avoiding
nothing and producing punishment in the bargain.

Although Mowrer discussed his results in terms of the self-perpetuating
effects of conditioned fear, it is likely that at least part of the "problem," if
vicious circle behavior may be so termed, lies in the organism's inability to
discriminate punishment from avoidance shock. Nevertheless, these results indicate that punishment does not automatically suppress the response that
precedes it. This conclusion is anomalous only if we base our expectations on the
unmodified law of effect (Thorndike, 1911). There have, however, been a
number of alternative positions proposed on the role of "satisfiers,"
"annoyers," and reinforcement in general (e.g., Staddon & Simmelhag, 1971;
Timberlake & Allison, 1974).

The vicious circle phenomenon has its counterpart in the modern operant
literature. A number of investigators have reported that the occasional delivery
of punishment may be sufficient to maintain responding which was previously
reinforced by shock avoidance. For example, McKearney (1968) trained
monkeys to avoid shock on a Sidman procedure. Following the establishment of
stable avoidance responding, a fixed interval (FI) 10-min punishment procedure
was introduced; that is, the first avoidance response made after each 10-min
period was punished. The shock-avoidance schedule was eventually terminated,
so that the only programmed consequence for responding was punishment every
10 min. This procedure not only maintained responding, but actually generated

a higher rate than had previously occurred under the avoidance schedule alone (see Figure 8.6). A similar experiment by Kelleher and Morse (1968) also reported that responding could be maintained and positively accelerated by a FI schedule of punishment. Kelleher and Morse's results are perhaps more surprising because subjects had no history of avoidance training. Their responding had been previously reinforced by food.

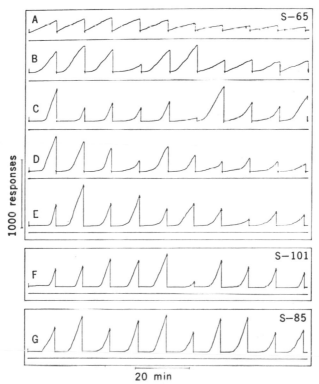

Figure 8.6. *Patterns of responding under different experimental conditions. Ordinate, cumulative number of responses per 10-min fixed interval; abscissa, time. The recording pen was reset to the baseline at the termination of each fixed interval. A. Schedule of shock-postponement and 10-min fixed interval (FI 10) schedule of shock-presentation programmed concurrently (tenth session after introduction of FI 10, monkey S-65). B. FI 10 shock-presentation only (21st session after elimination of shock-postponement schedule, monkey S-65). C. FI 10 shock-presentation, 30-sec time-out period after each shock (14th session after introduction of time-out, monkey S-65). D. FI 10 shock-presentation, no time-out period (16th session after removal of time-out period, monkey S-65). E. FI 10 shock-presentation, 30-sec time-out period reinstated (fourth session after reinstatement of time-out, 63rd session after elimination of shock-postponement schedule, monkey S-65). F. Terminal performance of monkey S-101 under the FI 10 schedule of shock-presentation with a 30-sec time-out after shock (57th session after elimination of shock-postponement schedule). G. Terminal performance of monkey S-85 under the FI 10 schedule of shock-presentation with a 30-sec time-out after shock (67th session after elimination of shock-postponement schedule). The variation in numbers of responses in successive intervals within a session is typical of fixed-interval schedules in general (4). [From McKearney, J. W. Maintenance of responding under a fixed-interval schedule of electric shock-presentation. Science, 14 June, 1968, 160, 1249–1251. Copyright 1968 by the American Association for the Advancement of Science. Reprinted by permission.]*

The ability to maintain responding paradoxically by shock delivery is not confined to punishment. For example, Hutchinson, Renfrew, and Young (1971) surveyed a variety of cases in which periodic deliveries of response-independent shock were sufficient to maintain stable response patterns in the absence of additional reinforcement contingencies. It is important to stress, however, that whereas both response-independent and response-dependent shock may successfully maintain responding, the properties of such responding may differ considerably between the two procedures. In fact, within-subject comparisons that examine the transition between response-independent and dependent-shock deliveries report differences in the temporal pattern, as well as rate of responding. Thus, while it may appear anomalous that subjects will respond at all under such conditions, they are, at least, keenly sensitive to the procedural nuances under which shock is being delivered (Byrd, 1969; McIntire, Davis, Cohen, & Franch, 1968; Morse & Kelleher, 1970).

Collectively, these results are quite puzzling. We find FI punishment and noncontingent-shock schedules generating positively accelerated patterns of responding in the absence of any other reinforcement contingency. Part of the basis for this anomaly no doubt rests on our assumptions about the nature of shock. As McKearney (1972) has noted, "Because the assignment of a given stimulus to the positive or negative category is often based on *a priori,* hedonistic, and non-empirical criteria, exceptions to the usual effects of these stimuli are often regarded as anomalous or paradoxical [p. 11]." Two studies speak clearly to this issue. One is the early work of Muenzinger (1934), who demonstrated that punishment of correct responses was equally as effective as punishment of incorrect responses in training a visual discrimination. Further evidence comes from Holz and Azrin's (1961) demonstration that shock is not only an effective suppressor of responding, but may also function as a discriminative stimulus that signals the availability of food. Using this technique, Holz and Azrin generated what may be termed *masochism,* a presumably pathological state. Its basis, however, was quite reasonable. When shock signals the availability of food to a hungry organism, it should not surprise us to find an increase in the rate of the very response that produces shock.

D. SCHEDULE-INDUCED AGGRESSION

Schedules of positive reinforcement specify contingencies between particular classes of behavior and environmental events. Schedules have been in wide use for over two decades now and are known to produce stable and characteristic patterns of operant behavior (Ferster & Skinner, 1957). It has become increasingly clear, however, that schedules of reinforcement also generate a variety of non-operant behaviors. These responses may have clearly identifiable features or topographies which enable the investigator to analyze them separately or to ignore them (e.g., Pear, Moody, & Persinger, 1972). On the other hand, they may interact with the primary operant response in such a manner as to produce spurious response counts (e.g., Davis & Burton, 1974; see also Figure 8.7).

Perhaps the most commonly observed class of nonoperant schedule-induced behavior is "aggression." This category is noticeably broad; that is, its motorics are determined typically by the cage topography and species of the subject. For example, using a single rat in a conventional operant-test chamber, one is likely to see gnawing and biting of the lever and grid floor. If a second animal or surrogate is available in the test chamber, however, aggression is more likely to take the form of attack.

Just as a father may praise or otherwise reinforce his son for "acting tough" with his peers, aggressive behaviors may also be brought under direct control of reinforcement. For example, Reynolds, Catania, and Skinner, (1963) trained a pigeon to attack a second pigeon in order to receive grain. There is some question, however, whether explicitly reinforced aggressive behavior represents "real" aggression, or, more germanely, whether it has the same topography as aggressive behavior that occurs as a by-product of schedule control. It is this latter category of aggression that is of greater relevance to our discussion of anomalous behavior. Just as the child's sudden burst of aggressive behavior is more surprising when things are peaceful than when aggression is encouraged by a parent, so it is surprising to find a rat violently attacking the lever during a schedule of positive reinforcement. In short, when our expectation of schedule performance includes only temporal patterns of operant responding, a sudden burst of bar-biting may appear quite anomalous.

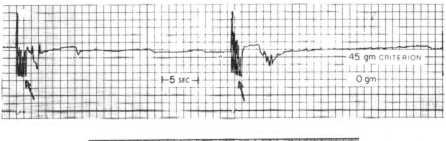

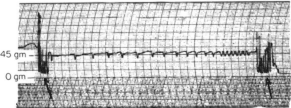

Figure 8.7. *Characteristic pattern of response force produced by postshock response bursts (at arrows) during a shock escape schedule. In addition to response counts produced by such nonoperant behavior, lower record also illustrates a response-force pattern produced by subject's respiration while leverholding. Twenty-two such "responses" were recorded following the postshock response burst on lower record, despite the subject's sustained contact with the lever. [From Davis & Burton, 1974. Reprinted by permission.]*

Actually, in the realm of experimentally produced anomalies, schedule-induced aggression may be less surprising than most. Its occurrence, in fact, may mesh quite comfortably with an intuitive view of schedules of reinforcement. For example, if one considers biting or attack behavior as an index of a subject's frustration or displeasure with its environment, then it is not surprising to learn that schedule-induced aggression has most commonly been reported under extinction conditions (Thompson & Bloom, 1966), or during the postreinforcement periods of fixed interval (Flory, 1969) and fixed-ratio food schedules (Pear & Roy, 1971). Such periods during reinforcement schedules, which are otherwise designated as positive, are not only likely to generate aggressive behavior, but are now known to have aversive properties that can actually suppress responding. For example, Auge (1977) demonstrated that neutral stimuli that were paired with the early portion of a fixed interval food schedule could be used to punish high rates of responding which occurred during the final third of the interval.

If positive reinforcement schedules contain aversive segments that are capable of inducing aggressive behavior, then it is a small step to predict that an aversive control schedule would be correspondingly likely to generate aggressive responding. This is precisely the case. Attack behavior has been reported in response to delivery of a variety of noxious stimuli, including shock (Azrin, Rubin, & Hutchinson, 1968). Aggression has also been identified during shock avoidance (Pear, *et al.*, 1972), and shock escape conditioning (Davis & Burton, 1974). In fact, experiments in our laboratory with leverpress escape have occasionally been disrupted when a 10 mm-wide metal response lever was literally chewed in half. Similar destructive results during escape conditioning have been observed by Domjan (1972, personal communication).

The ability to aggress in frustrating or painful situations may be beneficial to the organism's emotional state (i.e., "letting off steam"), or may be functionally beneficial insofar as aggressive behavior may actually terminate frustration or pain by attacking its source. If this were the whole case, then schedule-induced aggression, at least those cases involving noxious stimuli, might not be considered anomalous. There are situations, however, in which schedule-induced aggressive behavior has been plainly counterproductive; that is, has actively interfered with control or termination of the aversive event.

In shock escape and avoidance procedures, it has been observed repeatedly that the performance of paired animals deteriorates considerably from individual levels. Logan and Boice (1969) have reported such impairment with rats trained to turn a wheel in order to avoid shock, and I have found similar deterioration of performance with leverpress avoidance (Davis, 1969). The results are at times rather dramatic. Trained animals fight with each other frequently (not simply in response to shock), or interact in a manner that excludes making the avoidance response. Testing six different subjects in pairs over 23 half-hour sessions, I was able to report only one 5-min period during which subjects "cooperated"; that is, both remained in the front of the cage and alternated leverpressing. This brief period, during which shock was totally avoided, was immediately followed by fighting severe enough to cause us to terminate the session (Davis, 1969). Thus, the beneficial effects of cooperating do not seem sufficient to increase its likelihood or to eliminate counterproductive aggression.

Not surprisingly, similar maladaptive results of aggression have been reported under a leverpress shock-escape procedure. The results of an experiment by Ulrich (1967) are essentially similar to our "social-escape" results described earlier (Davis & Hirschorn, 1973). Rats fight at and between shock occurrences and are extremely inefficient at emitting the simple leverpress response that terminates shock.

As previously noted, shock-induced aggression is arguably not as surprising as schedule-induced aggression. It is, therefore, worth noting that aggressive behavior and the resultant disruption of performance may not simply represent "reflexive" (i.e., shock-elicited) fighting. Thus, aggression in our escape and avoidance experiments may be considered anomalous in terms of both its origin and its effects on performance. Data reported by Davis and Hirschorn (1973) bear directly on this point. We found that pairs of rats in which both animals had been pretrained to escape shock did indeed fight at every instance of shock onset (as well as during the shock-free intertrial intervals). However, these were the only conditions under which our relatively mild shock (.4 mA) reliably elicited aggression. Shock did not instigate fighting in pairs of untrained animals, and trained–untrained pairs fought on approximately 50% of shock presentations. The fact that the incidence of aggression was related to the amount of prior escape training suggests that aggression, in this case, might be more closely tied to experience or schedule-related factors than to shock, per se (cf. Powell, Francis, Francis, & Schneiderman, 1972).

III. Autocontingencies

If an anomaly is born of violated expectations, then there is no surer way to generate anomalous behavior than to underestimate our subject's abilities. For example, reports that behavior modification can produce visual discrimination in a functionally blind patient (Stoltz & Wolf, 1969), or that pigeons can be trained to discriminate photographs of humans from those without humans (Herrnstein & Loveland, 1964) are in the front ranks of anomalous results. In both cases, the anomaly rests on inadequate prior assumptions about the subject.

For the past several years my colleagues and I have examined how subtle stimulus contingencies may control the behavior of rats. In general we have found that rats are capable of a variety of temporal and counting-like discriminations that are both impressive and somewhat surprising. We have termed this class of stimulus arrangements *autocontingencies,* and they are operationally defined in the manner described below.

Most of our research involves a modified condition-suppression technique; that is, uncontrollable shocks are superimposed upon a food-reinforced behavioral baseline. Unlike conventional conditioned suppression, which employs a *traditional* tone–shock contingency (Rescorla, 1967), an autocontingency involves no additional exteroceptive stimulus (e.g., light or tone) to predict the presence or absence of shock. The sole basis for predicting shock under an autocontingency is whatever pattern or logical constraint in the distribution of shocks the subject can detect. For example, in our initial research (Davis, Memmott, & Hurwitz, 1975), we found that subjects were able to detect a safe (shock-free) period immediately following each shock delivery. Safety in this case was based upon discrimination of a minimum 3-min intershock interval; that is, shocks occurred randomly throughout the session, but never closer together than 3 min. This constraint in a so-called "random" distribution created an *if shock–then no shock* autocontingency and resulted in periods of accelerated baseline responding immediately following each shock offset (see Figure 8.8). Animals also detected that only three shocks were programmed dur-

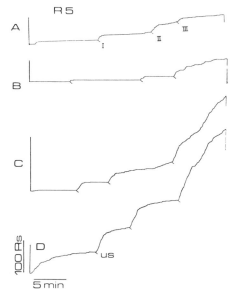

Figure 8.8. *Cumulative response record obtained while subject responded on VI food reinforcement schedule. Three unsignaled shocks were presented with a minimum 3-min. intershock interval. Record A was obtained during Session 17; Record B—Session 23; Record C—Session 130; Record D—Session 171. [From Davis H, Memmott J., & Hurwitz, H.M.B. Autocontingencies: A model for subtle behavioral control, Journal of Experimental Psychology: General, 1975. 104, 169–188. Copyright 1975 by the American Psychological Association. Reprinted by permission.]*

ing each 30-min session. This autocontingency (*if third shock–then no further shock*) resulted in sustained responding following the third shock, regardless of when in the session it occurred (Davis *et al.,* 1975; see Figure 8.9).

The investigation of autocontingencies, which has now become the major focus of our research, initially forced its way into our attention as an anomaly. In previous research with conditioned suppression, both Davis and McIntire (1969) and Seligman (1968) had examined the effects of unsignaled shock on a VI baseline. Both of these studies reported virtually total suppression of responding throughout the session. However, unlike the findings of Seligman, baseline responding in our experiment gradually began to recover across sessions. This data conflict was pursued and eventually resolved (cf. Davis *et al.,* 1975; Seligman & Meyer, 1970). Because Seligman's unsignaled shock distribution was truly random, subjects could not discriminate any safe periods for responding and, therefore, remained suppressed throughout testing (Seligman & Meyer, 1970). Our subjects, on the other hand, were tested in a slightly more accommodating situation. Although cues about shock occurrence were subtle, they were available (e.g., minimum intershock distribution, fixed number of shocks

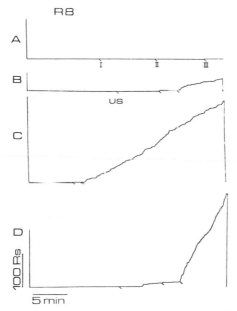

Figure 8.9. *Cumulative response record obtained while subject responded on VI food reinforcement schedule and received three unsignaled shocks per session. Unlike procedure illustrated in Figure 8.8, there was no restriction placed on intershock interval. Record A was obtained during Session 17; B—Session 36; C—Session 95; D—Session 133. [From Davis, H., Memmott, J., & Hurwitz, H. M. B. Autocontingencies: A model for subtle behavioral control, Journal of Experimental Psychology: general, 1975, 104, 169–188. Copyright 1975 by the American Psychological Association. Reprinted by permission.]*

per session). Our mistake was to assume that by withholding conventional predictive cues (e.g., a traditional tone–shock contingency), we could eliminate discriminative control. This oversight is rather humbling in light of the number of times I have cautioned experimental psychology students to avoid providing any information to rats in situations such as fixed interval (FI) or differential reinforcement of low rates (DRL) reinforcement schedules. The student's surprise at finding that rats could and readily did attend to such minimal cues as clicks in relay programming equipment was certainly no greater than our own chagrin at discovering that our subjects had analyzed our reinforcement contingencies with greater care than we had.

There is considerable generality to the premise that subjects often become "aware" of environmental stimuli or contingencies before the investigator who programmed them did. On some occasions the problem is compounded even further. It is not simply that the effects of an autocontingency were not anticipated, it is that even after behavioral control is in evidence, its source is often misunderstood. The resultant behavior is often both puzzling and persistent and is likely to be viewed as anomalous. At the very least, it supports the notion that autocontingencies involve subtle relationships, subtle to subject and experimenter alike.

A. AUTOCONTINGENCIES AND "FREELOADING"

We have recently completed some further autocontingency experiments that have again produced unexpected findings. Don Shattuck and I have explored the effects of superimposing both traditional tone–shock and autocontingency procedures upon a baseline that includes not only leverpressing, but also free-feeding. Our subjects were placed in a chamber in which they could either leverpress for food pellets or eat them freely from a dish in the rear of the cage. To those unfamiliar with the burgeoning literature on "freeloading" such an arrangement may seem preposterous. Why should an organism work for the very reward that is freely available in the same cage? The fact that organisms often do prefer to work for what is freely offered is known as "contra-freeloading," and because of its anomalous nature has earned a place in the motivational literature (Osborne, 1977).

The general question behind our research was this: Would the suppressive and accelerative effects that traditional and autocontingencies are known to have on food-reinforced leverpressing transfer directly to free-feeding? Or would eating, because it is a more "biological" response, be less vulnerable to the effects of these two conditioning procedures? This question has an interesting history. Although a number of investigators have compared the effects of punishment on instrumental and consummatory behaviors (e.g., suppression of leverpressing for vs. eating food), there are few who have made this comparison with regard to conditioned suppression. This extension has theoretical utility. It relates not only to the generality between unconditioned and conditioned stimuli, a concern at the core of many motivational hypotheses (e.g., Miller, 1951), but also to the generality between operant and Pavlovian procedures.

It is not totally clear whether punishment is more effective in suppressing instrumental or consummatory acts. Intuitively, either outcome is defensible, which virtually guarantees that whatever result is reported will be considered anomalous in some quarters. For example, Solomon (1964) noted that consummatory acts, because of their biological importance, might be less vulnerable to the effects of punishment than would instrumental acts. However, what evidence he surveyed appeared to suggest otherwise. More recently, Bertsch (1976) has reviewed this literature and similarly concluded that with strong punishers at least, consummatory behaviors are more readily suppressed than their instrumental counterparts.

Whether one can find comparable data for the effects of conditioned suppression on instrumental and consummatory behaviors is questionable. Only two studies appear to have addressed the question. DeCosta and Ayres (1971) compared conditioned suppression of leverpressing reinforced by sucrose with conditioned suppression of a licking response, when sucrose was freely available. They reported that leverpressing was more extensively suppressed. Similarly, Jackson and Delprato (1974) reported that although a CS paired with shock suppressed leverpressing, it did not eliminate the consumption of food pellets which were freely delivered during the CS. Thus, both of these studies suggest that unlike punishment, conditioned suppression may be more effective with instrumental than with consummatory acts.

Our research has examined the effects of conditioned-suppression and autocontingency procedures upon both leverpressing and free-feeding (i.e., instrumental and consummatory) behaviors. The first aspect of our data which deserves comment is the rather unusual finding that subjects spent nearly the entirety of each session eating free food rather than working for it. As previously noted, this result may sit well with our intuitions, but it is not consistent with a substantial body of literature that reports either a preponderance of leverpressing, or some degree of alternation between leverpressing and free-feeding (Jackson, 1976). This inconsistency may be due to our examining "free-loading" under conditions that are far more aversive than those generally employed. In any case, the lack of a stable leverpressing baseline forced us to forego a within-session comparison between instrumental and consummatory responses and to concentrate on the general question on how conditioned suppression and auto-contingency procedures affect free-food consumption.

Previous data from our subjects, collected prior to the introduction of free-food into the cage, indicated that leverpressing was clearly under control of both the traditonal and autocontingencies; that is, conditioned suppression occurred to the CS and conditioned acceleration followed shock offset. The effects of these two procedures upon free pellet consumption were virtually identical to their effects on lever pressing. Subjects ate free-food continuously until the CS-tone appeared, at which point they stopped eating for the duration of the 1-min signal. Immediately following shock, subjects typically lunged for the food tray and ate at extremely high rates for several minutes, often doubling or tripling their baseline rates. In short, our results indicate that consummatory and instrumental responses are affected similarly not only by conditioned suppression, but also by autocontingency procedures. They suggest that whatever manner of control is exerted by stimulus contingencies involving shock, its effects appear to be central (i.e., motivational) and transfer readily from the instrumental response to the consummatory behavior related to its reinforcement.

IV. Conclusions

Whenever subject and experimenter perceive the environment differently, an anomalous behavioral outcome is likely to occur. Since most of us are more likely to be experimenters than subjects, we occasionally hold to our own expectations about so-called reasonable behavior and shake our heads in amused disbelief at our subjects' anomalous responses. Certainly there have been analyses that suggest that the investigator's view of the stimulus situation is closer to the "truth" than the subject's. For example, the traditional view of "superstitious behavior" (Davis & Hubbard, 1972; Skinner, 1948) might be read in these terms. Because the experimenter has programmed rewards to occur independently of the subect's behavior, any repeated behavior patterns must be adventitiously reinforced (i.e., superstitious) and reflect the subject's misperception of the environment. However, as our data on autocontingencies confirm, simply having created a stimulus environment by no means guarantees that the investigator's view of it will be more accurate than the subject's.

In fact, a seemingly innocuous environment may conceal potent sources of control. Cronbach recounts a fascinating example, which was first discussed by Vesell in 1967:

> Investigators checking on how animals metabolize drugs found that results differed mysteriously from laboratory to laboratory. The most startling inconsistency of all occurred after a refurbishing of a National Institutes of Health (NIH) animal room brought in new cages and supplies. Previously a mouse would sleep for about 35 minutes after a standard injection of hexobarbital. In their new homes, the NIH mice came miraculously back to their feet just 16 minutes after receiving a shot of the drug. Detective work proved that red cedar bedding made the difference, stepping up the activity of several enzymes that metabolize hexobarbital. Pine shavings had the same effect. When the softwood was replaced with birch or maple bedding like that originally used, drug response came back in line with previous experience [Cronbach, 1975, p. 121].

We have surveyed anomalous behavioral results that occur under a variety of aversive control procedures. The review was not meant to be exhaustive; in fact, the wealth of material that was excluded for space considerations alone sug gests that seemingly anomalous results are widespread in the experimental literature.

It might be argued that discovering anomalous behavior is less likely in situations involving human subjects. Although I know of no data that bear directly on this comparison, it seems that there is at least one advantage in working with animal subjects. Although we often have to fight to keep out anthropomorphisms and inappropriate expectations, we are far less likely to label an animal "crazy" or "deviant" when we are faced with a bizarre bit of behavior. Such labels are anathema to a behavioral analysis since they eliminate the attempt, as well as the need, for a detailed experimental analysis of the situation. "Crazy" or "abnormal" are often viewed as *reasons* for the very behavior they were invoked to describe. Such general labels, as well as more exotic categories, such as "paranoid schizophrenic," not only obviate the subject's legal responsibility, but also the psychologist's experimental obligation. It is as if to say "lawfulness stops here: there is no need to analyze any further. The individual is crazy." [2] At least 50% of introductory psychology students in my experience have this belief: "Crazy" is a reason for doing things; not simply a description of things done. Thankfully, we do not seem to have as much of this glib option in dealing with animal subjects. Whatever attributes a creature must have to be considered "crazy" or "abnormal," most of us are unwilling to vest infrahumans with them. This has clearly worked to the benefit of animal psychology.

We have implied throughout that most situations in which the label "anomalous" is used reflect more tellingly upon our ignorance than upon our subject's behavior. This is not to suggest that the concept "anomaly" is not useful at this stage in the development of psychology. We may actually benefit from the fact that most investigators are sufficiently provoked by anomalies to explore further the experimental situation. By simply considering why our expectation has been violated, we usually learn more about the species and/or the environment, and in the process may refine our expectancies. Although such knowledge may ultimately lead to finding fewer anomalies, in the long run we will understand far more about behavior.

ACKNOWLEDGMENTS

Thanks to Harry Hurwitz and Donald Shattuck for their thoughtful criticisms.

[2] There may be one sense in which an individual may be viewed as "crazy" or "abnormal" without foresaking a behavioral analysis. If we are willing to label a stimulus environment, as we might a subject, as being "crazy," then we have only to apply the existential tenet that defines an individual in terms of his experiences. By this reasoning, an individual who has experienced "crazy" stimulus conditions may himself be viewed as being "crazy." The label, when derived in this manner, is not simply descriptive, but has analytical depth as well, insofar as it makes direct reference to the experiential history of the individual (Frankl, 1969).

REFERENCES

Auge, R. J. Stimulus functions within a fixed-interval clock schedule: Reinforcement, punishment, and discriminative stimulus control. *Animal Learning and Behavior,* 1977, *5,* 117–123.

Azrin, N. H., & Hake, D. F. Positive conditioned suppression: Conditioned suppression using positive reinforcers as the unconditioned stimuli. *Journal of the Experimental Analysis of Behavior,* 1969, *12,* 167–173.

Azrin, N. H., Rubin, H., & Hutchinson, R. Biting behavior by rats in response to aversive shock. *Journal of the Experimental Analysis of Behavior,* 1968, *11,* 633–639.

Badia, P., Culbertson, S., & Harsh, J. Choice of longer or stronger signaled shock over shorter or weaker unsignaled shock. *Journal of the Experimental Analysis of Behavior,* 1973, *19,* 25–33.

Bertsch, G. J. Punishment of consummatory and instrumental behavior: A review. *Psychological Record,* 1966, *26,* 13–31.

Bolles, R. C. Species-specific defense reactions and avoidance learning. *Psychological Review,* 1970, *77,* 32–48.

Bolles, R. C., & McGillis, D. B. The non-operant nature of the barpress escape response. *Psychonomic Science,* 1968, *11,* 261–262.

Brown, J. Factors affecting self-punitive locomotor behavior. In B. A. Campbell & R. M. Church (Eds.), *Punishment and aversive behavior,* New York: Appleton, 1969. Pp. 467–514.

Byrd, L. D. Responding in the cat maintained by response-independent electric shock. *Journal of the Experimenal Analysis of Behavior,* 1969, *12,* 1–10.

Campbell, S. L. Leverholding and behavior sequences in shock escape. *Journal of Comparative Physiological Psychology,* 1962, *55,* 1047–1053.

Cronbach, L. J. Beyond the two disciplines of scientific psychology. *American Psychologist,* 1975, *30,* 116–127.

Davis, H. Conditioned suppression: A survey of the literature. *Psychonomic Monograph Supplements,* 1968, *2,* 283–291.

Davis, H. Social interaction and Sidman avoidance performance. *Psychological Record,* 1969, *19,* 433–442.

Davis, H. Leverpress escape behavior in a clinically unconscious rat. *Physiology and Behavior,* 1979, *22,* 599–600.

Davis, H., & Burton, J. The measurement of response force during a leverpress shock escape procedure in rats. *Journal of the Experimental Analysis of Behavior,* 1974, *22,* 433–440.

Davis, H., & Hirschorn, P. Social behavior in rats during escape from shock. *Canadian Journal of Psychology,* 1973, *27,* 262–271.

Davis, H., & Hubbard, J. An analysis of superstitious behavior. *Behavior,* 1972, *43,* 1–12.

Davis, H., & Kenney, S. Some effects of different test cages on response "strategies" during leverpress escape. *Psychological Record,* 1975, *25,* 535–543.

Davis, H., & McIntire, R. W. Conditioned suppression under positive, negative and no contingency between conditioned and unconditioned stimuli. *Journal of the Experimental Analysis of Behavior,* 1969, *12,* 633–640.

Davis, H., Memmott, J., & Hurwitz, H. M. B. Autocontingencies: A model for subtle behavioral control. *Journal of Experimental Psychology: General,* 1975, *104,* 169–188.

Davis, H., & Porter, J. *Leverholding behavior during transition from escape to avoidance.* Paper presented at the meeting of the Psychonomic Society, St. Louis, 1976.

Davis, H., & Wheeler, L. Social interaction between rats on different schedules of reinforcement. *Psychonomic Science,* 1966, *4,* 389–390.

DeCosta, M. J., & Ayers, J. J. B. Suppression of operant *vs* consummatory behavior. *Journal of the Experimental Analysis of Behavior,* 1971, *16,* 133–142.

Dinsmoor, J. A., & Hughes, H. L. Training rats to press a bar to turn off shock. *Journal of Comparative and Physiological Psychology,* 1956, *49,* 235–238.

Estes, W., & Skinner, B. F. Some quantitative properties of anxiety. *Journal of Experimental Psychology,* 1941, *29,* 390–400.

Feldman, R. S., & Bremner, F. J. A method for rapid conditioning of stable avoidance barpressing behavior. *Journal of the Experimental Analysis of Behavior,* 1963, *6,* 393–394.

Ferster, C. B., & Skinner, B. F. *Schedules of reinforcement,* New York: Appleton, 1957.

Flory, R. K. Attack behavior as a function of minimum inter-food interval. *Journal of the Experimental Analysis of Behavior,* 1969, *12,* 825–828.

Frankl, V. *From deathcamp to existentialism.* Boston: Beacon, 1969.

Harsh, J. Preference for signaled shock: A well established and reliable phenomenon. *Psychological Record,* 1978, *28,* 281–290.

Herrmann, T., Davis, H., & Woods, B. A re-examination of the effects of septal lesions on leverpress shock escape. *Physiology and Behavior,* 1978, *21,* 587–592.

Herrnstein, R. J. Method and theory in the study of avoidance. *Psychological Review,* 1969, *76,* 49–69.

Herrnstein, R. J., & Loveland, D. H. Complex visual concept in the pigeon. *Science,* 1964, *146,* 549–551.

Hoffman, H. S. The analysis of discriminated avoidance. In W. K. Honig (Ed.), *Operant behavior: Areas of research and application.* New York: Appleton, 1966. Pp. 499–530.

Holz, W. C., & Azrin, N. H. Discriminative properties of punishment. *Journal of the Experimental Analysis of Behavior,* 1961, *4,* 225–232.

Hurwitz, H. M. B. Leverholding under free operant avoidance. *Journal of the Experimental Analysis of Behavior,* 1967, *10,* 551–554.

Hutchinson, R., Renfrew, J. W., & Young, G. A. Effects of longterm shock and associated stimuli on aggressive and manual responses. *Journal of the Experimental Analysis of Behavior,* 1971, *15,* 141–166.

Jackson, D. E. Within-session observations of rats leverpressing in the presence of free food. *Bulletin of the Psychonomic Society,* 1976, *8,* 292–294.

Jackson, D. E., & Delprato, D. J. Aversive CSs suppress leverpressing for food but not the eating of free food. *Learning and Motivation,* 1974, *5,* 448–458.

Keehn, J. D. Running and barpressing as avoidance responses. *Psychological Reports,* 1967, *20,* 591–602. (a)

Keehn, J. D. Is barholding with negative reinforcement preparatory or perseverative? *Journal of the Experimental Analysis of Behavior,* 1967, *10,* 461–465. (b)

Kelleher, R. T., & Morse, W. H. Schedules using noxious stimuli. III. Responding maintained with response-produced electric shocks. *Journal of the Experimental Analysis of Behavior,* 1968, *11,* 819–838.

Keller, F. S. Light aversion in the white rat. *Psychological Record,* 1941, *4,* 235–250.

Lockard, J. S. Choice of warning signal or no warning signal in an unavoidable shock situation. *Journal of Comparative and Physiological Psychology,* 1963, *56,* 526–530.

Logan, F. A., & Boice, R. Aggressive behavior of paired rodents in an avoidance context. *Behaviour,* 1969, *34,* 161–183.

McIntire, R. W., Davis, H., Cohen, S. I., & Franch, E. O. Sidman avoidance performance under punishment and non-contingent shock conditions. *Psychological Reports,* 1968, *22,* 897–903.

McKearney, J. W. Maintenance of responding under a fixed-interval schedule of electric shock presentation. *Science,* 1968, *160,* 1249–1251.

McKearney, J. W. Schedule-dependent effects: Effects of drugs, and maintenance of responding with response-produced electric shocks. In R. M. Gilbert and J. D. Keehn (Eds.), *Schedule effects: Drugs, drinking and aggression.* Toronto: Univ. of Toronto Press, 1972.

Meyer, D. R., Cho, C., & Wesemann, A. F. On problems of conditioning discriminated leverpress avoidance responses. *Psychological Review,* 1960, *67,* 224–228.

Migler, B. Experimental self-punishment and superstitious escape behavior. *Journal of the Experimental Analysis of Behavior,* 1963, *6,* 371–385.

Miller, N. E. Learnable drives and rewards. In S. S. Stevens (Ed.), *Handbook of Experimental Psychology.* New York: Wiley, 1951.

Morse, W., & Kelleher, R. T. Schedules as fundamental determinants of behavior. In W. N. Schoenfeld (Ed.), *The theory of reinforcement schedules.* New York: Appleton, 1970. Pp. 139–185.

Mowrer, O. H. On the dual nature of learning—a reinterpretation of "conditioning" and "problem solving." *Harvard Educational Review,* 1947, *17,* 102–148.

Muenzinger, K. F. Motivation in learning: I. Electric shock for correct response in the visual discrimination habit. *Journal of Comparative Psychology,* 1934, *17,* 267–277.

Orme-Johnson, D. *Conditioned suppression on punished and unpunished baselines.* (Space Research Laboratory Technical Report No. 67-12) College Park: Univ. of Maryland, 1967.

Osborne, S. R. The free food (contrafreeloading) phenomenon: A review and analysis. *Animal Learning and Behavior,* 1977, *5,* 221–235.

Pear, J. J., Moody, J. E., & Persinger, M. A. Lever attacking by rats during free-operant avoidance. *Journal of the Experimental Analysis of Behavior,* 1972, *18,* 517–523.

Pear, J. J., & Roy, G. W. Operandum attacking may contribute to schedule effects on response rate. *Perceptual and Motor Skills,* 1971, *33,* 849–850.

Perkins, C. C., Lewis, D., & Seymann, R. Preference for signal shock versus shock signal. *Psychological Reports,* 1963, *13,* 735–738.

Powell, R. W. Analysis of warm up effect during avoidance in wild and domesticated rodents. *Journal of Comparative and Physiological Psychology,* 1972, *78,* 311–316.

Powell, D. A., Francis, M. J., Francis, J., & Schneiderman, N. Shock-induced aggression as a function of prior experience with avoidance, fighting, or unavoidable shock. *Journal of the Experimental Analysis of Behavior,* 1972, *18,* 323–332.

Rescorla, R. A. Pavolian conditioning and its proper control procedures. *Psychological Review,* 1967, *74,* 71–80.

Rescorla, R., & Solomon, R. Two-process learning theory: Relationships between Pavlovian conditioning and instrumental learning. *Psychological Review,* 1967, *74,* 151–182.

Reynolds, G., Catania, A. C., & Skinner, B. F. Conditioned and unconditioned aggression in pigeons. *Journal of the Experimental Analysis of Behavior,* 1963, *6,* 73–74.

Seligman, M. E. P. Chronic fear produced by unpredictable shock. *Journal of Comparative and Physiological Psychology,* 1968, *66,* 402–411.

Seligman, M. E. P. On the generality of the laws of learning. *Psychological Review,* 1970, *77,* 406–418.

Seligman, M. E. P., & Binik, Y. M. The safety signal hypothesis. In H. Davis & H. M. B. Hurwitz (Eds.), *Operant-Pavlovian interactions.* Hillsdale, New Jersey: Erlbaum, 1977. Pp. 165–187.

Seligman, M. E. P., & Meyer, B. Chronic fear and alceration in rats as a function of unpredictability of safety. *Journal of Comparative and Physiological Psychology,* 1970, *73,* 202–207.

Sidman, M. Two temporal parameters of the maintenance of avoidance behavior by the white rat. *Journal of Comparative and Physiological Psychology,* 1953, *46,* 253–261.

Sidman, M. Normal sources of pathological behavior. *Science,* 1960, *132,* 61–68.

Sidman, M. Avoidance behavior. In W. K. Honig (Ed.), *Operant behavior: Areas of research and application.* New York: Appleton, 1966. Pp. 448–498.

Skinner, B. F. "Superstition" in the pigeon. *Journal of Experimental Psychology,* 1948, *38,* 168–172.

Skinner, B. F. *Beyond freedom and dignity.* New York: Knopf, 1971.

Solomon, R. L. Punishment. *American Psychologist,* 1964, *19,* 237–253.

Staddon, J. E. R., & Simmelhag, V. L. The "superstition" experiment: A re-examination of its implications for principles of adaptive behavior. *Psychological Review,* 1971, *78,* 3–43.

Stoltz, S., & Wolfe, M. M. Visually discriminated behavior in a "blind" adolescent retardate. *Journal of Applied Behavior Analysis,* 1969, *2,* 65–77.

Thorndike, E. L. *Animal intelligence.* New York: Macmillan, 1911.

Thompson, T., & Bloom, W. Aggression behavior and extinction-induced response rate increase. *Psychonomic Science,* 1966, *5,* 335–336.

Timberlake, W., & Allison, J. Response deprivation: An empirical approach to instrumental performance. *Psychological Review,* 1974, *81,* 146–164.

Ulrich, R. Interaction between reflexive fighting and cooperative escape. *Journal of the Experimental Analysis of Behavior,* 1967, *10,* 311–317.

V. A. COLOTLA

Experimental Depression in Animals

9

I. Introduction

According to National Institute of Mental Health statistics (Williams, Friedman, & Secunda, 1970), "depression" is one of the most prevalent mental illnesses in the United States. It may also be a common condition in other parts of the world, where official statistics are not readily available or where, because other needs are more pressing, depressives do not receive enough attention from psychologists or physicians.

The 1960s has witnessed vigorous attempts at understanding the mechanisms underlying depressive conditions (Depue & Monroe, 1978), and hopes have been raised that, through work with infrahuman subjects in the laboratory, the basis of depression may soon be understood. In the present chapter, I shall attempt to provide an evaluation of two promising behavioral models of depression that derive from laboratory studies with animals: the learned-helplessness model of Seligman and his associates (e.g., Miller, Rosellini, & Seligman, 1977) and the social deprivation studies of Harlow and his group (e.g., Suomi & Harlow, 1977). I shall delineate how phenomena produced in the laboratory and those found in clinical practice act in opposite directions in each of these examples.

PSYCHOPATHOLOGY IN ANIMALS
Research and Clinical Implications

A. EXPERIMENTAL PSYCHOPATHOLOGY

Even though Pavlov's work with his collaborators on experimental neurosis was reported in the 1920s (Pavlov, 1927), very little work on neurosis and other experimental psychopathologies was accomplished by scientists outside Russia in the decade that followed. Notable exceptions are Liddell's group at Cornell (e.g., Liddell, James, & Anderson, 1934), Masserman (1943), and Gantt (1944). Much work was devoted to the analysis of audiogenic seizures (Finger, 1944) and to frustration-induced abnormal fixations (Maier, 1949), but researchers were reluctant to ascribe such concepts as "mental conflict," "abnormal personality," and "inadequate ego," which are readily applied to human neurotic patients, to infrahuman counterparts developed in the laboratory (Hunt, 1964).

Since the 1960s, however, interest in experimental models of psychopathologies has been renewed (e.g., Baruk, 1967; Kietzman, Sutton, & Zubin, 1975; Kimmel, 1971; Maser & Seligman, 1977; Zubin & Hunt, 1967), and numerous animal analogues of human psychiatric conditions have been proposed (cf. Keehn, 1979, and other chapters in this volume). The two models of depression that I review in this chapter attest to this renewal of interest and suggest that it will not be without effect.

B. OTHER EXPERIMENTAL MODELS OF DEPRESSION

Learned helplessness and social isolation are not the only experimental approaches to depression, so other laboratory and conceptual models should be briefly mentioned for the benefit of readers interested in depression from alternative viewpoints. Among them are pharmacological models of depression that have linked brain monoamine depletion to depressive states. Ellison (1975), for instance, suggests that low norepinephrine levels are associated with "drive deficit" and lethargy in rats, reminiscent of man's depressive condition. Accounts of Ellison's recent experiments appear in Ellison (1977) and in Chapter 4 of this volume. Other researchers (e.g., Harris, 1957) have observed sedation and depletion of brain levels of norepinephrine, serotonin, and dopamine in animals following administration of reserpine. The reserpine model is one of the main pharmacological models of depression, and a direct relationship between depressive conditions and brain monoamine levels in human patients would be of enormous clinical importance if proven.

Klinger's (1975) work on the consequences of disengagement from incentives has also been offered as a potential model of depression (Klinger, Barta, & Kemble, 1974). Basically, these researchers found that after an increase in activity commonly observed during the first few extinction trials of an instrumental response (the frustration effect, Amsel, 1962) there follows a decrease in activity to below baseline levels. To account for this, Klinger (1975) postulates an incentive-disengagement cycle in response–reinforcer interactions that involves invigoration, aggression, depression, and recovery. He views depression as a normal part of disengagement that may be either adaptive or maladaptive for a particular individual, depending on circumstances.

There are some other important conceptualizations of depression, either behavioral (Costello, 1972; Eastman, 1976; Ferster, 1973, 1974; Lewinsohn & Libet, 1972; Lewinsohn, 1974, 1975) or cognitive (Beck, 1967). Ferster (1966), for example, defines clinical depression as "an emotional state with retardation of psychomotor and thought processes, a depressive emotional reaction, feelings of guilt, self-criticism and delusions of unworthiness" and believes that "these qualities refer to a change in complex performances with which the individual customarily interacts with his environment [p. 345]." The interactions that underpin depressions, he argues, are (a) insufficient behavioral repertoire to achieve reinforcement; (b) infrequency of behavior occasioned by the presence of aversive stimuli; (c) sudden changes in response requirements for reinforcement; and (d) punishment. Ferster's account of depression derives from technical terms generated by the experimental analysis of behavior in the animal laboratory, a terminology that cognitive theorists like Lewinsohn, Beck, and Seligman do not completely accept. A recent comparison of Lewinsohn's, Seligman's, and Beck's formulations of depression has been published by Blaney (1977), to whose informative commentary the interested reader is referred.

II. The Learned-Helplessness Model

A. THE PROTOTYPE EXPERIMENT

Seligman's prototype experiment has been described fully in several publications (e.g., Overmier & Seligman, 1967; Maier & Seligman, 1976; Seligman, 1975; Seligman & Maier, 1967), so it will be described only briefly here. In the Seligman and Maier (1967) experiment, for instance, three groups of eight dogs each were used. In one group, the dogs were restrained in a hammock and trained to turn off (escape) electric shocks by pressing in a panel with the nose or side of the head. Members of a second, yoked, group received the same number of shocks with the same durations and patterns as those received by their partners in the escape-trained group. Responses of the yoked group were inconsequential as to escaping the shocks. The third, control, group dogs were restrained in the hammock but were not exposed to shocks. Twenty-four hours after the specified treatment, all three groups were subjected to escape–avoidance training in a shuttlebox. In this situation, the escape and control group dogs rapidly learned to jump the barrier to escape from shock. Six of the eight dogs in the yoked group, however, completely failed to learn: After a few initial attempts to escape they stopped trying, lay down, and passively accepted shocks as they were administered. They had, the theory claims, learned to be helpless.

B. GENERALITY OF THE PROBLEM

1. *Species*

Essentially the same results as those obtained with dogs have been found with a number of other species, including man. The learned-helplessness phenomenon—the inability to escape from an aversive situation following exposure to inescapable trauma—has been observed with subject populations of cats (Thomas & DeWald, 1977), fish (Padilla, Padilla, Ketterer, & Giacolone, 1970), rats (e.g., Altenor, Kay, & Richter, 1977; Looney & Cohen, 1972), college students (Hiroto, 1974), and clinical patients (Price, Tryon, & Raps, 1978). Interestingly, the species most widely used in the social-isolation model of depression, the monkey (e.g., Harlow & Suomi, 1971), has not been studied in experiments employing the learned helplessness paradigm.

Despite the ubiquity of the learned-helplessness phenomenon it is worth remembering that Seligman acknowledges that it does not occur with all subjects: The regular finding with dogs is that about two-thirds of them exhibit learned helplessness and about one-third show normal escape learning after exposure to inescapable trauma. The literature on other species is obscure in this respect, but individual and species-specific differences between animals is a recurrent theme in the literature beginning with Pavlov (1927) onward (Gray, 1964; Kaufman & Rosenblum, 1966; Scott & Fuller, 1965; Fuller, Chapter 3 of this volume).

2. *Stimuli*

Generally, the most common aversive stimulus used as an unavoidable traumatic event with nonhuman subjects has been electric shocks. Alternatively, Weiss *et al.* (1976) forced rats to swim in cold water (2°C) for 30 min before escape–avoidance training and found learned helplessness in their subjects. They explain their results, however, as the result of depletion of norepinephrine in the brain, not as the acquisition of a cognitive set. In experiments with humans, the pretreatment typically consists of exposure to uncontrollable loud noise, insoluble discrimination problems, or forced failure to perform skilled tasks (e.g., Abramson, Garber, Edwards, & Seligman, 1978a; Hiroto, 1974).

3. *Situations*

Learned helplessness does not appear to be stimulus-specific in the sense that helplessness is restricted to the kind of aversive event employed in the pretreatment place. The Weiss, Glazer, and Poherecky (1976) study mentioned earlier is one example. Another is a study by Rosellini and Seligman (1975) in which experience in one kind of aversive situation, uncontrollable electric shock, generalized to another, frustration. Also, in an experiment reported by Altenor, *et al.* (1977), different groups of rats were exposed to different stressors: shock or confinement under water. Shock–escape failure subsequently occurred in either case. Another experiment, reported by Maier, Anderson, and Lieberman (1972), showed that rats pre-exposed to inescapable shock exhibited, in a test situation, less shock-elicited aggression than did rats that received no shock or escapable shock in the pretest phase of the experiment.

There are exceptions, however, to these generally positive results concerning situation generality. In the Cole and Coyne (1977) study with humans, subjects who displayed more impairment in solving anagrams after receiving inescapable noise than did control subjects who received escapable noise, were not worse than the controls when tested away from the original noise-exposure setting.

C. PARALLELS BETWEEN LEARNED HELPLESSNESS AND DEPRESSION

Seligman (1975) proposes (a) that helplessness results because animals learn during inescapable shock treatments that shock termination is independent of their behavior; and (b) that this learning transfers to the subsequent escape–avoidance training situation. Furthermore, Seligman contends that such learned helplessness manifests itself as three classes of deficit in the organism: motivational, cognitive, and emotional. The motivational deficit pertains to the failure of the helpless organism to respond to signals of aversive events even when the events become controllable. That is, the motivation to initiate voluntary responding to control future events is undermined (lowered initiation of voluntary responses). The cognitive deficit consists of a difficulty in learning that control is possible, even when escape or avoidance responses have actually been successful (negative cognitive set). Emotional involvement is inferred from the finding that learned helplessness has a time course. That is, a rest period between the pretreatment with uncontrollable shocks and the subsequent escape-avoidance learning test greatly reduces the degree of helplessness exhibited in the test situation (Maier & Seligman, 1976).

Altogether, Seligman points to six aspects of learned helplessness in animals that seem to parallel symptoms of depression in humans: (1) initiation of voluntary responses; (2) negative cognitive set; (3) time course; (4) lowered aggression; (5) loss of appetite; and (6) some common physiological foundations. These correspond in depressed people to:

1. Passivity and psychomotor retardation (cf. Ferster, 1966).
2. Human feelings of worthlessness (Ferster, 1966) and belief in the futility of their own behaviors (Beck, 1967). According to Beck, this is the critical and most prominent feature of depression.
3. Although there is disagreement among clinicians on the time course of depression and its relationship with mania (Depue & Monroe, 1978), the spontaneous dissipation of depression has been a noted characteristic of depression ever since Kraepelin advanced his diagnostic classification.
4. Reduced aggressiveness, sexuality, and social interest in general, and
5. Weight loss and anorexia are common accompaniments of human depressive conditions.

6. In both learned helplessness and depression there is a marked depletion of brain norepinephrine. Fuller accounts of these parallels are given by Seligman (1975) and Seligman, Klein, and Miller (1976).

D. PROBLEMS WITH THE LEARNED-HELPLESSNESS MODEL

The learned-helplessness model of depression has been criticized from a theoretical point of view (Buchwald, Coyne, & Cole, 1978; Costello, 1978; Rippere, 1977), and is contraindicated by the results of a number of experiments (Gatchel, McKinney, & Koebernick, 1977; Rizley, 1978; Sacco & Hokanson, 1978; Willis & Blaney, 1978).

The conceptual criticisms include the complaint that there are several meanings of "helplessness" in Seligman's writings, and that such terms as "outcome" and "uncontrollable outcome" are incompletely defined (Buchwald *et al.*, 1978). Costello (1978) contends that Seligman fails to identify the hypothesized cognitive deficit, ignores the various subtypes of human depression, and disregards the possibility that reactions other than helplessness can occur when responses and reinforcers are independent. Seligman's emphasis on cross-species generality of learned helplessness and on environmental factors are criticized by Rippere (1977), who points to important differences among species (especially socialization in man) and to nonenvironmental mediators of behavior.

Some empirical findings that do not support the learned-helplessness model of depression are: lack of a difference in measures of perceived noncontingency between behaviors and outcomes between depressed and nondepressed undergraduate students (Willis & Blaney, 1978); no evidence that depression-related behavioral deficiencies in a private measurement situation are a function of perceived noncontingency between response and outcome (Sacco & Hokanson, 1978); the attribution of failure by depressed students to internal personal inadequacies rather than to the absence of external contingencies (Rizley, 1978); and the absence of depression-based perceptual deficits in college students (McNitt & Thornton, 1978). In addition, O'Leary, Donovan, Krueger, and Cysewski (1978) did not find deficits in a skill task related to response–outcome independence in a group of depressed alcoholics, and Kilpatrick-Tabak and Roth (1978) found that a treatment procedure that induced elation in helpless subjects was ineffective with depressed subjects. Finally, in a study by Gatchel *et al.* (1977), learned helplessness was associated with a reduction in phasic skin conductance, whereas depression was associated with an increase in phasic skin conductance in the face of uncontrollable aversive events.

E. SELIGMAN'S REFORMULATION OF THE MODEL

The criticisms and the evidence not easily accounted for by the learned helplessness model of depression led Seligman and his colleagues to reformulate the model. Abramson, Seligman, and Teasdale (1978b) added an attributional framework to the original model: Once noncontingency of response and outcome is perceived then the cause of depression is attributed to helplessness. Once attributed, they say, helplessness can assume any of the following characteristics: It can be stable (permanent, such as a self-acknowledged feature of personality) or unstable (transient, such as fatigue); it can be global (all-encompassing, such as "lack of intelligence") or specific (focused on a single failing, for instance, lack of mathematical ability); or it can be located internally (attributed to personal characteristics) or externally (attributed to environmental characteristics).

The attributes of helplessness chosen by an individual are hypothesized to influence whether the expectation of future helplessness will be chronic or acute, whether it will be broad or narrow in spectrum, and the extent to which self-esteem is lowered. Thus, an individual attributing failure to global causes will have broad-spectrum behavioral deficits. If he or she also attributes stability to helplessness the person will show chronic motivational impairments, the intensity of which will depend on the certainty of the expectations of response–outcome noncontingency. Since helplessness attributed to internal sources is often stable and global, according to the theory, helplessness attributed to personal characteristics can cause more severe psychological deficits than helplessness attributed to characteristics of the environment.

In other responses to his critics, Seligman (1978) argues that experimental results at variance with the original model (e.g., O'Leary *et al.,* 1978) can easily be explained by the reformulated model, and also reminds Costello (1978) that far from ignoring the clinical subtypes of depression he has explicitly stated (Seligman, 1975) that his model more closely resembles *reactive* than it does *endogenous* depression. To that, Seligman (1978) now adds that perhaps learned helplessness is a model of a to-be-identified subclass of depressions, perhaps "helplessness depressions." Thus we come full circle: from an animal model of human depression to a human model of learned helplessness in animals.

III. The Social Isolation Model

A human form of depression of quite different origin from that which Seligman and his colleagues have tried to model is anaclitic depression in human infants as described by Spitz (1945; Spitz & Wolf, 1946). Before Spitz, Bakwin (1942) drew attention to the high mortality rates of orphaned babies committed to institutions in the late nineteenth and early twentieth century, and since Spitz, Bowlby (1969, 1973) has elaborated on a protest–despair–detachment syndrome shown by human children separated from their families. McKinney and Bunney (1969) reviewed several accounts of separation reactions in animals in the light of childhood depression and tabulated a number of behavioral reactions to loss observed in different species of animals. Their tabulation is shown in Table 9.1.

Apart from the studies reviewed by McKinney and Bunney (1969), Scott

Table 9.1
Some Reports of Animal Reactions to Separation[a]

Reference	Animals	Changes	Course or Duration
Seay & Harlow (1965)	Rhesus monkeys	Crying, withdrawal, appetite and sleep loss	Until reunion
Hinde, Spencer-Booth, Bruce (1966)	Rhesus monkeys	Huddling	Separation period (6 days)
Jensen & Tolman (1962)	Rhesus monkeys	Screaming	Less than 1 hour
Kaufman & Rosenblum (1967)	Pigtail monkeys	Agitation, huddling, withdrawal	6 to 8 days
Dilger (1960)	African parrot	Plumage loss and death	Death or indefinite
Saul (1962)	Dog	"Depressed"	3 months
Lorenz (1952)	Geese Jackdaws	"Grief" and appetite loss	Continuous
Hebb (1947)	Chimp	Loss of appetite and responsivity	Recurrent
Mason (1968)	Monkey	Huddling and appetite loss	High mortality
Tinklepaugh (1928)	Rhesus monkey	Self-mutilation, agitation, and withdrawal	14 months
Senay (1966)	Dog	Various	Until reunion (2 months)

[a] Adapted from McKinney and Bunney (1969).

and Fuller (1965) have compared separation syndromes in dogs and humans, noting differences in developmental characteristics of the respective species; and Scott, Stewart, and Ghett (1973) have reported distress vocalization to separation in the beagle, a withdrawal–fearfulness–untrainability syndrome in kennel-raised sheepdogs, and a depressive syndrome (listlessness, apathy, anorexia) in an "underdog" fox terrier. In addition, stereotyped rocking and posturing have been observed in several studies with isolated infant monkeys and chimpanzees (Berkson, 1967). Such stereotypes are characteristic of human autistic children.

More recently, Suomi and Harlow (1977) have wondered if helplessness could be a factor in the isolation syndrome. In this case, the isolated animals did not have helplessness thrust upon them, as with Seligman's dogs, but were raised in environments in which there were limited opportunities for adaptive responses to be learned.

The social-isolation model of depression stems from Harlow's (1958) pioneer work on the development of love in the infant monkey, in which the consequences of raising monkeys with artificial mother surrogates were explored. The behavioral disturbances that. Harlow and his colleagues observed in these experiments led to an impressive body of research on experimentally induced "depression," some of which I will describe later. It is worth remarking first, though, that in contrast to Seligman, Harlow did not set out to create a model of human psychopathology in monkeys but to analyze the sources of behavioral deficits that his monkey subjects displayed as a consequence of rearing procedures. It transpired that these deficits bore remarkable resemblance to those of certain human children (Bowlby, 1976).

A. THE EXPERIMENTAL EVIDENCE

Early experiments were concerned with the effects on infant rhesus monkeys of separation from their natural mothers (e.g., Seay & Harlow, 1965). The separation produced an initial "protest" stage, rarely lasting more than a few days, followed by a "despair" stage characterized by a sharp decrease in vocalization, exploration, locomotion, and play. Bowlby's third stage of "detachment" was not elaborated, but the two-stage reaction was remarkably similar to anaclitic depression in humans (Spitz 1945; Spitz & Wolf, 1946). Kaufman and Rosenblum (1967) reported a similar finding in that four pigtail infant monkeys living in a group reacted initially with agitation when their mothers were first removed from the home pen. The mothers were kept away from the pen for 4 weeks, in which time three of the infants became severely withdrawn. When the mothers were reintroduced into the pen, marked and prolonged intensification of the mother–infant relationship appeared in all four dyads.

Similar results have been obtained in other laboratories (see Table 9.1), although the depressive phenomenon is not seen in some monkey species, such as the bonnet macaque, the patus monkey, or the squirrel monkey (Kaufman, 1973; Suomi & Harlow, 1977). Apparently, such species differences depend on complex social interactions among infants and adults other than the mothers in the monkey colonies (Kaufman & Rosenblum, 1967; McKinney & Bunney, 1969).

Among the important variables that have been explored in social isolation and separation experiments are attachment relationships, characteristics of separation. and the isolation environment (Harlow & Suomi, 1974; Suomi & Harlow, 1977; McKinney, Suomi, & Harlow, 1973). These variables will now be briefly reviewed.

1. Attachment Relationships

Infants may be separated from their mothers either by removing the mothers and leaving the infants with other group members (e.g., Kaufman & Rosenblum, 1967) or by removing the infants and placing them in isolation. The second case involves not only mother–infant separation but peer–peer separation as well, and Suomi and Harlow (1977) point out that whereas mother–infant separation may provide a model for human infantile anaclitic depression, adult depression in humans may be better modeled by more severe forms of social isolation.

After the early studies of surrogate-mother rearing in Harlow's laboratory further studies (e.g., McKinney, Suomi, & Harlow, 1973) were developed more fully to explore the effects of peer–peer separation. In these experiments, groups of motherless infant monkeys were reared together from birth to 3 or 6 months of age and then separated from each other. According to Suomi and Harlow (1977), the behavior pattern observed upon separation was qualitatively identical to the two-stage reaction to maternal separation shown by both monkey (rhesus) and human infants. Moreover, virtually all variables found to influence reactions to separation from the mother have been demonstrated to have similar effects on peer–peer separations, at least among monkeys less than 1 year old (Suomi & Harlow, 1977).

2. Characteristics of the Separation

The duration of separation has been systematically studied. Harlow and Suomi (1974) used either a single 6-day separation period, two separate 6-day periods, or one 13-day period and found that the longer the period of separation, the more serious was the monkey's reactions to it.

McKinney et al. (1973) studied the living situation from which the target individual is removed. They reared infant monkeys in adjoining cages so that they could see but not touch each other, and allowed them 10 hours of social interaction per week. When the animals were removed one at a time in rotation and housed in a different experimental room, the separated monkeys showed the usual two-stage protest–despair reaction, but the stages were apparently less distinct than those observed in prior experiments.

All in all, severe and prolonged clinical depression has not been a prominant characteristic result of Harlow's rearing experiments, although a variety of abnormal postural, gestural, and social behaviors have been produced. Mason (1968) recognizes four components of the separation syndrome in primates: (a) abnormal postures and movements; (b) disturbances of emotion, particularly excessive fearfulness; (c) poor integration of motor patterns of behavior; and (d) defective social communication. Clinical depression is conspicuously absent from Mason's list, although it is a possible feature of the psychopathology induced by another experimental situation devised in Harlow's laboratory: the vertical pit.

3. Isolation Environment: The Vertical Chamber

Since depression in humans has been characterized as a state of "helplessness and hopelessness, sunken in a well of despair [Schmale, 1970, quoted by Harlow & Suomi, 1971]," Harlow transformed metaphor into substance and designed an apparatus to produce such a psychological well: the vertical chamber. The apparatus, "basically a stainless steel chamber open at the top with sides that slope downward and inward to form a rounded bottom [Harlow & Suomi, 1974, p. 284]," is pictured in Suomi and Harlow (1977) where a photograph of a monkey in a typical huddled depressive posture also appears.

In one study with the vertical chamber (Harlow & Suomi, 1971), four socially unsophisticated monkeys between 6–13 months of age were individually confined in vertical chambers for a total of 30 days each. When released, the monkeys showed profound and pervasive behavioral effects: self-clasping and huddling were far above baseline levels and remained so throughout following tests. In addition, locomotion and exploration decreased below normal levels. All these changes have been observed in other separation experiments and have been termed "depressive." Other effects of vertical chamber confinement—increases in destructive behavior and immature self-directed behavior—are perhaps characteristic of the manic aspect of manic–depressive psychosis.

The vertical chamber provides a means for uniting the social-isolation and learned-helplessness models of depression. It is a situation that engenders helplessness without traumatic physical pain and could serve as a pretreatment condition ahead of learned helplessness tests. Such tests need not involve escape–avoidance learning; helplessness, presumably, extends to positive tasks. Like aversive stimuli, sudden changes in response requirements for reinforcement, and punishment (Ferster, 1966), vertical chamber experience could disrupt an organism's complex interactions with its environment to produce the behavioral manifestations of depression in an infrahuman animal.

B. RELATIONSHIP TO DEPRESSION

The isolation-rearing model clearly relates to the anaclitic depression syndrome in human infants more than it does to the adult reactive-depression syndrome that the learned-helplessness paradigm is supposed to model, and corresponds even more clearly to the protest–despair stages that Bowlby (1969, 1973) describes for human children separated from their families. With nonhuman primates the Bowlby's third stage, attachment, appears to be missing in monkeys although it is characteristic of human children who renew acquaintanceship with their mothers. Harlow has been less insistent than Seligman in proposing his laboratory preparation as a model of a human clinical condition and so has encountered less criticism from clinicians who do not see animals as merely uncomplicated humans. To the contrary, Bowlby (1976) applauds work such as that of Harlow as highlighting a human state of affairs that has not gathered the attention it deserves. The wheel that turned full circle with Seligman is reversed in the case of Harlow: Seligman thinks he has found an undiscovered human condition through his studies of animals; Bowlby thinks Harlow has found in animals a condition in human children that has not received the attention it deserves.

IV. Conclusion

We have seen how experimental work with animals relates to depressive episodes in humans, and how the work by Seligman and his associates ends up with a human model of learned helplessness in animals, whereas Harlow and his collaborators arrive at an animal model of depressive conditions in children.

There are some important considerations from this kind of research for child-rearing practices. For instance, Seligman (1975) states: "If a young adult has no experience of coping with anxiety and frustration, he will not be able to cope with failure, boredom or frustration when it becomes crucial. Too much success, too coddled an existence, makes a child helpless when he is finally confronted with his first failure [pp. 157–158]." There is an implication here that children should not be spared frustrating experiences that would enable them to adapt to aversive situations as adults. This implication is reminiscent of the suggestion by Richelle (1966) in a review of errorless learning, that subjects learning without errors are not exposed to frustration, and hence do not develop frustration tolerance. The implication of Richelle's comment is, again, that organisms that have learned with errors, that have had exposure to the aversiveness of failure, are more able to cope later on with new situations engendering frustration.

One should be careful, however, not to issue any strong statements regarding child training and rearing from any kind of psychological research. Clarke-Stewart (1978) has pointed out the enormous popularity that books and articles by child-care "experts" have for parents in their child-rearing practices, and it should be borne in mind that there have been cases where some wrong, even dangerous for the psychological health of the infants, statements have been carefully followed by parents. John B. Watson (1928), for instance, cautioned parents against the unconsidered display of affection, a suggestion which he later publicly regretted.

Although the results to date have been encouraging, much more carefully controlled research with infrahuman and with human organisms is needed with regard to depressive conditions and the "immunization for depression," before any tentative statements are given to be applied on a large scale.

REFERENCES

Abramson, L. Y., Garber, J., Edwards, N. B., & Seligman, M. E. P. Expectancy changes in depression and schizophrenia. *Journal of Abnormal Psychology*, 1978, *87*, 102–109. (a)

Abramson, L. Y., Seligman, M. E. P., & Teasdale, J. D. Learned helplessness in humans: Critique and reformulation. *Journal of Abnormal Psychology*, 1978, *87*, 49–74. (b)

Altenor, A., Kay, E., & Richter, M. The generality of learned helplessness in the rat. *Learning and Motivation*, 1977, *8*, 54–61.

Amsel, A. Frustrative nonreward in partial reinforcement and discrimination learning: Some recent history and theoretical extension. *Psychological Review*, 1962, *69*, 306–328.

Bakwin, H. Loneliness in infants. *American Journal of Diseases in Children*, 1942, *63*, 30–40.

Baruk, A. La psychiatrie animale. *Annales de Therapeutique Psychiatrique*, 1967, *3*, 165–166.

Beck, A. T. *Depression: Clinical, experimental and theoretical aspects*. New York: Hoeber, 1967.

Berkson, G. Abnormal stereotyped motor acts. In J. Zubin & H. F. Hunt (Eds.), *Comparative psychopathology: Animal and human*. New York: Grune & Stratton, 1967. Pp. 76–94.

Blaney, P. H. Contemporary theories of depression: Critique and comparison. *Journal of Abnormal Psychology*, 1977, *86*, 203–223.

Bowlby, J. *Attachment* (Vol. 1). New York: Basic Books, 1969.

Bowlby, J. *Attachment and loss* (Vol. 2). *Separation, anxiety and anger*. New York: Basic Books, 1973.

Bowlby, J. Human personality development in an ethological light. In G. Serban & A. Kling (Eds.), *Animal models in human psychobiology*. New York: Plenum, 1976.

Buchwald, A. M., Coyne, J. C., & Cole, C. S. A critical evaluation of the learned helplessness model of depression. *Journal of Abnormal Psychology*, 1978, *87*, 180–193.

Clarke-Stewart, K. A. Popular primers for parents. *American Psychologist*, 1978, *33*, 359–369.

Cole, C. S., & Coyne, J. C. Situational specificity of laboratory-induced learned helplessness. *Journal of Abnormal Psychology*, 1977, *86*, 615–623.

Costello, C. G. Depression: Loss of reinforcers or loss of reinforcer effectiveness. *Behavior Therapy*, 1972, *3*, 240–247.

Costello, C. G. A critical review of Seligman's laboratory experiments on learned helplessness and depression in humans. *Journal of Abnormal Psychology*, 1978, *87*, 21–31.

Depue, R. A., & Monroe, S. M. The unipolar–bipolar distinction in the depressive disorders. *Psychological Bulletin*, 1978, *85*, 1001–1029.

Dilger, W. C. The comparative ethology of the African parrot genus *Agapornis*. *Zeischift für Tierpsychologie*, 1960, *17*, 649–685.

Eastman, C. Behavioral formulations of depression. *Psychological Review*, 1976, *83*, 277–291.

Ellison, G. Behavior and the balance between norepinephrine and serotonin. *Acta Neurobiologiae Experimentalis*, 1975, *33*, 499–515.

Ellison, G. D. Animal models of psychopathology. The low-norepinephrine and low-serotonin rat. *American Psychologist*, 1977, *32*, 1036–1045.

Ferster, C. B. Animal behavior and mental illness. *Psychological Record*, 1966, *16*, 345–356.

Ferster, C. B. A functional analysis of depression. *American Psychologist*, 1973, *28*, 857–870.

Ferster, C. B. Behavioral approaches to depression. In R. J. Friedman & M. M. Katz (Eds.), *The psychology of depression: Contemporary theory and research*. Washington, D.C.: Winston, 1974.

Finger, F. W. Experimental behavior disorders in the rat. In J. McV. Hunt (Ed.), *Personality and the behavior disorders* (Vol. II). New York: Ronald, 1944. Pp. 413–430.

Gantt, W. H. *Experimental basis for neurotic behavior: Origin and development of artificially produced disturbances of behavior in dogs*. New York: Hoeber, 1944.

Gatchel, R. J., McKinney, M. E., & Koebernick, L. F. Learned helplessness, depression and physiological responding. *Psychophysiology*, 1977, *14*, 25–31.

Gray, J. A. *Pavlov's typology: Recent theoretical and experimental developments from the laboratory of B. M. Teplov*. Oxford: Pergamon, 1964.

Harlow, H. F. The nature of love. *American Psychologist*, 1958, *13*, 673–685.

Harlow, H. F., & Suomi, S. J. Production of depressive behaviors in young monkeys. *Journal of Autism and Childhood Schizophrenia*, 1971, *1*, 246–255.

Harlow, H. F., & Suomi, S. J. Induced depression in monkeys. *Behavioral Biology*, 1974, *12*, 273–296.

Harris, T. H. Depression induced by Rauwolfia compounds. *American Journal of Psychiatry*, 1957, *113*, 950–951.

Hebb, D. O. Spontaneous neuroses in chimpanzees: Theoretical relations with clinical and experimental phenomena. *Psychosomatic Medicine*, 1947, *9*, 3–16.

Hinde, R. A., Spencer-Booth, Y., & Bruce, M. Effects of 6-day maternal deprivation on rhesus monkey infants. *Nature*, 1966, *210*, 1021–1023.

Hiroto, D. S. Locus of control and learned helplessness. *Journal of Experimental Psychology*, 1974, *102*, 187–193.

Hunt, H. F. Problems in the interpretation of 'experimental neurosis.' *Psychological Reports,* 1964, *15,* 27-35.

Jensen, G. D., & Tolman, C. W. Mother–infant relationships in the monkey *Macaca Nemestrina:* The effect of brief separation and mother–infant specificity. *Journal of Comparative and Physiological Psychology,* 1962, *55,* 131-136.

Kaufman, I. G. Mother–infant separation in monkeys: An experimental model. In J. P. Scott & E. C. Senay (Eds.), *Separation and depression: Clinical and research aspects.* Washington, D.C.: American Association for the Advancement of Science, 1973. Pp. 33-52.

Kaufman, I. C., & Rosenblum, L. A. A behavioral taxonomy for *M. nemestrina* and *M. radiata* based on longitudinal observations of family groups in the laboratory. *Primates,* 1966, *7,* 205-258.

Kaufman, I. C., & Rosenblum, L. A. The reaction to separation in infant monkeys: Anaclitic depression and conservation-withdrawal. *Psychosomatic Medicine,* 1967, *29,* 648-675.

Keehn, J. D. *Origins of madness: Psychopathology in animal life.* Oxford: Pergamon, 1979.

Kietzman, M. L., Sutton, S., & Zubin, J. (Eds.). *Experimental approaches to psychopathology.* New York: Academic Press, 1975.

Kilpatrick-Tabak, B., & Roth, S. An attempt to reverse performance deficits associated with depression and experimentally induced helplessness. *Journal of Abnormal Psychology,* 1978, *87,* 141-154.

Kimmel, H. D. Introduction. In H. D. Kimmel (Ed.), *Experimental psychopathology: Recent research and theory.* New York: Academic Press, 1971.

Klinger, E. Consequences of commitment to and disengagement from incentives. *Psychological Review,* 1975, *82,* 1-25.

Klinger, E., Barter, S. G., & Kemble, E. D. Cyclic activity changes during extinction in rats: A potential model of depression. *Animal Learning and Behavior,* 1974, *2,* 313-316.

Lewinsohn, P. M. A behavioral approach to depression. In R. J. Friedman & M. M. Katz (eds.), *The psychology of depression: Contemporary theory and research.* Washington, D.C.: Winston/Wiley, 1974.

Lewinsohn, P. M. The behavioral study and treatment of depression. In M. Hershen, R. Eisler, P. Miller (Eds.), *Progress in behavior modification.* New York: Academic Press, 1975.

Lewinsohn, P. M., & Libet, J. Pleasant events, activity schedules and depression. *Journal of Abnormal Psychology,* 1972, *79,* 291-295.

Liddell, H. S., James, W. T., & Anderson, O. D. The comparative physiology of the conditioned motor reflex: Based on experiments with the pig, dog, sheep, goat and rabbit. *Comparative Psychology Monograph,* 1934, *11* (Whole No. 51), 1-39.

Looney, T. A., & Cohen, P. S. Retardation of jump-up escape responding in rats pretreated with different frequencies of noncontingent electric shocks. *Journal of Comparative and Physiological Psychology,* 1972, *78,* 317-322.

Lorenz, K. Z. *King Solomon's ring.* London: Methuen, 1952.

Maier, N. R. F. *Frustration: The study of behavior without a goal.* New York: McGraw-Hill, 1949.

Maier, S. F., & Seligman, M. E. P. Learned helplessness: Theory and evidence. *Journal of Experimental Psychology: General,* 1976, *105,* 3-46.

Maier, S. F., Anderson, C., & Lieberman, D. A. Influence of control of shock on subsequent shock-elicited aggression, *Journal of Comparative and Physiological Psychology,* 1972, *81,* 94-100.

Maser, J. D., & Seligman, M. E. P. *Psychopathology: Experimental models.* San Francisco: Freeman, 1977.

Mason, W. A. Early social deprivation in the non-human primates: Implications for human behavior. In D. C. Glass (Ed.), *Environmental influences.* New York: Russell Sage Foundation, 1968. Pp. 70-100.

Masserman, J. H. *Behavior and neurosis: An experimental psychoanalytic approach to psychological principles.* Chicago: Univ. of Chicago Press, 1943.

McKinney, W. T., & Bunney, W. E. Animal model of depression. I. Review of evidence and implications for research. *Archives of General Psychiatry,* 1969, *21,* 240-248.

McKinney, W. T., Suomi, S. J., & Harlow, H. F. New models of separation and depression in rhesus monkeys. In J. P. Scott & E. C. Senay (Eds.), *Separation and depression: Clinical and research aspects*. Washington, D.C.: American Association for the Advancement of Science, 1973.

McNitt, P. C., & Thornton, D. W. Depression and perceived reinforcement: A reconsideration. *Journal of Abnormal Psychology*, 1978, *87*, 137-140.

Miller, W. R., Rosellini, R. A., & Seligman, M. E. P. Learned helplessness and depression. In J. D. Maser & M. E. P. Seligman (Eds.), *Psychopathology: Experimental models*. San Francisco: Freeman, 1977. Pp. 104-130.

O'Leary, M. R., Donovan, D. M., Krueger, K. J., & Cysewski, B. Depression and perception of reinforcement: Lack of differences in expectancy change among alcoholics. *Journal of Abnormal Psychology*, 1978, *87*, 110-112.

Overmier, J. B., & Seligman, M. E. P. Effects of inescapable shock upon subsequent escape and avoidance learning. *Journal of Comparative and Physiological Psychology*, 1967, *63*, 28-33.

Padilla, A. M., Padilla, C., Ketterer, T., & Giacolone, D. Inescapable shocks and subsequent avoidance conditioning in goldfish (*Carrasius auratus*). *Psychonomic Science*, 1970, *20*, 295-296.

Pavlov, I. P. *Conditioned reflexes*. London: Oxford Univ. Press, 1927.

Price, K. P., Tryon, W. W., & Raps, C. S. Learned helplessness and depression in a clinical population: A test of two behavioral hypotheses. *Journal of Abnormal Psychology*, 1970, *87*, 113-121.

Richelle, M. L'apprentissage sans erreur. *Année Psychologique*, 1966, *66*, 535-543.

Rippere, V. Comments on Seligman's theory of helplessness. *Behavior Research and Therapy*, 1977, *15*, 207-209.

Rizley, R. Depression and distortion in the attribution of causality. *Journal of Abnormal Psychology*, 1978, *87*, 32-48.

Rosellini, R., & Seligman, M. E. P. Frustration and learned helplessness. *Journal of Experimental Psychology, Animal Behavior Processes*, 1975, *104*, 149-157.

Sacco, W. P., & Hokanson, J. E. Expectations of success and anagram performance of depressives in a public and private setting. *Journal of Abnormal Psychology*, 1978, *87*, 122-130.

Saul, L. J. Psychosocial medicine and observation of animals. *Psychosomatic Medicine*, 1962, *24*, 58-61.

Schmale, A. *The role of depression in health and disease*. Paper presented at the 137th annual convention of the American Association for the Advancement of Science, Chicago, 1970.

Scott, J. P., & Fuller, J. L. *Genetics and the social behavior of the dog*. Chicago: Univ. of Chicago Press, 1965.

Scott, J. P., Stewart, J. M., & DeGhett, V. J. Separation in infant dogs: Emotional response and motivational consequences. In J. P. Scott & E. C. Senay (Eds.), *Separation and depression: Clinical and research aspects*. Washington, D.C.: American Association for the Advancement of Science, 1973. Pp. 3-32.

Seay, B. M., & Harlow, H. F. Maternal separation in the rhesus monkey. *Journal of Nervous and Mental Disease*, 1965, *140*, 434-441.

Seligman, M. E. P. *Helplessness: On depression, development and death*. San Francisco: Freeman, 1975.

Seligman, M. E. P. Comment and integration. *Journal of Abnormal Psychology*, 1978, *87*, 165-179.

Seligman, M. E. P., & Maier, S. F. Failure to escape traumatic shock. *Journal of Experimental Psychology*, 1967, *14*, 1-9.

Seligman, M. E. P., Klein, D. C., & Miller, W. R. Depression. In H. Leitenberg (Ed.), *Handbook of behavior modification and behavior therapy*. Englewood Cliffs, New Jersey: Prentice-Hall, 1976.

Senay, E. C. Toward an animal model of depression: A study of separation behavior in dogs. *Journal of Psychiatric Research*, 1966, *4*, 65-71.

Spitz, R. A. Hospitalism. An inquiry into the genesis of psychiatric conditions in early childhood. *Psychoanalytic Study of the Child*, 1945, *1*, 53-74.

Spitz, R. A., & Wolf, K. M. Anaclitic depression: An inquiry into the genesis of psychiatric conditions in early childhood, II. *Psychoanalytic Study of the Child*, 1946, *2*, 313-342.

Suomi, S. J., & Harlow, H. F. Production and alleviation of depressive behaviors in monkeys. In J. D. Maser & M. E. P. Seligman (Eds.), *Psychopathology: Experimental models.* San Francisco: Freeman, 1977.

Tinklebaugh, O. L. The self-mutilation of a male macacos rhesus monkey. *Journal of Mammalogy,* 1928, *9,* 293–300.

Thomas, E., & DeWald, L. Experimental neurosis: Neuropsychological analysis. In J. D. Maser & M. E. P. Seligman (Eds.), *Psychopathology: Experimental models.* San Francisco: Freeman, 1977. Pp. 214–231.

Weiss, J. M., Glazer, H. I., & Pohorecky, L. A. Coping behavior and neurochemical changes: An alternative explanation for the original "learned helplessness" experiments. In G. Serban & A. Kling (Eds.), *Animal models in human psychobiology.* New York: Plenum, 1976.

Williams, T. A., Friedman, R. J., & Secunda, S. K. *Special report: The depressive illnesses.* Washington, D.C.: National Institute of Mental Health, 1970.

Watson, J. B. *Psychological care of infant and child.* New York: Norton, 1928.

Willis, M. H., & Blaney, P. H. Three tests of the learned helplessness model of depression. *Journal of Abnormal Psychology,* 1978, *87,* 131–136.

Zubin, J., & Hunt, H. F. (Eds.). *Comparative psychopathology: Animal and human.* New York: Grune & Stratton, 1967.

DAVID HOTHERSALL
DAVID S. TUBER

Fears in Companion Dogs: Characteristics and Treatment

10

I. Introduction

Among the animals that have played a significant role in the ascent of man, the dog has been especially important (Bronowski, 1973). Recent discoveries at fossil sites show that man's association with dogs predates even the domestication of food and draft animals, and may have begun as much as 14,000 years ago. This association continues today with the majority of dogs being kept as companion animals. Dogs often have a close, reciprocal, supportive relationship with their owners. Such relationships are, no doubt, engendered by the dog's sensitivity to human social cues (Marr, Lierly, & Price, 1971) and to the emotional tenor of the family unit (Speck, 1964). In many cases a dog's acceptance into the family may be such that the distinction between the dog as a differentiated species and the dog as a family member becomes blurred. The remarkable capacity of dogs to interact socially in a supportive manner is shown by their ability to provide therapeutic support for disturbed children (Levinson, 1972; Corson, Corson, Gwynne, & Arnold, 1977), and to be accepted as suitable attachment surrogates for isolated monkeys (Mason & Kenney, 1974). In short, the dog is exquisitely adapted to the role of companion animal.

Such a role necessarily entails close interaction with humans and so a dog may be subjected to many of the stresses and throes of human society. While such stresses are often indirect, they are nevertheless real. In humans such situa-

PSYCHOPATHOLOGY IN ANIMALS
Research and Clinical Implications

tions may cause behavioral problems; it is not surprising that they have the same effect in some dogs. In the opening remarks of their classic monograph on the behavioral genetics of the dog, Scott and Fuller (1965) state: "Anyone who wishes to understand a human behavior trait or hereditary disease can usually find the corresponding conditions in dogs with very little effort. Dogs are timid or confident, peaceful or aggressive, and may be born with undershot jaws, club feet or hemophilia [p. 4]." Our experience in studying dogs kept as companion animals has clearly confirmed their statement. Dogs are indeed both a genetic and behavioral "goldmine." They display a variety of behavioral problems and disorders: At times their behavior is remarkably similar to the behavior of humans in similar situations; at other times, of course, it is clearly a reflection of the species characteristics of dogs. The intense fear shown by a dog in the presence of a thunderstorm is strikingly similar to the response of a human phobic in the presence of a feared stimulus: At times both responses are overwhelmingly intense, they are not subject to spontaneous remission, and they often result from just one traumatic experience. It is not surprising that the procedures we have found to be successful in overcoming such behavioral problems in dogs have conceptual parallels to the clinical procedures used in treating humans. Possibly, behavioral problems in companion animals may provide an excellent animal model of some human clinical conditions. In other cases the direct parallels between animal and human clinical problems are not as clear—aggression, for example, is certainly a common behavioral problem in both dogs and humans, but its expression obviously takes very different forms.

In this chapter we will describe the main class of behavioral problems we have seen in dogs kept as companion animals and will illustrate the methods used to overcome them. It is our hope that consonant with the theme of this volume, lessons relevant to human clinical work may be drawn from this work with companion animals.

II. Reactions to Separation

One of the endearing, indeed cultivated, characteristics of the companion animal is of course the development of strong attachments to members of the family. And yet while such attachments may stand as a tribute to the strength of the relationships, they appear to play a major role in contributing to the most common behavioral problem we encounter in the companion animal: maladaptive behaviors related to the absence of the owner. This class of problems comprises approximately 35% of the behavioral problems presented for treatment.

The behaviors that occur during the owner's absence reflect a varied constellation of whining, barking, defecation and urination, voluminous salivation, and, invariably, destruction of household and personal belongings. The frequency and temporal characteristics of such a reaction to the owner's departure are shown in Figure 10.1, which describes the audible characteristics of the reac-

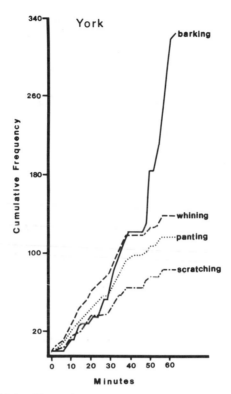

Figure 10.1. The reactions to separation in the Llewellyn Setter, York.

tions of York, a 6-year-old Llewellin setter during the first 60 min after the owner's departure. The prominent characteristics of the record are the immediacy of onset and the persistence of the distress vocalizations. While the owner was away, York was a severely disturbed dog; at other times his behavior was exemplary; in fact York was nationally ranked in obedience competition.

In the case of Pirate, a 14-month-old dalmatian, no item was immune from his daily destructive onslaught. Pirate's owners were both employed, and so he had been left alone for 8–10 hours each day since being acquired as a puppy. In addition to intense whining, Pirate chewed everything within reach including stereo equipment, furniture, woodwork, clothing, and the carpet. Of special interest was the owner's report that on those occasions when they had unexpectedly returned home prematurely, the destructive behavior had already begun—once within 10 min of their departure. Ironically, taking Pirate along and leaving him in the car was without incident despite extended absences. The destructive behavior was specifically a reaction to the owner's leaving the dog alone in the home.

In some cases, destruction begins when there is a major change in the dog's life. Medusa is an excellent example of the effects of such a change. When we first saw her, Medusa was an 18-month-old Irish setter. She spent her early pup-pyhood living with her owner in a college dormitory and was very much the dar-ling of the dorm. Students pampered and played with her all day long; she re-ceived a great deal of exercise and almost constant attention. At the age of 6 months, quite abruptly, her fortunes took a turn for the worse. She and her owner moved to an apartment, and her owner took a full-time position in addi-tion to his studies. The din and activity of dormitory living was replaced by the relative solitude of an apartment. Medusa now had to stay in an apartment all day long with the pleasure of companionship with the owner necessarily being deferred to weekends. In her owner's absence, Medusa explored cupboards, shelves, closets, and drawers. Most of the contents were simply strewn about the home, but records, shoes, a guitar, wooden articles, and leather goods were totally destroyed. Each week her destructive behavior seemed to focus on a new area of the home. The kitchen, however, proved to be a special favorite: Dishes, pots and pans, and garbage were carried throughout the home. Medusa's behavior had been a daily occurrence for the 6 months prior to our initial meeting.

While such reactions are often attributed to boredom—and in some cases we suspect just that—the reaction that we are most interested in is very different. In fact, the consistency of the circumstances surrounding the appearance of the behavior, the characteristics of the reaction during the absence, and its similarities to reactions to separation in other species, all suggest that we are dealing with a behavior that is much more fundamental than simply a desire to seek entertainment during the quiet hours when the owner is away.

The behavioral reaction in these dogs has several common features:

1. Prior to the owner's departure, the dog typically begins to exhibit signs of distress: pacing, whining, or trembling.

2. In general, the reaction occurs immediately or very soon after the owner's departure. In the case of whining or other audible behaviors as presented in Figure 10.1, tape repordings can accurately confirm this in addition to corroborating a high level of distress. For many of these dogs, there is neither eating nor drinking during the absence period.

3. By the time these dogs are presented for treatment, the reaction occurs reliably during each and every absence.

4. Finally, the dog exhibits a strong dependency reaction upon the owners when they return to the house. Even following brief absences of only a few minutes duration, the reunion is one of extreme excitement and protracted greeting. Characteristically, at other times around the house, the dog is virtually a shadow of the owner, following constantly from room to room. If the owner does settle for any period of time, so does the dog. If the dog should leave or wander off in pursuit of other activities, he continually returns to the owner briefly as if to assure himself of the owner's presence.

It is intriguing to consider the parallels between these separation reactions and those described in rhesus monkeys by Harry and Margaret Harlow and their colleagues (Harlow & Harlow, 1971). Such animals when separated from their mothers, or from a cagemate with whom they have been raised from birth, respond to separation with prolonged distress vocalizations, frantic pacing, and other signs of acute emotional distress. Ultimately such separations may lead to withdrawal and autistic behaviors. Similarly the reunions between separated cagemates are marked by periods of intense clinging. The "together–together" or "choo-choo train" clinging postures of these monkeys are an exaggerated caricature of a dog's reaction to an owner's return. Similar reactions to separation from the mother have been described in human infants (Spitz, 1946; Robertson & Bowlby, 1952), further suggesting the relevance of an animal model of human attachment.

While such considerations may be of interest to psychologists, they provide little comfort to an owner whose primary concern is to stop a dog from destroying the house. Typically, such an owner has few techniques to resort to and they are generally ineffective. Punishment, necessarily delayed, has little effect on the dog's future destructive behavior. In the extreme case we have witnessed a "wait until your father gets home" punishment procedure. A wife, returning home at 5:00 p.m., would completely ignore the extensive damage done by their dog until her husband, the disciplinarian in the family returned home at 8:00 p.m. Then the dog would be punished! Clearly what the dog is most likely to learn is an association between the owner's arrival and punishment; what the dog does not learn is an association between its behavior during the owner's absence and punishment. The submissive posture or hiding shown by the dog upon the owner's return—behaviors commonly interpreted by many owners as signs of guilt—are more likely anticipations of the punishment to come. The destroyed items may actually acquire conditional stimulus properties for the impending punishment (Vollmer, 1977).

In addition to the ineffective punishment procedure there are also very few rewards in this situation. The actions of the owner preparatory to leaving the house can only signal to the dog the inevitability of the stress which follows; the stimulus conditions during the absence can only signal future punishment. In the face of repeatedly encountering damage when returning home, it is understandable that the owner's feelings toward the dog are less than amicable. But the dog, happy at the owner's return, is met by an owner who is likely to administer punishment. The result for the dog is conflict—a classical prerequisite for emotional stress. From the point of view of behavior theory, there is simply nothing working in the dog's favor.

A common alternative to punishment is the use of confinement during the owner's absence. However, this does little to ameliorate the dog's stress and serves only to restrict the range of the dog's objectionable behavior. It may, in fact, potentiate it: The basement, made bare to minimize any misbehavior, or a small cage, are, at best, harsh, isolation environments.

One of the primary goals of our remedial treatment is the reduction of stress associated with the owner's absence. Accordingly, the training procedure we have developed is constructed within the framework of the desensitization paradigm and is conceptually analogous to the approach used by Lazarus (1960) in treating a young girl's fear of separation. Working with nonverbal animals however, imposes a variety of constraints: The dog must be exposed to a graded series of departures and absences by the owner, which gradually increase in intensity. In these training sessions, owners simulate all of the preparatory behaviors relating to departure and absence, often including actually leaving in a car. Initially, training absences are extremely short to ensure that the owner's return to the house occurs prior to any misbehavior by the dog. Our aim is to establish a strong positive association between the owner's departure, contrived good behavior by the dog, and the owner's return which culminates in an extraordinary reward period for the dog. As training progresses, the absences are extended as long as the dog's objectionable behavior remains under control. Progress to longer training absences is always followed by rehearsal at shorter absences; misbehavior, indicating that the dog's tolerance has been exceeded, is always followed by extensive remedial practice at much shorter absence durations. As training continues, absences become longer but they do so erratically. Although our goal is to achieve errorless learning, use of such a graded series of exposures to the feared situation ensures that any misbehavior by the dog will be likely to occur in close temporal contiguity with the owner's return. At such times the necessary reprimands can at least be used effectively.

Because these training absences must occur in conjunction with the owner's routine daily absences, a stable cue is presented during every training absence that serves to differentiate the training periods. Thus, at one level of analysis, the dog's behavior is under the control of a discriminative stimulus which sets the occasion for differential reinforcement of any behavior which is not objectionable; at another level the situation is one of a transfer paradigm using stimulus conditions which have been shown to maximize retroactive interference (Wickens, Tuber, Nield, & Wickens, 1977). Once we are satisfied with the dog's performance during these training absences, we can then gradually fade out the training stimulus. As is easily imagined, this training procedure is unwieldy, demanding, and especially tedious. It is also very effective.

We have seen 63 dogs presented for separation reactions. Although the behavior of these dogs shows some common features and characteristics, such uniformity belies the varied and complex origins of the problem. In the absence of quantitative, normative data, conclusions as to the etiology of this behavior must be regarded as preliminary, highly tentative, and largely illustrative.

It seems intuitively reasonable to expect that abandonment and impoundment would contribute to the subsequent development of strong attachments that might, in turn, exacerbate stress reactions to an owner's absence. Nine of the dogs showing separation reactions had, in fact, been acquired as strays. Similarly, it might be expected that a dog kept in a restricted environment beyond the first 4 months of life would have difficulty in adjusting to a family situation. The effects of partial isolation, the kennel syndrome, have been well documented (Fuller, 1967; Pfaffenberger & Scott, 1959). Four of the dogs showing separation reactions had histories of prolonged confinement in kennels.

However, in 27 of these cases the puppy entered the home situation between 5 and 12 weeks of age, a time typically considered to be optimal for transfer to a new environment and for the establishment of strong bonds or attachments to humans. Yet in 19 of these dogs, a strong reaction to the owner's absence was reported to have appeared immediately after the dog entered the home. The only normative data we have been able to find as to the incidence of such separation reactions in dogs come from a study by Scott and Bielfelt (1976). They report destructive behavior in reaction to an owner's absence in 21% of a group of dogs raised under controlled conditions preparatory to training as guide dogs. In the case of our dogs it is interesting to note that whether these dogs were acquired from a pet store or from a private breeder made little difference—separation reactions were almost equally likely in dogs from both sources. Nor was it important whether or not the dogs were subjected to regular or erratic absences by the owner. Why these dogs, introduced to the family situation at an optimal age, and apparently not subjected to any stressful or traumatic experiences, exhibited the separation reaction is an intriguing question which we are unfortunately unable to answer. However, an indication of the extreme sensitivity of puppies to change is shown by a result reported by Pfaffenberger (1963). Withholding a once per week handling session between the ages of 12 and 16 weeks profoundly influenced their later behavior. Due to their dependency upon their human handlers and their timidity in novel environments, these dogs were unsuitable for further training as guide dogs.

The separation reactions in eight of these dogs first occurred some time after their introduction into the home. In all of these cases the appearance of the problem behavior was coincidental with a specific event: Drastic changes in the owners' schedules or changes in residence were the significant events for six of these dogs. Whereas it seems probable that these events did indeed cause the separation reactions, the question of why they had such an effect remains unanswered.

The remaining 23 dogs resist meaningful categorization for a variety of reasons: incomplete life histories, varied ownership and environments, different treatments, etc.

Although our success in overcoming many such separation reactions is reassuring, the complexity of the determinants of these reactions is somewhat overwhelming. Given such a situation one can only empathize with the problems that surely confront the human clinician in attempting to isolate "causes" of a human behavioral problem.

III. Phobic Reactions

We will now consider a second type of behavior problem involving fear—excessive fears of specific stimuli. Such fears are often very intense. Indeed one distinction between such "home-grown" fears and those frequently studied by experimental psychologists in laboratory situations is their intensity and diffuseness. Before we appreciated this distinction we presented a moderately weak recording of a thunderstorm to a 110-pound Old English sheepdog named Higgins whose owner reported that he had an intense fear of thunder. At the first sound of artificial thunder, Higgins decided to leave the room and physically overcame the three people who were attempting to restrain him. His fear was overwhelmingly real. We have seen other dogs, and particularly such heavily muscled breeds as labradors, tremble to the point of collapse in the presence of a feared stimulus. Profuse salivation, frantic pacing, and attempts to escape are all common. One such dog having an acute fear of trains had actually broken two teeth in an attempt to get into a house and thus escape from a train which was passing about half a mile away. These fears are tremendously intense and appear more like the fears of human phobics than the relatively controlled fears of laboratory animals.

Such fears also have a number of other characteristics similar to those of human phobias (Marks, 1970, 1977; Seligman, 1971): They persist in the face of repeated nontraumatic encounters with the feared stimulus and they are usually acquired in one trial, whereas one trial conditioning of laboratory fears is rare. In many of the dogs we see, a full-blown fear response is established after only one traumatic exposure. The case of Frosty is an excellent example.

Frosty was a mature Great Pyrenees who was not originally afraid of anything. He was a friendly, affectionate dog. One spring, Frosty was out in the garden with his owner who was planting some seeds. A storm was approaching with the usual thunder and lightning. Frosty had no fear of storms and remained out in the garden with his owner as she worked to complete the planting. Suddenly a bolt of lightning struck an electric power transformer mounted on a utility pole in the garden. The transformer exploded with a loud bang and a bright flash of light. The owner was terrified and ran into the house with Frosty close behind. From that time on Frosty was frightened of thunderstorms. A single traumatic experience was sufficient for the establishment of a strong phobic response.

A single traumatic experience was also sufficient to establish a strong fear response in Major, a 4.5-year-old Labrador retriever. He had shown the acute fear since the age of 6 months, making the spring and summer months in Ohio a time of great stress for his owners. As a puppy he had not shown any fear of storms or of loud noises, in fact his owner, who is a keen hunter, had taken him out on trials and had actually shot over Major's head without any problems. At the age of 6 months, Major was chained to a bench in a body shop while his owner did some welding work. The 220-V cable to an air compressor shorted out causing an arc welder to explode with a loud bang and a flash of light. Since that one experience Major has been afraid of loud noises, storms, and gunshots. His reaction to a storm consisted of panting, shaking, constant seeking of attention, profuse salivation, and vigorous attempts to escape from the storm. Tranquilizers had no effect upon this reaction, which the owner reported would carry over to the day after the storm. Both at home in the presence of a real storm, and in our clinic during the artificial storm, Major's fear could be blocked by a game of fetch or retrieving. He would vigorously retrieve, but if at any time he lost the ball or dummy the fear would emerge and he would then reject all attempts to continue the game. Also living in the family was a female Labrador with none of these fears, but her companionship was of no help to Major.

Then there are other cases where the origin of the fear is unknown. Cindy was a gentle 4-year-old German shepherd, who was acutely afraid of sudden loud noises and of thunderstorms. Long before the storm became apparent Cindy would begin to pant, whine, and pace. As the storm became imminent she became increasingly disturbed and would begin to discharge from the nose and mouth; each thunderclap would elicit strong and uncontrollable trembling. Her owner was an aeronautical engineer of a precise cast of mind and had classified Cindy's reactions into four stages. Stage 4 was a final collapse into a flaccid, trancelike state after which she would remain completely unresponsive for periods up to 24 hours. She would then gradually recover.

The origins of Cindy's fears are vague. They first appeared when she was 2.5 years old after her return from a stay with her owner in Hawaii. It is interesting to note that thunderstorms do not occur in Hawaii. Her flight to and from the island appeared not to have been stressful. Cindy's owner was a pilot and before her fear became apparent he flew her everywhere, and the owner was satisfied that the quarantine period had been uneventful. How her fear originated neither we, nor her owner, were ever able to determine.

A final similarity between phobias in dogs and humans is that the set of potentially phobic stimuli appears to be limited and nonarbitrary. Certain associations are formed with great readiness, for example, between sudden loud noises and intense fear reactions, whereas others are more resistant to the formation of an association. A number of psychologists including Marks (1970, 1977) and Seligman (1971) have pointed out that a similar situation exists with respect to human phobias, with the set of feared objects and situations being limited and nonarbitrary. The following passage clearly shows that this fact was also well known to the American writer James Thurber (1937):

> I would like to end with the case history of a friend of mine in Ohio named Harvey Lake. When he was only nineteen, the steering bar of an old electric runabout broke off in his hand, causing the machine to carry him through a fence and into the grounds of the Columbus School for Girls. He developed a fear of automobiles, trains and every other kind of vehicle that was not pulled by a horse. Now, the psychologists, would call this a complex and represent the fear as abnormal, but I see it as a perfectly reasonable apprehension. If Harvey Lake had, because he was catapulted into the grounds of the Columbus School for Girls, developed a fear of girls, I would call that a complex, but I don't call his normal fear of machines a complex. Harvey Lake never in his life got into a plane (he died in a fall from a porch) but I do not regard that as neurotic, either, but only sensible [Copyright © 1937 James Thurber. Copyright © 1965 Helen W. Thurber and Rosemary T. Savers. From *Sex Ex Machina*, in *Let Your Mind Alone*, published by Harper & Row. Originally printed in the *New Yorker*.].

Upon meeting a phobic dog our first step is to discuss with the owner the stimulus situations that elicit the fear. For purposes of illustration we will consider the examples of Cindy and Major. First the dog is tested using a stereophonic recording of a storm to see if the fear can be elicited by the artificial stimulus. We realize, of course, that in presenting the recording we are simulating only a part of the stimulus complex associated with a real storm— changes of temperature, humidity, barometric pressure, etc., are obviously part of the natural storm, but sound is the stimulus element we can present and control most easily. Once we are convinced that we can indeed elicit the fear we embark upon a counterconditioning or desensitization procedure to overcome the fear. The procedure is very similar to that used by such behavior therapists as Wolpe (1958) in overcoming human fears. Historically it is based on the famous experiment by Watson and Mary Cover Jones (Jones, 1924, 1974) who used a counterconditioning procedure to successfully overcome a fear of animals in the case of Peter, a 3-year-old with an intense fear of animals but a great liking for food.

Cindy's owner was first instructed to work at home rewarding her with slices of hot dogs for remaining calmly on a distinctly colored rug, which provided a stable training and transfer cue—much like the novel stimulus in the absence training procedure. In addition this preliminary training ensured that a stimulus-specific response antagonistic to the fear was well rehearsed. This postural response was also necessary in order for subtle changes in respiration and muscle tension to be detected. Once this had been accomplished, the owner brought Cindy, the rug, and a copious supply of hot dogs to our office for the training. We began with Cindy lying calmly on the rug. Stereophonically recorded thunderstorms (spliced from sound effects records) were then presented at very weak intensities—the owner rewarding Cindy for remaining calm on the rug during each clap of thunder. At low levels we ensure that the fear will not be elicited and that the thunder can quickly be associated with the reward. The sound level was to be increased only when we were satisfied that she was calm and making the association between thunder and the hot dog: This could be observed by a simple turning of the head toward the owner's hand at the thunderclap. Should any sign of fear or apprehension appear, the storm would immediately be reduced to a safe level for further practice. Cindy's fear was extreme; the first four 1-hour sessions showed very slight gains in raising her threshold. The records we kept of her progress were characterized by very delicate excursions of increasing intensity followed by a hasty retreat. However, by the ninth session Cindy was completely indifferent to storms in the 80-dB range and appeared to be enjoying her hot dogs. Records of the initial sessions, each of which was 50 min long, are shown in Figure 10.2.

At this stage Cindy's training was transferred to her home. Her first exposure to the artificial storm in the home evoked an intense reaction, although subsequent exposures were increasingly ineffective. Cindy's first exposure to a real storm came that same week. She showed an initial intense reaction which progressed quickly to the trembling stage. Although she was periodically unresponsive, her reaction did not persist after the end of the storm.

Cindy

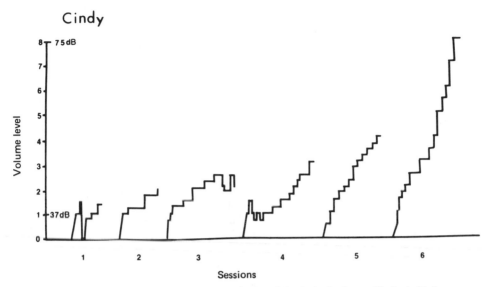

Figure 10.2. *Course of counterconditioning of a fear of thunder in the German Shepherd, Cindy.*

We continued to use the desensitization procedure with Cindy in her home, and our efforts were reflected in a substantial improvement in her behavior. Formerly a storm in the night would arouse her immediately, sending her in terror to the owner's bedroom. The owner's descriptions of being awakened at such times by a terrified German shepherd were graphic. Cindy is now more difficult to arouse and during a particularly intense night storm at least asks permission to join the owner in bed. Once there she now sleeps during the rest of the storm. In her reactions Cindy no longer reaches what the owner termed Stages 2, 3, and 4, and there is no indication of a persistent response after the storm has passed.

Realistically, there is still much to be done with Cindy. Even after a total of 19 hours of work with her both in our clinic and her home using both artificial and real storms, there are vestiges of the fear we would like to alleviate. She still relies heavily upon her owner for comfort and security and her responsiveness to other loud noises is still surprisingly high. We have not yet determined whether Cindy will ever fly again—she still finds the percussive sounds and backfires an aircraft engine makes during warm-up, disturbing—and the degree of specificity of the desensitization effects was unexpected. While our procedure clearly made Cindy less brontophobic, her other fears were only minimally attenuated.

We used a similar desensitization procedure with Major, except that in his case the food reward was pepperoni and cheese. Every dog has his price, and Major's was pizza. Figures 10.3 and 10.4 show the course of his desensitization. These records have a number of interesting aspects.

1. The change in the dog's behavior over time is clear, but the laborious nature of this procedure is also obvious. What is true for dogs is also true for

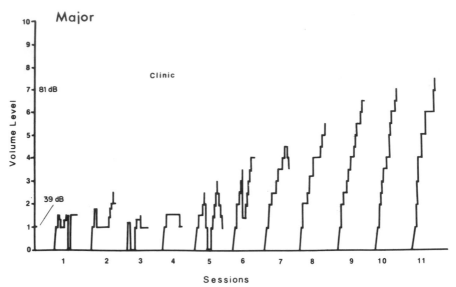

Figure 10.3. *Course of counterconditioning of a fear of thunder in the Labrador Retriever, Major.*

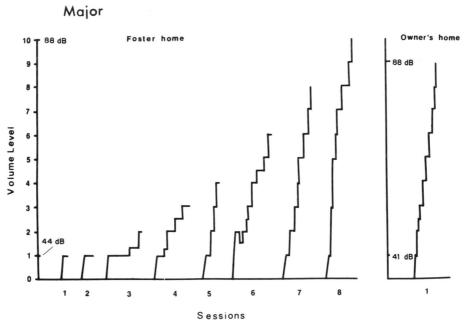

Figure 10.4. *The effect of changes in context on counterconditioning in Major.*

children and for cats. Consider, for example the 45 sessions administered by Mary Cover Jones in overcoming Peter's fear (Jones, 1924), or Figure 10.5 which shows the progress of the cat, Septima during the first 30 desensitization sessions conducted by Joseph Wolpe as part of the pioneer animal research he performed prior to the development of the techniques of psychotherapy through reciprocal inhibition (Wolpe, 1958). This record of training was derived from protocols recently reported by Wolpe (1976). The time and effort expanded in overcoming Major's, Peter's and Septima's fears, and the general characteristics of their desensitization records, are remarkably similar. Canines, children, and cats—similar behaviors, similar procedures, and similar outcomes.

2. The changes in the dog's behavior when the transfers were made from our clinic setting to the home of a student working with us, and then finally to the owner's home show the subtlety of the stimulus control. The problem of facilitating transfer from the clinical to the nonclinical setting is of similar concern to the human behavior therapist. Once again the parallels between the animal and human clinical settings are noteworthy.

3. One of the theoretically interesting features of Figure 10.3 is that the initial sessions show little if any progress. However, Major's behavior on Session 5 shows that indeed some progress was being made. It would appear that some form of consolidation was taking place early in training. The similarity of the training patterns during these initial sessions and those conducted after the transfer (Figure 10.4), suggests that such consolidation may, in fact, be related to the situational or contextual aspects of the training.

We have tested 15 dogs showing fear reactions to noises. As in the case of separation reactions, the origins of these fears are both varied and complex.

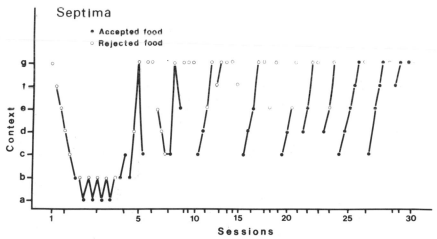

Figure 10.5. *Counterconditioning of an experimentally established fear in the cat, Septima. The ordinate represents a hierarchy of situations from "g," the chamber in which the cat was originally shocked, to "a," the room most dissimilar from the conditioning situation. Connected points represent exposures within the same session (after Wolpe, 1976).*

For seven of these dogs the onset of fear was attributed to a specific stimulus event. In six dogs, the presenting problem was their reaction to thunderstorms, but in only two of them did the fear first appear in reaction to storm-related trauma. In the remaining four dogs showing a fear of storms, the initial fear reaction appeared in response to very intense, percussive stimuli in other contexts. Typically these were gunshots, firecrackers, or the electrical explosion suffered by Major. Thus, for these four dogs the fear of thunderstorms can be viewed as a secondary or generalized fear. A seventh dog subjected to an explosion of a Molotov cocktail-like device showed an intense fear of loud noises, but did not exhibit any generalization to thunderstorms and also failed to respond to even gunshots when tested outside its home environment.

In the remaining eight dogs the fear first appeared in reaction to a routine storm and in the absence of any obvious trauma. All but one of these dogs showed the fear reaction to other loud noises as well. Three dogs failed to react to our artificial storm despite the fact that their owners described them as reacting intensely to real storms.

Descriptively, these two groups of dogs are similar in age of onset of the fear reaction. For 12 of the 14 dogs the fear of storms first appeared after at least one uneventful, summer season. Characteristically, exposures to thunderstorms during subsequent seasons produced no attenuation of the fear. At the time of presentation the average duration of the fear was 29 months with a range from 9 to 65 months.

At this stage we are reluctant to assign too much significance to whether or not a traumatic first experience can be identified for these fears: Our population of dogs is too small and the data too dependent on the owners' reports. Our knowledge of what makes a stimulus event traumatic for some dogs is similarly limited. Why some dogs react to such events with intense, long-lasting fear responses is yet another unanswered question. Although there is some evidence that suggests that sensitivity to sound in dogs may be inheritable (Humphrey & Warner, 1934), clearly the relationship between genetic predisposition and environmental events is a complex one.

IV. Conclusions

A century has now passed since Darwin published *The Expression of the Emotions in Man and the Animals* [Darwin, 1872]. His work heralded a major change in our perspective on the behavior of humans and also provided formal, intellectual legitimacy to the study of other species in the search for an understanding of our own emotional legacy. It is perhaps too soon to assess just how far we have traveled toward that understanding, but we believe that the landmarks suggest that we are on the correct path.

The characteristics of fears occurring in the companion dog and their amenability to behavior therapy have striking parallels to the characteristics and treatments of fears occurring in man. The treatment procedures, issuing largely from a common source in the laboratory, have only slightly diverged to accommodate the characteristics of the species being treated. Refined and adapted, they represent a common conceptual bond and continue to promote a mutual reciprocity between human and animal clinicians. It is but a small source of comfort that, like our counterparts in the human clinic, we too are haunted by the myriad of vagaries and uncertainties attending the development of behavior problems in the natural setting. We are no less plagued by the often arduous and protracted course of the remedial treatment.

However, it is this latter concern that must necessarily cement our ties to the laboratory. For example, the nature of contextual control, so critical to the effectiveness of any remedial procedure, remains largely unexplored. The disturbing regression shown by Major (Figure 10.4) when the site of training was changed, was unexpected. That such an effect is not simply related to the conditions of training imposed by the constraints of dealing with a nonverbal animal is indicated by a similar finding in the treatment of human phobias. Lick and Unger (1975) report similar, large contextual effects when conditions of exposure to feared stimuli are changed in an even more subtle manner in human phobics. In view of the impact of such influences, the tenacity with which fears resist treatment is not surprising. The very essence of behavior therapy pivots critically on our understanding of such fundamental processes as contextual control, transfer of training, and memory (Wolpe, 1958; Wickens *et al.*, 1977) — processes all too often overlooked or taken for granted.

Coursing throughout our concerns is the nature of the relation between temperament and sensitivity to traumatic experience. One of the outstanding similarities between canines and humans is their high degree of individual variability (Scott & Fuller, 1965). Within a given breed, individual dogs will emerge unscathed from the most stringent conditions of isolation (Fuller, 1967); within even a given litter the effect of severing a well-established man–dog relationship results in different reactions in different dogs (Senay, 1966). Such effects permeate our experience as they do those of the human clinician. Experimental recognition of the importance of such differences has long been a part of the Pavlovian tradition within Russian psychology (Gray, 1964), but only to a lesser degree has this been true in the United States (Corson & Corson, 1976).

Since our first report on behavioral problems in companion animals (Tuber, Hothersall, & Voith, 1974), our perspective has been enriched by a growing appreciation of the companion dog as a potential resource in refining our understanding of behavior. Our efforts and experiences, together with those of others in this emerging area of applied animal behavior (Borchelt, 1977), carry the promise that this understanding may extend beyond a single species.

ACKNOWLEDGMENTS

We would like to express our sincere appreciation to Debra S. Boehm, Pamela S. Fisher, Wendy Keller, and Marie F. Peters for their dedicated and enthusiastic assistance.

REFERENCES

Borchelt, P. *Applied animal behavior symposium,* presented at the 49th annual meeting of the Midwestern Psychological Association, May 1977.

Bronowski, J. *The ascent of man.* Boston: Little, Brown, 1973.

Corson, S. A., & Corson, E. O'L., Constitutional differences in physiologic adaptation to stress and distress. In G. Serban (Ed.), *Psychopathology of human adaptation.* New York: Plenum, 1976. Pp. 77–94.

Corson, S. A., Corson, E. O'L, Gwynne, P. H., & Arnold, L. E. Pet dogs as non-verbal communication links in hospital psychiatry. *Comprehensive Psychiatry,* 1977, *18,* 61–72.

Darwin, C. *The expression of the emotions in man and the animals.* London: J. Murray, 1872.

Fuller, J. L. Experiential deprivation and later behavior. *Science,* 1967, *158,* 1645–1652.

Gray, J. A. *Pavlov's typology: Recent theoretical and experimental developments from the laboratory of B. M. Teplov.* Oxford: Pergamon, 1964.

Harlow, H. F., & Harlow, M. K. Psychopathology in monkeys. In H. D. Kimmel (Ed.), *Experimental psychopathology: Recent research and theory.* New York: Academic Press, 1971. Pp, 287–334.

Humphrey, E., & Warner, L. *Working dogs: An attempt to produce a strain of German Shepherds which combine working abilities with beauty of confirmation.* Baltimore: Johns Hopkins Press, 1934.

Jones, M. C. A laboratory study of fear: The case of Peter. *Pedagogical Seminary,* 1924, *31,* 308–315.

Jones, M. C., Albert, Peter, & John B. Watson. *American Psychologist,* 1974, *29,* 581–583.

Lazarus, A. A. The elimination of children's phobias by deconditioning. In H. J. Eysenck (Ed.), *Behavior therapy and the neuroses.* New York: Pergamon, 1960. Pp. 114–122.

Levinson, B. M. (Ed.). *Pets and human development.* Springfield, Illinois: Thomas, 1972.

Lick, J. R., & Unger, T. E. External validity of laboratory fear assessment: Implications from two case studies. *Journal of Consulting and Clinical Psychology,* 1975, *43,* 864–866.

Marks, I. *Fears and phobias.* New York: Academic Press, 1970.

Marks, I. Clinical phenomena in search of laboratory models. In J. D. Maser & M. E. P. Seligman, (Eds.), *Psychopathology: Experimental models.* San Francisco: Freeman, 1977. Pp. 174–213.

Marr, J. N., Lierly, J. A., & Price, R. A. Man-man models for man-animal team research: Accurate empathy in dog trainers. Paper presented at the meeting of the Midwestern Psychological Association, Detroit, May 1971.

Mason, W. A., & Kenney, M. D. Redirection of filial attachments in rhesus monkeys: Dogs as mother surrogates. *Science,* 1974, *183,* 1209–1211.

Pfaffenberger, C. J. *The new knowledge of dog behavior.* New York: Howell, 1963.

Pfaffenberger, C. J., & Scott, J. P. The relationship between delayed socialization and trainability of guide dogs. *Journal of Genetic Psychology,* 1959, *95,* 145–155.

Robertson, J., & Bowlby, J. Responses of young children to separation from their mothers. *Courrier de la Centre Internationale,* (Paris), 1952, *2,* 131–142.

Scott, J. P., & Bielfelt, S. W. Effects of experience in 4-H foster homes. In C. J. Pfaffenberger, J. P. Scott, J. L. Fuller, B. E. Ginsburg, & S. W. Bielfelt, (Eds.), *Guide dogs for the blind: Their selection, development, and training.* Amsterdam: Elsevier, 1976. Pp. 101–126.

Scott, J. P., & Fuller, J. L. *Genetics and the social behavior of the dog.* Chicago: Univ. of Chicago Press, 1965.

Seligman, M. E. P. Phobias and preparedness. *Behavior Therapy,* 1971, *2,* 307–320.

Senay, E. C. Toward an animal model of depression: A study of separation behavior in dogs. *Journal of Psychiatric Research,* 1966, *4,* 65–71.

Speck, R. V. Mental health problems involving the family, the pet and the veterinarian. *Journal of the American Veterinary Medical Association,* 1964, *145,* 150–154.

Spitz, R. A. Anaclitic depression. *Psychoanalytic study of the child,* 1946, *2,* 313–342.

Thurber, J. Sex Ex Machina. In *Let Your Mind Alone.* New York: Harper & Row, 1937.

Tuber, D. S., Hothersall, D., & Voith, V. L. Animal clinical psychology: A modest proposal. *American Psychologist,* 1974, *29,* 762–766.

Vollmer, P. J. Do mischievous dogs reveal their "guilt"? *Veterinary Medicine/Small Animal Clinician,* 1977, June, 1002–1005.

Wickens, D. D., Tuber, D. S., Nield, A. F., & Wickens, C. Memory for the conditioned response: The effect of potential interference introduced before and after original conditioning. *Journal of Experimental Psychology,* 1977, *106,* 47–70.

Wolpe, J. *Psychotherapy by reciprocal inhibition.* Palo Alto: Stanford Univ. Press, 1958.

Wolpe, J. *Theme and variations: A behavior therapy casebook.* New York: Pergamon, 1976.

DONALD J. LEVIS

The Infrahuman Avoidance Model of Symptom Maintenance and Implosive Therapy

11

I. Introduction

Human psychopathology represents a range of complex and mystifying behaviors that have eluded scholarly and scientific understanding for centuries. Consider the behavior of a male forced to relinquish his professional career because he is afraid to leave his home for fear that dog feces will be deposited in his yard; or the case of a woman so panic-stricken by the obsession she has cancer that psychiatric hospitalization is required. Attempt to comprehend how one could become so frightened of smelling odors in public that leaving home elicits terror; or how a fear of bath water necessitates the wearing of a life preserver; or how blood flow from the vagina on a daily basis without detectable medical cause results in the need for a blood transfusion. There are individuals who tremble at the sight of bugs, airplanes, or tall buildings, and others who fear expressing feelings of sexuality, anger, love, or compassion. Still others fear thoughts about failure, loss of love, loss of control, taking responsibility, death, and afterlife; or are afraid that they might molest or hurt their own children. And then there are those who are so affected by their pathology that they think themselves to be someone else, hear voices, see visions, or simply remain immobile in a fetal position (Stampfl & Levis, 1973a; Levis, forthcoming).

The diversity and complexity of behaviors labeled psychopathological would appear to argue against the possibility of constructing a general model of

PSYCHOPATHOLOGY IN ANIMALS
Research and Clinical Implications

the development and maintenance of such behavior. Although the issue of whether or not a common etiology for various behavior pathologies exists has yet to be resolved, few investigators would object to the statement that learning plays an important role in the development of both normal and abnormal human behavior.

The issue at hand is whether it is feasible to apply existing learning or conditioning laws to complex behavior. Of course, the resolution of this issue depends upon the predictive and explanatory power of the model offered. However, given the current state of the field, I take the position that attempts to extrapolate existing learning laws represents a reasonable strategy, one that already has proved profitable. The extension to the area of psychopathology of Miller's studies of fear and conflict and Skinner's studies of operant conditioning are cases in point. As Eysenck (1960) reasoned:

> If the laws which have been formulated are, not necessarily true, but at least partially correct, then it must follow that we can make deductions from them to cover the type of behavior represented by neurotic patients, construct a model which will duplicate the important and relevant features of the patient and suggest new and possibly helpful methods of treatment along lines laid down by learning theory [p. 5].

One advantage of postulating a learning analysis of psychopathology is that the conditioning laws so far developed in the laboratory do rest upon considerable research data. This state of affairs is not the case for many nonlearning-based clinical theories. Another advantage inherent in the learning approach is the ability to start from the more well-defined and controllable examples of behavior and then to work systematically and progressively to build on these. In contrast, the nonlearning-oriented theories of psychopathology are usually complex, all encompassing models designed to analyze the complete human organism. The resulting illusory sense of understanding with the latter strategy is usually achieved by sacrificing clarity, precision, and predictability.

II. Animal Models and Clinical Relevance

A learning analysis is not, without its own set of problems. The learning principles developed so far are, to a large extent, supported by infrahuman research data that frequently utilize the laboratory rat as subject material. Critics (Koch, 1956; Hunt, 1964) are skeptical about the applicability of generalizing to human behavior from laws developed in the infrahuman laboratory. They argue that there are developmental differences between rats and humans. Yet, related disciplines like medicine, genetics, biology, and psychopharmacology have achieved considerable success in advancing knowledge of human behavior via animal models. It may also transpire for psychology that data collected from infrahuman species will prove more useful for generalizing than the vast amount of research presently being conducted on the college sophomore.

The argument has been made that if maladaptive behavior is tied, at least in part, to conditioning of emotional or autonomic responses, and if mediated internal cues (such as words, thoughts, images, and memories) in the human follow essentially the conditioning laws developed with extroceptive stimuli, the case for animal models of human maladies becomes much stronger. The rat not only provides a less complex organism which may be more advantageous for deciphering basic laws, but it is also equipped with an emotional nervous system similar to that of the human. Additionally, infrahuman subjects are subject to experimentation that for ethical reasons cannot be conducted on humans. Even if such experimentation only provides a vehicle for illustration and confirmation of suspected hypotheses about the human, the effort is more than worthwhile (Levis, 1970a; Stampfl, 1970).

Despite the obvious need for confirmation at the human level, infrahuman research has already had a considerable heuristic influence on the development of human behavioral treatment techniques. This is certainly no small accomplishment. But whatever heuristic and predictive powers have been achieved, continual improvement in the "animal model" approach must be forthcoming. Such questions as how the laws of learning interact with genetic, personality, and physiological variables must, at some point, be addressed as well as the issue of the human's cognitive complexity. To avoid sterility, infrahuman researchers should become familiar with human psychopathology and must develop analogues capable of generalization across species and situational variables.

A. THE AVOIDANCE-CONDITIONING PARADIGM

The most common ingredient among individuals receiving the label of "neurotic" is that they suffer from some form of extreme emotional or anxiety state. Freud (1936) not only agreed with this clinical observation but suggested the additional component that human symptoms develop because they serve the important function of helping the inflicted individual to ward off or reduce this painful emotion. The conceptualization of symptom execution as avoidance behavior has received considerable support and acceptance since Freud's original hypothesis. Clinically, this phenomenon becomes apparent when symptom execution is blocked. If the obsessive–compulsive ritual of a person, like hand-washing, is prevented, a great surge of anxiety will follow; or if a phobic individual is exposed to the feared object an emotional panic state usually results.

Viewing symptom formation as emanating not from an outgrowth of anxiety but rather from a learned mechanism designed to bind or avoid anxiety is consistent with what is known about emotional learning at an infrahuman level. Rather than describe an animal model that attempts to duplicate the *topography* of human behaviors that are labeled symptoms, the strategy adopted for this chapter is to evaluate infrahuman theory and data that are believed to illuminate the general *processes* of human avoidance development, maintenance, and removal.

The discrete-trial, avoidance-conditioning paradigm provides a basic procedure for investigating those variables responsible for developing a conditioned emotional state. In the typical procedure, the animal subject is placed into one side of a double-compartment apparatus for a short period, at the end of which the experimenter presents a "neutral" stimulus (CS) for a predetermined duration such as 6 sec. Shock (UCS) is presented following the 6th sec. The shock remains until the rat escapes by jumping over a hurdle into the shock-free compartment. This escape response terminates both shock and tone. The tone–shock period is repeated again in the new compartment, and to escape again the rat must jump back into the original compartment, which is now safe. If the animal enters the safe compartment prior to shock onset, the response immediately terminates the tone and avoids shock on that trial. With repeated trials the avoidance response is gradually learned.

B. DIFFERENCE BETWEEN INFRAHUMAN AND HUMAN LEARNING SITUATIONS

My hypothesis is that human methods of dealing with stressful, anxiety- or fear-provoking situations follow essentially the strategy of the rat. That is to say, an adaptive response to a perceived dangerous situation is to escape as quickly as possible from the presence of the danger signal (CS) and to eliminate the possibility of exposure to an inherently painful stimulus (UCS). However, important differences do exist between the laboratory- and the human-conditioning situation. The topography of the human avoidance response or symptom may take a different form from that required in the infrahuman experiment. Human responses not only involve physical removal from anxiety producing cues but also take the shape of cognitive defense mechanisms, obsessions, compulsions, depression, somatic complaints, and other noted clinical symptoms.

The stimuli to which human patients have been previously conditioned also may be qualitatively different from those used in the laboratory. Clinical experience suggests that such danger cues not only involve external stimuli (e.g., sight of a tall building, sexual odor cues, or the sound of a train), but also internal cues like thoughts and images. As Dollard and Miller (1950) suggested, the adult human frequently has been punished for acts that occurred in childhood, so that punishment (UCS) becomes associated with the thought or symbolic representation of the act and not the act itself. Such aversive thoughts or images remain elicitors of anxiety and, in turn, are frequently avoided through the response of "not-thinking about them." This latter avoidance mechanism is similar to the Freudian concept of repression.

Despite the topographical differences between running and jumping in a rat and thinking (or not thinking) in a human, the mechanism for conditioning (CS–UCS pairing) and the resulting principles derived, I believe, are operative in both the laboratory and real-life situations.

III. Two-Factor Avoidance Learning Theory

Maladaptive behavior that is likely to be labeled symptomatic is believed to be motivated by a strong secondary drive-state. Secondary drives differ from primary or innate drives—like hunger, thirst, and sex—in that their ability to serve as motivators is dependent upon learning (Brown, 1961). Secondary drives play an important role in the development of human behavior and are believed to be behind the strivings for prestige, social mobility, money, power, status, and love. But perhaps the more pervasive drive is learned fear, or anxiety, which is hypothesized to be the main motivator of maladaptive behavior. As Dollard and Miller (1950, p. 190) suggested, fear is important to symptom formation because it can be attached to new cues so easily through learning, and because it is the source of motivation that produces the inhibiting response in most conflicts.

A. FEAR AND AVOIDANCE ACQUISITION

Although a variety of theoretical accounts are available to explain avoidance behavior (Bolles, 1971; Herrnstein, 1969; Schoenfeld, 1950; Seligman & Johnston, 1973) the most useful model for my present purpose is Mowrer's two-factor theory (Mowrer, 1947, 1960; Rescorla & Solomon, 1967). The first factor consists of the organism's learning to fear previously nonfeared stimuli. The second factor, or behavior the organism learns, is how to avoid these feared events. Thus, fear onset serves as a drive to activate the avoidance response, whereas fear reduction provides the necessary condition for reinforcement and maintenance of the avoidance response.

I view symptoms and defensive maneuvers reflected in psychopathology of humans as equivalent to avoidance behavior (Freud, 1936; Stampfl & Levis, 1967; Wolpe, 1958). The two-factor theory represents an excellent working model for understanding such behavior. However, fear conditioning and subsequent avoidance behavior is not in and of itself a sign of psychopathology. In fact, human survival is, in large part, dependent upon such learning for it protects the individual from potential sources of physical pain and tissue damage. Psychopathology can be defined as little correlation between the occurrence of the above response classes and the actual presence of physical danger to the organism. For example, if being on the tenth floor of a building leads to a strong emotional reaction and subsequent avoidance of the building, the behavior can be described as maladaptive since there is no physical danger to the individual. Or, consider the compulsive behavior of an individual who has to wash his or her hands over and over after turning on a light switch or touching money. Normally, failure to engage in such behavior does not involve physical danger. It is labeled maladaptive because it is not biologically protective and because it frequently interferes with the functioning of desired, socially adaptive responses (Levis & Hare, 1977).

B. THE UTILITY OF AVOIDANCE FORMATION

As noted earlier, considerable differences exist between the response topographies measured in the laboratory and the variety of those observed in clinical settings. In theory, the principle for establishing and reinforcing such behaviors is believed to be the same in each case. The typical human phobic reaction represents perhaps the closest analogy with the avoidance paradigm of the laboratory. The organism, either rat or human, actively avoids the CS whether it is a tone in the context of a box with grid floors, or an airplane, tall building, or car. Such avoidance behavior is believed to be functional in both settings in that it immediately reduces the stress of the organism.

Other more complicated symptoms of the human also make functional sense if the source of the conditioned aversive stimulation is considered. Take the case of an individual who, upon touching a dollar bill, has to wash his hands repeatedly. If the CS pattern involved in the etiology of the hand-washing symptom were known and if these events were associated with strong fear of dirt or disease, the act of hand-washing to remove a potential source of contamination makes sense. If one is afraid of thinking sexual or aggressive thoughts then the compulsion to count heartbeats serves to reduce the occurrence of the dangerous material.

Perhaps a better illustration of symptom utility is seen in cases of hysterical conversions. For example, to avoid combat, one may develop a paralysis of arm or leg, or if one is an aviator, a visual disturbance. Such avoidance behavior has the immediate effect of preventing the individual from reentering the feared combat situation. Such conversion cases are also frequently accompanied by the inability of the patient to understand the relationship between the avoidance behavior and the conversion reaction. The addition of these cognitive avoidances also has the effect of reducing accompanying sources of anxiety generated by feelings of guilt (Levis & Hare, 1977).

Fear reduction not only strengthens active avoidance behavior but it can also account for passive avoidance learning. Passive avoidance learning is seen in cases of depression. Here, inactivity and despondency make sense from a symptom utility viewpoint if the patient fears rejection or failure in work or interpersonal relationships. Such symptoms, in addition to avoiding aversive cues, may generate a source of secondary reinforcement (gain) in that friends may take a supportive position. Cognitive defense mechanisms such as repression, projection, rationalization, and displacement serve a similar avoidance function in that they block aversive thoughts, memories, or images.

In summary, I believe that the essential ingredients in the development and maintenance of human psychopathology involve fear learning and subsequent avoidance of aversive conditioned stimulation. Although the CS complex in humans frequently results in a variety of fear-eliciting cues, through the processes of generalization, higher-order conditioning, and secondary learning, an underlying common fear pattern or theme usually develops. Fear of bodily injury, rejection, and failure are examples of such themes.

I acknowledge that the etiology of symptom formation at the human level can be motivated by learning paradigms more complex than that suggested by the simple avoidance model outlined. This point has been illustrated by Levis and Hare (1977), who outline five different learning paradigms believed to be embedded in the development of symptomatology. Although most of these models conceptualize pathology as involving an approach–avoidance conflict paradigm, fear-elicited avoidance behavior still represents the critical ingredient. Thus, the establishment of principles of avoidance conditioning represents an important first step in understanding human psychopathology and in determining suggestions for treating such behavior. The active and passive avoidance paradigms of the laboratory, I believe, serve as valuable research tools in fostering these objectives.

C. FEAR AND AVOIDANCE EXTINCTION

Considerable data have been amassed at the infrahuman level to support the motivational or energizing effects of fear (Amsel & Maltzman, 1950; Brown, Kalish, & Farber, 1951; Meryman, 1952, 1953) as well as the reinforcing effects of fear reduction (Brown & Jacobs, 1949; Kalish, 1954; Miller, 1948). An abundance of laboratory evidence also shows that both fear and instrumental responding can be extinguished by presenting the CS without the UCS (Baum, 1970; Black, 1958; Denny, Koons, & Mason, 1959; Hunt, Jernberg, & Brady, 1952; Knapp, 1965; Weinberger, 1965).

According to two-factor theory, repeated exposure of the total CS complex without the UCS weakens the conditioned-fear response. When the CS fails to elicit fear, fear ceases to serve as cue for escaping the CS and thereby avoiding the USC. Data are available that support the contention that if the avoidance response is blocked or prevented during extinction and the CS is repeated, both the fear and the avoidance response will extinguish (Corriveau & Smith, 1978; Shipley, Mock, & Levis, 1971).

IV. Critical Issues Related to Maintenance of Avoidance Behavior

Unfortunately, unlike the maintenance of human symptoms, the laboratory conditioning of avoidance responding tends to extinguish fairly rapidly following removal of the UCS (Mackintosh, 1974; Uhl & Eichbaure, 1975). In this sense, the avoidance laboratory model falls short in producing results comparable to those reported from the clinical literature. First, learning is very slow in the shuttlebox situation previously described. Our experience (Levis, 1970a; Levis & Stampfl, 1972) is that one-fourth of the rats fail to reach a learning criteria of 10 consecutive avoidance responses after 150 consecutive training trials (also see Brush, 1966). Second, following removal of the UCS for these animals that learn, rarely does a subject emit more than 50 consecutive avoidances before stopping to respond. In fact, reports of nearly complete failures to obtain successful avoidance conditioning and of short-lived conditioning with rats and other animals are strikingly in evidence, both in the shuttlebox and in other experimental situations (Anderson & Nakamura, 1964; D'Amato, Keller, & DiCara, 1964; Feldman & Bremmer, 1963; Fitzgerald & Brown, 1965; Hurwitz, 1964; Keehn, 1972; Meyer, Cho, & Wesemann, 1960).

Humans, on the other hand, emit symptoms for years in the absence of any physical danger (UCS). Clinical evidence also suggests that when patients fight their symptom by not engaging in avoidance behavior the result is an unbearable anxiety reaction that frequently progresses to a panic-like intensity. The increased CS exposure from blocking responding appears to result in an increase rather than a decrease in anxiety.

Part of the previously cited discrepancy may well be a function of the experimental situation used for conditioning avoidance responding. Fear theory assumes that conditioning occurs to a complex set of stimuli not just to the nominal CS. For example, laboratory evidence supports the importance of apparatus cues as part of the total CS complex eliciting fear (Denny, Koons, & Mason, 1959; McAllister & McAllister, 1962, 1971). Unfortunately, the shuttlebox, bar press, and wheel-turning apparatuses represent complex learning tasks with numerous uncontrolled contingencies. For one thing, the situation cues do not change markedly following responding, resulting in a relatively minor stimulus change involving only the nominal CS. According to fear theory, without a marked stimulus change following responding, the magnitude of the reinforcement (fear reduction) will be small. Furthermore, if part of the CS complex (like the apparatus cues) is present during the intertrial interval, the speed of the reduction in the fear response will be retarded. As McAllister, McAllister, and Douglass (1971) have argued, the animal may be immobile by the time the maximum reinforcement effect occurs resulting in the reinforcement of passive responding (immobility) rather than active avoidance.

If this analysis is correct then learning and resistance to extinction can be improved by producing a large stimulus change before and after responding. This hypothesis was directly tested and supported in the shuttlebox situation by Modaresi (1975) and Boyd and Levis (1979). This expectation is also supported by data obtained from a one-way avoidance situation, which usually produces a substantial stimulus change following responding. Rats typically learn a one-directional response after an average of three or four shock trials, and once the UCS is discontinued some subjects respond for 100 trials before stopping.

Making it easier for the rat to discriminate between a situation that is safe and one that is noxious clearly is a step in the right direction. But even 100 trials of consecutive avoidance responding before an animal extinguishes is stretching the point that a good analogue situation exists between avoidance learning in the laboratory and human symptom maintenance.

A. CONSERVATION OF ANXIETY HYPOTHESIS

Relatively fast avoidance extinction is not always the case with rats (Mowrer & Keehn, 1958; Sidman, 1955), but the most notable exceptions to rapid extinction of avoidance behavior in the shuttlebox have been reported with dogs (Solomon & Wynne, 1953; Solomon, Kamin, & Wynne, 1953). These authors demonstrated that following a few intense shocks during acquisition of avoidance, dogs' mean latency of responding in extinction was still getting shorter 200 trials later. One dog made 490 extinction trials before a punishment procedure was introduced. Solomon and Wynne noted three important observations in the above cited studies. First, the avoidance latencies of the dogs shortened considerably. Second, overt signs of anxiety rapidly disappeared with training and seemed nonexistent in extinction following the frequently occurring short-latency responses. Third, if a dog happened to produce a long-latency response on a particular extinction trial, signs of anxiety behaviorally became apparent immediately following the instrumental response, with short latency responses returning for the next few trials.

These observations led to the conservation of anxiety hypothesis. According to Solomon and Wynn (1954), extinction of the avoidance response is directly related to the repeated exposure of the fear response. However, short exposures to the CS resulting from quick avoidance responses do not permit time for the elicitation of the classically conditioned fear reaction. Since the short-latency instrumental act does not elicit fear it will not be followed by fear reduction, thereby weakening the habit strength of the avoidance response. This weakened habit strength is manifested through progressively increasing response latencies that, in turn, account for enough CS exposure to elicit the anxiety reaction. The instrumental response is again followed by anxiety reduction with a resultant increment in strength of the avoidance habit. This increased habit strength is reflected by progressively shorter response-latencies as the anxiety reaction associated with the longer CS segments secondarily conditions anxiety to the shorter CS segments.

The conservation of anxiety notion appears to explain the observations described so far, yet the problem remains as to why little extinction was noted for some dogs after 200 trials (cf. Eysenck, 1976; Rachman, 1976). Solomon and Wynne (1954) suggested the principle of *partial irreversibility* to resolve this problem. According to these authors, a very intense or "traumatic" pain–fear reaction to a given CS pattern will result in a *permanent* increase in the probability of occurrence of a fear reaction in the presence of the conditioned stimulus pattern.

The importance of Solomon's group's contributions were realized quickly by workers in the area of psychopathology. First, an experimental procedure was provided that produced extreme resistance to extinction of discrete-trial avoidance behavior. Second, the critical factor for producing the effect appeared to be the occurrence of a traumatic event, similar to speculations made about the etiology of human symptoms. Finally, the conservation of anxiety hypothesis could explain symptom (avoidance) maintenance, as well as explain why, when humans fight their symptoms by not avoiding, increases occur in the fear response.

B. CONSERVATION OF ANXIETY HYPOTHESIS REINTERPRETED AND EXTENDED

There are difficulties with the Solomon and Wynne interpretation of avoidance behavior. F. R. Brush (1957) found that shock intensity was not a critical variable in sustaining avoidance behavior. Even the subtraumatic shock level of .7 mA maintained avoidance responding for a substantial number of trials. Other investigators (Levis, 1966a, b; Maatsch, 1959) have also produced prolonged avoidance behavior in extinction following exposure to moderate UCS levels.

Stampfl, in an unpublished manuscript written in 1960, reinterpreted and extended the conservation principle. Stampfl divided the studies conducted in Solomon's laboratory during the 1950s into two groups, those that demonstrated extreme resistance to extinction (Solomon & Wynne, 1953; Solomon et al., 1953; Brush, Brush, & Solomon, 1955; F. R. Brush, 1957) and those that obtained relatively fast extinction (Kamin, 1954; Church, Brush, & Solomon, 1956; E. S. Brush, 1957). He observed that a critical factor separating the two groupings was whether or not a drop-gate was used in the procedure. If used, extreme resistance to extinction was reported. Church et al. (1956) were aware of this factor and interpreted the critical role of the drop-gate as preventing generalized extinction of the avoidance response by blocking intertrial responses.

Stampfl suggested that the drop-gate may also increase the complexity of the CS, thus producing greater resistance to extinction. Intertrial responding may not have been the critical factor. Levis (1971) supported this latter conclusion: He found that as CS complexity increased intertrial responding decreased, but the absolute level of avoidance responding was found to be independent of the level of intertrial responding.

Stampfl also observed that most of the conditioning laws developed in the laboratory stem from procedures that manipulate only one nominal CS. However, work at a clinical level suggests that the avoided CS pattern includes a complex of varied stimulus elements that are frequently ordered in a serial pattern in terms of accessibility from memory. Unfortunately, the variable of CS complexity has remained a relatively unexplored parameter in the American conditioning literature (Baker, 1968; Razran, 1965).

Following this reasoning, Stampfl (see Levis, 1966a) maintained that if short-latency avoidance responses conserve fear to longer CS exposures then the conservation should be maximized by dividing the CS–UCS interval into distinctive sequentially ordered components, (e.g., tone followed by flashing lights). He argued that after the attainment of short-latency responses to the first stimulus in the chain (S_1) subsequent extinction effects to this component should result in little generalization of extinction to the second component in the sequence S_2 if S_2 is highly dissimilar to S_1. The greater the reduction in generalization of extinction effects from the early to the latter part of the CS–UCS interval, the greater the amount of anxiety will be conserved to the components closer to UCS onset. As fear to S_1 extinguishes, response latencies will become longer, eventually resulting in the exposure of S_2. At this point, a stimulus change from a low fear to a high fear state will occur. The S_2 component is viewed by Stampfl as functioning as a second-order conditioning stimulus "recharging" S_1, which will again be capable of producing short-latency responses. Theoretically, as long as sufficient fear remains to S_2, the process should continue to repeat itself. By adding further distinctive components (S_3) to the original conditioning sequence, the process of reacquiring shorter avoidance response latencies should be increased via the principles of anxiety conservation and intermittent secondary reinforcement.

However, unlike the Solomon and Wynn (1954) interpretation, Stampfl's position is that the fear response is elicited by the CS when short-latency avoidance responses occur. Short CS exposure is viewed as eliciting a fractional anticipatory fear response which at an asymptotic response-level is capable of motivating avoidance responding for some time. Each exposure of the fractional anticipatory fear response should weaken the avoidance response, and eventually latencies will progressively increase, exposing the subject to a greater level of fear. At some point, this increased fear level will re-reinforce short-latency responses.

Stampfl's model explains why, after learning, the organism does not show signs of fear when short-latency responses occur. The fractional anticipatory fear response notion also explains how avoidance responses are elicited by short-latency CS exposures. The prediction that serial CS presentation will enhance resistance to extinction when compared to a nonserial CS procedure has been supported, with serial CS subjects responding for more than 100 consecutive trials (Kostanek & Sawrey, 1965; Levis, 1966a; Levis & Stampfl, 1972; Levis, Bouska, Eron, & McIlhon, 1970). Like the Solomon and Wynne model, Stampfl's position proposes that the level of fear associated with a particular segment of the CS–UCS interval decreases as that segment's temporal distance from the UCS onset increases. Evidence does exist for such a relationship in the classical conditioning literature with both single CS (Bitterman, 1964; Pavlov, 1927; Siegel, 1967) and serial CS presentations (Frey, Englander, & Roman, 1971; Williams, 1965). Findings in the avoidance literature also suggest that such a relationship may exist during shuttlebox acquisition training (Dubin & Levis, 1973; Levis, 1970b; Levis & Dubin, 1973; Levis & Stampfl, 1972) and during one-way avoidance extinction (Boyd & Levis, 1976).

The serial CS hypothesis has been postulated by Stampfl (Stampfl & Levis, 1967, 1969) to account for the lengthy maintenance of human symptoms; it provides a rationale for why increase in anxiety occurs with initial blocking of symptom execution. The successful avoidance by the human of many elements of the CS complex helps conserve the fear to the unexposed components of the chain.

For examples and details of this extension to psychopathology see Levis (forthcoming) Stampfl and Levis (1967, 1969, 1973a,b) and Stampfl (1970).

V. Support for the Modified Version

Central to the issue of the utility of fear theory is the need to obtain empirical support for the anxiety conservation hypothesis. Although some attempts
have been made to test implications of the model (Delude & Carlson, 1964;
Weinburger, 1965), experimental support is notably lacking. Fear theorists must
do more than simply point to examples of sustained avoidance responding in extinction and note casual observations of the effects of long-latency avoidance
responses. A recent series of experiments in our laboratory attempted to analyze
some of the implications of the model presented by Stampfl by comparing a
serial and a nonserial CS procedure in a one-way avoidance apparatus.

Stampfl's prediction that avoidance maintenance will be enhanced by a
serial CS procedure has already received empirical support in a one-way (Levis,
1966a,b; Levis *et al.,* 1970) and shuttling situations (Levis, 1970b; Levis &
Boyd, 1973; Levis & Dubin, 1973; Levis & Stampfl, 1972). However, the one-
way apparatus is better suited to generate extremely high levels of responding
because the stimulus situation immediately preceding and following a response
can be made highly distinctive. Such an experimental arrangement not only permits a greater per trial reinforcement effect (fear reduction), but minimizes
generalization of extinction effects occurring to apparatus cues during the intertrial interval. Unfortunately, the few studies conducted with serial procedures in
the one-way situation have usually placed a ceiling effect on trials to extinction.
In the Levis *et al.* (1970a) study, animals were discontinued after 200 extinction
trials, with 40% of the animals failing to extinguish by the 200th trial. In the first
study to be reported, in order to determine whether animals would develop functional autonomy or eventually extinguish, as an S–R position must maintain, an
artificial ceiling was not imposed. We also attempted to analyze the effects of a
long-latency response on subsequent avoidance behavior, as well as to determine
changes in response topography across testing. The first two studies were conducted in collaboration with Thomas L. Boyd (see Levis & Boyd, 1979).

Three groups each consisting of 18 rats were tested. Group 1, the serial condition, consisted of an 18-sec CS–UCS interval divided into three 6-sec CS
segments comprising different stimulus components (tone, flashing lights,
buzzer). Group 2 received a single nonserial stimulus (either a tone, flashing
lights or buzzer) throughout the 18-sec interval. Group 3 subjects were conditioned solely to the apparatus cue. All stimuli manipulated were approximately
counterbalanced among conditions. The apparatus was an automatic one-way
avoidance box described in Boyd and Levis (1976). The intertrial interval
averaged 60 sec. Each subject was trained to a criterion of 10 consecutive
avoidance responses, at which point shock was eliminated. One hundred trials

were run each day, or until an extinction criterion of five consecutive responses greater than a latency of 18 sec was reached.

The results indicated that none of the groups differed on the acquisition indices measured. The mean number of extinction trials and range of responding (in parentheses) for Groups 1, 2, and 3 were 248.6 (76–560), 74.3 (19–149), and 69.7 (11–105) trials, respectively. These means are plotted on the left side of Figure 11.1. As can be seen, the serial group produced over three times more responses to extinction when compared to the nonserial conditions (Groups 2 and 3). The left side of Figure 11.1 plots the longest consecutive series of avoidance responses (latency less than 18 sec). These findings are similar to the relationship obtained for trials to extinction, with the serial group reliability differing from the nonserial CS condition. All subjects eventually reached the extinction criterion. However, it should be noted that, if the experiment had stopped after 200 trials, one might have concluded that extinction would not occur. These data support the contention that given time and sufficient CS exposure extinction is inevitable.

A careful analysis of the data also provides strong support for the contention that the serial procedure maximizes the conservation of anxiety by reducing the generalization of extinction across the CS interval. First, the percentage of responding to the three components of the serial were identical to the percentage of responding to the same time-frame for the nonserial groups. However, on an absolute level, considerably more short-latency responses were recorded for the serial subjects. Second, analysis of the response latencies in extinction reveals that serial subjects took reliably longer before producing a response greater than 6 sec (response to S2), and once this occurred it was followed by a reliably greater number of short-latency responses less than 6 sec when compared to the

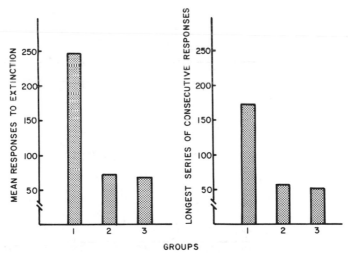

Figure 11.1. *The mean number of extinction trials (left panel) and mean number of consecutive responses in extinction (right panel) are plotted for each group in Experiment 1 of the Levis and Boyd (1979) study.*

nonserial groups. The finding that S2 and S3 in the serial procedure function as powerful second-order conditions can be seen in Figure 11.2.

For illustrative purposes, this figure plots the individual trials of the subjects from each group who provided the greatest number of extinction trials. Not only can the serial back-up effect be seen in this figure, but it should be noted that extinction reflects a gradual rather than sudden increase in response latencies. Finally, the total amount of CS exposure received prior to reaching extinction for the serial group was triple the amount required for the nonserial conditions.

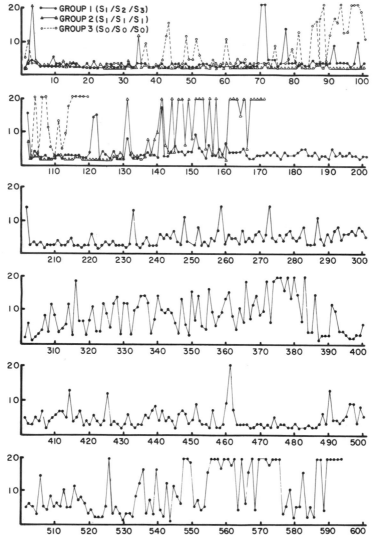

Figure 11.2.   *The trial by trial response latency in extinction is plotted for that subject in each group which produced the greatest number of extinction trials in Experiment 1 of the Levis and Boyd (1979) study.*

We ran a second experiment to determine whether fear was motivating the high percentage of short latency responses (1–4 sec) noted in the previously cited experiment. Cognitive theorists, like Seligman and Johnston (1973, p. 95), argued that fear, as indexed by autonomic responses or conditioned suppression, will not be present during asymptotic acquisition or extinction. To their way of thinking, fear has long extinguished via CS exposure, and avoidance behavior is maintained by the expectancy that a response will prevent shock onset.

We attempted to provide a differential test of this critical point. The CS–UCS interval length was 8 sec. A trace procedure was used with the first 4 sec of the interval consisting either of a tone or of a white noise stimulus. The remaining 4 sec involved exposure only to the background cue. A response within the first 4 sec terminated the CS and the trial. All rats were trained to a criterion of 50 consecutive avoidance responses with latencies of 4 sec or shorter. Following this phase they were transferred to a suppression procedure in which the CS was superimposed on an ongoing appetitive response of water licking. Half the subjects, Group C, received a control stimulus not previously presented. Fear was measured by indexing the amount of suppressive effects on licking behavior that occurred during the stimulus period (30-sec duration). The left side of Figure 11.3 presents the suppression data for the two groups: the right side of the figure measures time to the first lick following CS offset (recovery latencies). As can be seen from this graph (.00 = maximum suppression; .50 = no suppression), the data reliably support the contention that at asymptotic responding fear to the CS is still present. Jane E. Smith, Wendy Epstein, and I attempted to replicate and extend this suppression experiment. Subjects (24 per group) were trained to a criterion of either 5, 25, or 50 consecutive, short-latency, avoidance responses (4 sec or less) using the procedure described in Experiment 2. The effects of the CS on suppression of licking were then tested. Half the subjects in

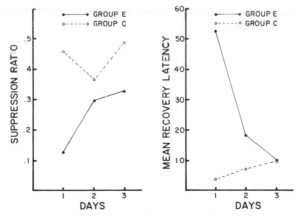

Figure 11.3. The mean suppression ratio [B/(1/2 A + B)] during CER testing (left panel) and the mean time to first lick following CS offset during CER testing (right panel) is plotted for Group E (experimental) and Group C (control) of Experiment 2 for each of the three test trials (days) of the Levis and Boyd (1979) study.

each group were exposed to the CS used in avoidance training (the experimental groups), and half were exposed to a novel stimulus (the control groups).

The suppression ratios for the experimental groups on Day 1 for Conditions 5, 25, and 50 were .03, .21, and .08, respectively. The corresponding control condition's ratios were .27, .45, and .31. Surprisingly, the experimental group with the greatest number of short-latency responses (50) suppressed more than the subjects who received 25 trials. Further data analyses are required before this latter finding can be interpreted, but the critical point is made—fear is still present to the CS.

VI. Response–Prevention Technique of Extinction

The studies reported provide important support for the contention that fear is still present following extended responding to short CS exposure periods, and that upon longer CS exposures, increases in the level of fear occur resulting in the reconditioning of short avoidance–response latencies. With sufficient exposure of the total CS complex, extinction of fear, and therefore of avoidance responding, is believed to be inevitable. In the context of an avoidance paradigm, the organism controls, through instrumental responding, the amount of CS exposure presented and, therefore, the degree of fear extinction. It would follow from fear theory, that one way to hasten extinction would be to prevent responding while repeatedly presenting the total CS complex. This procedure is commonly referred to as a response–prevention technique of extinction. Considerable evidence exists at the infrahuman level that a response–prevention technique hastens extinction of conditioned avoidance responses (Bankart & Elliott, 1974; Baum, 1969a,b, 1970; Berman & Katsev, 1972; Monti & Smith, 1976; Schiff, Smith, & Prochaska, 1972; Shipley, Mock, & Levis, 1971).

However, Page (1955) and Coulter, Riccio, and Page (1969) have argued that a response–prevention procedure leads not to fear extinction but to development of incompatible response tendencies. Their data are cited frequently as being opposed to two-factor theory. But, according to fear theory, CS termination reinforces whatever response is closely associated with the resulting reduction in aversiveness. If an active avoidance procedure is used and if sufficient reinforcement directly follows responding, an increase in avoidance behavior will occur as a function of reinforced trials. A response–prevention procedure prevents active avoidance responding, but reinforcement is still present when the CS is terminated. If the animal is immobile at the time (which appears to be the usual state of affairs), postural inactivity will be reinforced by drive reduction. Thus, in the typical response– prevention study, the acquisition phase should lead to the development of one response (active avoidance) and the prevention phase to a different and incompatible response (immobility).

The response required in the test phase is critical, and whatever fear is left will activate the most dominant response tendency (the larger value of the two habits). In theory, CS exposure in extinction must lead to a weakening of both habits, but unless one measures at the end of prevention the response topography that is dominant, predictions cannot be readily made. Shipley *et al.* (1971) demonstrated by measuring both activity and inactivity during response–prevention that CS exposure can lead to both the development of immobility and fear extinction. Furthermore, when CS exposure and trials are controlled, active responding does not, at least in their study, effect extinction of the fear response.

From the preceding discussion it would seem critical for the understanding of the data generated from the complex avoidance paradigm that the dominant response tendency present at the "treatment" phase be measured. This measurement will permit a prediction of how the animal will behave during the "fear-test" phase. It would then follow that complete fear extinction during prevention would be operationally defined as occurring when random activity is present to the CS, or activity involving the same topography as that of an appropriate control condition. Such an analysis should lead to powerful predictions that will eventually determine the merits of fear-theory.

Theorists who take the position that response–prevention does not result in extinction of the fear response also fail to consider the abundance of data collected using a classical conditioning procedure that shows clearly that fear and instrumental behavior both extinguish with CS exposure. A classical-conditioning extinction procedure is procedurally identical in principle to a response–prevention procedure.

Although the residual fear issue has resulted in either modification (Riccio & Silvestri, 1973) or rejection (Seligman & Johnston, 1973) of two-factor theory, the basic premise for these alternative viewpoints is predicated on the proposition that fear is not present following extended short-latency avoidance response. The data reported from our laboratory suggest that this proposition is false.

Further research on this topic is of course needed, but consideration should be given to controlling for the total amount of nonreinforced CS exposure and establishing the differential extinction rates of various fear measures.

In closing, I reitereate my position: Sufficient nonreinforced CS exposure will lead to the extinction of the fear response and all previously conditioned avoidance behavior. Stampfl has argued the same point and has extended the response–prevention procedure of extinction to the treatment of human symptoms. His extrapolation has been labeled "implosive" or "flooding" therapy and essentially involves an imagery or in vivo procedure designed to induce forced CS exposure (see Levis, forthcoming; Stampfl & Levis, 1967, 1969, 1973a,b; Stampfl, 1970). The technique has received support at both the animal analogue and human patient levels of analysis (see Levis & Hare, 1977), although, the underlying principles of the therapy are still in need of more direct experimental investigation.

It should be noted that the avoidance model of the laboratory described in this chapter directly stimulated the development of the above treatment approach. Whether, in last analysis, the deductions made from the model will be confirmed at the human level is uncertain. But the initial success of the model is encouraging and supportive of further work.

REFERENCES

Amsel, A., & Maltzman, I. The effect upon generalized drive strength of emotionality as inferred from the level of consummatory response. *Journal of Experimental Psychology,* 1950, *40,* 563–569.

Anderson, N. H., & Nakamura, C. Y. Avoidance decrement in avoidance conditioning. *Journal of Comparative and Physiological Psychology,* 1964, *57,* 196–204.

Baker, T. W. Properties of compound conditioned stimuli and their components. *Psychological Bulletin,* 1968, *70,* 611–625.

Bankart, B., & Elliott, R. Extinction of avoidance in rats: Response availability and stimulus presentation effects. *Behaviour Research and Therapy.* 1974, *12,* 53–56.

Baum, M. Extinction of an avoidance response motivated by intense fear: Social facilitation of the action of response prevention (flooding) in rats. *Behavior Research and Therapy,* 1969, *7,* 57–62.(a)

Baum, M. Extinction of an avoidance response following response prevention: Some parametric investigations. *Canadian Journal of Psychology,* 1969, *23,* 1–10. (b)

Baum, M. Extinction of avoidance responding through response prevention (flooding). *Psychological Bulletin,* 1970, *74,* 276–284.

Berman, J. S., & Katsev, R. D. Factors involved in the rapid elimination of avoidance behavior. *Behavior Research and Therapy,* 1972, *10,* 247–256.

Bitterman, M. The CS–US interval in classical and avoidance conditioning. In W. F. Prokasy (Ed.), *Classical conditioning: A symposium.* New York: Appleton, 1965. Pp. 1–19.

Black, A. H. The extinction of avoidance responses under curare. *Journal of Comparative and Physiological Psychology,* 1958, *51,* 519–525.

Bolles, R. G. Species-specific defense reactions. In F. R. Brush (Ed.), *Aversive conditioning and learning.* New York: Academic Press, 1971. Pp. 183–233.

Boyd, T. L., & Levis, D. J. The effects of single-component extinction of a three-component serial CS on resistance to extinction of the conditioned avoidance response. *Learning and Motivation,* 1976, *7,* 517–531.

Boyd, T. L., & Levis, D. J. The interactive effects of shuttlebox situational cues and shock intensity. *American Journal of Psychology,* 1979, *92,* 125–132.

Brown, J. S. *The motivation of behavior.* New York: McGraw-Hill, 1961.

Brown, J. S., & Jacobs, A. The role of fear in the motivation and acquisition of responses. *Journal of Experimental Psychology,* 1949, *39,* 747–759.

Brown, J. S., Kalish, H. I., & Farber, I. E. Conditioned fear as revealed by magnitude of startle response to an auditory stimulus. *Journal of Experimental Psychology,* 1951, *41,* 317–328.

Brush, E. S. Traumatic avoidance learning: The effects of conditioned stimulus length in a free-responding situation. *Journal of Comparative and Physiological Psychology,* 1957, *50,* 541–546.

Brush, F. R. The effect of shock intensity on the acquisition and extinction of an avoidance response in dogs. *Journal of Comparative and Physiological Psychology,* 1957, *50,* 547–552.

Brush, F. R. On the differences between animals that learn and do not learn to avoid electric shock. *Psychonomic Science,* 1966, *5,* 123–124.

Brush, F. R., Brush, E. S., & Solomon, R. L. Traumatic avoidance learning: The effects of CS–UCS interval with a delayed-conditioning procedure. *Journal of Comparative and Physiological Psychology,* 1955, *48,* 285–293.

Church, R. M., Brush, F. R., & Solomon, R. L. Traumatic avoidance learning: The effects of CS–US interval with a delayed-conditioning procedure in a free responding situation. *Journal of Comparative and Physiological Psychology,* 1956, *49,* 301–308.

Corriveau, D. P., & Smith, N. F. Fear reduction and "safety-test" behavior following response prevention: A multivariate analysis. *Journal of Experimental Psychology: General,* 1978, *107,* 145–158.

Coulter, X., Riccio, D. C., & Page, H. A. Effects of blocking an instrumental avoidance response: Facilitated extinction but persistence of "fear." *Journal of Comparative and Physiological Psychology,* 1969, *68,* 377–381.

D'Amato, M. R., Keller, D., & DiCara, L. Facilitation of discriminated avoidance learning by discontinuous shock. *Journal of Comparative and Physiological Psychology,* 1964, *58,* 344–349.

Delude, L. A., & Carlson, N. J. A test of the conservation of anxiety and partial irreversibility hypothesis. *Canadian Journal of Psychology,* 1964, *18,* 15–22.

Denny, M. R., Koons, P. B., & Mason, J. E. Extinction of avoidance as a function of the escape situation. *Journal of Comparative and Physiological Psychology,* 1959, *52,* 212–214.

Dollard, J., & Miller, N. E. *Personality and psychotherapy.* New York: McGraw-Hill, 1950.

Dubin, W. J., & Levis, D. J. Influence of similarity of components of a serial CS on conditioned fear in the rat. *Journal of Comparative and Physiological Psychology,* 1973, *85,* 304–312.

Eysenck, H. J. (Ed.) *Behaviour therapy and the neuroses.* New York: Pergamon, 1960.

Eysenck, H. J. The learning theory model of neurosis—a new approach. *Behaviour Research and Therapy,* 1976, *14,* 251–261.

Feldman, R. S., & Bremner, F. J. A method for rapid conditioning of stable avoidance bar pressing behavior. *Journal of the Experimental Analysis of Behavior,* 1963, *6,* 393–394.

Fitzgerald, R. D., & Brown, J. S. Variables affecting avoidance conditioning in free-responding and discrete-trial situations. *Psychological Reports,* 1965, *17,* 835–843.

Freud, S. *The problem of anxiety* (H. A. Bunker trans.). New York: Psychoanalytic Quarterly Press and W. W. Norton, 1936. Pp. 85–92.

Frey, P. W., Englander, S., & Roman, A. Interstimulus interval analysis of sequential CS compounds in rabbit eyelid conditioning. *Journal of Comparative and Physiological Psychology,* 1971, *77,* 439–446.

Herrnstein, R. Method and theory in the study of avoidance. *Psychological Review,* 1969, *76,* 49–69.

Hunt, H. F. Problems in the interpretation of experimental neurosis. *Psychological Reports,* 1964, *15,* 27–35.

Hunt, H. F., Jernberg, P., & Brady, J. V. The effect of electroconvulsive shock (E.C.S.) on a conditioned emotional response: The effects of post-E.C.S. extinction on the reappearance of the response. *Journal of Comparative and Physiological Psychology,* 1952, *45,* 589–599.

Hurwitz, H. M. B. Method for discriminative avoidance training. *Science,* 1964, *145,* 1070–1071.

Kalish, H. I. Strength of fear as a function of the number of acquisition and extinction trials. *Journal of Experimental Psychology,* 1954, *47,* 1–9.

Kamin, L. J. Traumatic avoidance learning: The effects of CS–US interval with a trace-conditioning procedure. *Journal of Comparative and Physiological Psychology,* 1954, *47,* 65–72.

Keehn, J. D. Schedule-dependence, schedule-induction, and the law of effect. In R. M. Gilbert & J. D. Keehn (Eds.), *Schedule effects: Drugs, drinking and aggression.* Toronto: Univ. of Toronto Press, 1972.

Knapp, R. K. Acquisition and extinction of avoidance with similar and different shock and escape situations. *Journal of Comparative and Physiological Psychology,* 1965, *60,* 272–273.

Koch, S. Behavior as "intrinsically" regulated: Work notes towards a pretheory of phenomena called "motivational." In M. R. Jones (Ed.), *Nebraska Symposium on Motivation.* Lincoln, Nebraska: Univ. of Nebraska Press, 1956.

Kostanek, D. J., & Sawrey, J. M. Acquisition and extinction of shuttlebox avoidance with complex stimuli. *Psychonomic Science,* 1965, *3,* 369–370.

Levis, D. J. Implosive therapy, Part II: The subhuman analogue, the strategy, and the technique. In S. G. Armitage (Ed.), *Behavioral modification techniques in the treatment of emotional disorders.* Battle Creek, Michigan: V. A. Publication, 1966. Pp. 22–37. (a)

Levis, D. J. Effects of serial CS presentation and other characteristics of the CS on the conditioned avoidance response. *Psychological Reports,* 1966, *18,* 755–766. (b)

Levis, D. J. Behavioral therapy: The fourth therapeutic revolution? In D. J. Levis (Ed.), *Learning approaches to therapeutic behavior change.* Chicago: Aldine, 1970. (a)

Levis, D. J. Serial CS presentation and the shuttlebox avoidance conditioning: A further look at the tendency to delay responding. *Psychonomic Science,* 1970, *20,* 145–147. (b)

Levis, D. J. The effects of CS complexity on intertrial responding in shuttlebox avoidance conditioning. *American Journal of Psychology,* 1971, *84,* 555–564.

Levis, D. J. Implementing the technique of implosive therapy. In E. Foa & A. Goldstein (Eds.), *Handbook of behavioral interventions.* New York: Wiley, forthcoming.

Levis, D. J., Bouska, S., Eron, J., McIlhon, M. Serial CS presentation and one-way avoidance conditioning: A noticeable lack of delayed responding. *Psychonomic Science,* 1970, *20,* 147–149.

Levis, D. J., & Boyd, T. L. Effects of shock intensity on avoidance responding in a shuttlebox to serial CS procedure. *Psychonomic Bulletin,* 1973, *1,* 304–306.

Levis, D. J., & Boyd, T. L. Symptom maintenance: An infrahuman analysis and extension of the conservation of anxiety principle. *Journal of Abnormal Psychology, 1979, 88,* 107–120.

Levis, D. J., & Dubin, W. J. Some parameters affecting shuttle-box avoidance responding with rats receiving serially presented conditioned stimuli. *Journal of Comparative and Physiological Psychology,* 1973, *82,* 328–344.

Levis, D. J., & Hare, N. A review of the theoretical rationale and empirical support for the extinction approach of implosive (flooding) therapy. In M. Hersen, R. M. Eisler, & P. M. Miller (Eds.), *Progress in behavior modification.* New York: Academic Press, 1977.

Levis, D. J., & Stampfl, T. G. Effects of serial CS presentation on shuttlebox avoidance responding. *Learning and Motivation,* 1972, *3,* 73–90.

Maatsch, J. L. Learning and fixation after a single shock trial. *Journal of Comparative and Physiological Psychology,* 1959, *52,* 408–410.

Mackintosh, N. J. *The psychology of animal learning.* New York: Academic Press, 1974.

McAllister, W. R., & McAllister, D. E. Role of CS and apparatus cues in the measurement of acquired fear. *Psychological Reports,* 1962, *11,* 749–756.

McAllister, W. R., & McAllister, D. E. Behavioral measurement of conditioned fear. In F. Robert Brush (Ed.), *Aversive conditioning and learning.* New York: Academic Press, 1971.

McAllister, W. R., McAllister, D. E., & Douglass, W. K. The inverse relationship between shock intensity and shuttle-box avoidance learning in rats: A reinforcement explanation. *Journal of Comparative and Physiological Psychology,* 1971, *74,* 426–433.

Meryman, J. J. *Magnitude of startle response as a function of hunger and fear.* Unpublished master's thesis, State Univ. of Iowa, 1952.

Meryman, J. J. *The magnitude of an unconditioned GSR as a function of fear conditioned at a long CS–UCS interval.* Unpublished doctoral dissertation, State Univ. of Iowa, 1953.

Meyer, D. R., Cho, C., & Wesemann, A. F. On problems of conditioning discriminated lever-press avoidance responses. *Psychological Review,* 1960, *67,* 224–220.

Miller, N. E. Studies of fear as an acquirable drive: I. Fear as motivation and fear-reduction as reinforcement in the learning of a new response. *Journal of Experimental Psychology,* 1948, *38,* 89–101.

Modaresi, H. A. One-way characteristic performance of rats under two-way signaled avoidance conditions. *Learning and Motivation,* 1975, *6,* 484–497.

Monti, P. M., & Smith, N. F. Residual fear of the conditioned stimulus as a function of response prevention after avoidance or classical defensive conditioning in the rat. *Journal of Experimental Psychology: General,* 1976, *105,* 148–162.

Mowrer, O. H. On the dual nature of learning—a re-interpretation of "conditioning" and problem-solving." *Harvard Educational Review,* 1947, *17,* 102–148.

Mowrer, O. H. *Learning theory and the symbolic processes.* New York: Wiley, 1960.

Mowrer, O. H., & Keehn, J. D. How are intertrial "avoidance" responses reinforced? *Psychological Review,* 1958, *65,* 209–221.

Page, H. A. The facilitation of experimental extinction by response prevention as a function of the acquisition of a new response. *Journal of Comparative and Physiological Psychology,* 1955, *48,* 14–16.

Pavlov, I. P. *Conditioned reflexes.* London: Oxford Univ. Press, 1927.

Rachman, S. The passing of the two-stage theory of fear and avoidance: Fresh possibilities. *Behavior, Research, and Therapy,* 1976, *14,* 125–131.

Razran, G. Empirical codification and specific theoretical implications of compound-stimulus conditioning: Perception. In W. F. Prokasy (Ed.), *Classical conditioning: A symposium.* New York: Appleton, 1975.

Rescorla, R. A., & Solomon, R. L. Two-process learning theory: Relationships between Pavlovian conditioning and instrumental learning. *Psychological Review,* 1967, *74,* 151–182.

Riccio, D., & Silvestri, R. Extinction of avoidance behavior and the problem of residual fear. *Behaviour Research and Therapy,* 1973, *11,* 1–9.

Schiff, R., Smith, N., & Prochaska, J. Extinction of avoidance in rats as a function of duration and number of blocked trials. *Journal of Comparative and Physiological Psychology,* 1972, *81,* 356–359.

Schoenfeld, W. N. An experimental approach to anxiety, escape, and avoidance behavior. In P. H. Hoch & J. Zubin (Eds.), *Anxiety.* New York: Grune & Stratton, 1950.

Seligman, M. E. P., & Johnston, J. C. A cognitive theory of avoidance learning. In F. J. McGuigan, & D. B. Lumsden (Eds.), *Contemporary prospectives in learning and conditioning.* Washington, D.C.: Scripta Press, 1973.

Shipley, R. H., Mock, L. A., & Levis, D. J. Effects of several response prevention procedures on activity, avoidance responding, and conditioned fear in rats *Journal of Comparative and Physiological Psychology,* 1971, *77,* 256–270.

Sidman, M. Some properties of the warning stimulus in avoidance behavior. *Journal of Comparative and Physiological Psychology,* 1955, *48,* 444–450.

Siegel, A. Stimulus generalization of a classically conditioned response along a temporal dimension. *Journal of Comparative and Physiological Psychology,* 1967, *64,* 461–466.

Solomon, R. L., Kamin, L. J., & Wynne, L. C. Traumatic avoidance learning: The outcomes of several extinction procedures with dogs. *Journal of Abnormal and Social Psychology,* 1953, *48,* 291–302.

Solomon, R. L., & Wynne, L. C. Traumatic avoidance learning: Acquisition in normal dogs. *Psychological Monographs,* 1953, *67, 354,* 19.

Solomon, R. L., & Wynne, L. C. Traumatic avoidance learning: The principle of anxiety conservation and partial irreversibility. *Psychological Review,* 1954, *61,* 353–385.

Stampfl, T. G. Implosive therapy: An emphasis on cover stimulation. In D. J. Levis (Ed.), *Learning approaches to therapeutic behavior change.* Chicago: Aldine, 1970.

Stampfl, T. G., & Levis, D. J. The essentials of implosive therapy: A learning-theory-based psychodynamic behavioral therapy. *Journal of Abnormal Psychology,* 1967, *72,* 496–503.

Stampfl, T. G., & Levis, D. J. Learning theory: An aid to dynamic therapeutic practice. In L. D. Eron & R. Callahan (Eds.), *Relationship of theory to practice in psychotherapy.* Chicago: Aldine, 1969.

Stampfl, T. G., & Levis, D. J. Implosive therapy. In R. J. Jurjevich (Ed.), *Handbook of direct and behavior psychotherapies.* Raleigh: North Carolina Press, 1973. (a)

Stampfl, T. G., & Levis, D. J. *Implosive therapy: Theory and technique.* New Jersey: General Learning Press, 1973. (b)

Uhl, C. N., & Eichbaure, A. Relative persistence of avoidance and positively reinforced behavior. *Learning and Motivation,* 1975, *6,* 459–467.

Weinberger, N. M. Effects of detainment on extinction of avoidance responses. *Journal of Comparative and Physiological Psychology,* 1965, *60,* 135–138.

Williams, D. R. Classical conditioning and incentive motivation. In W. F. Prokasy (Ed.), *Classical conditioning: A symposium.* New York: Appleton, 1965. Pp. 340–357.

Wolpe, J. *Psychotherapy by reciprocal inhibition.* Palo Alto: Stanford Univ. Press, 1958.

Psychotherapy from the Standpoint of a Behaviorist

12

I. Introduction

The processes by which the behavior of organisms is acquired, shaped, and eliminated during its transaction with the environment is the central theme of behavioral formulations of psychopathology and psychotherapy. The traditions of Pavlov, Hull, and Skinner emphasize the plasticity of human behavior, primarily through the discoveries of the animal laboratory. Pavlov's conditioned reflex experiments with dogs and the extensions by Watson to human behavior led the applications of learning principles to psychopathology. Both created models of behavioral pathology in the laboratory and treated them by manipulating the same variables by which the pathology was created. Pavlov observed "neurotic" by products of the salivary conditioning procedures. Watson, in the experiment that made the child Albert fearful of furry objects, created a dysfunction by conditioning a reflex response to a loud noise. The attempt to reverse the dysfunction utilized the same processes in a procedure very similar to the one that Wolpe later termed reciprocal inhibition and progressive relaxation. Despite Pavlov's epistemology of cerebral causes of behavior and Hull's (1943) construction of neurological intervening variables, all of these early programs of research espoused that behavioral processes were orderly and controlled by the environment. Skinner's functional analysis of behavior, the most recent exposition of the same theme, asserted that the discovery of how environmental variables con-

PSYCHOPATHOLOGY IN ANIMALS
Research and Clinical Implications

trolled behavior could substitute for mentalistic and inferred physiological explanations. Skinner's radical behaviorism set an example for research programs that achieved large magnitudes of control of the behavior of the individual organism.

II. Behavioral Therapies as Metaphors of Behavioral Control

A prominent characteristic of those who made the first behavioral contributions to the study of mental illness was their sustained involvement in basic animal research early in their careers and their later concern with applying this knowledge to human problems. Despite Pavlov's total preoccupation with technical laboratory research, 7 out of the 23 lectures, in which he summarized his life's work, concerned human pathology and applications to human problems (Pavlov, 1927). In Lecture 20, for example, he wrote of "imagined pregnancy and all sorts of imaginary diseases." John B. Watson (1968), who spent the first 20 years of his career in basic research with animals, contributed the experiment, in collaboration with Raynor, with the infant Albert just as he was leaving academic laboratory work. *Behaviorism* (Watson, 1919, 1930), which was destined to become the clarion call of behaviorism, was published *after* he left the work of the laboratory behind. By 1953, Skinner had turned his attention to writing *Science and Human Behavior* and to applying operant conditioning principles to education, psychotherapy, and other broad social enterprises. The careers of those, like Azrin, Ferster, and Sidman who turned from intense occupation with basic animal research to work in mental hospitals, schools for the retarded, education, psychotherapy, and theoretical extensions of principles of operant reinforcement to the problems of depression, obesity, and the genesis of mental illness, mirrored Skinner's divided career. For each of these scientists, the accomplishments of animal research led to the conviction that the methods could be extended with great effect and power to human concerns. Operant conditioning had a special impact on those interested in extensions of laboratory findings to clinical problems, perhaps because so many of the characteristics of the laboratory work of operant psychology were so consonant with clinical procedures—particularly the emphasis on the behavior of individual subjects rather than group averages and inferential statistics (Ferster, 1974).

The experience, often reported by novice and professional alike, of conditioning a pigeon illustrates the special valence that connected many operant experimental psychologists to the clinical field. The experimenter, contacting the animal only through a button, instantly increases the frequency of an act and shapes it into a new complex form, all in a matter of minutes. A certain amount of art, rather than a mechanical application, is needed even though the experimenter knows with certainty that sooner or later he or she will produce the conditioned behavior. The interaction has a strong clinical flavor because the experimenter needs to observe the details of the pigeon's behavior and to adjust his or her actions to the peculiarities of the individual bird. No pigeon is too difficult to succeed with an no tour de force too difficult to attempt. The demonstration shows the lawful control of behavior and clarifies how the reinforcement procedures interact with the bird's behavior to produce the planned result. But what is especially important is that the experiment also demonstrates another aspect of control—the mastery that the conditioner achieves. He or she sets out to increase the frequency of a particular act, presses a button, and instantly sees it increase dramatically. When the conditioner stops pressing the button, the behavior becomes less frequent and disappears. He has a sense that he had created behavior and taken it away. It is a dramatic event, shared by many of those with intense investments in behavioral psychology, which explains how so many operant conditioners came to sit on the boundary between natural science and clinical practice.

This metaphor of control took a further turn with research with pigeons on schedules of reinforcement (Ferster & Skinner, 1957), which could maintain a million or more pecks per month in an individual subject as well as control the moment-to-moment fine-grain aspects of the animal's behavior. The experience reinforced the conviction, like the result of the Watson–Raynor experiment with Albert, that behavior was plastic and that human pathology would be equally reversible if we subjected it to analogous contingencies of reinforcement. This style of research, in which the dependent variable was the frequency of the performances of an individual subject, gave a clinical cast to laboratory operant conditioning research. The experimental procedures were adjusted continuously, depending on the behavior of the subject; factors responsible for each animal's uniqueness were taken into account, deviant animals were not automatically discarded; and changes in behavior were of a large enough size to be useful practically.

Walden Two (Skinner, 1948), a fictional account of a model society in which an optimal life was constructed by basing its practices and types of control on principles of behavior, functioned as a powerful stimulant, much like Watson's experiment with Albert, to the idea that such a utopian life could be accomplished by applying behavioral principles.

It is not so surprising that so many scientists have reacted to the success with which they controlled behavior in the laboratory as a prelude to extending their skills and findings to human problems. Besides its inherent usefulness, the solution of practical human problems is an escape from the social isolation of the theoretical laboratory, where the primary task could, indeed, be defined as "finding out more and more about less and less." The laboratory enterprise is a lonely one in which discoveries are abstract, often without any direct connection to practical affairs, and where it is not only possible but also largely desirable to create and study phenomena that may not have heretofore existed in nature. Significant laboratory achievements usually require sustaining long, intense effort in which the investigator works without the collaboration and support of colleagues at large.

It is paradoxical that Freud, who served as the foil of so many of those espousing the study and treatment of human behavior as a natural science, came from a tradition very similar to Pavlov, Watson, and Skinner. For a 20-year period, from medical school to his entrance to clinical practice, Freud was primarily engaged in histology, neurophysiology, neuroanatomy, and neurology, spending more time at a microscope than as a clinician. It is generally accepted that Freud's epistemology of mental life is a metaphor of his knowledge of the reflex arc. With Freud, like Pavlov, Watson, and Skinner, it was the success with the power of natural science in the laboratory, coupled perhaps with the social isolation of that work, that led him to practical work with people.

It is tempting to speculate that the slight impact that Lewin (1935), Guthrie (1935), and Tolman (1932) have had on the extensions of basic laws of learning to clinical problems is connected with the absence of any substantial involvement in the technical laboratory research that achieved explicit control of behavior. In a similar vein, it is not surprising that Miller (1941, 1944) and Solomon (1977), whose animal laboratory research achieved considerable control of the behavior of the individual subject, wrote more about the clinical implications of their work than did Hull's other students.

III. Behavioral Approaches to Psychopathology as a Reaction Against the "Medical Model"

Behavioral approaches to clinical problems, in addition to their emphasis on applying learning principles, also opposed the use of the epistemology of the mental life and the "medical model," a legacy of Freud's medical practice with patients who complained of somatic difficulties, such as anethesias or paralyses. Further impetus for defining neuroses as medical pathology came from the conceptual scheme that Freud adopted from his neurological training, modeled on a failure of nerve discharge, in turn causing somatic reactions from the unchannelled impulses. The advent of ego psychology, with its emphasis on a wider range of human transactions beyond resolution of conflicts, was the development that opened up psychotherapy to nonmedical practitioners (Hartman, 1950).

The opposition to the medical model was not restricted to behavioral psychologists but took the form of sensitivity groups, nondirective therapy, biofeedback, assertive training, primal scream methods, rational–emotive therapy, and many others. It is tempting to think of cognitive behavior modification (Mahoney, 1977) as another example of opposition to the medical model, since in other respects, the assumptions are so similar to Freud's. The similarity between *cognitions* as a major datum, and Freud's assertion that he dealt with a mental representation of the patient's actual experience, places cognitive theory closer to the theoretical structure of psychodynamic psychology than to behaviorism. All of these approaches to psychotherapy are called behavioral, not in the sense that they lean on principles of learning and the objective description of behavior but because they reject the assumptions of Freudian theory involving the central place of conflict resolution that is connected with the Freudian epistemology of motor discharge.

IV. Principles of Learning and a Natural Science Framework to Clarify Clinical Practice

The applications of behavioral principles under the guise of behavior therapy and behavior modification are in contrast to a broader use of behaviorism as a natural scientific concept of human nature.

Primarily through the pioneering work of Eysenck (1957) and Wolpe (1958) the implications of Pavlov's and Watson's writing found expression in actual clinical practice as behavior therapy. As is inevitable in clinical practice, it is difficult to say how much of therapy is governed by the guiding theory and how much by the interaction and discovery with the patient. Increasingly, behavior therapists are acknowledging the importance of clinical skill in interaction with the patient and the necessity of continual adjustment of the clinical procedure. Similarly, with behavior modification practice, Azrin (1977) has emphasized the importance of letting clinical methods evolve and of interactions in which the changes in the behavior of the patient shape the therapist's clinical procedure. The implication of these trends is a continued separation of the tasks of behavior therapy and behavioral psychology. Clinical procedures are becoming practically and experientially oriented, perhaps even adopting some of the practices of conventional psychotherapy. Behavior modification and therapy appears to be focusing more on practical procedures discovered in the field.

What, then, is the relevance and applicability of a science of behavior? It is not in a position to discover the kinds of complex phenomena that novelists, social commentators, philosophers, and clinicians describe. An important use of behavioral psychology is a language about human conduct, a lingua franca that is an alternative to common language and to the mentalistic epistemology of psychodynamic psychology and philosophy. Clinical experts seem to be able to communicate successfully to each other, and there is often assurance that something substantive is being communicated when a proven clinician is speaking. But it is usually difficult to know in detail what parts of the therapy cause the benefit to the patient. To the extent that it is possible to describe what happened, effective transmission seems to occur between persons who already know much of what is being said.

Behavioral language has the same advantage in clinical work as physiology has for internal medicine. Reinforcement, as the instant immediate consequence of a performance, is the cornerstone of a scientific language about behavior because it allows us to observe the component details of a complex activity in addition to its larger function. The basic principle of a behavioral description is a separation of human conduct into the act itself and the change in the environment it produces, whether this change is in the external environment, within the individual, or in another person. Many clinicians complain that describing the fine details of a complex act takes away its essential human quality—and there is reason to share that concern. For the fine detail of the experiment and the overall view of the practitioner illustrate how science and practice complement each other. The one side is illustrated by the metaphor of the Ph.D. scholar as the person who knows more and more about less and less, and the other side by the practitioner as a source of knowledge gained by day-to-day interactions with the problems of human existence. It is useful to look beyond the particular clinical or colloquial or mentalistic language to the observation of the patient that prompted the clinician to speak. It is reasonable to assume that effective practitioners, moved to speak, have seen something of importance. The experimental psychologist requires the collaboration of the clinician to know what are the important human experiences to formulate scientifically, and which dimensions of them have particular salience. Otherwise, how would natural scientists know what specimen to put under the microscope? One sense of control is illustrated when food is used to condition behavior, say in the pigeon demonstration that was described previously. The other sense of control is the functional analysis, after the fact, which relates what happened to the variables of which it is a function. It is in this latter sense that the functional analysis of operant behavior can serve as a language to convert experiential knowledge to objective terms so that practices can be refined by experience and communicated. One function of learning theory has been to analyze various modes of psychotherapy.

A. PSYCHOLOGICAL ANALYSES OF PSYCHODYNAMIC THERAPY

Since the publication of Masserman's text on psychiatry (1943), in which he attempted to relate human psychopathology to animal laboratory experiments, there has been a steady progression of theorists who have attempted to bridge experimental and clinical psychology conceptually, in the sense of a functonal analysis of the phenomena.

Dollard and Miller's (1950) pioneering book, *Personality and Psychotherapy* was one of the first explicit attempts to apply principles of learning to psychotherapy in a broad conceptual way. They followed Watson's lead that the principles of learning that govern all of a person's commerce with the environment would also clarify how abnormal patterns emerge and how the changes in the environment could be arranged in therapy to alter the individual's patterns of behavior to ones that would more effectively sustain his behavior in the current environment. Unlike Watson and the behavior therapies that followed Wolpe's (1958) lead, Dollard and Miller accepted psychodynamic therapy as a practical enterprise and used principles of learning to make the theory and practice communicable. Like those who attempted to apply science to practice before, they assumed that pathological modes of conduct were learned just like normal ones and that all therapies influenced behavior through the processes that described how learning took place. Dollard and Miller brought together two traditions. First there was psychoanalysis as an influential mode of treatment and the theoretical schematization of· the causes of psychopathology. Like learning theory, it sought causes for abnormal behavior in the child's early social and personal history. Dollard and Miller applied the traditions of Pavlov, Thorndike, Hull, and social learning to attempt to bring the pathological conduct, uncovered by Freud, into view as natural events that could be described scientifically. The underlying assumption of both views—psychodynamic and behavioral—was that the phenomena obeyed definite laws.

Wachtel (1977), a practicing psychoanalyst who also came under the influence of Dollard and Miller, continued a similar enterprise, except that his book, *Psychoanalysis and Behavior Therapy,* emphasized information from clinical practice to which learning principles might, in some instances, contribute clarity. Wachtel, from his vantage point as a therapist, was able to describe the behavior of patient and therapist in more detail than is usually found, either in clinical case histories or in behavioral writings. His presentation of the major themes of psychodynamic theory and practice benefits from the connections he finds to behavior theory, mainly in the form of Dollard and Miller's account and some of the practices of behavior therapy. Wachtel's account of psychodynamic theory could serve as a primer for behaviorally oriented psychologists who would like to think about the phenomena there behaviorally, much as Dollard and Miller did.

B. OPERANT CONDITIONING

The operant-conditioning approach to a behavioral conception of human conduct could be represented by two books. The first is Keller and Schoenfeld's (1950) classical introductory textbook which began with the explication of principles of learning, mostly with animals, and ended with chapters on human emotion and social behavior in the natural setting. The second is Skinner's (1953) *Science and Human Behavior* which formulated the major dimensions of human personal and social life in the framework of operant principles. Like Dollard and Miller's application of Hullian learning theory to psychoanalytic practices, both Keller and Schoenfeld and Skinner used principles of learning to clarify knowledge of human behavior acquired from other sources. Keller and Schoenfeld emphasized observations made by psychological specialties other than operant conditioning, while Skinner explicated the behavioral control involved in common observations of human agencies, such as law, government, psychotherapy, and religion, as well as the complex individual behavior of self-control, private events, and multiply caused repertoires. These panoramic views of large areas of behavioral control that Skinner presented served to delineate the kinds of independent variables that should be examined and the empirical data that had to be observed. The chapter on self-control, in *Science and Human Behavior* for example, served as a paradigm for Ferster's (1962) work on the control of eating, which, in turn, stimulated a series of applications to empirical research. The functional analysis of the repertoire of the depressed person (Ferster, 1972), which set out to functionally analyze the component behaviors with the basic processes of operant behavior represents a similar use of a basic paradigm. The functional analysis of depression represents a shift in the use of operant conditioning principles from treatment techniques toward its complementary use with clinical observations. The discussion of depression began:

> The first task in a behavioral analysis is to define behavior objectively, emphasizing functional (generic) classes of performances *consistent with the prevailing clinical facts,* the component behaviors of which can be observed, classified and counted. Then the basic behavioral processes can be applied to discover the kinds of circumstances that can increase and decrease the frequency of particular ways of acting. Finally, an objective account of the depression phenomenon can provide a framework for experiments that measure complex, *valid clinical* phenomena. An objective account of the functional relation between the patient's behavior and its consequences in the physical and social environment can *identify the effective parts of therapy* so that it can be applied more frequently and selectively [p. 85; emphasis added].

The same paradigm is represented by the description of the autistic child's repertoire and its development in the natural environment (Ferster, 1967a). Despite the large number of experiments attempting to develop therapies for enlarging the repertoire of autistic children that these early reports stimulated it is important to note that the early experiments—demonstrating the successful laboratory modification of an autistic child's repertoire with arbitrary reinforcers, such as food or tokens—were presented as tours de force. The behavioral repertoires developed in these children, although still not nearly as complex as those involved in a normal social repertoire, were used to indicate the existence of the normal processes at a basic level. The discussion of the experiment concluded:

> We do not consider these techniques as attempts at rehabilitation but rather as experimental analyses of the actual and potential repertoires of these children. If it proves possible to develop and widen behavioral repertoires significantly in the experimental room, then this would seem to indicate the possibility that the same potential for behavioral change would exist in the social milieu if the proper conditions could be generated [p. 97].

Recommendations for specific therapies are virtually absent in Skinner's publications, despite his general support for these modes of treatment. It is only in the field of education, one in which Skinner had firsthand experience, that he suggested specific methods of practice (Skinner, 1968). Otherwise, he wrote about systems of classification about existing practice, such as in *Science and Human Behavior.*

1. Operant Psychology's Emphasis on the Positively Reinforced Repertoire

An important contribution of operant conditioning to clinical therapy is the emphasis on the development and maintenance of a total repertoire. Partly, this emphasis appears to be a natural result of the instructional bias of operant approaches; partly it is a by-product of the experience with the fine-grain, technical control of behavior that was discussed earlier. The large emotional impact of *Walden Two* (1948) on so many of its readers appears to come from its promise that a whole society could reinforce positively so as to enhance the capability of all its members. Pavlov, Watson, Masserman, and Miller and Dollard were concerned, in their applications of laboratory research to human problems, with the disruptive effects of aversive experiences. But until Skinner opened the possibility of the technical study of positive reinforcement in the individual subject, there was little means of studying the shaping and maintenance of the underlying repertoire, whose disruption was the reason for the concern about the impact of aversive stimuli. Not only was there the possibility that some disruptions could be the result of a weak underlying repertoire, but the realization began to appear that many important repertoires might be absent because the individual never encountered the experience necessary for their development—essentially a lacuna of development. Although Hull dealt with this issue, mostly in his discussion of ''habit strength,'' the emphasis on inferred hypothetical constructs and experiments that tested hypotheses statistically without dealing directly with the behavioral processes of the individual weakened the impact of his work on clinical matters. Many of those for whom *Walden Two* became the vision of the new society that could be at hand if the principles of positive reinforcement were broadly applied to social problems had the experience of shaping the behavior of an individual pigeon and maintaining it strongly. They had the opportunity of observing firsthand, or through reading a cumulative record, knowledge of basic behavioral processes such as the studies of the *Behavior of Organisms* (Skinner, 1938) and by Estes (1944).

Operant psychology's emphasis on the ongoing repertoire as a product of a person's interaction with the social and physical environment has a parallel in the history of psychodynamic psychology. Freud's formulation emphasized the overriding disruption of major parts of a socially effective repertoire as a byproduct of the conflicts they engendered. Behavior therapy has the same thrust as Freud's early view when it seeks to remove the disruptive residues of past traumatic episodes. Later psychodynamic formulations of ego psychology (Hartmann, 1950) formulated a sphere of behavioral development that could proceed independently of the biological and instinctual drives and the conflicts they engendered. The formulations of the ego psychologists are consistent with the processes that emerge from interaction with the environment through the basic processes of positive reinforcement.

V. Technical Analysis of Behavior: A Way to Describe a Complex Therapeutic Interaction Objectively, Communicably, and in Detail

A major contribution of operant-conditioning principles is the precision that can be achieved in the description of ongoing natural events. If behavioral analysis is a complement to clinical practice, then it will need to contribute to the observation and description of clinical phenomena as they occur in the full complexity of the natural environment. Keehn and Webster (1969) made the same distinction when they differentiated between behavior therapy and behavior modification. They defined the task of behavioral analysis (modification) as a means of understanding how behavior is acquired and altered, and hence as applicable to the goals of psychodynamic as to behavioral therapy. An account by Ferster (1967b) describing the details of the interaction of a gifted therapist with an autistic child exemplifies how objective description at the level of a performance's proximal reinforcers contribute to the communicability and refinement of a therapy. It is important to emphasize that descriptions were of the fine grain of the performances of therapist and child and that the functional significance of the interaction consisted of a framework that complemented the objective account of the immediate events.

Consistent with such a collaborative effort, therapist and experimentalist contributed and gained advantages. The experimentalist learned ingenuous ways in which the therapist influenced the child. In addition to the functional analysis of the interactions with well-known behavioral principles, a content emerged that could only be discovered experientially, artfully, and serendipitously by patient and therapist shaping each other by the differential reinforcers of their respective repertoires. From the perspective of the therapist, the behavioral description of the therapy allowed the small component parts of it to be visible and communicable in detail. The therapist, describing the way that behavioral analysis influenced her work, reported that she could now explain little step-by-step procedures so that her therapy was less intuitive and mysterious. As a result, she was more aware of the detailed events that made her work with children effective, could refine it, make it more intensive, and teach others similar skills. Speaking of her experience with behavioral analysis she said: "And I am able to see the tiny little steps and explain much better what I am doing with the children so the magic is out of Linwood—which I think is wonderful [Ferster, 1967b, p. 149]."

VI. Arbitrary and Natural Reinforcement and the Generic Nature of Operant Behavior

The distinction between arbitrary and natural reinforcement (Ferster, 1967a, 1972a, 1974) concerns the generic definition of operant behavior (Skinner, 1938; Findley, 1962) and is a crucial concept for applying behavioral principles to the behavioral changes that occur in clinical practice. In brief, therapy procedures are arbitrary when the behaviors they reinforce are different operants than those in the patient's daily life about which the clinical problem exists.

The analysis of relatively simple instances of animal behavior illustrates the principle that an operant performance is a class of activities defined, not by topographic features, but by the alteration in the environment (reinforcer) that, in turn, increases its frequency. Thus, the sound of the food dispenser that operates when a rat presses a lever increases the frequency of those movements that displace the lever far enough to close the switch that energizes the food delivery mechanism. There is a natural connection between those of the rat's movements that will increase in frequency and the physical properties of the lever and the electrical switch that it closes. Because the reinforcer increases the frequency of those performances that it follows, it becomes possible to describe leverpressing as a kind of behavior that closes the switch, rather than by the topography of the movements. A similar relation between performance and reinforcer exists when we turn the steering wheel or press the brake pedal of an automobile. The topography of the movements of the hand and foot that are reinforced is determined by the change in the car's direction or its deceleration. The performance and its outcome are an integral behavioral unit, one in which each defines the other. The maintenance of such forms of behavior is virtually automatic and as stable as the natural relation between the performance and the change in the environment that supports it.

Examples abound of such performances reinforced by the natural physical connection to the change in the environment they produce. The movements required to ride a bicycle are reinforced by the changes they produce in the rider's balance with gravity; the movement of a screwdriver is shaped by its position in the slot of the screw; the initial movements of "putting on a coat" are reinforced by the position of the arm in the sleeve; the movements of the water pitcher are reinforced by the flow of water into the glass; the movements of the seal's neck and body are reinforced by the balance of the ball on the seal's nose; the magnitude of squinting or shading is controlled by the intensity of light falling on the eyes; and the movement of the pen on paper is reinforced by the shapes of the characters that appear and their correspondence with normal practices of the verbal community to which the person using the pen belongs. In all of these cases there is an exquisitely fine interplay between the performance and the change in the environment that is physically connected to it. The behavioral unit is stable and precise and is maintained for as long as the physical laws that are involved hold. The disruptive effects of mirror drawing, attempts to write blindfolded, and speaking without hearing the sounds, illustrate what happens without a natural, generic connection between performance and reinforcer.

The contrasts and alternatives to such generic reinforcements are virtually unthinkable. There is no practical way food reinforcement, even applied as a conditioned reinforcer preceding it, could shape the nuances of writing. It is hard to conceive of how the nuances of the movements of the vocal musculature could be reinforced other than by the fine-grain generic connection to the resulting auditory patterns. For this reason, most attempts at arbitrary reinforcement occur later in the behavioral chains of which these examples are only the first members. But the same properties of generic reinforcement operate even when these activities are the initial behaviors in a chain contributing to other practical effects or to social interactions. Consider, for example, the behavior of a child putting on a coat, reinforced by food. Clearly, food could be used to teach the child to put on his or her coat by using successive approximations of the complete act. The coat is held in the ready position and some conditioned reinforcer, derived from food, can reinforce the required approximations precisely. At this stage, the position of the child's hand in the sleeve of the coat can be a reinforcer in a chain of behaviors leading to food or tokens just as bar-pressing for the rat could be reinforced by watching the position of the lever and manually operating the food magazine when it moves the required distance. The problem is not whether one reinforcer or another can differentially reinforce the behavior of putting on a coat but of undesirable side effects and how much overlap there is between putting on a coat for food and putting it on to stay warm. Technically, both cases are chains of performances in which the first components are reinforced by the position of the coat on the child's limb. The second component is either the token, in the arbitrary case or the relief from the cold in the natural case.

A. NATURAL REINFORCEMENT

Figure 12.1 diagrams the way the repertoire of the child and therapist interact with each other when the reinforcement is natural. All of the reinforcers sustaining dressing are on the bottom part of the diagram. Putting on the coat is the initial member of a chain, the second part of which is a negative operant—avoidance of cold temperatures. The therapist's task is entirely instructional, providing collateral support that is diminished as the child takes over more of the dressing. At first, the therapist puts the coat on for the child, except for the last sleeve. He places the child's arm into the sleeve's entrance so that simply by extending his arm, the child completes dressing. With the coat on, the child can go outside without being cold. With successive approximations of the terminal repertoire, the therapist contributes progressively less until dressing occurs, unsupported, and the therapist's intervention is no longer required. The intervention is educational because the therapist does not actually reinforce the child's behavior but facilitates reinforcement that occurs when the child goes outside in the cold. He provides collateral support that amplifies the child's behavior to allow it to be reinforced naturally, elsewhere. In more general language, we

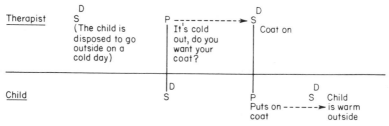

Figure 12.1. Natural control.

would say that the therapist facilitates behavior which, when it occurs, will be supported independently of him by the inherent relationships between cold air, skin temperature, and wearing a coat. Similar examples could be as readily constructed around the use of eating utensils, getting on and off a rocking horse, drinking from a cup, putting on shoes, or climbing stairs from one part of a house to another.

B. ARBITRARY REINFORCEMENT

Figure 12.2 is a diagram illustrating the arbitrary reinforcement of the same performances. Dressing is reinforced, in a chain, like the example of natural reinforcement presented earlier but with the difference that the final member of the chain is "eating cookies" rather than staying warm. In order to maintain the child's dressing activity, the therapist needs to continue to reinforce it with cookies in contrast with the natural case, where the therapist had only to provide collateral support to temporarily mediate its interaction with the cold weather.

C. THE SOCIAL ASPECTS OF THE THERAPEUTIC INTERACTION

The important complication of arbitrary reinforcement procedures comes from the social nature of the therapy interaction. Therapy is an interaction in which the reinforcement of the therapist's behavior by the performances that develop in the child's repertoire is as important a component as the child's performances reinforced by the contingencies or instructions arranged by the therapist. It is in these interactions, in which the therapist and child provide the reinforcers for each other's participation, that an analysis of the generic relation between the performances and their reinforcers may have large, practical importance for the outcome of therapy. The therapist's performances are reinforced because they induce the child to put on its coat. The child's performances with the coat are reinforced by the food or tokens that the therapist gives. Whether the child eats is not, of itself, important for the therapist; and whether the child puts on its coat is not, of itself, very important for the child. The therapist would stop giving food if the child dressed for other reasons, and the child would stop dressing if it received food without doing so.

One consequence of arbitrary interpersonal control, is a fine-grain, point-to-point correspondence of the child's performance with the reactivity of the

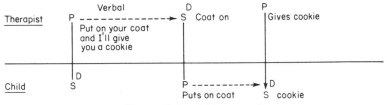

Figure 12.2. *Arbitrary control.*

therapist, rather than the stable effects that come from staying warm outside. While the development of an interactive repertoire between the child and others may be one of the most important objectives of psychotherapy, such interactions have inherent undesirable by-products that, in the long run, will be anti-therapeutic. The disadvantages of arbitrary control go beyond the absence of a generic connection between wearing a coat and the child's experience outside in the cold air that occurs when food is substituted for the warmth of the coat.

D. POWER STRUGGLE

One unfortunate by-product of arbitrary control is the countercontrol that can occur when the therapist attempts to increase the frequency of some behavior that the patient is not inclined to emit. The particular property of arbitrary reinforcement that leads to a struggle between the participants is highlighted in the diagrams of arbitrary interactions that was shown in Figure 12.2. The reinforcement of each participant's activity depends on the other. The child, whose accustomed ways of getting food have been disrupted, can tease or obstruct the therapist by withholding the therapist's reinforcer—compliance with the objectives of the reinforcement therapy. This property of the interaction is especially prominent and serious when the child, for other reasons, is inclined to act aggressively toward the therapist. The difficulty is even more serious because the aggressive activity the child directs to the therapist may of itself be an important issue for therapy. Such a conflict between child and therapist can escalate because the child can differentially reinforce extreme forms of control by withholding the behavior that the therapist is attempting to increase in frequency. When the therapist escalates the struggle by applying more restraint and deprivation, the child's aggressiveness will usually increase, in turn requiring more stringent levels of coervice control by the therapist. Eventually the interaction could be accurately described as a "struggle of wills." The result is parallel to the process that occurs when a child nags his parent, who differentially reinforces whining and nagging by complying with the child's demands, or by attending to him only when the demands become aversive enough to increase the frequency of a performance that will terminate or avoid the nagging. The primitiveness and paradox of these struggles is that the parent, intentionally or not, reinforces the very behavior of the child that is most aversive to him or her until extremes of aversive control are practiced by both parties.

Although such power struggles, as they are described clinically, are most prominent when they involve control by aversive stimuli, this feature is by no means the defining characteristic of arbitrary control. Aversive stimuli can increase the frequency of behavior generically and naturally as, for example, when we shade our eyes from the bright sun, hold our fingers in our ears to attenuate a loud noise, put on or take off clothes to be warm or cool, and pinch our nostrils to escape a noxious odor. The relation between these behaviors and the aversive control they attenuate is stable and totally predictable, in contrast to interpersonal control where one participant influences another's behavior with aversive stimuli to increase the frequency of some performance relevant to the reinforcement of his own repertoire. Conversely, events that nominally can function as positive reinforcers may be a component in arbitrary control, as for example, the uses of food discussed in the preceding sections, to reinforce dressing or speaking. These procedures have the characteristics of arbitrary control because the customary ways the child feeds are discontinued or blocked, thereby giving the therapist latitude to arrange whatever contingency between eating and performance he desires. It is the therapist's latitude, when he or she adjusts the reinforcement contingency for the purposes of creating the target repertoire the therapist seeks to develop, that leads to an adversary engagement in which each party can exert aversive control over the other. The repertoire that results, therefore, shifts from the ways that the child's normal environment feeds the child to one that comes from the reactivity of the particular therapist and the specific reinforcement procedure the therapist applies.

E. FOOD AS A NATURAL REINFORCER

Food, if it is generically related to the performance it reinforces, could also be a natural reinforcer. For example, if children are given some responsibility for preparing their meals, paced with the existing repertoire and in successive approximations of more complicated forms, the resulting behavioral development will be similar to the generic reinforcement of putting a coat on described previously.

F. ARBITRARY REINFORCEMENT AS A TRANSITION

It may be possible that arbitrary reinforcement in therapy could be used as a transition to the same topography reinforced naturally. Unfortunately, we have little clinical knowledge about the process by which the reinforcement of a topography of behavior maintained by one reinforcer contributes to its maintenance by an entirely different reinforcer elsewhere. We do know, however, that the problem is easily avoided by the use of the same behavioral principles with natural reinforcers. We have evidence that such reinforcers have the potential of maintaining behavior as durably as food, for example, in the experiments reported by Creed and Ferster (1972) and Ferster and Hammer (1966), without the serious side effects of arbitrary control.

The strategy for applying behavioral principles in natural settings is to begin with some behavior in the patient's repertoire and to provide collateral variables that will allow it to be reinforced in an environment to which the patient has normal access. Potential reinforcements for almost any kind of behavioral repertoire exist in some environment. It may be possible to build a repertoire by proceeding in small steps from a performance that is currently maintained in one part of the patient's environment to a slightly more complex one that could be reinforced in another part, also accessible (Ferster, 1979). The task is that of arranging collateral support for the patient's existing capability that can bring it to a form that can be naturally reinforced by a stable feature of the patient's ambience. In that case, the collateral support can be faded, paced with the patient's capability, until a repertoire emerges that will be reinforced without the therapist's intervention, Unfortunately, "inertial" aspects of many kinds of behavioral deficits complicate such a straightforward remedy (Ferster, in press), although the main principle still appears applicable.

G. TWO SENSES OF CONTROL

Implicit in the different properties of natural and arbitrary reinforcement are the two senses of control that reinforcement procedures convey. The one sense is pejorative, when the behaviors to be increased in frequency are for the benefit of the controller with less attention for the purposes of the controllee. The teacher deems that the pupils should be quiet in class; the ward attendant deems that the patients should keep their clothes clean; the behavior therapist deems that the mute patient should speak. The other sense, more consonant with natural reinforcement and the use of behavioral principles as a descriptive framework, elucidates the functional relation between the patient's conduct and the variables of which it is a function. For better or for worse, all of the patient's behavior is controlled. The main issues are whether a clear account of the control can be communicated and for whose benefit and for what reasons are the control exercised. Arbitrary reinforcement is not, of course, limited to behavioral therapy procedures.

The following account by Jeanne Simmons (Ferster, 1967a) concerns the use of natural reinforcement in psychotherapy from other points of view than behavioral therapies.

> And that's why we walk behind the child. He feels your protection when you walk behind. If you give him a chance to go any direction, he may be wrong when he goes this way or that. Just follow him. If it's a dead end, pick him up gently and bring him to a main route. But never think that you know the answer, because you are dealing with an individual who may want to go very different routes which for him may be better. That's why I feel more comfortable behind children so I can see where they are going [p. 346].

This statement about the goals of therapy accents the crucial importance of natural reinforcement, generically related to the child's existing repertoire even though the language is that of a clinician totally involved in personal interactions with the children. The statement of the goal of therapy implies that she begins with the existing behaviors in the child's repertoire, maintained by current reinforcers. The procedures describe collateral support of the child's repertoire by the therapist, which anticipates difficulties the child may encounter and encourages the most effective parts of the child's current capability (looking for health in the child, she might say). The same theme is a recurrent one elsewhere in the clinical literature (Searles, 1965; Glover, 1955; Rogers, 1965).

VII. The Fundamental Role of Verbal Behavior in Psychotherapy

Psychodynamic and other conventional therapies consist, avowedly, mostly of a patient's complaints about difficulties in life and a verbal interaction with the therapist about them. Most behavioral approaches also have a patient talking to a therapist, despite the theoretical framework that emphasizes observable behavior that is capable of objective enumeration. Behavioral approaches to self-control, delinquency, and sexual problems begin with reports from an interview about the patient's complaints and either talk about them, as in desensitization therapy, or instruction to the patient about what actions to take elsewhere. The observation that verbal interactions predominate both in diagnosis and therapy has large implications for how a science of human behavior can provide support for clinical treatment. The first step in such a venture is a behavioral account of how therapist and patient alter each other's behavior in the immediate context of their interaction. After that, the enterprise can turn to account for how the verbal behaviors that emerge as a product of therapy can ameliorate problems in the patient's daily life.

Since the starting point of a behavioral analysis is the immediate interaction between patient and therapist, it is useful to begin with a general review of how verbal reinforcement occurs before discussing the reinforcement of the patient's speech in the therapeutic interview. Verbal behavior, like simpler operant behavior, is defined by its reinforcer, rather than by the topographies of the performances. Its topography, the movements of the mouth, lips, tongue, and diaphragm is much too complex to be reinforced by anything other than its fine-grain relation to the sound it produces, in a manner analogous to the balance of the ball on the seal's nose or the rider on a bicycle. The reaction of the listener is the generic counterpart of speaking. In the sense of its finest grain and immediacy, verbal behavior is reinforced by "the speaker as his own listener," who bridges the reinforcing practices of the larger verbal community. The issues of arbitrary and natural reinforcement are even more crucial in verbal behavior than in nonverbal forms. Stably maintained properties of the therapist's repertoire provide the reactions that sustain and shape the patient's speech. Or, alternatively, the patient's speech reflects the control by past listeners, inductively. The parts of the two repertoires that engage each other represent a reinforcer that has a fine grain, equal to the therapist's sensitivity and training as a listener. Deficit in interpersonal control is an obvious behavioral objective that can be developed through the natural reinforcers inherent in the therapeutic interaction. The differential reactivity of the therapist as a trained listener has the potential of remedying those parts of the patient's speech that are more con-

trolled by his or her deprivation than by the circumstances when it can be reinforced. Particularly relevant for such differential reinforcement are the various
impractical expectations or unrealistic demands made on the therapist. Conversely, the reactions the patient evokes in the therapist are data about the patient's repertoire. The residue, in the therapist's repertoire, is also verbal. The
tight control between the speaker–listener, patient–therapist pair creates a situation in which the reinforcers are natural, in the sense that they are maintained
by stable properties of both repertoires.

A. CONFUSION BETWEEN THE EVENTS OF THE PATIENT'S LIFE
AND WHAT HE SAYS ABOUT THEM

If the verbal interaction between patient and therapist is observable and
behaviorally objective, the events talked about, those of the patient's life elsewhere, are inferences subject to distortion and incomplete descriptions, no matter how objective are the terms. If the description of ordinary events is subject to
distortion, then the patient's account of why he or she acts is even more in
doubt. There is often the loosest of correspondence, for example, between a patient's description of what led to a missed appointment or the reason why certain
topics are overlooked, and the independent variable that may be eventually uncovered. The failure to differentiate what is being talked about from the talk
itself is a serious technical difficulty which may occur in any verbal therapy, but
it is more visible in behavioral therapies than in others because behavioral
language amplifies the discrepancy.

One reason for the confusion between the events of the patient's life and the
talking that occurs in psychotherapy is that the verbal reinforcers are arbitrary in
respect to the behaviors talked about in the patient's daily life, and vice versa.
The generic counterpart of the patient's behavior in therapy are the influences
on the therapist who is listening and on the patient as his own listener. The
generic counterparts of the ongoing events of the patient's daily life are the day-
to-day occurrences there. Obviously what is said about the patient's life influences what the patient might do subsequently, and vice versa, but the connection is a repertoire that needs to be examined separately.

B. AN ANALYSIS OF THE BEHAVIORS OCCURRING
IN THE IMMEDIATE INTERACTION BETWEEN
PATIENT AND THERAPIST

The behavior that occurs in therapy is an objective datum in which most of
the activities and their reinforcers can, at least potentially, be observed by both
parties. Perhaps, because we are accustomed to searching beyond the immediate
events of the therapeutic interaction, its potentially objective and behavioral
nature is overlooked.

1. Initial Control of the Patient's Speech

When we say that a patient "talks to a therapist" the implication is that the
patient's speech is sustained by the way it influences him. When we say that

the therapist listens to the patient, the immediate events are the control of the therapist by the patient. Yet, to begin with, neither party has a history of control by the other. Clearly, the control over the patient is not at first entirely specific to that particular therapist. Otherwise, it would not be likely that a patient would talk at length, frequently with little comment by the therapist, during the first interview. Much of this behavior appears to function as a magic mand, such as "I wish it would stop raining," or "Gosh, I'm hungry," all generalized complaints which are extensions beyond the normal circumstances where there might be any realistic expectation that a normal listener could comply with relief (Skinner, 1957, Chap. 3). Such generalized complaints have a connection to past circumstances where similar succor had been forthcoming. The therapy situation, as well as the examples of magical mands that were mentioned before, are different from the usual situations where negatively reinforced operants occur. In these cases, the level of deprivation of the speaker–patient has exceeded the normal history of audience control so as to cause the emission of the complaint or request for relief despite the lack of history with this particular therapist. It is for this reason that first interviews are so technically difficult in psychotherapy.

The initial repertoire out of which the connection between the two parties is to emerge is a fantasy to which a listener could not conceivably comply with relief. Yet, it is this repertoire, the initial one, from which further behavioral development needs to emerge. An obvious quality of the patient's initial repertoire is its inertia. So much of it seems to be controlled by deprivation rather than by the audience which governs where and when it can be reinforced. A corollary of such a repertoire is the failure to observe in full detail and at some distance from personal deprivations, the characteristics of other persons in whose repertoires there are potential reinforcers. Repertoires with such inertial properties are reminiscent of the infant's feeding patterns, where the level of deprivation pre-empts all playful behavior and notice of any events other than feeding. Even complex forms of speech may be functionally equivalent to the infant feeding if the reinforcers maintaining it are closely controlled by high levels of the speaker's deprivation rather than by generalized reinforcement. An elegant turn of phrase or a poem could function as a complaint or demand, despite its complex topography. The therapist, as a trained listener who functionally analyzes the verbal interaction with the patient, is in a position to react differentially to the patient depending on the thrust of what is being said.

2. Reinforcement of Verbal Behavior by the Therapist–Listener

The change from generalized complaints to performances reinforced by their generic effect on the listener–therapist is, in itself, an exercise in the analysis of generic reinforcement. Even though complaints and requests for relief may require the participation of the therapist–listener, they function differently than the verbal interactions that can occur later in therapy when the immediate interaction with the therapist begins to sustain the patient's speech. The initial repertoire of the patient is relatively insensitive to the reaction of the therapist largely because it is a negatively reinforced operant, a *mand* is verbal jargon, largely under the control of the patient's deprivation and aversive stimulation. The final line by the therapist in *Portnoy's Complaint,* Philip Roth's novel about psychoanalysis, after virtually an entire novel of a soliloquy of complaints, "Now we can begin," illustrates the same shift in the functional control between the patient's speech and its relation to the therapist's repertoire. The change from generalized complaints to performances mediated by the therapist is an example of the refined definition of verbal behavior discussed earlier (Skinner, 1957, pp. 224–226) in which the form and characteristics of the speaker's (patient's) behavior are determined by the uniquely verbal reactivity of the listener (therapist). The analogy, from the example of the seal balancing the ball, is to the pressure on the nose as the reinforcer rather than the food. The refined definition of verbal behavior involves the immediate effect of the interaction between the two persons, such as occurs in the flash of an eye, the turning of the head, and how the content of a reply corresponds to the variables that control the patient's statement. The same process occurs, of course, with even more immediacy and fine grain when the speaker listens to himself.

To the extent that the interaction with the therapist is similar to that which occurs with others, it is an increment in social capability. The sheltered context of the therapeutic interview, particularly with respect to the collateral support provided by the therapist, can create a social capability that will overlap with other persons and situations. The behavioral events in the immediate therapeutic situation provide an opportunity for interpretation and description because they are an approximation of the kinds of observations that can be made elsewhere. Of equal clinical significance is the actual behavior of telling the events to the therapist. The patient's speech "to the therapist" has two simultaneous functions. First, it is a tact, usually quite distorted and impure, under the control of a current or childhood event (or any other past event the patient is talking about); perhaps it is even some intraverbal residue of the past event. Second, and more important, it is a performance whose form has been shaped by speakers whom the patient has influenced in the past. If the latent reactivity of the therapist is similar to those individuals who have maintained the patient's behavior in the past, the verbal episode will be successful and stable. To the extent that the therapist does not react in the same way as the patient's past listeners have, there is an opportunity, first, for differential reinforcement, and second, for observation of the discrepancy between the patient's behavior and reinforcement by the therapist.

When a patient is telling a therapist, for example, about his or her childhood, the effect that is generated in the therapist, as a listener, is a more important characteristic of the verbal behavior than of the event which it describes. The reinforcer in such a verbal episode is a subtle one, and it is at the heart of the definition of verbal reinforcement. The delicate interactions between two people that occurs when someone tries to explain something illustrates the process. There is give and take as the speakers and listeners play on each other until the listener says he understands and the speaker is no longer inclined to explain because the listener can now say what was being explained. Functionally, the patient's speech is primarily a performance reinforced by "making the therapist understand" and only secondarily a performance describing the patient's past life. The advantage of such a functional relation between therapist and patient, listener and speaker, is that the interaction reinforces (hence increases the frequency) of explanations and observation of the patient's life. The therapist's ability to make a functional analysis of the emitted behavior he or she is observing in the immediate situation and the therapist's interest in the patient's observations gives a unique advantage to the therapist's verbal reactivity.

3. Teaching the Patient to Observe His Own Behavior and to Describe Its Interaction with That of the Therapist

The immediate events of the psychotherapeutic interaction provide specific opportunities for the therapist, as a trained listener and observer, to prompt or reinforce the patient's verbal activities which are descriptive of his private and public experiences. When the therapeutic pair is a dyad in which the reactivity of one reinforces the activity of the other, one outcome is an increased verbal repertoire under the control of the immediate events that occur. The differential reaction of the therapist can reinforce descriptions of current happenings, talk about private events within the patient's own skin of which the patient may not be aware, the external variable of which such private events are a function and the behaviors of others that interact in the process. Although we talk, colloquially, about how the patient notices his or her own behavior, the reality, behaviorially, is the reverse because it is the differential reaction of the therapist that reinforces verbal behavior under the control of private events, the previously covert action and influences, and the variables controlling the patient's behavior. Such increased verbal activity emerges as tacts and intraverbal behavior under the control of the interactions between therapist and patient as they deal with the immediate events surrounding their common task. The therapist, as a trained listener who is making a functional analysis of the interaction between them, can bring the patient's attention to one aspect of behavior rather than to another. The control by the therapist of the patient is that of a generically defined performance, including the reinforcer of which it is a function, rather than the content, topography, or "surface meaning" of what the patient is saying.

One of the objectives of psychotherapy, distinguishing it from educational procedures, is to enable the patient to talk about covert processes by creating conditions by which he can observe otherwise unnoticed aspects of his conduct and their functional antecedents. Prolonged silences, conflicts over appointment or fee schedules, discrepancies between the patient's demands and a practical view of what kinds of help are possible, arriving late or missing appointments, for example, frequently occur because some current events are too aversive to talk about. Once the therapist becomes a listener whose attention is generically connected to the patient's speech, there is the possibility of a verbal repertoire that can allow the patient to observe the multiple determinants of the lateness or the silence and to talk about the variables of which it is a function. Discriminative control of human behavior is predominately verbal. In fact, much of the differential control of human behavior by the physical as well as the social environment can occur only verbally, particularly with those behaviors that are social and verbal.

Desensitization of the aversive control of verbal behavior is another potential product of any therapeutic interview or procedures where the patient's talk about difficult matters is paced with the ability to tolerate it. As was pointed out in the earlier section on behavior therapy, an increase in the amount of verbal activity will contribute to many other therapeutic functions.

C. HOW VERBAL BEHAVIOR WITH A TRAINED LISTENER
CAN INFLUENCE THE PATIENT'S LIFE ELSEWHERE

Since the behaviors that occur in therapy are different from the activities that occur elsewhere, a crucial task of a behavioral analysis is to describe the process by which the two repertoires influence each other. If there were not a large discrepancy between what actually happens to a patient in daily living and the patient's report of what happened, there would not, in all likelihood, be a problem of the sort that required therapy.

1. The Interpersonal Repertoire with the Therapist

The interaction between the two parties is in itself an increase in repertoire and a model, for better or worse, of what may happen between any two people. To the extent that the patient learns to influence the therapist, there are elements of repertoire that can influence other persons in other situations. To the extent that the patient can observe the details of the therapist's conduct, how he or she has influenced it and the reverse process, the patient has made progress toward the ability to make the same observations elsewhere. If a patient observes his own drowsiness or boredom and learns to search for provocative antecedents for this evidence of his anxiousness, there is a likelihood that he may be able to do a similar search at other times when he gets drowsy or bored. The therapist as a trained observer, who constantly is making functional analysis of the current events between them, is in a position analogous to the violin teacher who can help the student hear nuances of pitch that are at first audible to the teacher and not the student. The necessary condition, however, is that there is a significant disposition to play the violin so that the notes that are played that can be scrutinized.

2. The Verbal Repertoire from Psychotherapy Enhances Observation

The patient's ability to observe events in his or her life is intimately connected to the patient's ability to talk about them, just as touching something, point-to-point with the forefinger, like the beginning reader, brings behavior under a finer grain control of the component details than if the only movement was that of the eyeball and its focus. An educational advantage of a verbal repertoire, tacts and intraverbals, is that it allows discrete, point-to-point correspondence with the interpersonal items that emerge between them. Descriptions, if they can be extended from psychotherapy to daily life, will move the functional control of the patient's behavior from the covert to overt forms outside of the therapeutic situation.

3. A Verbal Repertoire Increases Positive Reinforcement and Decreases Aversive Control

There are large practical consequences to the presence or absence of a verbal repertoire that corresponds to one's own behavior, that of others, and the way that they control each other. Without such a repertoire, there is little possibility of reducing either the amount of aversive control or the amount of intermittent reinforcement and extinction. The process is analogous to a free shock in an animal experiment as compared with one preceded by a warning stimulus; or an uncertain occurrence of a positive reinforcer as compared with a clear event that cues when a performance can be reinforced. A verbal repertoire that corresponds closely to the conditions of reinforcement and punishment is an orderly, predictable view of events that maximizes the frequency of positive reinforcement and minimizes aversive control. When such a repertoire is absent, a corollary is the emotional by-products, related to extinction and intermittent reinforcement, that are described colloquially as loss, isolation, and hopelessness. The contrast between a daily life amplified by verbal behavior about it and an absence of such verbal amplification is the contrast between a world that is orderly and predictable and one that is capricious (Beck, 1967).

It is commonly observed, for example, that a patient interrupted during therapy by frequent telephone calls may not be able to talk about his or her complaints, either overtly or intraverbally. The persistence and magnitude of the annoyance may be so great, however, that it preempts almost all other kinds of interactions with the therapist, and the patient will talk about being bored, about having nothing to say, or about quitting therapy—or the patient may be late for the next appointment. If the patient can talk about his own reaction and its connection to the therapist's telephone activity, there is some possibility of seeing both behaviors clearly and of actively influencing the important events—the interruptions and the anger over them. The alternative is a confused mixture of three corners of the triangle: the patient's observation of the interruption, his or her annoyance at it, and a view of the therapist as a responsible person.

REFERENCES

Azrin, N. H. A strategy for applied research. Learning based but outcome oriented. *American Psychologist*, 1977, *32*, 140–149.

Beck, A. *Depression*. Philadelphia: Univ. of Pennsylvania Press, 1967.

Creed, T. L., & Ferster, C. B. Space as a reinforcer in a continuous free-operant environment. *Psychological Record*, 1972, *22*, 161–167.

Dollard, J., & Miller, N. *Personality and psychotherapy.* New York: McGraw-Hill, 1950.

Estes, W. K. An experimental study of punishment. *Psychological Monographs,* 1944, *57* (Whole No. 263), 40-107.

Eysenck, H. J. *The dynamics of anxiety and hysteria.* New York: Praeger, 1957.

Ferster, C. B. Arbitrary and natural reinforcement. *Psychological Record,* 1967, *17,* 341-347. (a)

Ferster, C. B. The transition from laboratory to clinic. *Psychological Record,* 1967, *17,* 145-150. (b)

Ferster, C. B. Clinical reinforcement. *Seminars in Psychology,* 1972, *4*(2), 000-000. (a)

Ferster, C. B. The experimental analysis of clincial phenomena. *Psychological Record,* 1972, *22,* 1-16. (b)

Ferster, C. B. The difference between behavioral and conventional psychology. *Journal of Nervous and Mental Diseases,* 1974, *159,* 153-157.

Ferster, C. B. A functional analysis of the verbal aspect of depression. In *Laboratory models of depression.* New York: Academic Press, in press.

Ferster, C. B. A laboratory model of psychotherapy. The boundary between clinical practice and experimental psychology. In P. O. Sjöden, S. Bates, & W. S. Dockens, III (Eds.), *Trends in behavior therapy.* New York: Academic Press, 1979.

Ferster, C. B., & Hammer, C. E. The synthesis of arithmetic behavior in chimpanzees. In W. K. Honig (Ed.), *Operant behavior: Areas of research and application.* New YorK: Appleton, 1966. Pp. 634-676.

Ferster, C. B., & Simmons, J. An evaluation of behavior therapy with children. *Psychological Record,* 1966, *16,* 65-71.

Ferster, C. B., Nurnberger, J., & Levitt, E. B. The control of eating. *Journal of Mathetics,* 1962, *1,* 87-110.

Ferster, C. B., & Skinner, B. F. *Schedules of reinforcement.* New York: Appleton, 1957.

Findley, J. An experimental outline for building and exploring multi-operant behavior repertoires. *Journal of the Experimental Analysis of Behavior,* 1962, *5,* 113-166.

Glover, E. *The technique of psychoanalysis.* London: Bailliere, Tindall and Cox, 1955.

Guthrie, E. R. *The psychology of learning.* New York: Harper, 1935.

Hartmann, H. Comments on the psychoanalytic theory of the ego. In Ruth S. Eissler *et al.* (Eds.), *Psychoanalytic study of the child* (Vol. 5). New York: International Universities Press, 1950.

Hull, C. L. *Principles of behavior.* New York: Appleton, 1943.

Keehn, J. D., & Webster, C. B. Behavior therapy and behavior modification. *The Canadian Psychologist,* 1969, *10,* 68-73.

Keller, F. S., & Schoenfeld, W. N. *Principles of psychology.* New York: Appleton, 1950.

Lewin, K. *Dynamic theory of personality.* New York: McGraw-Hill, 1935.

Mahoney, M. J. Reflections on the cognitive-learned trend in psychotherapy. *American Psychologist,* 1977, *32,* 5-13.

Masserman, J. M. *Behavior and neurosis.* Chicago: Univ. of Chicago Press, 1943.

Miller, N. E. Experimental studies in conflict. In J. McV. Hunt (Ed.), *Personality and the behavior disorders* (Vol. 1). New York: Ronald Press, 1944.

Miller, N. E., Dollard, J. *Social learning and imitation.* New Haven, Conn.: Yale Univ. Press, 1941.

Pavlov, I. P. *Conditioned reflexes.* London: Oxford Univ. Press, 1927.

Rogers, C. R. *Client-centered therapy.* Boston: Houghton-Mifflin, 1965.

Searles, H. Neutral therapist responses. In *Collected papers on schizophrenics and related subjects.* New York: International Universities, 1965.

Skinner, B. F. *The behavior of organisms.* New York: Appleton, 1938.

Skinner, B. F. *Walden two.* New York: Macmillan, 1948.

Skinner, B. F. *Science and human behavior.* New York: Macmillan, 1953.

Skinner, B. F. *Verbal behavior.* New York: Appleton, 1957.

Skinner, B. F. Teaching machines. *Science,* 1958, *128,* 969-977.

Skinner, B. F. *The technology of teaching.* New York: Appleton, 1968.

Solomon, R. L. An opponent-process theory of acquired motivation: The affective dynamics of addiction. In J. D. Maser & M. E. P. Seligman (Eds.), *Psychopathology: Experimental models.* San Francisco: Freeman, 1977. Pp. 66–103.

Tolman, E. C. *Purposive behavior in animals and men.* New York: Century, 1932.

Wachtel, P. *Psychoanalysis and behavior therapy.* New York: Basic Books, 1977.

Watson, J. B. *Psychology from the standpoint of a behaviorist.* Philadelphia: Lippincott, 1919.

Watson, J. B. *Behaviorism* (2nd ed.). New York: Norton, 1930.

Watson, R. *The great psychologists.* Philadelphia: Lippincott, 1968.

Wolpe, J. *Psychotherapy by reciprocal inhibition.* Palo Alto: Stanford Univ. Press, 1958.

F. L. MARCUSE

J. J. PEAR

Ethics and Animal Experimentation: Personal Views[1]

13

I. Introduction

We as authors of this chapter, while differing in theoretical orientation, think of ourselves as humanists and in our various "give and take" discussions of the varied points posed in this chapter have found that similarities outweigh differences. Although one of us (J. J. Pear) is a radical behaviorist, he does not see this as incompatible with humanism; in fact, he believes that a behavioristic analysis provides the only sound basis for *effective* humanism (Skinner, 1978). The other (F. L. Marcuse) stressing the fact that this is 1979 not 7919 would simply say that he is a multiple determinist. This, however, is not in any way to deny that there were some unresolved controversies about the meaning of certain concepts, some dispute about usage of words—as indicated, such points were settled by compromise or by "slugging it out"—in short, there were emendations. Neither of us claims to be a moral messiah, but both of us would agree with the sentiment expressed by G. B. Shaw when he said that some people saw things as they were and asked why, but that he saw things as they could be and asked why not.[2]

A possible criticism the reader may make is that what we say here repre-

[1] Preparation of this chapter was supported by Grant No. A7461 from the Natural Sciences and Engineering Research Council of Canada to J. J. Pear.

[2] The authors, however, differ sharply with his views against vivisection.

PSYCHOPATHOLOGY IN ANIMALS
Research and Clinical Implications

sents only a "playing around with words" or only stating tautologies. To this our plea is only "half-guilty." While one of us (F. L. Marcuse) has contributed to the semantic journal, *Etc.*, he does not consider himself a semanticist; rather he thinks of words as representing *a* but not *the* factor contributing to, or standing in the way of, fuller understanding of the concept under discussion. Too often the definition of ethics is "that which is moral," whereas morality is defined as that which is ethical. This is similar to defining pornography as that which is obscene and turning around and saying that the obscene is that which is pornographic; obviously more than circular reasoning is required.

Inasmuch as this chapter is rather unusual, representing as it does a collaboration between a radical behaviorist and an eclectic humanist, let us begin with a conclusion; namely, that animal research is not only desirable but is ethically mandatory. We differ somewhat in the probable benefits foreseen from animal research, but we both agree that present-day knowledge of the factors producing human suffering (physical, psychological, and social), and how it may be alleviated, is so limited that if animal research has even the vaguest possibility of contributing to the human field, it should be done.

II. On Values

It was once widely believed by Western philosophers that there were two orders of law in the universe: natural law and moral law. Both could be discovered largely or entirely through reason. With the recognition that reason by itself (logic and mathematics) can establish only tautologies, the emphasis in efforts to comprehend natural law shifted to scientific experimentation. The field of ethics was seen as being distinct from science, and a strict dichotomy was drawn between reality statements and value statements (Hume, 1958, Book 3, pp. 456–468). This view, which is now the traditional view, is succinctly summarized in the modern cliché that science can tell us how to make a bomb, but not whether we should make one.

Skinner (1953, 1971) has challenged this traditional view of ethics. In systematically developing the social implications of his behavioral theory, he indicated that a valid objective ethics can be established by means of a scientific analysis of values. (A remarkably similar position has been formulated by the philosopher Stephen C. Pepper, 1958, 1960; for other related viewpoints see Handy, 1969.) The purpose of this section is to briefly explore the implications of this approach for the use and treatment of animals in research.

To begin to develop an objective ethics, we start by asking not what our values should be, but rather why do we have ethical values at all? The answer is that we are conditioned by our social environment to make ethical statements and to engage in corresponding ethical behaviors. This is not to deny that certain genetic predispositions may play an important role in the establishment of ethical behavior. Whatever our genetic predispositions are, however, strong sup-

t some point in the
begin actively work-
most radical revolu-
strive to bring about
heir behavior reper-
s they help to bring
culture will survive,

s to specific types of
ved partly because it
t accordingly. If this
essentially the same
would give for the
, due to variations in
oned in the same way
izing is sufficient to
ls of their culture. As
lest answer to some-
survival of his or her
ncerned, but if your
rse for your culture

alues "should" be in
h in practice the task
les ultimately will be
Anyone who accepts
o concede the provi-
he or she might ad-
value the survival of
provide a basis for
e culture is the value

e values of a particular
alues of that culture be if
Skinner (1953) states

the long-term effect
if the culture is to
le group which does
the point of view of
the survival value of
nonstrating the con-
that such a science
The current culture
e, that in which the

sary to fully establish and main-
e no distinction between ethical
ginates in the conflict between
it. Accordingly, ethical training
r in children that is immediately
dults and reinforce behavior in
nforcement but is reinforcing to
bel behavior that is punished by
that is reinforced by adults as
s discriminative stimuli control-
his conditioning are maintained
ng throughout the lifetime of the
social reinforcers and punishers
d.

seems to play an important role
behavior. Because of having ex-
others similarly hurt or injured
experienced reinforcement our-
be reinforcing to us. But such
reinforcements require strong
s operating in the environment.
on to being socially punished, be
that to you." The golden rule is
cilitate generalizing one's own

what accounts for the relevant
ition of human cultures—a pro-
ies. As some traits are more con-
of a species, similarly, some
rs to the existence of a culture.
of a culture are: (a) its ability to
ssive internal competition and
strength of its members; (c) its
tract new members; (d) its abili-
to induce its members to work

in which a culture induces its
al. It would be difficult to argue
culture is the one that is optimal
gue that the physiological struc-
al to its survival. In both cases,
ocess.
e more advantageous mutations
s manner a culture may acquire

new practices that more effectively promote its survival. /
cultural evolutionary process, some members of the culture
ing to bring about improvements in its practices. Even the
tionaries are products of their culture, and the changes they
stem from ethical principles their culture has implanted in
toires. If they are successful and if on balance the change
about are indeed improvements, the probability that their
and with it the new practices, will have been increased.

Thus, the reason we respond with specific moral labe
behavior is that we are members of a culture that has survi
has conditioned its members to apply such labels and to a
explanation seems circular, it is well to remember that it i
type of explanation that specialists in biological evolutio
specific physiological structure of a given species. Of course
social conditioning, not everyone has been ethically conditi
or to the same degree. Probably no amount of philosoph
change those whose behavior is "unethical" by the standar
Skinner (1971) pointed out, there seems to be only one ho
one who asks why he or she should be concerned about the
culture: "There is no good reason why you should be co
culture has not convinced you there is, so much the wc
[p. 137]."

A scientific analysis of values cannot tell us what our v
any absolute sense. What in principle it can tell us, althou
will be immensely difficult and complex, is what sets of val
incorporated by our culture or some superseding culture.
the validity of this analysis would, at the very least, have
sional or transitory nature of any alternative set of values
vocate. For those who have already been conditioned to
their particular culture, a scientific analysis of values ca
moral or ethical behavior. In any event, the survival of th
from which all other values will ultimately follow.

From this point of view, the question *What should t*
culture be? can be meaningfully translated into *What will the*
it survives? Thus, concerning the issue of cultural design,
that the question of

> "Who should control?" is a spurious question. . . . If we look a
> upon the group, the question becomes, "Who should control
> survive?" But this is equivalent to asking, "Who *will* control in
> survive?" . . . In the long run, . . . the most effective control fror
> survival will probably be based upon the most reliable estimates o
> cultural practices. Since a science of behavior is concerned with de
> sequences of cultural practices, we have some reason for believin
> will be an essential mark of the culture or cultures which survive
> which, on this score alone, is most likely to survive is, therefo

methods of science are most effectively applied to the problems of human behavior [p. 446].

Just as such a science eventually will tell us who should control, it will also be able to tell us what our other values should be if our culture is to continue to evolve. What values will prevail in a highly evolved culture? Undoubtedly, we would like to think that the values civilization ultimately endorses will be very similar to our present values. There is no guarantee, however, that this will be the case. History contains a record of values various cultures once held to be supreme, but which are now viewed as irrelevant, passé, misguided, or immoral. However, *concern for the well-being of other humans* seems to be one value that is especially important to the survival of a culture. Its long endurance, at least as an ideal stressed in moral writings since antiquity, attests to its strong survival value.

Desire for acquiring knowledge is another value that is likely to be endorsed by a highly evolved culture. Knowledge has strong survival value because of the control it affords over the environment. "Knowledge for its own sake" is often expressed as a value, but this merely reflects the fact that, since all the contingencies in the environment are interrelated, all knowledge is potentially useful. In the final analysis, immediacy of application is the main distinction between practical and purely theoretical knowledge. By endorsing knowledge for its own sake a culture is simply taking care of its long-range interests as well as its short-range interests. Thus, scientific knowledge is among the most highly valued types of knowledge in our culture.

The acquisition of scientific knowledge was profoundly enhanced by the advent of the experimental method, which was, therefore, a cultural innovation possessing great survival value. Once the experimental method had taken hold in the physical sciences and thereby contributed to the development of physical technology, it was by relatively short steps that it then came into its own in the biological sciences and, finally, in the behavioral sciences. Perhaps it is too early to say for certain, but on the basis of the available data—such as described in the previous chapters—the use of the experimental method in the behavioral field is likely to be as important to the culture as it has been in the physical and biological fields.

The two values just mentioned—concern for others and desire for knowledge—sometimes come into conflict when the use of the experimental method to obtain knowledge about humans is contemplated. In such cases, the priority of values in our culture is quite clear: No experiment may be done that might harm a member of our species. The appropriateness of this priority seems obvious, since the mistreatment of any person is a potential threat to other people and, hence, to the culture. It is generally accepted, however, that any type of potentially informative experiment may be performed on a nonhuman animal.

Thus we come to the topic of animal experimentation. What do the ethics we have outlined imply about the prospects of the prevalent morality regarding our right to experiment on nonhuman animals? And what moral considerations, if any, are implied regarding the treatment of the subjects of such experiments?

Recently, the issue of "animal rights" or "animal liberation" has been receiving increasing attention in the general press (e.g., Gwynne & Begley, 1978) and in philosophical (e.g., Fox, 1978; Singer, 1975) and scientific (e.g., Keehn, 1977; Wade, 1976, 1978a, b) writings. Following the example of those who champion the rights of oppressed groups within the culture, various individuals and groups are challenging the morality of exploiting animals for research and other human purposes. For example, some writers have attacked "speciesism," which is defined as "a prejudice or attitude of bias toward the interests of members of one's own species and against those of members of other species."

In considering the issue of animal rights, it is important to note that rights are not intrinsic to any individual or group whatever its species. Rights are culturally defined, and the process by which a particular group achieves specific rights within a culture usually involves direct participation by the members of that group acting in an organized manner. There is, however, no meaningful sense in which animals can participate in such a process. Although animals have advocates within the culture, advocates of science have cogent arguments they can use to make other members of the culture aware of the benefits the culture can gain from animal experimentation. These arguments, in effect, relate to the survival value of a particularly cultural practice—namely, that of animal experimentation—and, therefore, to the likelihood that the culture that endorses that practice will survive in the long run.

Of course, the ability to participate in the culture is not the only basis for according significant rights to an individual or group. For example, it is obvious that human infants, even though lacking the ability to participate fully in the culture, are very important to its survival—which is why it is considered highly moral for adults to undergo extreme risk and hardship to protect and care for them.

But what about those humans who, due to genetic defects or physical injury, can never attain the level of verbal and other behavioral development necessary to participate fully in the culture? There are a number of factors that would seem to ensure that a highly evolved culture would accord these people moral rights (including the right not to be subjected to harmful or aversive experimentation) comparable to the moral rights it grants to other members of the culture. First, not to do so would threaten other members of the culture, since the acceptance of criteria for denying moral rights to some humans sets a dangerous precedent for expanding the criteria to include increasing numbers of people. Second, many people with severely limited behavioral development have close relatives who are intimately concerned with their welfare and who are capable of taking social action to secure moral treatment for them. Third, many people with severely limited verbal development establish close personal (i.e., uniquely human) relations with normally functioning people, who, therefore, also act to secure moral treatment for them.

Although according significant moral rights to animals appears not to have survival value for the culture, this does not imply that concern for their welfare will have no place in a highly evolved culture. On the contrary, it can be expected to be an important feature of it for at least two reasons. First, conserving the wide variety of species that inhabit our planet is important to the culture. Species are interrelated, and a drastic decrease in the numbers of one often adversely affects others, including our own. The presence of a large variety of species on our planet is also esthetically reinforcing to many people, perhaps at least partly because our species evolved in an environment that was rich in life forms. And, of course, the availability of a large variety of species to observe and study is useful for instructional and scientific purposes. Second, many of the similarities that permit us to generalize experimental results with animals to humans argue for giving members of many species the best treatment that is compatible with other considerations regarding the good of the culture. Children are taught as part of their ethical training to be kind to animals, one possible reason being that behavior toward animals tends to generalize to humans. People to whom the mistreatment of animals is not aversive may tend not to find the mistreatment of humans aversive.

In this context, perhaps it is not surprising that as the rights of various disadvantaged groups receive increasing emphasis in our culture, our treatment of nonhuman animals is also seen to be an important ethical issue. Although one might well question the motivation of those who devote much time and energy to advocating animal rights rather than concentrating their efforts on bringing about better treatment for humans, the two issues (namely, treatment of animals and humans) are not separate. Yet there is a value conflict within the culture that must be resolved if the biological and behavioral sciences are to benefit humanity to the greatest possible extent.

Behavioral science will likely be an important factor in resolving this conflict. Presumably, behavioral science will tell us, in time, precisely how values originate, how they interact, and how they relate to the survival of the culture. If the strong contribution of animal research to behavioral science thus far is any indication, we can confidently predict that animal research will be an important part of this process of resolving ethical questions.

III. On Priorities

If, as has been indicated, values can be objectified because over time they are a function of survival possibilities, then this would allow for their being ordered. The issue that is then involved becomes straightforward. Simply put, it is as follows: *Should the good and well-being of humans be placed over that of animals?*

The answer of most people (at least in our culture) is definitely yes. To certain others, to whom humans and nonhumans (animals) "are all God's creatures" the answer, at least implicitly, is no; and to still others, who are not familiar with the problem, it remains to show the advantages as well as the disadvantages of experimenting with animals. At this point the reader may observe somewhat of a logical non sequitur, for some individuals will put the needs of humans over those of animals, but will at the same time, maintain that we are all equal in God's sight. Should this not then lead to equal treatment!? Pitfalls and the like that may be present in animal investigation do not constitute a reason for not using animals, but rather they are merely a reason for increased experimental caution.

It often seems quite ironical and meaningless to even pose the question of ethical responsibility to individuals who may at that very time be involved in creating (geneticists), perpetuating (social workers), or destroying (military), human life itself for they have already taken positions expressing the values inherent in such actions! The issue here is whether such values and their priorities that are present are recognized or expressed verbally, for often the problem is disguised. A case in point may be seen in the following. A psychologist (Corsini) who at the time was working in the prison system tells of the warden who professed no theoretical bias whatever, but who referred to a prisoner as a "no good rat who was born that way." Or consider the president of an American university who had been asked to state the university's position vis-à-vis the United States involvement in the war in Vietnam. His reply to this question was to say that the university had to maintain its objectivity and could not afford to "take sides." The university in question was not only training officers at that time for this "brush war" but it had also accepted contacts that involved research which would lead to the possibility of discovering a more efficient defoliant! In effect, the decision, be it witting or unwitting, to make no value judgments is, in itself, a value judgment.

This lack of recognition of such evaluations is especially likely when these values are in support of the status quo. The issue of values and their priorities is explicitly expressed by a recent president of the American Psychological Association who said that if psychology is to survive "it is important that it throw its resources into the effort to terminate the war [in Vietnam], to control population, and to combat racism [Albee, 1970]." Sabine, the political economist (1937), suggested that the claim to neutrality in values was at best a myth.

One should also remember that psychology is widely regarded as a means of "contributing to human welfare [e.g., Washington State Psychological Association, 1967]." Some psychologists would question whether this contribution is being implemented; otherwise, they ask, why the autonomous appearance of an association concerned with advancing the role of the black psychologist in the United States? Other psychologists state that by accepting values one is surrendering a "tough, hardheaded" scientific approach, but one wonders whether in reality this does not represent acquiescing to a thick-headed approach (Marcuse, 1977).

It is of interest to note that within the past few years a group of operant behaviorists, feeling that pragmatism alone is not sufficient, have raised the question of directionality (Behaviorists for Social Action, 1977). In short, they are concerned that their procedures are often used to support those very institutions whose existence or practices they question. In their statement of purpose they proclaim: "We resist the application of science and technology, including behavioral science, when used to worsen social injustices. We do however defend the operant analysis of behavior against undue attack."[3]

IV. On Advantages and Disadvantages

If we are to raise the question of ethics of working with animals, we, as indicated, had first better answer the question: Why use animals in the first place? That is, what are the advantages and disadvantages of doing so? A few of these positive and negative features follow: Animals obviously have a much simpler life space. As a reductio ad absurdum, we do not select, or ask the animal caretaker for, 10 Protestant pigeons, or 20 Republican rats, or 30 anxious ants. Such characteristics may be of importance in human investigation; however, there is an advantage in studying simpler systems before studying more complex ones. Moreover, animals usually have a shorter life span and this, to the scientist interested in the genetic transmission of certain behaviors, may be of importance if one is to obtain results in one's lifetime. There is also the fact that one can control the animal's environment more easily than that of the human. We can dictate how many other animals are to be present, the degree of heat, the intensity of light, the quantity of food that is to be available, and so on. In addition to the possibility of greater environmental control, there is also the fact that one can use larger numbers when one uses animals as compared to humans. Most important is the fact that one can use animals for critical experiments. Thus, to mention but two examples, animals may be used for surgery or for the induction of abnormal behavior (elaborated on in a later section). There may also be disadvantages and these essentially stem from the simple fact that animals are not humans. One such difficulty is the question of anthropomorphism, the tendency to see in the behavior of animals, via projection, reasons for acts which would generally be true in humans (e.g., a cat licks itself "to keep clean"). This problem is especially obvious when the lower phyla are under consideration. For example, an amoeba extending a pseudopod for "more" food is not like Oliver

---

[3] This issue of priorities in values was very clearly pointed out by the United Nations Disarmament Action Group (Calgary) when, in a brochure they said "It'll be a great day when our schools get all the money they need and the airforce has to hold a bake sale to buy a bomber."

Twist asking for more soup! There is also the unfortunate fact that there is a tendency to generalize from single outstanding cases of animal behavior. Finally, there is the ignoring of the law of parsimony in interpreting the why of animal behavior. This last violation is seen most clearly in the failure of the experimenter to recognize the presence of minimal cues. This was best illustrated in the celebrated case of the "educated" horse—Clever Hans. On balance, although we have not weighed them all, advantages far outweigh disadvantages; and, as has been indicated, it may even be questioned whether or not such disadvantages are not in reality merely experimental precautions.

V. On Vivisection

Etymologically, the word *vivisection* connotes experimental surgical intervention, whereas its antonym, *antivivisectionism,* has taken on a broader meaning. It represents the objection to most kinds of animal experimentation.

Antivivisectionists, while small in number, appear to have many contacts with the news media and governmental committees. In their portrayal of the vivisectionist at work one can usually count on (a) that he or she will be "fiendishly" operating; (b) that the experimental subject will be a household pet; (c) that the experimenter, in addition to being described as "amoral," "vicious," and "sadistic," will be shown as burly; and (d) that the helpless animal's eyes will be rolled heavenward. There are many facets under which the topic of vivisectionism and antivivisectionism can be discussed, but for the purposes of this chapter we will restrict ourselves to commenting on: medical history, baby harp seals, sexuality in cats, the "Baboon Seven," head-on car collisions, and the question of misuse.

The antivivisectionist's stance often shows a woeful ignorance of medical history. This was succinctly shown in capsule form by the tongue-in-cheek oath that Carlson, the physiologist, would have antivivisectionists take. He would have them foreswear the use of any drug that had first been tested on animals for purity and side effects, he would have them shun any operative procedure that had been standardized on animals, he would have them refuse to take insulin for diabetes, etc. (an example, subsequent to Carlson's pledge, would be the coronary bypass which has already helped innumerable human beings and was pioneered on animals). The last item in Carlson's pledge is "I will make out my will immediately!"

Often, objections to exploitation of animals for human purposes appear to be based on emotionalism with very little rational support. Objection of an active nature has been made in recent years about the annual killing of baby harp seals. With their big brown eyes, white fur, cuddly nature, and general appearance, these animals represent "innocence incarnate." It is ironic that some of the most vehement protest is made by perfume-scented, fur-wearing, leather-shod, meat-eating, wallet-bearing, lard-using, purse-adorned, belt-wearing individuals. It should be realized that by the hunt thousands of individuals supplement an income (rather meager at that) in this way. Harp seals are not an endangered species; indeed, they need to be thinned out because of their overabundance. It should also be remembered that the minister of the Canadian Department of Fisheries, besides making the above points, has defended the use of the club in terms of its resulting in instantaneous death and not injuring the pelt. Seal hunting is neither a luxury trade nor a sport, rather it is a livelihood. The height of irony regarding the "murder" of baby seals happened to one of the writers (F. L. M.) in 1970 when he was living in the United States. He was asked to sign a petition requesting the Canadian government to cease and desist from this inhumane practice. It so happened that at this very time the United States was using napalm to reduce the Vietnamese population! Priorities and values obviously come into play. What if baby seals were spiny-skinned, pink-eyed, skunk-smelling, green-furred animals, loathsome in all human respects—would there have been the resultant hue and outcry anymore than in the slaughter of cows for meat, the preparation of pigs for bacon, or the forced feeding of geese for our tables?

More recently (Wade, 1976) the prestigious American Museum of Natural History came under attack by antivivisectionists when it was revealed that its researchers had been studying sexuality in the cat. Opposition to this investigation took the form of demonstrations, picketing, letter-writing campaigns, attempts to eliminate the museum's funding, and so on. The museum had three strikes against it: Cats are household pets, sex is still, to many, a rather dubious area for research, and operations were performed on the cats. Specifics of the criticisms involved cruel and unusual procedures by insensitive investigators, etc. The experimentation, said the antivivisectionists, was ethically unacceptable and furthermore, the knowledge that it has generated to date was said to be nonexistent, or at best very trivial. The statement was also made that the investigation was "Nazi-like." To all these various charges one could and should say the following: The animals were well provided for (see Section VIII), and it is not clear exactly what "cruel and unusual experimental manipulation" meant, given that operations such as castration on household pets are not uncommon in our society. Furthermore, the fact is seldom mentioned, or if it is it is minimized, that such experimentation may throw some light on an ambiguous human condition. Granted that there are experimental projects involving animals which turn out to be valueless, one must still be on guard against post hoc reasoning. It is difficult to measure the contributions of any given investigation or to know them in advance. As to the statement that such research is "Nazi-like" it only befuddles the issue by equating humans and nonhumans.

The case of the "Baboon Seven" involved strong protest against some research with baboons who were being used at different universities in the United States to study the physiological effects of head-on car collisions—a leading cause of death for humans under the age of 45. The investigation involved strapping the animals to impact sleds that were then hurled at a high speed into barriers.

The animals had been anesthetized before the crash, were medically examined after the crash, and then put to death before regaining consciousness. The antivivisectionists were apparently successful in having this potentially valuable research stopped. Ironically enough, one of the goals of this investigation was how to avoid the future use of animals as research subjects.

Antivivisectionists sometimes assert that animals should not be "made to pay" for human "sins." People have car accidents because of human "foolishness." People smoke too much and get lung cancer because they lack "willpower." But we live in a deterministic world, and the concept of "retribution" is not appropriate. Human life is more important to the culture than animal life is, regardless of the conditions that cause humans to engage in behavior that is dangerous to themselves.

Vivisectionists believe that something of value for humans may be learned by working with animals. Such investigation may take the form of drug-testing, developing new operative procedures, induction of "experimental neuroses," research into the role of certain cortical areas, the purposeful creation of phobias, investigation of certain hormonal or vitamin deficiencies, and so on. In short, vivisectionism encompases both physiological and psychological processes as well as their interaction. It hopes that it may find something of value that may add to understanding both normal and abnormal behavior in animals and humans.

Every year or so one hears about some antivivisection bill that was only narrowly defeated. Furthermore, it should be realized that the very consideration of such bills, even when defeated, takes up the time of the researcher when he or she is required to testify, often in a distant city, as to just why the particular investigation is being carried out, etc. Sometimes it is said that the issue is passé—would it were so!

In certain instances the shoe may even be on the other foot. Thus, for example, Gifford-Jones (1978), a physician, in discussing death, agony, and the administration of strong pain-killers in terminal cancer in humans makes the following pointed comment: "How can society be so kind to animals in pain yet so immensely cruel and insensitive to human agony."

It is entirely conceivable, however, that animals may sometimes be used unnecessarily or inappropriately for experimental purposes. For example, what about putting irritating substances in the eyes of animals to test for the possible harmful effects of yet another "new improved" shampoo or similar product? Who needs it? Along the same lines, Shapiro (1978) asks: What about the use of animals in testing out a drug which may lessen respiratory problems that beset members of a minority group, when all along it is known that poor sanitation is important in the etiology of such diseases? It might well be said in this instance that if there is no attempt to correct the problem of sanitation, the use of animals is highly dubious. Again, what if animals are expended in testing out the destructive efficacy of the neutron bomb? Here the use of test animals is at best a secondary issue and the objection should be to the idea of the use of this bomb in the first place—obviously values and their priorities come into play. With regard to these and similar questions, however, misuse is not a satisfactory reason for disuse.

VI. On Generalizing

Over 110 years ago Claude Bernard (1865/1957) made the following points:

1. While experimentation on animals admittedly is more applicable to animals than to humans, "moral law" prohibits experimentation on the latter.
2. Research on all kinds of animals is "indispensable," for different species of animals have different potential pathologies.
3. Certain kinds of experiments demand certain kinds of animals because of different species' special characteristics and susceptibilities.
4. Without a comparative study of animal reactions, "practical" medicine can never be scientific.

These are all points which today are still relevant to those who are concerned with the ethics of animal experimentation. Point 2 may be observed in the different kinds of animals studied in many different research settings. Bernard's statement in point 3 is illustrated for example, in the selection of rats to study quasi-epileptic reactions. While at first higher phyla might seem to be more desirable, they do not show this particular motor reaction. Bernard's first and fourth points represent, in part, the justification of animal experimentation encountered today. With proper precautions, Bernard concluded, generalizations are almost limitless. It should be noted that although he said this, Bernard in no way ignored the differences that exist between humans and animals. Where Bernard speaks of "vital units" (i.e., physiological units), Schnierla (1948), for one, talks of both physiological and psychological levels. This latter concept is defined in Warren's *Psychological Dictionary* (1934) as "the general field or background in which a quality appears." By levels we refer to the different stages in the evolutionary process from the one-celled to the many-celled, from the amoeba to the human. Emphasis on differences alone leads unfortunately to a speculative philosophy which regards humans as unique entities. According to Bernard, higher species differ from lower ones in possessing a greater number of distinct vital units; that is, they are more complex (p. 124). This emphasis on both similarities and differences allows for viewing behavior throughout the phylogenetic scale with some continuity.

One obviously important practical use of animals is in the evaluation of drugs. Here, as in other areas concerned with direct application to humans, the question immediately arises as to what kind of animal should be used. The dictum that can be followed, allowing for the nature of the investigation, is that the greater the resemblance, at least physiologically, to humans the more meaningful and, hence, the more ethical the generalization. At present, unfortunately, one suspects that such extraneous considerations as the cost of maintaining animals (e.g., a rat colony as compared to a chimpanzee colony) are adjudged. In addition, it may be recalled that it was not too long ago that thalidomide (a tranquilizer) was prescribed for pregnant women. This drug had disastrous consequences. It was then revealed that the drug had not been tested on pregnant animals. Had this feature been allowed for, generalization would have been more meaningful and much human suffering avoided (Sjöström & Nilsson, 1972). One cannot help but think that financial considerations (which turned out not to be advantageous) were being placed ahead of human values. It may be naive to expect a private institution to manifest social responsibility.

VII. On Disturbed Behavior

The investigator of animal behavior concerned with the propriety of inducing disturbed animal behavior is immediately confronted with the issue of terminology. Just what is meant when a researcher refers to: experimental neuroses (Liddell, 1947); tantrum behavior (Marcuse, 1944); "freezing" (Riess, 1946); audiogenic seizure (Cook, 1939b; Maier & Longhurst, 1947); tonic immobility (Lindsley, Finger, & Henry, 1942); myotonia congenita (Kolb, 1938); animal hypnosis (Gilman & Marcuse, 1949); and so on. Are the symptoms that are described acute or chronic? Is a given phylogenic level presupposed in the use of these terms? For example, phobias in the dog and chimpanzee are somewhat understandable, but this is certainly not too clear when we talk about phobias in the cockroach! These are questions which animal investigators concerned with the ethical implications of what is being done have to anwer. In short, he or she is faced with dubious definitions and discrepant data, that is, a sea of semantics. To satisfy antivivisectionist objections, he or she would also have to ascertain whether the behavior in question was experimentally produced (on purpose) or resulted from "an act of God" (not purposely produced), for example, a flood.

What are some of the characteristics of these various disturbances? They may be: loss of gregariousness, presence of tics, absence of previously acquired discriminating ability, hyperpnea, tachycardia, upset of nocturnal motor activity ("insomnia" as shown by kymographic recordings), apnea, agitation, stiff-legged conditioned response, motor paralysis, inappropriate ejaculation of semen, inhibition of salivary flow, plasticity, loss of weight, death, etc. Admittedly, such characteristics are generally negative, but it must be remembered that the research is undertaken with two thoughts in mind: Can it fill in gaps in our knowledge (i.e., add to basic research findings) and, second, are the findings applicable to human behavior? Induction of any kind of disturbed animal behavior has been justified time and time again because of its possible application to human psychopathology (see Liddell, 1936, 1938, 1947, 1951, 1954; Kolb, 1938; Cook, 1939a; Marcuse, 1955; Chertok & Fontaine, 1963; Keehn, 1977;[4]

[4] This has almost 30 pertinent references.

etc.). Let us make this concrete with an example with which one of the authors (F.L.M.) is familiar. He was asked to test the efficacy of a certain drug in combating motor seizures in known seizure-susceptible rats before it was tried on a human. Dosage and side effects, if any, were to be noted. (This work was carried out for Dr. Cone at the Neurological Clinic at the Allan Memorial Institute in Montreal.) While the results, in this instance, were not conclusive, it is such a procedure that is being argued for. In short, most researchers tend to agree with Liddell, who firmly believed that from animal study it would be possible to identify traumatic factors responsible for both animal and human erratic behavior. In this fashion, he said, such research on animals may contribute to psychotherapy.

The *specialité de la maison* of the Cornell Behavior Farm was "experimental neurosis." Its "heyday" in terms of research output was roughly the mid 1930s to the middle 1950s, and it was during this period that one of the authors (F.L.M.) spent 10 years at this location. Research work that was done encompassed such varied species as dogs, rats, sheep, goats, pigs, and cows.

Methodologically and logically the work left something to be desired—at least from the viewpoint of the 1970s. While it appeared that Liddell (its director) "had something," one was never quite sure just what it was, for Liddell seldom used controls or even a single animal as its own control. Liddell might describe how some of his prized "experimentally neurotic animals" (sheep in this case) had "lost their gregariousness" because they had strayed from the flock and become prime targets for attack by packs of wild dogs.

This observation had led to the conclusion that "lost gregariousness" was one of the characteristics of experimental neurosis. However, this would also occur in animals that were not experimentally neurotic; unfortunately the frequency of occurrence of this loss was never established for either kind of animal. A selective sampling of events and animals might well have occurred. This possibility became painfully obvious to the writer who, at the time, was carrying out an extinction procedure with three litter mates (goats). One showed 100% extinction, another approximately 50%, and the third 0%—depending which animal was focused on, theory formulation might be different! Such selective sampling might also occur in the graphs that Liddell presented and even in how much of the graph was shown.

In physiological recordings per se there often is, in addition to selective sampling, a lack of understanding of the normal range of physiological systems. Certainly, before one can discuss abnormal behavior, physiologically or psychologically, one should know the characteristics of the "norm" from which one is "abbing." Heartbeats that occurred in groups of two or more were thought to characterize an experimentally neurotic animal, yet these were also found in animals that had never been exposed to stimuli that produce so-called experimental neurosis! This error in attributing certain characteristics to experimentally disturbed animals is typical of many investigations. For example, N.R.F. Maier stated that "retiring cage behavior" was present in rats that showed motor seizures after being exposed to certain sounds. Ironically, F.L.M., completely unaware of Maier's work, was at that very time using this particular characteristic (retiring cage behavior) *to select* seizure-susceptible rats! What is cause and what is effect is not always clear.

Another highly dubious point in the methodology used by Liddell and others may be seen in the procedures whereby "experimental neurosis" was elicited. Such techniques might involve the use of constant time intervals between trials of simple classical conditioning, difficult discriminations, the clashing of biologically antagonistic unconditioned responses, stressful instrumental conditioning, etc. In all of these procedures a common factor was present—inhibition. This exogenous inhibition of a physical nature was often provided by the restraint of a Pavlovian harness. In point of fact, F.L.M. was so convinced of the importance of the role of exogenous inhibition that he attempted to extrapolate its possible significance to his own work on "audiogenic seizure." What he did was to strap the source of seizure stimulation (a bell) on the back of known motor-seizure-susceptible rats. In short, the inhibition that had been due to the cage was no longer present as the rats now had the freedom of the room. The excitatory stimulus (bell) was then turned on. No seizure occurred to two known 100% susceptible rats (however, the problem of physiological recording in freely moving rats forced the discontinuation of the investigation). Another type of error in logic at the Cornell Behavior Farm was in the nature of "damned if you do and damned if you don't" type of reasoning. Liddell at times might describe an animal as quiet on the *outside* but rebellious and erratic on the *inside* or sometimes an animal would be said to be *passively quiet* though really actively alert. This type of reasoning made it impossible to evaluate results.

On the positive side, it is to Liddell's credit that he was interested in all forms of disturbed behavior in all kinds of animals and as a result one would find many kinds of animals at the Cornell Behavior Farm. Still another point on the positive side was the fact that Liddell was interested in atypical animal behavior, both physiologically and psychologically. His animal "therapy," which he hoped could be extrapolated to humans, was broad and all inclusive. It might consist of the use of drugs, methodological change, vacations for the disturbed animals (i.e., periods of no testing), surgery, etc. While his emphasis did not preclude theory formulation it stressed the empirical—Liddell wanted more data and was willing to accept it from any source. He fully believed that with more facts he would have greater understanding of disturbed behavior and that the accumulation of such data from different levels of altered animal behavior made application to human behavior more likely. His breadth of interest was an asset experimentally—but academically it was a liability. Believing that it would be highly unethical to omit research of any kind in this relatively unexplored area he would permit his graduate students to pursue their own interests in the field of animal psychopathology. However, as a result of this kind of belief on Liddell's part, his students felt the situation to be too unstructured and this, unfortunately, led to a paucity of doctoral students.

Probably one of the most important positive features of the work at the Cornell Behavior Farm was the semiverbalized admonition that obtaining of results depended, in part, on human–animal relationships. Mystical factors of any kind in this relationship were not implied. What was being said, however, was this: The relationship (positive or negative) might determine whether or not the experimenter succeeded in getting the subjects to the laboratory on a given day and consequently being able to obtain data.

VIII. On Care

The question that immediately arises when animals are kept in laboratories for experimental purposes, be it psychological or physiological, is "Are they well housed and fed?" Rules concerning the maintenance and upkeep of any kind of animal colony are designed to help guarantee this. The Canadian Council on Animal Care (Shore, 1978) has its counterpart in the United States (American Psychological Association, 1971) as well as in many other countries. These animal care groups, in addition to surveillance, make trips to centers of experimentation to make sure that their guidelines are being followed. Their goal is simply to prevent unnecessary pain and suffering in animals, as well as to ensure the animals' well-being. Animal caretakers nowadays are much better qualified than in the past and are no longer mere "purveyors of feces." Whereas in the past an empty room, generally in the basement, sufficed for animal care, within the last few years appropriate ventilation, satisfactory cleaning facilities, good light, adequate temperature and humidity levels, and so on are now usually present. In short, there is a large measure of environmental control, and these innovations are generally initiated at the blueprint stage when buildings are being planned or renovated. This applies to both indoor and outdoor facilities. In short, an animal (be it frog, dog, cat, chimp, or fish) may be said to typically receive care that is as good as, if not better than, that it would receive in the public pound. Apart from the humanitarian factor promising satisfactory animal care, the simple fact exists that if a research project requires financial funding, it is in the researcher's best interest to adhere to the guidelines set down by the various councils on animal care. Equally important is the simple fact that if generalizable data are to be obtained, it is almost mandatory that healthy animals be present and this, in turn, demands effective care.

This is not to say that abuse in the treatment of animals does not occur, be it wittingly or unwittingly. A case in point often not realized concerns the physical restraints imposed on an animal when it is confined. Although an animal may be apparently well kept when caged, it still may be deprived of freedom of movement, social interaction with other members of its species, etc. To what extent should these be provided in order for the treatment to be considered humane? Does the answer to this question depend on the phylogenic level of the organism? One somehow feels that it is less humane to keep a chimpanzee in solitary confinement with "nothing to do" than it is to treat a rat in the same way. In any event, it is possible to specify housing conditions that can be agreed upon by most informed people who are concerned with the humane care of animals.

IX. On Method and Procedures

Unlike the matter of developing acceptable standards of animal care, the problem of preventing unnecessary suffering caused by experimental manipulations on animals is extremely difficult and complex. Perhaps this is why the American Psychological Association, to mention one noteworthy organization concerned with the care and treatment of experimental animals, says little about the experimental treatment of animals. On this issue its code of principles (1971) states simply: "Research procedures subjecting animals to discomfort shall be conducted only when such discomfort is required, and is justified by the objectives of the research." But who decides whether the discomfort is justified by the objectives of the research and how is that decision made? And what about the objectives themselves—should there not be some assurance that they justify the animal suffering involved in achieving them?

Presently, at least, the objectives of the research and the procedures used to achieve them are usually decided solely by the researcher with perhaps "veto power" being held by a granting agency if financial support is required. Generally, the review board of the granting agency is composed largely or entirely of scientists in areas related to the researcher's area of investigation. Clearly no competent scientists deliberately sets out to conduct or to support useless or sadistic research. Good research and humane practices go hand in hand.

This point was spelled out very clearly by Russell and Burch (1959) in their comprehensive treatment of humane experimental techniques; for example, "the humanest possible treatment of experimental animals, far from being an obstacle, is actually a prerequisite for successful animal experiment [pp. 3-4]." Russell and Burch discussed in great detail the manner in which inhumanity in animal experimentation can be reduced under three broad headings they call "the three Rs": *replacement, reduction,* and *refinement.*

Replacement refers to the substitution of living conscious animals with less conscious or insentient material. There are two general types of replacement: relative replacement in which completely anesthetized animals (see Section V) or preparations made from painlessly killed animals are used; and absolute replacement in which higher animals are replaced by less sentient lower organisms or by nonliving physical and chemical systems. Replacement occurs almost inevitably with advances in knowledge. For example, as understanding of the physical and chemical processes underlying biological entities increases, it becomes increasingly possible to by-pass living organisms by studying those processes more directly and extrapolating the results to living organisms. Similarly, as understanding of the biological systems constituting higher living organisms increases, it becomes increasingly possible to study directly those or similar systems wherever they most conveniently can be found in nature. Often the most convenient place to find them is in lower organisms. For example, a great deal of knowledge in neurophysiology has been gained by studies of the giant squid because of its enormous nerve fiber that can be dissected out and studied more easily than the nerve fibers of species more closely related to humans. Regarding this point, Lane-Peter (1972) noted: "There should be no conflict between the claims of science and the obligation of humanity towards animals, for both should ask the same question; is this animal the best experimental system for the job? If its use is scientifically inappropriate or objectionable on humanitarian grounds its use is probably—almost certainly—irrational: and so it should not be used [p. 41]."

In the behavioral sciences, replacement by nonliving material appears to be not yet possible. Although Russell and Burch suggested that research on mechanical models of behavioral systems might prove fruitful, we feel it is extremely doubtful that sufficient knowledge of behavioral systems exists to begin to build accurate models of them. Nevertheless, replacement of higher by lower organisms occurs in the behavioral sciences in the sense that many experimental psychologists frequently use animals such as pigeons and rats in lieu of higher organisms to study basic behavioral processes such as reinforcement, punishment, and stimulus control; much, however, depends on the particular problem being investigated.

Reduction, the second of the three Rs, refers to reducing the number of animals required to obtain information of a given amount and precision. In addition to humanitarian grounds, this is important for scientific reasons because of the resulting reduction in the time and money needed to conduct the research. Reduction centers on the problem of reducing the variance in the data. One way to do this is by using more sophisticated statistical designs that permit greater amounts of variance to be factored out of the error term. Another approach involves greater control of the variance produced by genetic and environmental variables. Such control can be accomplished by selective breeding and by controlled rearing and housing conditions (see Section VIII).

A point that Russell and Burch might have made is that when major results can be obtained reliably in individual organisms it is not necessary to employ the large numbers of subjects that are usually required in research using statistical designs. In their classic texts on experimental methodology, Bernard (1865/1957) and Sidman (1960) extensively described techniques for studying physiological and behavioral processes, respectively, in individual organisms. These methods use successful replication of a finding rather than its statistical significance as the criterion of its reliability. One quite powerful approach discussed by both authors is called (by Sidman) *systematic replication*. This involves repeating an experiment under new conditions so that both the original finding can be confirmed and new information can be provided about the conditions under which it occurs. For example, instead of using three new rats to replicate a finding obtained with one rat, the experimenter might use a pigeon, a cat, and a monkey. If the same result is obtained in all cases, it can be concluded not only that the finding is reliable, but also that it has wide generality across species. Of course, to be used most effectively and successfully, systematic replication requires a great deal of experimental skill and sound judgment.

Refinement, the third of the three Rs, refers to the development of techniques for reducing the distress produced by experimental manipulations. This also has good scientific as well as humane rationale, since there is reason to believe that the presence of distress is likely to interfere with any study which is not specifically concerned with distress. This category includes the development of more effective anesthetics and techniques of euthanasia. It also includes refinement in the experimental manipulations themselves. For example, Russell and Burch recommend that rather than relying heavily on the use of electric shock as an aversive stimulus, investigations of behavioral processes might make more use of stimuli which commonly evoke flight and attack when encountered in the animal's natural environment. Such experiments might be regarded as more humane because they do not present the animal with a situation markedly different from that which it would have encountered had it been in its natural environment, and, in addition, the results might generalize more readily to the behavior we wish to predict.

Russell and Burch recommend the three Rs to researchers who wish to be as humane as possible to their subjects and still obtain important scientific information. It does not seem likely that adherence to these or similar principles of humane experimentation can be enforced with anything approaching the precision with which animal care can be and has been enforced (see Section VIII). Nor would it, in our opinion, be desirable to attempt to do so. History indicates that the effectiveness of science depends to a great extent on the freedom of the individual scientist to tackle problems that he or she feels are important with procedures he or she feels are appropriate. Most of the burden of humane experimentation thus must be carried by the individual researcher.

What measures can be taken to ensure that researchers will be guided by humane principles in their experimental manipulations on animals? One recommendation is that prospective researchers should be well trained in the importance of humane considerations in good scientific practice. Scientists should be encouraged to question the humaneness of their own and others' procedures with the same intensity that they question the scientific soundness of those procedures. Another recommendation is that scientists should be completely open with the general public concerning their procedures and the reasons for using them. It is unfortunately true that interviews with the media and representatives of the public take up valuable time that otherwise could be used for research, and also that the media sometimes misquote scientists and misrepresent their work. Yet, as many scientists have found to their sorrow, secrecy breeds suspicion and hostility which sooner or later must be allayed by openness.[5] In the long run it is the culture as a whole that will resolve the ethical issues involving research with animals (see Section II). The scientist can exert the maximum possible influence on this process only by keeping the public well informed concerning the methods of science and their justifications.

X. On Some "Iffy" Issues

It would seem to the authors that iffy questions can be treated as being of two types. The first is at present purely in the realm of science fiction—a sort of iffy squared. The second has a slightly stronger basis in present day factual knowledge; for example, the apparent possession of some humanlike language abilities by certain nonhuman species. Speculation concerned with these two situations follows.

Antivivisectionists sometimes pose the following type of question: "What if a group of extraterrestial invaders arrived, demonstrated that they were intellectually superior to us, and informed us that they would have to use a few million humans in a basic research project of considerable merit—would we consider it moral for them to do this?" The intended implication is that since presumably we would not consider it moral, to be consistent we should likewise regard as immoral the use of animals in all noxious experiments. There are several problems with this argument. First, it assumes that the intellectual superiority (however that may be defined) of humans over animals is the proposed moral justification for animal experimentation. However, such a justification is not proposed in this chapter nor do we believe that it is a valid one (see Section II). Second, the intended analogy is incorrectly drawn. For the analogy to be appropriate, the question is not whether it would be immoral from the human point of view for intellectually superior extraterrestials to experiment on humans, but rather whether it would be immoral from *their* point of view—and this we cannot know without being given more information about the nature of these hypothetical invaders. Third, and perhaps most important, the argument can be seen merely as a variation of the moral exhortation "How would you like it if someone did that to you?" But such an exhortation does not logically constitute a valid argument. As pointed out in Section II, the frequent use of this exhortation in our culture is probably maintained as a means of supplementing generalization from oneself to others *within* the culture. It is as though, in effect, we have been taught to apply the following rule of thumb: If you want to know whether or not a particular ac-

[5] One of the authors (F. L. M.) felt differently on this point and agreed to disagree. He drew the analogy with going for a dental check-up. We generally allow the dentist's expertise to decide what should be done. Admittedly, such a procedure would run the danger of elitism but would also ensure judgment by peers as well as recognize individuality. Methodology other than this is thought by F. L. M. to reflect a mistaken interpretation of democratic principles.

tion toward another member of the culture is considered ethical by the culture, ask yourself whether you would find that action aversive if it were performed toward you. The rule has arisen because it helps minimize dissension within the culture, and it has nothing to do with hypothetical invaders from outer space.

The other side of the "invasion-from-outer-space" question has also been posited. Suppose that in future explorations of other worlds we discover a race of nonhumans that appears to be intellectually similar to our own species. Would it be ethical for us to exploit these nonhumans for research (or, for that matter, other purposes) that might be harmful to them? This question may best be approached by considerations closer to our experience. It is generally considered unethical to undertake actions that would harm members of other human cultures, even though those cultures may be quite different in many respects from our own. Why is this the case? One reason is that, as indicated in Section II ("On Values"), we have been conditioned to value humans strongly because any action which threatens another human, even if he or she is not a member of our own culture, directly or indirectly threatens members of our culture. (Recall, for example, the famous placard carried by a black protester of the United States participation in the Vietnamese civil war: "The Viet Cong never called me 'nigger'!" Many blacks and other minority group members perceived the racial undertones in the American involvement in that war and responded to the implied threat on themselves.) Another reason is that in being conditioned to value the survival of our culture, we have been conditioned to value a particular set of cultural practices and may, therefore, value similar practices when they are encountered outside of our culture. "They are people like us" is a frequently invoked exhortation to accord certain rights to other human cultures; what it apparently means is that members of those cultures appear to engage in the same types of everyday activities that members of our own culture perform.

How similar to the practices of our culture, and along what stimulus dimensions, does a set of cultural practices have to be in order for us to highly value the individuals who engage in those practices? To a large extent this is an empirical question. It is, therefore, impossible to specify precisely the characteristics a culture must possess in order for us to accord it significant moral rights. The adjective "intelligent," although its meaning is vague, probably conveys as much precision as we can presently give to the behavioral characteristics critical to according moral rights. It seems likely that, to return to the question at the beginning of this discussion, if "intelligent" life were found on another planet it would be accorded significant moral rights by a highly evolved culture on our own planet.

Another point raised by antivivisectionists concerns the hypothetical proposition that if animals could talk to us they would inform us that they do not like participating in noxious experiments. As it is usually posed this argument has little or no bearing on the position taken here, since it is usually directed toward the fact that many species probably experience pain in a manner similar to that in which humans experience it. This fact is not at issue in this chapter (see Section II). However, the position taken here does appear to have implications for our treatment of certain nonhuman animals if it could be shown that they can learn a human or humanlike language. Verbal behavior is—at least so far—a unique attribute of human cultures and is also crucial to their existence. Because of its great social importance it is highly valued, and any nonhuman organism that possessed it to a substantial degree would probably tend to receive a great deal of moral consideration from our culture. The present lack of highly developed verbal behavior in any nonhuman species presently excludes them from the benefits of this cultural tendency as well as from organizing in ways necessary to secure significant rights. Moreover, it also precludes strong similarities between their cultural organizations and our own which, to the extent that such correspondences existed, might lead us to value their culture in the same sense that we value our own and other human cultures.

Recently the hypothetical of "iffy" aspect of talking animals has been considerably reduced with regard to at least one species. Ethical concern about the treatment given chimpanzees is increasing because, in large measure, of research showing that it is possible to teach American Sign Language and other forms of communication to these animals (e.g., Gardner & Gardner, 1969, 1975; Rumbaugh, von Glasersfeld, Warner, Pisani, & Gill, 1974). For example, in an article on ethical considerations regarding the use of chimpanzees in research, the well-known ethologist Jane Goodall was quoted (Wade, 1976b) as follows:

> There are occasions when it is justified to use chimps, but what upsets me is the conditions in which they are kept. They should be kept very well but in fact they get lousy treatment. They are kept in small cages with nothing to do, and they are usually put in solitary confinement when they get older. *Yet these are creatures which we now know can communicate in sign language—that seems very wrong to me* [p. 1078; emphasis added].

It it interesting to speculate where research on nonhuman language-using primates will lead and what ethical implications it will have for their treatment. To the extent that they eventually come to interact with the human culture in a manner approximating that of its members, they may receive moral rights comparable to those granted to members of the culture. Aside from this possibility, it seems likely that chimpanzees and other animals that show certain significant similarities to humans will begin to be accorded better treatment than animals that are less similar to humans. It is sometimes said that the complexity of an organism's nervous system should be an important ethical consideration in how we treat that organism. But the critical dimension may be the similarity of its overt behavior to behavior we regard as most typical of our species. It seems to follow from the principle of generalization that a culture that treats its own members well will tend to give good treatment to members of other species that strongly exhibit "humanlike" behavior.[6]

---

[6] One of the authors (F.L.M.) is dubious about this point, believing that what is thought to be sentiment often turns out to be sentimentality.

XI. Some Conclusions

1. Individuals concerned with ethical issues and the unnecessary use of animals in research should demand a high degree of experimental rigor.

2. The newsletter of the Medical Research Council of Canada (1978) pointedly noted: "Experimental animal models constitute a major asset in biomedical science and food related research [p. 8]." Experimental animal models are also important in the behavioral field, as indicated by the contents of this book.

3. Strong emphasis should be placed on giving animals the best treatment that is compatible with other considerations regarding the good of the culture.

4. Animal investigation, while at present often only suggestive, is ethically mandatory.

REFERENCES

Albee, G. W. The uncertain future of clinical psychology. *American Psychologist,* 1970, *25,* 1071–1080.

American Psychological Association. *Principles for the care and use of animals.* Washington, D.C.: Author, 1971.

Behaviorists for Social Action. Kalamazoo, Michigan: Department of Psychology, Western Michigan Univ., 1977.

Bernard, C. *An introduction to the study of experimental medicine.* (H. C. Green, trans.). London: Dover, 1957. (Originally published, 1865.)

Chertok, L., & Fontaine, M. Psychosomatics in veterinary medicine. *Journal of Psychosomatic Research,* 1963, *7,* 229–235.

Cook, S. W. A survey of methods used to produce "experimental neurosis." *American Journal of Psychiatry,* 1939, *96,* 1259–1276. (a)

Cook, S. W. The production of "experimental neurosis" in the white rat. *Psychosomatic Medicine,* 1939, *1,* 293–308. (b)

Fox, M. Animal liberation: A critique. *Ethics,* 1978, *88,* 106–118.

Gardner, R. A., & Gardner, B. T. Teaching sign language to a chimpanzee. *Science,* 1969, *165,* 664–672.

Gardner, R. A., & Gardner, B. T. Early signs of language in child and chimpanzee. *Science,* 1975, *187,* 752–753.

Gifford-Jones, W. Pain killers: Must we suffer to enter eternity. *Winnipeg Free Press,* Nov. 7, 1978, p. 16 (Leisure).

Gilman, T. T., & Marcuse, F. L. Animal hypnosis. *Psychological Bulletin,* 1949, *46,* 151–165.

Gwynn, P., & Begley, S. Animals in the lab. *Newsweek,* 1978 (March 27), pp. 84–85.

Handy, R. *Value theory and the behavioral sciences.* Springfield, Illinois: Thomas, 1969.

Hume, D. *A treatise of the human understanding.* Oxford: Clarendon Press, 1958.

Keehn, J. D. In defense of experiments with animals. *Bulletin of the British Psychological Society,* 1977, *30,* 404–405.

Kolb, L. C. Congenital myotonia in goats. *Bulletin of the Johns Hopkins Hospital,* 1938, *63,* 221–237.

Lane-Peter, W. The rational use of living animals in bio-medical research. In *The rational use of living animals in bio-medical research.* Hertfordshire, England: Universities Federation for Animal Welfare, 1972.

Liddell, H. S. Nervous strain in domesticated animals and man. *Cornell Veterinarian,* 1936, *26,* 107–112.

Liddell, H. S. The experimental neurosis and the problem of mental disorder. *American Journal of Psychiatry,* 1938, *94,* 1035–1041.

Liddell, H. S. The experimental neurosis. *Annual Review of Physiology,* 1947, *9,* 569–580.

Liddell, H. S. The influence of experimental neuroses on respiratory function. In H. A. Abramson (Ed.), *Somatic and psychiatric treatment of asthma.* Baltimore: Williams & Wilkins, 1951. Pp. 126–147.

Liddell, H. S. Conditioning and emotions. *Scientific American,* January, 1954.

Lindsley, D. B., Finger, F. F., & Henry, C. E. Some physiological aspects of audiogenic seizures in rats. *Journal of Neurophysiology,* 1942, *5,* 185–198.

Maier, N. R. F., & Longhurst, J. U. Studies of abnormal behavior in the rat XX: Conflict and "audiogenic" seizures. *The Journal of Comparative and Physiological Psychology,* 1947, *40,* 397–412.

Marcuse, F. L. Animal hypnosis and psychology. In M. B. Klein (Ed.), *Hypnodynamic psychology,* New York: Julian Press, 1955.

Marcuse, F. L. Teaching psychology. *Teaching Psychology,* 1977, *1,* 3.

Marcuse, F. L., & Moore, A. U. Tantrum behavior in the pig. *Journal of Comparative Psychology,* 1944, *32,* 235–241.

Medical Research Council of Canada. New plan to preserve endangered animal models. *Medical Research Council Newsletter,* 1978, *8*(2), 7–8.

Pepper, S. C. *The sources of value.* Berkeley: Univ. of California Press, 1958.

Pepper, S. C. *Ethics.* New York: Appleton, 1960.

Riess, B. F. "Freezing" behavior in rats and its social causation. *Journal of Social Psychology,* 1946, *24,* 249–251.

Rumbaugh, D. M., von Glasersfeld, E., Warner, H., Pisani, P., & Gill, T. V. Lana (chimpanzee) learning language: A progress report. *Brain and Language,* 1974, *1,* 205–212.

Russell, W. M. S., & Burch, R. L. *The principles of humane experimental technique.* London: Methuen, 1959.

Sabine, G. *History of political theory.* New York: Holt, 1937.

Schneirla, T. C. Psychology, comparative. *Encyclopedia Britanica,* 1948.

Scientists and humane societies work together. *University Affairs,* February, 1978, p. 5.

Shapiro, E. Lectures on social and preventive medicine. Univ. of Manitoba, Medical School, personal communication, 1978.

Shore, V. Scientists and humane societies work together. *University Affairs,* 1978, *19*(2), 5–6.

Sidman, M. *Tactics of scientific research: Evaluating experimental data in psychology.* New York: Basic Books, 1960.

Singer, P. *Animal liberation.* New York: New York Review of Books, 1975.

Sjöström, H., & Nilsson, R. *Thalidomide and the power of the drug companies.* Middlesex, England: Penguin, 1972.

Skinner, B. F. *Science and human behavior.* New York: Macmillan, 1953.

Skinner, B. F. *Beyond freedom and dignity.* New York: Knopf, 1971.

Skinner, B. F. Humanism and behaviorism. In B. F. Skinner (Ed.), *Reflections on behaviorism and society.* Englewoods Cliffs, New Jersey, Prentice-Hall, 1978. Pp. 48–55.

Wade, N. Animal rights; NIH cat sex study brings grief to New York museum. *Science,* 1976, *194,* 162–167.

Wade, N. Briefing: NIH considers animal rights; A new militancy in England. *Science,* 1978, *199,* 279. (a)

Wade, N. New vaccine may bring man and chimpanzee into tragic conflict. *Science,* 1978, *200,* 1027–1030. (b)

Warren, H. C. *Dictionary of psychology.* New York: Houghton Miflin, 1934.

Washington State Psychological Association, constitution and by-laws, *Newsletter,* Feb. 1967.

Index